THE LISTENING SELF

Personal growth, social change, and the closure of metaphysics

In a study that goes beyond the ego affirmed by Freudian psychology, Dr Levin offers an account of personal growth and self-fulfillment based on the development of our capacity for listening.

Drawing on the work of Dewey, Piaget, Erikson and Kohlberg, he uses the vocabulary of phenomenological psychology to distinguish four stages in this developmental process and brings out the significance of these stages for music, psychotherapy, ethics, politics, and ecology. This analysis substantiates his claim that the development of our listening capacity is a process that fits Foucault's conception of a practice of the self, forming our character as social beings and moral agents.

Dr Levin contends that our self-development as auditory beings is necessary for the achievement of a just and democratic society. Arguing that our ethical ideals and political principles require the realisation of our communicative potential, he demonstrates how listening can contribute to the ideal speech situation and rational consensus formation modelled on Habermas's theory of communicative action. Taking up the work of Merleau-Ponty Levin examines how the listening process introduces us to procedures of reciprocity.

David Michael Levin is Professor of Philosophy at Northwestern University, Illinois.

Jacket illustration:
The Intertwining:
Symbol of our Rootedness, the Weave of Feminine Wisdom, the Interrelatedness of all Beings, the Interdependency of Self and Other, the Interactional Co-Emergence of Subject and Object, the Co-Ordination of Self and Society, the Oneness that is Manifold, the Consonance that is shaped to permit Dissonance, and the Difference that in-forms Consensus. Symbol, also, of the Labyrinth, the Immeasurable, the Ground whose Dimensions cannot be Sounded, and the Structure of the Inner Ear.

By the same author

The Body's Recollection of Being
(Routledge & Kegan Paul, 1985)
The Opening of Vision
(Routledge, 1988)

THE LISTENING SELF

PERSONAL GROWTH, SOCIAL CHANGE AND THE CLOSURE OF METAPHYSICS

DAVID MICHAEL LEVIN

ROUTLEDGE
London and New York

First published 1989
by Routledge

11 New Fetter Lane, London EC4P 4EE
29 West 35th Street, New York, NY 10001

Typeset in 10/11pt Palatino Linotron 202
by Input Typesetting Ltd, London
Printed in Great Britain
by Biddles Ltd, Guildford

British Library Cataloguing in Publication Data
Levin, David Michael, *1939–*
The listening self: personal growth,
social change and the closure of
metaphysics
I. Title
191

ISBN 0–415–02582–6
ISBN 0–415–02583–4 Pbk

Library of Congress Cataloging-in-Publication Data
also available

On 14 October 1947 Chuck Yeager piloted his plane faster than the speed of sound. On this day, with us behind him, he broke through the sound barrier. This book is written for the world that follows in the wake of this event; it is written for a generation which also takes pride in having broken through other kinds of barriers as well: barriers of ancient hatreds and dehumanizing injustice, barriers that divided neighbours, barriers that divided the self.

To Eugene Gendlin
Breaker of Barriers

Contents

Acknowledgements		xi
Opening Conversation		xiv
Introduction The Gift and the Art		1
Chapter 1	The Historical Call to Our Hearing	9
Part I	Narcissism: The Ego's Rise to Power	9
Part II	Nihilism and the Closure of Metaphysics	15
Part III	The Metaphysics of Presence	18
Part IV	The Western Vision of Reason: Questioning the Enlightenment	29
Part V	Communicative Ethics: A New Model of Rationality	35
Part VI	Social Change: The Potential in Perception and Sensibility	37
Part VII	Developing our Capacities: Listening as a Practice of the Self	39
Part VIII	The Listening Self: Four Stages of Self-Development	45
Part IX	Humanism Today	62

Chapter 2 *Zugehörigkeit*: Our Primordial Attunement 66
Chapter 3 Everydayness: The Ego's World 76
Chapter 4 Skilful Listening 81
Chapter 5 Communicative Praxis 90
Part I The Body Politic 90
Part II States of Deafness: Listening for the Excluded Voices 103
Part III The Conscience of Listening: The Self as Intersubjectivity 111
Part IV Needs and their Interpretation: Listening to Inner Nature 127
Part V Sounds of Truth 136
Part VI In the Depth of the Flesh: The Body Politic as Corporeal Image 140
1 The Narcissism of the Flesh
2 Freud: Primary and Secondary Narcissism
3 Lacan: The Mirror and the Self
4 Merleau-Ponty: Narcissism as Self-Deconstruction
5 The Intertwining and its Reversibilities: A Radical Political Order
6 A Sense of Justice
Part VII Consensus and Difference 186
Chapter 6 *Hearkening*: Hearing Moved by Ontological Understanding 205

CONTENTS

Part I	The Ontological Appropriation of Hearing	206
Part II	Our Natal Bonding	209
Part III	Feminine Archetypes: Earth, Plants, Body, Feeling, Intertwining	212
Part IV	*Gelassenheit*: Just Listening	223
Part V	The Echo and the Ego	235
Part VI	The Principle of the Ground: Setting the Double Tone	240
Part VII	The Gathering of the Logos	247
Part VIII	The Fourfold: A Gathering of Sound	255
Part IX	Time and the Echo: A Gathering of Time	258
Part X	Belonging to Culture: A Gathering of History	269

Notes 276
Bibliography 307
Index 321

Acknowledgements

Two people participated with decisive impact in the thinking that has made this book possible. I am especially indebted, before all others, to my brother, Roger Levin, and my friend, Eugene Gendlin. Our numerous conversations over the course of many years rescued me more than once from some terrible confusion, doubt, dogmatic certainty, and depression, as I struggled to articulate the experience I wanted to share in a phenomenological language that would be true to the concrete and deeply felt richness of this experience while continuing the dialogue with my philosophical tradition in a discourse dominated for centuries by the Cartesian-Newtonian paradigm and organized by consensually validated principles that have tended systematically to exclude or suppress precisely that claim of experience for the sake of which I have written this present work.

I am also grateful for the encouragement of my mother and father, who provided a wonderful home for my writing and broached some thought-provoking questions in response to the pages they heard me read.

David Wood, who read not only this volume, but also its two companion volumes, is also deserving of my thanks for his painstaking reading. It gives me great pleasure to acknowledge, here, his willingness to read so much so carefully and help me to say what it is that I want to say.

Northwestern University has given me much-needed support, providing very generous grants to cover a variety of research expenditures and a good deal of free time to complete my project. I am extremely grateful for this assistance.

Finally, I would like to thank my colleague Thomas McCarthy for his comments and suggestions regarding Chapter 5.

I am grateful to Alfred E. Knopf, Inc. for permission to reprint three lines from 'The auroras of autumn', a poem by Wallace Stevens published in *Collected Poems of Wallace Stevens* (New York, 1954).

For permission to reprint a long passage on the echo in Longchenpa, *Kindly Bent to Ease Us* (Berkeley, 1976), I am grateful to Dharma Publishing Co.

Excerpts from *Freedom to Learn* by Carl Rogers are reprinted by permission of the Charles E. Merrill Publishing Company. Revised edition available: *Freedom to Learn for the 80's*, © 1983.

Excerpts from *Paterson*, by William Carlos Williams, © 1951, 1958, are reprinted by permission of New Directions Publishing Corporation.

Excerpts from 'The dry salvages' in *Four Quartets* by T. S. Eliot are reprinted by permission of Harcourt Brace Jovanovich, Inc., © 1943 by T. S. Eliot; renewed 1971 by Esme Valerie Eliot. The passages are reprinted outside the United States, its dependencies, and the Philippine Islands by permission of Faber & Faber Ltd, London.

Winnahdin
Winter, 1987

Opening Conversation

Mental activities . . . each draws its metaphors from a different bodily sense. . . . Thus, from the very outset, in formal philosophy, thinking has been thought of in terms of *seeing*. . . . The predominance of sight is so deeply embedded in Greek speech, and therefore in our conceptual language, that we seldom find any consideration bestowed on it, as though it belonged among things too obvious to be noticed. . . . [But] if one considers how easy it is for sight, unlike the other senses, to shut out the outside world, and if one examines the early notion of the blind bard, whose stories are being listened to, one may wonder why hearing did not develop into the guiding metaphor for thinking.

Arendt, *The Life of the Mind*, 110–11

OPENING CONVERSATION

(everything comes down to the ear you are able to hear me with)

Derrida, *The Ear of the Other*, 4

The regression of the masses today is their inability
to hear the unheard-of with their own ears, to
touch the unapprehended with their own hands.
Horkheimer and Adorno, *The Dialectic of
Enlightenment*, 36

OPENING CONVERSATION

Today critical thought . . . demands support for the residues of freedom, and for tendencies toward true humanism.

Horkheimer and Adorno,
The Dialectic of Enlightenment, ix

Knowledge is humanistic . . . not because it is *about* human products in the past, but because of what it *does* in liberating human intelligence and human sympathy.

Dewey, *Democracy and Education*, 230

For this is humanism: meditating and caring [*Sinnen und Sorgen*] that man be human and not inhumane [*unmenschlich*].
Heidegger, 'Letter on humanism', *Basic Writings*, 199–200

A higher society . . . can hardly be conceived of without processes of spiritualization and interiorization.
Horkheimer, 'Egoism and the movement for emancipation', 190

OPENING CONVERSATION

. . . to think of perfections of bodily organs which surpass our own.
Leibniz, *New Essays on the Human Understanding*,
book III, ch. 6, 307

But do we know what *ta onta* [commonly translated as *beings, entities, the-things-which-are*] means? We would only come closer to the matter if we were to concern ourselves with the nose, the eyes, and with hearing.

Heidegger, *Heraclitus Seminar 1966–1967*, 19

OPENING CONVERSATION

In teaching philosophy in the gymnasium the abstract form is, in the first instance, straightaway the chief concern. The young must first die to sight and hearing, must be torn away from concrete representations, must be withdrawn into the night of the soul and so learn to see on this new level.

Hegel, *Letters*, 280

The madman . . . is clearly . . . for one who can hear, he who seeks God, since he cries out after God. Has a thinking man perhaps really cried out here *de profundis*? And the ear of our thinking, does it still not hear the cry? It will refuse to hear it so long as it does not begin to think. Thinking begins only when we have come to know that reason, glorified for centuries, is the most stiff-necked adversary of thought.
Heidegger, 'The word of Nietzsche: "God is dead" ', *The Question Concerning Technology and Other Essays*, 112

OPENING CONVERSATION

The tasks which face the human apparatus of perception at the turning points of history cannot be solved . . . by contemplation alone.

Benjamin, *Illuminations: Essays and Reflections*, 242

Only through the objectively unfolded richness of man's essential being is the richness of subjective human sensibility (a musical ear, an eye for beauty of form – in short – *senses* capable of human gratification, senses affirming themselves as essential powers of man) either cultivated or brought into being.

Marx, *Economic and Philosophical Manuscripts of 1844*, 139

OPENING CONVERSATION

The senses are not only the basis for the *epistemological* constitution of reality, but also for its *transformation*, its *subversion* in the interest of liberation.

Marcuse, *Counter-Revolution and Revolt*, 71

INTRODUCTION

The Gift and the Art

In the Book of Psalms (115:6), we find these words: 'they have ears, but they hear not.' According to the common and therefore dominant interpretation, these words refer to the idols of the idol-worshippers and are intended to strengthen the commitment of the Jewish people to a religion freed from the materialism of idolatry. But the greatness of this ancient text lies in its generosity, its availability to different, and even conflicting, interpretations. Could the God who has condemned these idols be heard to speak analogically? Is there a sense in which, although we have ears, we too do not hear?

Our hearing is a gift of nature; we receive it without having to ask for it. But such gifts make claims – moral claims, as Bernard Williams has argued – and there are different ways of receiving nature's gifts and responding to their claims.[1] How we receive and respond is a question of moral character. The gift of hearing is the gift of a capacity, a potential that calls for its existential realization. So an appropriate response, an appropriate reception, would be the development of that capacity. How, then, should we understand such development? Of what are we capable?

If our hearing is a capacity belonging to the life of the spirit, then it would be a grave error to believe that this capacity reaches its full maturity in the course of a process adequately understood in the terms of our biological sciences – or to believe that the maturity of this capacity, the fulfilment of our potential, could ever be properly measured by norms uncritically derived from the ontological insensitivity and indifference of everyday life. We cling tenaciously, despite the instructive words in the psalm, to our long-entrenched, popular notions about the 'essential nature' of our capacities and the 'inherent' ends and limits that determine their unfolding.

The gift of nature is the gift of an *unfulfilled* capacity, an *unrealized* potential, an *unfinished* task. The gift calls for existential work: the kind of work that could be described, adopting a term introduced by Foucault, as an ascetic 'practice of the Self'. Social interactions begin this work for us; but ultimately, each individual is responsible for the extent and character of its continuation. To the extent that we each take over this work in the process of our own individuation, our hearing becomes an 'art of living', a *technē tou biou*. The art of skilful hearing, a practical wisdom, a *phronēsis,* is our response-ability in relation to the original gift of nature.

Since we are social beings, processes of self-development are never only psychological, for they always take place in lives whose dimensions are also social and cultural. Thus, one of the principal claims I shall be making in this book is that, if we are to survive the challenges in our contemporary historical situation with a dignity redeeming our 'humanity' and successfully resolve the crisis now testing the rationality and legitimacy of our modern world-order, we must understand that the moral and spiritual development of our capacity for listening would be responsive to a need whose realization figures not only in the well-being of individual human natures, but also in the constellation of our present historical task.

Our time is a distinctively needful time. In summarizing the diagnosis of modernity that Habermas is proposing in his *Theory of Communicative Action*, Seyla Benhabib writes:

> The pathologies of the lifeworld arise in three domains: in the sphere of cultural reproduction, the consequence is a loss of meaning; in the sphere of social integration, anomie emerges; and as regards personality, we are faced with psychopathologies. Since each of these spheres contributes to the reproduction of the other two, the crises [of our time] are in fact more complex: loss of meaning in the cultural domain can lead to

> the withdrawal of legitimation in the sphere of social integration, and to a crisis of education and orientation in the person. Anomie can imply increasing instability of collective identities, and for the individual, growing alienation. Psychopathologies bring with them the rupture of traditions, and in the social sphere, a withdrawal of motivation.[2]

In the course of our present study, we shall be considering how our experience with hearing relates to the 'pathologies of the lifeworld' that appear in our time. In regard to the sphere of cultural reproduction, we shall reflect on how 'loss of meaning' – a symptom of nihilism – is connected with an ontologically 'forgetful' way of hearing: a hearing habitually indifferent to the ontological difference between beings and the Being of these beings as this difference manifests through the structuring, the *Gestaltung*, of the auditory situation. In regard to the sphere of social integration, we shall reflect on how our failure to cultivate the skill of listening is connected with the increasing problematization of rational consensus and the breakdown of traditional processes of legitimation; but we shall also consider how a better, more developed competence in listening could significantly improve the communicative infrastructures of the lifeworld that are necessary conditions for rational consensus, legitimation, equity, and justice. Finally, in regard to personality, we shall reflect on how the very limited development of our capacity for listening is responsible for much suffering and misery, and how the cultivation of this capacity can contribute to, and is in turn affected by, the forming of moral character, encouraging communicative relationships, awakening a compassionate sensibility and the understanding it bears within it, motivating a concern for reciprocity and respect for differences, enabling the recognition of authentic needs, reversing processes of alienation that disintegrate the Self, and transforming the patriarchal ego, the historically constellated source of a will to power that has turned itself more and more into an instrument of nihilism, raging self-destructively.

This book is the third volume in a trilogy of works exploring the human potential for self-development in its perceptual, affective, cognitive, moral, and spiritual dimensions, and motivated by the conviction that there is a causal connection, in both directions, between what we might call the 'evolutionary possibilities' of society – above all, the possibilities for achieving greater freedom, justice, and democracy – and the 'psychological' development of the individual; and that some further, deeper realization of this potential is therefore necessary, if we are to respond appropriately to the crisis demands of our historical time.

Like the two volumes which preceded it, namely, *The Body's Recollection of Being* and *The Opening of Vision*, this book on listening is intended as a contribution to the emerging of a new body of understanding. Each volume addresses the question of self-development by concentrating on an experiential dimension of our embodiment – a distinctive 'channelling' of the human potential. The first volume explores this potential, and attempts to provoke greater self-awareness, inherent in our experience with gestures and motility. The second volume reflects on this potential in our capacity for vision, diagnosing the visionary dimension of everyday life in the historical conditions distinctive of modernity, bringing to light the pervasive character of its psychopathology, connecting this psychopathology with the advent of nihilism, and beginning to engender a vision of radically different character – a vision, that is, which would be able to structure the visionary situation, the figure-ground difference, in an historically new way. This book, of course, takes up the potential in our capacity for listening, and likewise attempts to encourage greater self-awareness, spelling out the possibilities in terms of a logic, an implicate order, of developmental stages.

All three volumes attempt a critical diagnosis of the 'psychopathology' of everyday life prevailing at this time; and they attempt to understand, in terms of this critical interpretation of our lifeworld, how our individual and collective failure to develop these different capacities has given them a character, a 'psychology', that is responsible for the historical situation in which we find ourselves, and how, conversely, the prevailing conditions of social life are responsible for the pathologies of gesture, vision, and hearing distinctive of our time. However, going beyond critique, beyond what Adorno called 'negative dialectics', these volumes also attempt to think how the further development of our capacities, bringing out the potential implicate within them, could constitute not only our self-fulfilment as individuals, but also a new *historical* achievement – a stage in our social and cultural evolution that would be genuinely emancipatory, progressive, and life-enhancing for all. Thus, each volume attempts to articulate processes of personal growth – individuation and self-fulfilment – in ways that make explicit how they are inseparable from 'processes of Enlightenment' – using Horkheimer's term for processes advancing the work of emancipation, rational consensus, legitimation, and justice – that are taking place in the social and cultural lifeworld as a whole.

Sounding the more primordial depths of our listening capacity and its historical pathology, we will find, however, as the present study argues, that listening is a capacity whose development, and pathological failures to develop, call for interpretation in relation to the Question of Being. Thus, first, we will be considering a diagnosis that brings out our experiential, auditory *closure* to the dimensionality of Being as a whole; then we will initiate a *recollection* of Being in a process through which we make contact with this dimension and retrieve for present living the as yet unrealized potential that lies in our renewed belonging to, and being once again attuned by, the dimensionality, meaning, and wholeness of Being.

Here we are going to interpret what Heidegger calls our 'forgetfulness of Being' in terms of our experience with listening closures. Correlatively, we will interpret Heidegger's concepts of 'the Being of beings', 'Being as a whole', and 'Being as such' as terms referring to the immeasurable, primordial ground of our listening experience, the dimensionality of the auditory field in its wholeness. 'Being' is not another name for God, nor is it to be identified with some other (kind of) being or entity: in terms of our *traditional* metaphysical framework, it is, then, nothing: no thing. But let us avoid mystification: in the context of this study, 'Being' refers very specifically to the disclosure, the audible fact, that our auditory situations, and all the audible beings we encounter in them, constitute an essentially open dimension of meaningfulness. The 'presence' of Being, the Being of beings, is simply the audible manifestation of this dimensionality.

Within the context of this study, we shall assign to the *Es gibt*, to Heidegger's concept of the 'dispensations of Being' an auditory sense. Particular configurations of sounds and silences, events which take place in the auditory field of our present world-age, as well as the historically distinctive tonality of the field itself, which has, as ground, become increasingly flat, hollow, and empty, are therefore to be understood as historical 'dispensations of Being'. These 'dispensations' can never be brought totally under our individual or collective control; however, they are never totally outside the sphere of our influence, our capacity to determine their formation and impact.

The conception of 'Being' at stake in this book is therefore neither a continuation of the old metaphysics nor a fall into ontotheology. For what I am calling 'Being' is none of the following: an unconditional ground, an absolute and separate reality, a nonempirical or supersensible reality, a world-transcendent principle, a first cause, an immanent telos, an immanent and final reason, a total presence, a being, an ideal meaning, a highest genus, a universal form, an ultimate cognition, a deity, a divine power, a spiritual force, a foundation for knowledge, an absolute truth, or an encompassing mind.

Like the two preceding works, this study will connect the question of self-development – in this case, our self-development and maturity as beings gifted with a capacity to hear – with the Question of Being, Heidegger's *Seinsfrage*, in its twofold character, namely, as an historical experience of the advent of nihilism and as the most fundamental question in the history of metaphysics.

The crucial connection I am trying to make, therefore, is between an auditory closure to Being, a closure to the auditory ground or field, which manifests a limited development – a painful and self-destroying development – of our capacity for hearing, and an historical experience of nihilism, whose advent is manifest in a 'loss of Being', or a 'loss of meaning', and is reflected in the history of Western metaphysics as a closure in thinking that reduces the Being of beings to the condition of a being. In each of the volumes, then, there is an attempt to recollect an experience with the ground – the 'ground' of our standing and walking, the 'ground' of our visual experience, the 'ground' of our hearing – by virtue of which we might be able to learn, to awaken within ourselves, an historically new relationship to the 'ground' that figures in the Question of Being. In each of the volumes, there is a recollection of the ontological difference as it manifests through, and for, our embodied experience; in our visionary and auditory experiences, for example, of the structural differentiation of figure and ground, object and field. This recollection is different from Heidegger's, however, because it is a process which takes place by virtue of our embodiment, the gift of our embodiment: it is, in sum, the body's recollection of Being.

Now, in so far as 'metaphysics' is defined simply as the discourse which reflects on the Question of Being, the process of recollection into which I am attempting to gather our thinking is of course a *continuation* of the history of metaphysics, since it continues to question and measure our body of experience, our capacity for self-awareness and perceptivity, by reference to the Question of Being – or rather, to say this more concretely, by reference to the question of our openness to the dimensionality of Being as a whole. But if 'metaphysics' is identified with a discourse in which, despite the broaching of the ontological question, there is already at work a process of reflection, or speculation, that ensures, however unconsciously, a decisive *foreclosure* in our experience with Being, then there is a sense in which our work of recollection initiates a genuine *rupture*, a break with the traditional discourse. The history of metaphysics is a history which reflects the secret work of nihilism, a closure to Being. In the recollection we will be undertaking – undergoing – in this book, however, the Question of Being is asked in a way that invites us, and allows us, to *open* ourselves to an experience with Being. And since the question works in this way, our experience with Being can become an experience of Being in its openness, its opening dimensionality.

Our project of recollection *breaks* with the history of metaphysics by attempting to *think* the Question of Being in an *opening* way. By breaking with the dispassionate, disinterested, disembodied speculation – and first of all, perhaps, the methodology of totalization – definitive of traditional metaphysics, our recollection *salvages* the Question of Being and gives it new life. There is a primordial, rudimentary, unrealized 'understanding' of Being that is given to us with the gifts of nature. This 'ecstatic' *sense* of the openness of Being that is concealed within our capacities, the predispositions or 'moods' of our perceptual experience, is an ontological gift – the primordial *Es gibt*. It is in recollection that we take up and respond to the claim, the *Anspruch*, informing this primordial gift.

This study, then, weaves together four different narrative texts: (1) a phenomenology of perception primarily indebted to the work of Merleau-Ponty; (2) a phenomenological psychology which draws mainly on the work of Freud and

Jung in order to interpret ego process and the possibility of a journey constellating the Self beyond egocentric, ego-logical patterning; (3) a critical interpretation of society and culture drawing on the work of Marx, Benjamin, Horkheimer, Adorno, Marcuse, Habermas, and Foucault; and finally (4) a hermeneutical interpretation of nihilism and the history of Being as they are reflected in the mirror-history of metaphysics: an interpretation which is indebted, of course, to the thinking of Nietzsche and Heidegger, but which attempts to advance their thinking by channelling it through the body of felt experience.

In our present historical situation, there is a pervasive alienation of meaning. And because we are alienated from the production of meaning, oppressive operations continue to control it. This situation constitutes a difficult social and political task. It also articulates the need for a recollection of Being. I offer this present study with the conviction that the development of our capacity for listening is a meaningful way of reclaiming alienated meaning and assuming response-ability for the future.

CHAPTER 1

The Historical Call to Our Hearing

Part I
Narcissism: The Ego's Rise to Power

> Man's kinship with the gods is over. Our Promethean moment was a moment only, and in the wreakage of its aftermath, a world far humbler, far less grand and self-assured, begins to emerge. Civilization will either destroy itself, and us with it, or alter its present mode of functioning.
>
> Des Pres, *The Survivor: An Anatomy of Life in the Death Camps*[1]

When Protagoras proclaimed that Man is the measure of all things, he was claiming for Man a power, an authority, that seems not to have been claimed before. And yet, it would be unwise, I think, to hear in his words the same meaning they would affirm had he been the first to utter them at the dawn of the modern epoch. For Protagoras would still have conceded, I think, that our capacity to measure is ultimately extremely limited. What I suggest he meant was that, of all those things which are *within* the compass of our experience, we are *necessarily* the measure. On this reading, which makes his assertion shocking enough for his time, his statement does not deny that the extent of our measure is finite and that there may be things beyond our measure: things of which, given our mortal condition, our unavoidable finitude, we must for ever remain ignorant. As I read Protagoras, his assertion is not necessarily in conflict with the sentiments expressed centuries later by Pascal, who also wrote about this question of measure, and about the 'ratio' of heart and intellect, and who told us, in his *Pensées*, of his vision of 'terrifying spaces', an immeasurable abyss that shatters the composure of reason.

Man may be, then, as Protagoras declares, the measure of all things; but we of today have abolished all sense of how limited this measure really is. Without a God, without any sense of a transcendent dimension against which to measure our measuring, all limits are removed. As I argued in 'The horizon's embrace' (*The Opening of Vision*), by way of commentary on these words of Protagoras and on the feelings that moved Kant as he contemplated 'the starry heavens above me and the moral law within me' (*The Critique of Practical Reason*): having built our lives in such a way that we have lost sight of the horizon, and so flooded our dwelling-places with man-made lights that we have obliterated the sky of the night, the presence of the immeasurable, our vision is no longer moved by a sense of the proper measure.

In a note included in *Daybreak*, Nietzsche wrote:

> My eyes, however, strong or weak they may be, can see only a certain distance, and it is within the space encompassed by this distance that I live and move; the line of this horizon constitutes my immediate fate, in great things and small, from which I cannot escape. Around every being there is described a similar concentric circle, which has a mid-point and is peculiar to him. Our ears enclose us within a comparable circle, and so does our sense of touch. Now, it is by these horizons, within which each of us encloses his senses as if behind prison walls, that we *measure* the world, we say that this is near and that far, this is big and that small, this is hard and that soft: this measuring . . . is all of it an error.[2]

Nietzsche does more, here, than acknowledge that we are the measure of all things; rather, he asserts and accepts it – accepts it in a way that neither Protagoras nor Pascal ever could. What exercises Nietzsche – and this is the point that places him in the eye of the storm, the very centre of nihilism

– is that the measure we have made for ourselves, the measure we have assumed for ourselves, is tragically, unjustifiably small. For Nietzsche, Man is the absolute measure – and we have no reason, only an ancient, groundless, fear, to set limits on this measure.[3]

Beginning with the Renaissance, the first phase of 'modernity', a certain 'narcissism' emerged in western culture. Struggling on behalf of a 'universal Reason', the Enlightenment unwittingly reinforced it, for the unconditional value of 'Man' was the battle-cry of the revolutionary progress that was made in the light of Reason. In the unfolding of our modern history, however, the self-defeating tendencies within this culture of narcissism have increasingly prevailed over the more constructive and progressive. This narcissism has figured in the hegemony of a paradigm of knowledge, truth, and reality that now encourages a very aggressive, very destructive will to power. This will to power equates reason and justice with power, represses the body of feeling, denies the life of the spirit, reduces the Self to an ego which is socially adaptive but fragmented and self-alienated, and empties the Self and its world of all meaning and all value.

Thus, we can now begin to see that, after the first and most glorious phase of modernity, during which time western culture broke away from its medieval past and basked in the sun of a healthy self-affirmation, an 'excessive' pride, a culture of narcissism, gradually elevated Man to the position occupied by God. In many ways, of course, the original spirit of modernity, the spirit of the Renaissance and the Enlightenment, was extremely benevolent: a necessary phase in the progressive evolution of western society and culture, as well as a life-affirming moment for the individuation of the Self. In the modern spirit that awakened in the Renaissance, there was a noble assertion of emancipation from dogmatic, coercive authority and a passionate assumption of responsibility for the daily course of public life. But the historical form this spirit subsequently took – an inflation of Man's power – has increasingly revealed the fact that it is concealing within itself a constellation of dangers.

Cartesian metaphysics, reflecting the ambiguous tendencies latent in this culture of narcissism, conceived the Self as a (tacitly masculine) ego supremely sure of itself. Much can be said for the ontology of Cartesian thought. Its self-grounding self-assurance generated a method which freed us from dogmatic authority, and even its mechanistic picture of Man and world, without which the physical sciences and the sciences of Man could not have advanced, should for ever deserve our admiration. But this metaphysics of isolated subjects and objects bequeathed to us a Self locked into a world of self-defeating, virtually schizophrenic dualisms. The 'human' was split apart into animal-being and pure rationality, nature and culture, body and mind, matter and spirit, inner and outer, subject and object, ego and other, individual and society, private and public, feeling and reason. And Reason, the absolute method of a self-grounding subject, was identified with the clarity of logic, the exactness of mathematics, and the objectivity of physics, so that, by the middle of the twentieth century, it could be totally identified with instrumental validity. At the same time that western science denied the spiritual dimensionality of Man, *reducing* the human being to a machine of flesh and blood, it coupled with western humanism to *inflate* our collective sense of what we are capable of. With the power of science, we have created political economies that actively promoted the unscrupulous 'self-made man' and all forms of egotism, charted the course of world-wide colonialism, institutionalized social exploitation and domination, and found encouragement for our collective fantasies of planetary omnipotence and omniscience.

As a characterization of the western lifeworld, 'narcissism' signifies the rise to power, the self-assertion, of an ego-logical subject which can only be adequately understood if we recognize its masculinity, its patriarchal origin, its predominantly bourgeois personality and politics, and its obsessive will to power, to mastery, control, and domination. The 'Self' which has risen to power in the modern world is unmistakably, as Horkheimer and others have argued, a masculine, bourgeois ego.[4] In *The Eclipse of Reason*, Horkheimer boldly tied together the development of the modern ego, the rule of the patriarchy, the dominance of the masculine gender and character, the instrumentalization of Reason, the domination of nature, the domination of people, the will to power, and the symptomology of nihilism:

> the ego is felt to be related to the functions of domination, command, and organization. . . . Its dominance is manifest in the patriarchal epoch. . . . The history of Western civilization could be written

> in terms of the growth of the ego. . . . At no time has the ego shed the blemishes of its origin in the system of social domination.[5]

Narcissism, then, is a symptom of nihilism: a symptom that has increasingly displayed its latent self-destructiveness, its latent nihilism. The glorification of Man, Man as ultimate will to power, has encouraged technocracies of social domination and cultural fantasies of an absolute control over nature. Our cultural fantasies have been channelled into sciences and technologies that require total objectivity and impose it everywhere. This has meant, in time, as Nietzsche already realized in his life span, the death of God – and an increasing forgetfulness of Being, through its domination, reduction, and reification. The cultural experience of the death of God – or, more broadly conceived, the end of absolute finalities – has been a decisive factor in our pervasive sense today of drifting without purpose: our sense, that is, of homelessness and rootlessness. It has also meant the negation of any ultimate, transcendent source, any irrevocable guarantee, of meaningfulness – any unshakable foundation for knowledge, any absolute authority in truth, any fixed point of focus for the projection and mirroring of personal, social, and cultural ideals. We are compelled to live 'groundless' lives. In *The Will to Power*, where Nietzsche diagnosed the historical advent of nihilism, he noted, for example, a loss of 'faith' in the categories of reason. But now, this disillusionment is deeper and more perplexing, for we have begun to realize that Reason itself – the universal Reason of Enlightenment emancipation – has a darker, more negative aspect which we had not suspected. This aspect appears in the 'rationalization' of bureaucratic technocracies and in a rational universalism which is deaf and blind to all differences – especially those it cannot subsume without violence. In our time, Reason itself – or rather, Reason reduced to the question of techniques – has become an instrument of domination and violence.[6]

It is now becoming painfully clear that the institutional authority of science and technology has successfully effected a reduction of human beings to the dual status of subjectified, privatized egos and subjugated, engineerable objects. Thus, ironically, the rule of narcissistic subjectivity has inaugurated and institutionalized a rule of objectivity – a reduction of the

Being of beings to the condition of objecthood – that turns out to be inimical to genuine subjectivity.

In *The Politics of Experience*, R. D. Laing contends that 'if our experience is destroyed, our behaviour will be destructive'.[7] Today we are seeing and hearing this kind of rage. At the same time that the rule of objectivity is *subjectifying* the Self by *detaching* us from our body of lived experience, nullifying the *validity* of personal experience, and undermining our *trust* in what we actually experience, the rule of objectivity also *objectifies* the Self, reducing it to a machine and subjecting the once all-too-human subject to the terror of machines out of control.

The face of narcissism shows us its delusions of omnipotence; but this face is really just a mask. The face it conceals is the face of depression and despair. Suffering through the death of God and the loss of the traditional sense of Being, our society has increasingly experienced itself as living in a historical condition of extreme abandonment and deprivation. We have failed, somehow, to grow *beyond* the culture of ego-logical narcissism. Not surprisingly, symptoms of collective depression have begun to constellate: emptiness, deadness, despair, narcotization. The culture of narcissism has led us to nihilism, the negation of meaningful Being; and this, in turn, has been felt as a deep sense of immeasurable, unnameable loss: a 'loss', as Heidegger interprets it, 'of Being', a cancer of the spirit, then, around which our collective depression has slowly begun to form.[8]

The psychopathologies of the present time are related to the fact that the *being* of the Self has adopted the historical form of a monadic ego and totally identified itself with the ego's will to power – a will to master and dominate. As this will to power, the modern ego rose up to abolish the old gods, the old ideals, the old authorities and sources of meaning. But there was, and is, a self-destroying nihilism concealed within this self-assertion. The pathologies we are seeing and hearing today – the narcissistic character disorders, the schizophrenias, the depressions – are therefore pathologies distinctive of a society and culture in which the fate of the Self has been hitched to the ego's increasingly nihilistic will to power. This ego-logical will takes control by extending the domain in which objectivity rules. The rule of objectivity, however, is inimical to meaningfulness and the dimensionality of Being. In its rise to power, the ego has forgotten itself. 'All reification [*Verdinglichung*] is', as one of the authors of *The Dialectic of Enlightenment* pointed out, 'a forgetting.'[9]

These psychopathologies, forms of suffering and misery from which no one is exempt, need to be given an *ontological* interpretation, i.e. an interpretation in terms of our experience of (the meaning of) Being; because, in each case, the very *being* of the Self is at stake, and because the Self's being-at-stake manifests the fact that, in a world ruled by the institutions of instrumental Reason, a world determined by scientific objectivity and technological standards, a world where profit is more important than peace and justice, the dimensionality of Being itself, within which we live, is also at stake.

Part II
Nihilism and the Closure of Metaphysics

'All reification is a forgetting.'
Adorno, *Über Walter Benjamin*[10]

According to Heidegger's reading of the history of western metaphysics, the nihilism raging within the culture of narcissism is reflected in the 'forgetting', the reification and totalization, of Being within metaphysics itself:

> Philosophy is metaphysics. Metaphysics thinks being as a totality – the world, man, God – with respect to Being, i.e., with respect to the belonging together of beings in Being. Metaphysics thinks beings as being in the manner of representational thinking which gives reasons. Since the beginning of philosophy and with that beginning, the Being of beings has showed itself as the ground (*archē*, *aition*).[11]

Heidegger contends, in other words, that 'metaphysical thinking departs from what is present in its presence, and thus represents it in terms of its ground as something grounded'.[12] Formulated very succinctly, then, what Heidegger is arguing is that the history of metaphysics is the history of a discourse which opened – opened itself to Being – by asking the ontological question 'What is Being?', only to begin, at the very same time, the spelling out of an answer that forecloses any possibility of an opening experience with the dimensionality of Being as such. The discourse begins with an opening question, the Question of Being; but its history is marked by a way of thinking – speculative, representational – which spells its increasing *closure* to (the meaningfulness of) Being.

This closure to Being must not be confused with the *end* of metaphysics. Metaphysics can be said to continue, of course, as long as there are people to read the texts and join the conversation. But its 'closure' is another matter: metaphysics *can* continue, without ending, in a thinking that perpetuates its closure.

Is a reversal of this history possible? Can the closure of metaphysics be 'overcome'? Can the discourse somehow be reopened? Can we 'end' metaphysics by thinking the Question of Being in a way that reopens it – and reopens *us* to its reach and range? Can we deconstruct metaphysics – not in order to abandon the Question of Being, but precisely in order to let ourselves be *opened* by it? Can we breach metaphysics for the sake of our question? Is the kind of thinking which has prevailed in the history of metaphysics the only possible way to relate to the Question of Being?

Heidegger attempts a new kind of thinking: a way of thinking which attempts to reopen the discourse of metaphysics. To reopen it, that is, so that the Question can sound and reverberate in the openness. Heidegger attempts a 'recollection' of Being. For him, this recollection calls for an interpretation of the history of metaphysics by virtue of which the succession of steps contributing to the closure is made explicit and rendered perspicuous. Heidegger's etymologies are often attempts to trace the genealogy of a specific closure and make possible a moment of recollection, opening us to an experience with Being.

In the present study, we shall continue the 'task of thinking' Heidegger began and attempt to think the possibility of a recollection of Being by virtue of our capacity for listening. The working assumption, here, is that our hearing is in fact an *ontological* organ: an organ always already inherent in, belonging to, and attuned by, the openness of the dimensionality of Being as a whole, presencing for our hearing as an auditory field, a sonorous field. (Borrowing from Merleau-Ponty, we could say that this relation to Being is inherent in our hearing as an 'organismic a priori'. We may also, I believe, adopt the term 'pre-ontological understanding', a term Heidegger introduced in *Being and Time*, to describe this relationship between our hearing and Being-as-it-presences-for-us in the auditory situation.) Our hearing is an *ontologically orientated* capacity, in the sense that, although its (our) relationship to the dimensionality of the auditory field as a whole, i.e. to that field in and as which the meaningfulness of Being manifests, is not yet 'adequate' to the task, it (we) can nevertheless, through disciplined practices, 'practices of the Self', undergo further development. Indeed, since the suffering of nihilism lies in our closure to Being, I believe the conclusion is inevitable that we *need to learn* a way of listening that is more ontologically attuned, more open to Being.

The way of thinking for which Heidegger was searching, a way different from the speculative, representational thinking of traditional metaphysics, needs to be a way of listening. After asking why 'the ear of our thinking' still does not hear the 'cry', Heidegger observed, 'It will refuse to hear it so long as it does not begin to think.' And then he added that thinking 'begins only when we have come to know that reason, glorified for centuries, is the most stiff-necked adversary of thought'.[13] The way of thinking that will be open to an experience with Being, as speculative 'reason' never has been, needs to be a way of thinking deeply intertwined with an ontologically developed listening. Our listening can develop our capacity to think: think in a way that is not just more 'reasoning' and 'reflecting'. In *What Is Called Thinking?*, a work whose very title already makes unusual demands on our ability to hear its tone, the register into which it has been tuned, Heidegger calls hearing 'our need and necessity': 'our need and necessity, first of all, to hear the appeal of what is most thought-provoking'.[14] Thus, the lectures gathered under this title, this question, make an appeal to our hearing: an appeal that will not register until we have engaged in some work with our capacity to listen. *What Is Called Thinking?* is a text that calls us to practise a thinking hearing: a thinking which listens, a listening which is thoughtful. This practice is arduous, but if we work at it step by step, mindful of our experiencing process – and, in particular, our bodily felt sense of the listening dialectic – significant modulations will happen. It may be useful to keep in mind, in the course of such work, that, as Merleau-Ponty said in 'The intertwining – the chiasm' (a text we shall be working with later): 'in a sense, to understand a phrase is nothing else than to fully welcome it in its sonorous being'.[15] Even this, however, is not so easy.

In 'The word of Nietzsche: "God is dead" ', Heidegger indicates very clearly that the coupling of listening and thinking may be crucial in overcoming the reflection of nihilism in the future discourse of metaphysics:

> When we hear in the name 'nihilism' that other tone, in which the essence of the named begins to sound, then we will also hear differently the language of that metaphysical thinking which has experienced something of nihilism without being able to think its essence. Perhaps someday, with that other sound in our ears, we will be able to reconsider the epoch in which the consummation of nihilism is now beginning in another way than we have hitherto.[16]

Part III
The Metaphysics of Presence

> The disease of reason is that reason was born from man's urge to dominate nature; and 'recovery' depends on insight into the nature of the original disease, not on a cure of the latest symptoms.
>
> Horkheimer, *The Eclipse of Reason*[17]

> We need 'a theory of the pathology of modernity from the viewpoint of the realisation – the deformed realisation – of reason in history.'
>
> Habermas, 'The dialectics of rationalization'[18]

There are many different ways for us to relate to, or be 'with', people and things, and be 'in' the situations of our lives. There are many different ways, for example, of perceiving: different channels (auditory, visual, tactile; intellectual, emotional, bodily); different styles (aggressive, relaxed, manipulative, sceptical, indifferent); different orientations (idle curiosity, scientific); different perspectives (looking backwards, glancing sideways); different postures and positions (near, far, frontal, peripheral); different degrees of intensity and attentiveness (focused, diffuse, touching lightly, listening eagerly, staring, sniffing deeply); and different degrees of self-awareness. We can be 'with' absent people and things, and be 'in' situations that are not actual by exercising memory and imagination. Sometimes we are 'with' people and things, and 'in' situations, in a mode of intense participation and heightened attention; but sometimes our connection is distant, forgetful, or absent-minded. (A psychotherapist, reflecting on his method, stated: 'I don't always follow my own process all the time, but I always *try* to be there for the other person.')[19]

We sometimes encounter people and things, and enter into situations, with great openness, eager to enjoy a fresh experience; at other times, we tend to encounter people and things, and enter into situations, with closed minds and deaf ears – anxious, tense, defensive, perhaps, or perhaps with our minds already set, our course of action fixed, and our experience prejudged, predetermined. We sometimes begin an encounter absolutely certain of our knowledge and understanding, absolutely convinced that we have nothing to learn from the encounter itself: we enter the situation totally under the spell of our stereotype, our preconceptions. We can hear only what we want to hear, or what we already know and believe; we can hear nothing different, nothing new. There are some things we can hear only with great difficulty, only with great pain. There are some things we *need* to hear, but probably never will. There are things we would *like* to hear, but we are also too afraid to listen.

We are sometimes so defensive, so threatened or vulnerable, that we encounter people and things, and enter into situations, in a way that defers or postpones any genuine experience, any 'real' encounter. (We could consider 'representation' to be the re-presenting of what presents itself; the prefix would then signify a deferment by repetition, presumably more on our preferred terms.)

Sometimes, it is mostly 'in the head', i.e. intellectually or theoretically, that we are 'with' people and things, and 'in' situations; at other times, the channel, the contact, will be more 'emotional' – or more basically 'physical', a 'bodily presence'. Or, instead of being theoretical, abstract, merely speculative, it will be active, engaged, practical. Sometimes we are 'with' people and things, and 'in' situations, mainly to enjoy them for whatever they may offer, whatever they may be. (Works of art claim this kind of relationship. So do lovers, sometimes.) At other times, we encounter them with very definite intentions, interests, goals, and our relationship is then more instrumental, and perhaps more possessive, more controlling. (In his study on Walter Benjamin, Richard Wolin makes the assertion that 'the goal of knowledge is the possession of objects and not their emancipation'.)[20]

Since it is a reflection *on* life, metaphysics cannot avoid being a reflection *of* life, reflecting back to us the 'psychopathologies of everyday life' – and for us in particular, this means the 'pathologies' distinctive of modernity. How has metaphysics traditionally related to the beings (*ta onta*) coming within its purview? What does our reading, today, of the history of western metaphysics tell us about the way in which metaphysical reflection (speculation, contemplation) encounters – lets itself be with – persons and things?

Heidegger contends that 'starting from what is present, metaphysical thinking re-presents it in its presence'.[21] Consequently, he argues that the 'first step' in overcoming the metaphysical tradition of reflection must be 'the step back from the thinking which merely re-presents [*Vor-stellung*] to the thinking which responds and recalls'.[22] Here Heidegger sets in motion a contrast between two different ways, two different patterns, of relating, of 'being with'. In another text, he says:

> The course of the questioning [in metaphysical discourse] is intrinsically the way of a thinking which, instead of furnishing representations and concepts, experiences and tries itself as a transformation of its relatedness to Being.[23]

Basically, metaphysical reflection relates to people and things (*ta onta*, beings), and even to Being as such, the Being of these beings, in terms of a pattern, a *Gestalt*, that positions them within a structure of subject and object: a structure in which an isolated subject (ego) confronts, opposite it, an isolated object. Representation, as the German word *Vorstellung* says of itself, is precisely such a pattern: it is a *Ge-stalt* which involves positioning (*stellen*) something directly in front of (*vor*) a subject.

However, according to Heidegger, 'where anything that has become the object of representation, it first incurs, in a certain manner, a loss of Being'.[24] The authors of *The Dialectic of Enlightenment* echo this analysis, arguing that 'the capacity of representation is the measure of domination, and domination is the most powerful thing that can be represented'.[25] It is in the light of this interpretation, then, that Heidegger was wont to maintain that the 'truth' of Being 'will be given over to man' when we have 'overcome' ourselves as 'subjects' – 'and that means', he says, when we 'no longer re-present' that which is as 'object'.[26] But, given our historically prevailing, ego-logical will to power, it will not be easy for us to cease relating to, cease being with, people and things, and *a fortiori*, of course, the Being of these beings, in a way that represents them as objects. It will be necessary that we first overcome ourselves as subjects; and this means that we must first 'work' with ourselves. One such way of 'working with ourselves' is, of course, the problematic of concern in this study: the development of our capacity for listening, understood as a 'practice of the Self'.

In *What Is Called Thinking?*, Heidegger indicates that he has realized some clues to the kind of work, the kind of self-overcoming process, that needs to be followed. It involves, he says, 'remaining focused on the presencing of what is present [*in das Anwesen vom Anwesenden eingewiesen zu bleiben*]'.[27] If this is pointing in the right direction, as I think it is, then we must consider its implications for our traditional process of forming concepts (*Begriffe*), for the very concept of 'concept' calls for an activity of grasping, bringing together into a graspable, possessable unity. And, since we have already had occasion to recognize the intertwining of thinking and listening, we must consider – and will indeed, later in this study, consider – what 'remaining focused on the presencing of what is present' could possibly *mean* as a way of listening, a way of structuring the *Gestalt* of our listening. For the moment, perhaps it will suffice to say, anticipating our next few chapters, that what is called for is a practice of *Gelassenheit* (letting-go, letting-be) and 'recollection', gradually breaking the spell, the hold, of the ego-logical patterning that prevails in our time: the *Gestalt* type, namely, which Heidegger calls *das Ge-stell*, enframing, a positioning or positing that fixates, pins down, secures, and holds constant.

Heidegger tells us that, in his reading of Anaximander, he attempted to hear the words 'spoken in a preconceptual way'.[28] For it is his strong conviction that 'the saying first resonates when we set aside the claims of our familiar ways of re-presenting things'.[29] The listening which thinks, here, is a 'preconceptual' listening, a listening that involves the entire body, the body, that is, of felt experience. It is a listening structured not by the intentionality of conceptual grasping, but rather by the body's *felt sense* of the saying: it is a listening attuned through feeling. This way of structuring the listening situation allows the words to resonate; it gives the words the auditory space of a listening that has refrained from restricting them to the field of a subject-object structure. Words can resonate only when they are given such freedom, such openness. Otherwise, they are immediately caught, enframed, within the representational structure.

In 'The age of the world picture', Heidegger writes:

> That which is, is no longer that which presences; it is rather that which, in our representing, is first set over against, that which stands fixedly over against, and which has the character of the object [*das Gegen-ständige*]. Representing is making-stand-over-against, an objectifying that presses forward and masters.[30]

As a form of objectification, representation structures our encounters in a way that 'blocks us off', as Heidegger says, 'against the Open'.[31] For the most part, representational encounters are ruled by normalization and typification: classificatory closure to fresh experiencing.[32]

Let us now examine in more detail the way representational thinking – the way of thinking that prevails in the historical project of western metaphysics – projects the Question of Being. How does metaphysics structure the reflective situation in which it takes up its *Sache*, its matter for thought – Being? I want to suggest, here, that metaphysical reflection projects only two modes of Being – that it always *represents* the Being of beings as appearing, manifesting, showing itself, letting itself be encountered, in one of two possible modes. The one mode Heidegger calls *Vorhandensein*: sheer extantness, being-present-at-hand. The other mode he calls *Zuhandensein*: being-ready-to-hand. The latter is the mode of being in terms of which we experience, and in general relate to, the things that surround us in the everyday world: it is the way things appear to us, the way things are for us, when we relate to them, or are 'with' them, in practical, instrumental ways. Tools and equipment are the obvious paradigm for this mode of being. But of course, we often relate to people in manipulative, instrumental ways, treating them as means to our ends, rather than as ends in themselves. In other words, we often represent human beings as beings reducible to their being ready-to-hand and at our disposal. But we can also relate to people, things, and situations in a more 'theoretical' way. When a tool we are using suddenly breaks down, for example, then we may find ourselves considering it more abstractly, more theoretically. What *is* this tool, anyway? Why is it designed as it is? How does the design, and how does the material it is made from, serve the purpose, the use? Is this design essential? Is this material essential? Could I make something very different to accomplish the same task? And we might stare at it for a long time, looking at it, perhaps for the first time, in abstraction from its use in all our projects. We might even, in this state, be struck by its beauty, its graceful shape, its craftsmanship – aspects we had never noticed before.

Now, there is nothing intrinsically wrong – nothing wrong at all – with the instrumental, pragmatic relationship to things. Without such a way of experiencing and relating to the things of our world, we would not long have survived as a species. Even the 'lowest' animals of nature are involved in instrumental activities. What *is* wrong, however, is the assumption that, because the Being of all beings lends itself to our use, we may relate in this way to all beings and at all times. This overgeneralized attitude disposes us to be abusive, to misuse things. It disposes us to instrumentalize people, to be manipulative of them, and also possessive.

The pragmatic attitude, then, which discovers beings as ready-to-hand, encourages an understanding of 'Being' which in fact deeply *misunderstands* it, because it tends to take as universal, as paradigmatic, as metaphysically necessary and unchangeable, the relationship with Being – the 'projection' of Being – that prevails when we are absorbed and preoccupied with the things of our practical lifeworld. When we are hammering a nail into the wall, it is *appropriate* to be related to these things in an instrumental way. Their being *lends* itself to this treatment. In such circumstances, the fact that we are letting their being manifest *only* as ready-to-hand-being (*Zuhandensein*) is of course no cause for concern. But there *is* cause for concern when it is assumed that instrumental relationships are paradigmatic, are the only kind of relationship of which we are capable, and that Being itself, Being as such, may be adequately or totally understood in terms of our instrumental projection.

Whereas the conditions of daily living frequently tempt us

into an instrumental ontology, a misunderstanding of 'Being' as nothing more than *Zuhandensein*, the speculative metaphysician tends to fall into another misunderstanding, an error no less consequential. Like the rest of us, the metaphysician tends to 'forget' the contexts of things – the situations in which things are embedded and from which they are not really separable. And correlatively, like the rest of us, the metaphysician tends to 'forget' the background understanding that is a necessary condition of possibility for all entitative or ontological relationships, regardless of whether these be theoretical or practical.

Thus, the speculative metaphysician takes the peculiar way things manifest in correspondence to his adoption of a 'theoretical' (and supposedly disinterested, dispassionate) attitude, and to his assumption of a (disembodied) position which is everywhere and nowhere, as paradigmatic of the 'essential truth' of Being. Thus, the metaphysician also misunderstands 'Being' because of an overgeneralization: he assumes that, because 'Being' manifests for his thinking in its 'sheer extantness' (*Vorhandensein*), this is 'how Being is'; he assumes, in brief, that any other experience of 'Being' is naive, ignorant, and deluded.

The metaphysician will perhaps condescendingly tolerate the pragmatic (understanding of) ontology; but he is proud of his strength in resisting the ontology 'ordinary' mortals are tempted to believe in, and he is confident that, when he beholds persistent and 'eternally' unchanging objects, self-contained, self-sufficient substances abstracted and isolated from their world, he is seeing things as they really are – seeing the very 'essence' of Being as such.

These, then, Being as *vorhanden* and Being as *zuhanden*, are the two – and only two – ways in which, traditionally and for the most part, we of the western world have experienced, understood, and represented 'Being'. (I am of course leaving aside, here, the mystical experience of *coniunctio*, for, after all, this experience has never been common, or even commonly recognized as our ideal norm.) Heidegger, though, as we know, contests the claims of these two modes of Being to represent the 'truth' of Being: what he calls the 'presence', or 'presencing' (*das Anwesen*), of Being. For him, these representations are (ontic, ontologically forgetful) misunderstandings, to the extent that they lay claim to know the only truth, or the whole truth, of Being. And in *Being and Time*, Heidegger argues that in fact each and every one of us is always and already granted a pre-ontological understanding (or an ontological pre-understanding) of the truth of Being that is radically different from the two prevailing representations. Unfortunately, this different understanding is, as he argues, covered over – forgotten, suppressed, denied. Such is the effect of socialization, which works to achieve a 'consensually validated' reality in keeping with deeply ingrained habits.

In the next chapter, I will argue that this radically different understanding is carried by the experiential body, and that, in the particular case of hearing, it is borne by our primordial experience of *Zugehörigkeit*: our primordial inherence in, belonging to, and attunement by the dimensionality of Being as a whole. And in the chapters that follow, I will indicate, first of all, how this pre-understanding of Being 'normally' develops from infancy to adulthood, and, second, how this understanding, normally deeply concealed by the 'consensually validated', ontically forgetful misunderstanding into which we are socialized as ego-logical adults, can in fact be *developed* in a disciplined practice of the Self.

But for now, let us return to the question of the relationship between metaphysics and 'Being'. This section of the chapter is called 'The metaphysics of presence'. It is time to take note of the fact that the preposition makes this phrase ambiguous. According to one way of reading it, it suggests that presence is something which figures in the discourse of metaphysics, that it is a *topic* for metaphysics. By contrast, the other reading I make out refers to the metaphysical seizure and captivity of this concept, and says that metaphysics can grasp 'presence' only by representing it in a characteristically metaphysical way.

The second interpretation is the one that has been attacked by Derrida – or if not (any longer) by him, then at least (even now) by many writers under his spell. This interpretation appears, for example, in the assertion that 'What is common to metaphysics is the positing of Being (*Sein*) as presence, its self-positing as metaphysics of *presence*'.[33] But the second interpretation cannot be attributed to Heidegger. Heidegger does *not* think that 'presence' is, as such, metaphysical; rather, he holds that 'presence' can be – and has been – captured by metaphysics, and that the metaphysician's claim that *Zuhandensein* and *Vorhandensein* exhaustively represent the Being of beings is a grave and fateful misunderstanding, for the presencing (*Anwesen*) of Being *eludes* such a conceptual grasp. Indeed, it is precisely in order to make this point *against* traditional metaphysics that Heidegger introduces the term *Anwesenheit*, which refers to the way Being *is* (the way Being manifests, appears, shows itself) for a thinker able to relate to 'it', able to be with 'it', in a non-grasping, non-enframing, non-representational way, i.e. neither relating to it instrumentally nor relating to it theoretically, according to the methods of speculative metaphysics.

This study adopts, then, the neutral interpretation. But, in order to wrest the thinker's experience of 'presence' free from the grasping of metaphysics, we must distinguish between wholes and totalities. For what essentially characterizes metaphysics is that it totalizes and reifies 'presence'. If we do not first draw the difference, however, between wholeness and totality, then we will not appreciate the non-totalizable wholeness of presence, and we will conclude that even Heidegger's notion of *Anwesenheit* only perpetuates the ontology of traditional metaphysics.

Erik Erikson conceptualized the difference between wholes and totalities in the terms of Gestalt psychology as a way of reaching some understanding of totalitarianism. Formulated in terms of the *Gestalt*, the phenomenon of totalitarianism could be correlated with the authoritarian personality. Erikson contends that 'As a Gestalt, wholeness emphasizes a sound, organic, progressive mutuality between diversified functions and parts within an entirety, the boundaries of which are open and fluid. Totality, on the contrary, evokes a Gestalt in which an absolute boundary is emphasized. . . . A totality is as absolutely inclusive as it is utterly exclusive.'[34] I suggest that the *totality-Gestalt* corresponds to Heidegger's *Gestell* (enframing), and to the metaphysical representation of (the presence of) Being as *Vorhandensein*, and that the *wholeness-Gestalt* corresponds to Heidegger's *Geviert* (a gathering of the Fourfold), and to the experience of the presence (*das Anwesen*, presencing) of Being in so far as it can twist free of the metaphysical tradition and avoid the temptation to totalize and reify. Erikson argues that 'when the human being . . . loses an essential wholeness, he restructures himself and the world by taking recourse to what we may call *totalism*'.[35] This diagnosis of the totalizing pathology is particularly thought-provoking when considered in the light of Heidegger's analysis of the 'loss of Being' in modernity. In the narrative of this study, I shall attempt to illuminate, in terms of our experience with hearing, i.e. as auditory

Gestalten, the connection between Heidegger's history of the metaphysics of Being and the psychopathology Erikson has described. To be specific, I shall attempt to make explicit how, in the course of our patriarchal, ego-logical socialization, the development of our listening capacity *loses touch* with an essential dimension of its wholeness in relation to Being, and how this loss of contact with the meaningfulness, openness, and wholeness of Being sets us up for the temptation, which our speculative metaphysics reflects, to reify and totalize the presencing of Being.

Metaphysics reifies and totalizes the presencing of Being. This is brought out very well by John Sallis, in an analysis that he formulates with good reason (as the next section of this chapter will show) in terms of a visual paradigm. In *Delimitations: Phenomenology and the End of Metaphysics*, Sallis asserts that the metaphysical passion for a way of thinking which assumes 'that knowledge is essentially intuition means that ideally it is a pure seeing, a sheer beholding, of what is simply there, *present* to one's gaze, of what ideally would be totally open to one's gaze, something fully present'.[36] Sallis also writes, there, of a 'sheer intuition of full presence, utterly closed off from everything else, utterly self-enclosed, a perfect figure of closure': a 'full presence to what is present'; a 'fully and self-sufficiently present' seeing; and a gaze so relating to the Being of beings that 'it would present itself without reserve'.[37]

In an earlier paper, Sallis connected this metaphysical capture of presence to *Vorhandensein*, once again making use of vision to clarify the metaphysical paradigm of 'knowledge':

> This [*Vorhandensein*] is to be understood in its correlation with pure seeing, with *noein*, with intuition (*Anschauung*): When something gives itself to one's sheer gaze, when it is simply there for one's looking, displaying itself before and for apprehension, then it has the character of being present-at-hand.[38]

And in connecting with Derrida's critique of the 'metaphysics of presence', Sallis refers us to a 'sheer perceptual presence', a 'simple sensory presence (e.g. of a tone) in the living present'.[39] It is clear, when we take into account all the descriptions of 'presence' which Sallis provides, that the target of the critique is reification and totalism: a 'presencing' which is (or is understood and represented as) a totality, a 'presencing' without any hint of incompleteness or any trace of absence, a 'presencing' seen all at once and once and for all. But *this* experience of 'presencing' is not what *Anwesenheit* is all about. I would argue, however, that it was not until Heidegger had worked his way through to some understanding of *Gelassenheit*, letting-go and letting-be, that he could *oppose* to the metaphysical representations of 'presencing' an altogether *different* experience: an experience with presencing that does not reify and totalize, but instead gathers it into a sense of wholeness. Thus, in the course of our study here, we shall consider how *Gelassenheit* functions in the *Gestalt* formation of listening to make possible an experience with Being as a non-totalizable wholeness. (Derrida's contention that the 'metaphysics of presence' is 'phonocentric' will consequently turn out to be more problematic and controversial than he may have thought, because the temporality of sounds never lets us forget impermanence and never allows us a total grasp and possession, whereas the written or printed text always tempts us to see a total survey of words that are more permanently recorded and unchanging. Thus it would seem that writing would do more to encourage traditional ontology than speaking.)

Before leaving the problematization of metaphysics we have been considering in this part – and in Part II – of the present chapter, I would like to record, with my approval, the way David Wood has characterized the thinking that eludes metaphysical capture. Wood writes that

> Derrida says of Heidegger that one of his real virtues lies in his *intrametaphysical* moves. I would like to say the same of Derrida. . . . In *Ousia et Grammē*, Derrida, talking about Aristotle, says that what is truly metaphysical is not *the particular question* he evades . . . but the [fact that] the question [is] evaded, the covering up, the passing on, the failure to reflect. Conversely, what in Derrida's work *exceeds* metaphysics is his writing *as and insofar as it opens up* a space of *alternative theoretical possibilities* and bears witness to the scope of its own transformative possibilities. . . . Philosophy on the move is the only possible transgression of metaphysics.[40]

The way of thinking we are exploring here in terms of listening is a way of thinking which attempts to avoid the metaphysical grasp of 'presence' and learn how to be 'with' the presencing of Being in a way that opens up instead of shutting off – a way that lets go, lets move and change, instead of reifying.

Part IV
The Western Vision of Reason: Questioning the Enlightenment

> Above all, we value sight . . . because sight is the principal source of knowledge and reveals many differences between one object and another.
>
> Aristotle, *Metaphysics*[41]

> The exclusive emphasis on an optical connection to the universe . . .
>
> Benjamin, 'One-way street'[42]

> Enlightenment is totalitarian.
>
> Horkheimer and Adorno, *The Dialectic of Enlightenment*[43]

> Since Bergson, the use of the sight metaphor in philosophy has kept dwindling, not unsurprisingly, as emphasis and interest have shifted entirely from contemplation to speech, from *nous* to *logos*.
>
> Arendt, *The Life of the Mind*[44]

> Vision is a spectator; hearing is a participation.
>
> Dewey, *The Public and its Problems*[45]

Once upon a time, or so the story goes, we were an oral and aural culture, without writing and reading. There is some evidence to believe that the infant's development undergoes a similar shift from a primarily auditory awareness to a more vision-orientated consciousness, recapitulating the ancient history of civilization.[46] Be this as it may, we know that it is principally through seeing, the power to survey, that the infant first acquires a narcissistic sense of its capacity to control objects, and that, as early (at least) as the pre-Socratic philosophers, the Greeks were using words for knowing and the object of knowledge which also meant the act of seeing and the object of the gaze.[47] Vision and knowledge are inseparable as instruments of power.

In the body politic of the senses, vision, as we know, is sovereign, and the totalitarian empire of the panoramic gaze, the most reifying and totalizing of our sensory powers, continues to extend the hegemony of its metaphysics: its ontology, its paradigm of knowledge and truth, total visibility, a uniform field of absolute intelligibility. This ruling privilege, almost totally concealing all indications of the historical struggle between vision and hearing, has produced a succession of philosophical texts subservient to the visual paradigm. But even at its very beginning, the metaphysics that was emerging had already been engaged in a massive denial of temporality and impermanence, finitude and mortality. The victory of vision, however, ensured the enduring domination of *oculocentrism* – a paradigm based on the dual nature of the Gaze, the one practical and aggressively active, the other theoretical and contemplative, panoramic, stationary, unmoved, dispassionate, disembodied, outside time and space. In the empire proclaimed by our metaphysics, our vision, our *metaphysics* of vision, it is clear that no fundamental changes, no contradictions, no reserve of difference will be allowed to disturb the power of the contemplative Gaze or to question the groundplan of its comprehensive rationality.

Anticipating Freud, Nietzsche connected knowledge to a biological drive – a 'drive to appropriate and conquer'.[48] Nietzsche also anticipated Habermas, insisting that there is no such thing as knowledge which is 'disinterested'. An interest in orders of control is the character of knowledge based on the visual paradigm. The capacity of the gaze to *turn away* from the entities it has seen and yet retain an image of them in isolation, abstracted from their situational assignments, i.e. as present-at-hand, as *vorhanden*, enables and encourages our vision to assume a theoretical power that in turn amplifies its practical power over entities.[49] Our infant eyes open to the world fresh with wonder and fascination; but, very soon, this attitude narrows to curiosity. As Mallarmé once put it, *l'enfant abdique son exstase*.[50] Before long, as the ego-centre begins to constellate through a patriarchal legitimation of the masculine archetype, this curiosity becomes more interested in manipulating and controlling the visual spectacle and the intentionality of the gaze becomes more focused, more ray-like, more linear.

The 'knowledge' for which vision works is a 'knowledge' the Greeks called *epistēmē*. (*Epistēmē* should be compared, here, with *sophia*, a wisdom that understands.) This word comes from *epi*, meaning 'in front of', and *stā*, meaning 'set down', 'posited', 'standing', *gestellt*. The ontology belonging to this epistemology may therefore be called a *frontal* ontology, an ontology of entities which, at least in the ideal situation, are to be held 'front and centre': in the most ideal act of *beholding*, the object is to be *held* in place directly before the eyes. This is the metaphysics of vision: a metaphysics that tends to overvalue constancy, uniformity, permanence, unity, totality, clarity, and distinctness. Now, the nature of the visionary situation is such that the gaze always inhabits a field of contemporaneously coexisting entities, more or less immediately in continuous view, constant beholding. This situation, however, encourages a metaphysics of presence, a discourse of speculative thinking in which the apparently real panoptical omnipresence of entities is reflected – and not only reflected, but projected as the absolute truth.

Perhaps a different vision is possible, for vision, too, is a capacity that can be developed – developed, perhaps, far beyond the ego-logical stage maintained by our social 'consensus' and prevailing historical conditions. It is, in fact, with some hope of contributing to further visionary self-formation that I have, in *The Opening of Vision*, attempted to diagnose the character of vision in our time (namely, as *das Gestell*, enframing), and suggested possibilities for its transformation that are inherent in the process of *Gestalt* formation and related to our inveterate tendency to 'forget' the figure-ground difference.

However, given the many centuries of historical privilege for vision and given the inherent tendencies of vision that have contributed to a metaphysics of the will to power – tendencies, as I will argue, that are less forceful in hearing – we should also begin to think about the possibility of developing our capacity for listening and giving more normative weight, in our paradigm of knowledge, rationality, truth, and social reality, to the very different wisdom deeply inherent in listening.

In 'Ubi est qui natus est Rex Judaeorum', Meister Eckhart contrasts vision and hearing as kinds of power:

> Hearing brings more into a man, but seeing gives out more, even in the act of looking. And therefore we shall all be blessed more in the eternal life by our power to hear than by our power to see. For the power to hear the eternal word is within me and the power to see will leave me; for in hearing I am passive and in seeing I am active.[51]

Eckhart is pointing out two things: that we have less control over what we hear, and that hearing is inherently a less control-driven organ. This difference has been registered, as Erwin Straus once noticed, by our locutions: we speak of 'casting an eye', but about our hearing we speak, rather, of 'lending an ear'.[52] Straus also pointed out, in the same study, that the Latin word for 'obey', *obaudire*, also means 'to listen from below', i.e. in a relationship of respectful understanding.[53]

It is easier for us to shut our eyes than close our ears. It is easier for us to remain untouched and unmoved by what we see than by what we hear; what we see is kept at a distance, but what we hear penetrates our entire body. Sounds do not stop at the boundaries set by the egocentric body; but the egobody of vision can usually maintain its boundaries (inner and outer, here and there, ego and other) more easily. Hearing is intimate, participatory, communicative; we are always *affected* by what we are given to hear. Vision, by contrast, is endistancing, detached, spatially separate from what gives itself to be seen. Thus, in terms of the characteristics that have constellated into archetypes within the prevailing conditions of our lifeworld, vision has been the representative of our phallic energies, while hearing has been the representative of our feminine spirit. *A fortiori*, then, the task of this study, the project of developing our capacity for listening and achieving a better integrated balance between the power in listening and the power in vision, calls for a recollection of the feminine wisdom, the *sophia*, carried by the listening body-Self; a recollection that will re-member the listening body in relation to Being, the dimensionality of its wholeness. The task can only be accomplished if personal growth is accompanied by correspondingly needful changes in our social and cultural life, overcoming the masculine will to power.

The Enlightenment certainly constellated a new historical vision: a vision that took the 'light of Reason' as its guide.

But this vision covertly arrogated for itself some of the power to determine the norms by which the very character of Reason was to be thought and enacted. I see the Enlightenment as the consummate moment in the historical dominance of the visual paradigm, for it was during, and as a result of, this visionary moment that the western world, moved to revolutionary changes, assumed responsibility for 'processes of Enlightenment' which began to realize its emancipatory potential.[54] The glorious vision of the Enlightenment was a vision that accepted, and never saw the need to question, the legitimacy and benevolence of a 'universal' Reason. It therefore imagined the emancipation and humanization of 'Man' through the progressive rationalization of life. It did not see what became apparent only in the next century, and perhaps not until Marx and Weber began to analyse the institutionalization of Enlightenment Reason: namely, the terrible violence, the subtle repression of difference and otherness, hidden within the 'benevolent universality' of Reason. The heirs of the Enlightenment have paid a dear price for this moment of glory and blindness.

The motility of the gaze, its distinctive intentionality, has unquestionably motivated a monological and instrumental (*zweckrational*) rationality. With the development of our capacity for hearing, however, we may be able to overcome the historical dominance of what *The Dialectic of Enlightenment* calls an 'alienated ratio' – an alienated and alienating rationality by which the lives of modernity, our lives, have for too long been measured.[55] By virtue of developing our listening, we may find ourselves granted the sense of a different norm, a different measure, a different principle for thinking the 'ratio' of rationality. I intend to argue, in this study, for a new paradigm of Reason: a principle of Reason grounded in the dimensionality recollected through our experience with listening. Habermas has worked out a procedural definition of the principle we need in his recent theory of a communicative rationality; but he has not taken into account the listening side of the 'ideal speech situation'.

In this regard, it may perhaps be worth pondering the fact that *Vernunft*, the German word for 'Reason', comes from *vernehmen*, a word with a range of meanings that includes 'hearing'. *Vernunft* therefore ought to mean a Reason that listens and hears. But in fact, the 'Reason' of the Enlightenment, the *Vernunft* of Kant's *Critique* and Hegel's *Phenomenology*, was a Reason whose powers of synthesis and reconciliation worked under the spell of oculocentrism and its paradigm. Moreover, for Kant and Hegel, the unifying administration of 'Reason' means that what they called the 'understanding', *Verstand*, is a faculty whose function is subordinate to that of *Vernunft*.[56] In our present study, however, we shall be using the word 'knowledge' to designate the totalizing, metaphysical functioning of 'Reason' as it has been embodied in the visual paradigm, correlatively reserving the words 'thinking' and 'understanding', the latter with its resonances that echo the Latin *obaudire*, to designate the functioning of a non-metaphysical Reason, a capacity to unify, integrate, reconcile, and harmonize without imposing totality.[57] Such a capacity is embodied, schematized, in the underlying character of our listening nature. And it is called for by the communicative conditions of our social existence. Thus, in the course of this study, we shall be working out the implications of these two relationships: the one between knowing and seeing, the other between hearing and a thinking that understands.

Now, I have argued (1) that totalism is an inveterate tendency inherent in seeing and (2) that this totalism is reflected in the totalism of a metaphysics under the spell of an optical paradigm of Reason. What remains to be touched on briefly here is how the nature of our experience with listening *subverts* the will to totalism and the closure of metaphysics, and indeed *encourages* a different ontological attitude, a different relationship to the Being of beings. Let us take up a point made by Erwin Straus: 'Sound', he wrote, 'is somewhere *between* thing and nothing. . . . [It] *is* something, yet it is not a thing one can manipulate; . . . it is not a thing, but neither is it no-thing.'[58] In other words, the nature of sound is such that it denies our hearing an experience of objectivity similar to the experience we enjoy with our vision. Unlike the things that we see, things that endure in the contemporaneous coexistence of spatial entities and belong to the 'omnipresence' of space itself, sounds are transitory and impermanent, ever insubstantial, belonging to the realm of temporality: they cannot be grasped, held, possessed. Thus, the nature of sounds deconstructs the ego's sense of identity, its sense of itself as a substantial, self-grounded subjectivity, enjoying an undisputed certainty in a world under its control.

St Bernard of Clairvaux is said to have remarked: 'You wish to see? Listen then: hearing is a step in the direction of vision.'[59] The point of *The Opening of Vision* is that, if we need a principle of the ground, then we need a new *vision* of the ground, a new *experience* of the ground *as* the ground of the ontological difference. But it is the point of this present study that, if we are ever to breach our metaphysics, then we also need to overcome its oculocentrism and work toward a new relationship to the ground, born out of our experience with listening as a practice of the Self.

The future of the world which the humanism of the Enlightenment inaugurated seems to call, now, for the restitution of the Hebraic tradition, a tradition that has always emphasized the communicativeness of listening more than the possessiveness of vision.

Part V
Communicative Ethics: A New Model of Rationality

The 'Reason' of the Enlightenment turned out to be overbearing, oppressive, and even violent, as well as emancipatory and humanizing. Advancing the diagnosis first articulated by Horkheimer and Adorno, Habermas discerned the need for a new model of rationality. Whereas the 'Reason' of the tradition – I am thinking mainly of Descartes and Kant – was monological, the new paradigm must be a dialogue, a conversation, an exchange of arguments. Whereas the 'Reason' of the tradition spoke in terms of a priori principles and assumed in advance the universality of their application, the new paradigm must make universalizability an achievement of genuine consent (*Einverständnis*), reached through open, democratic processes of communication in which all those affected, concerned, or influenced by the matter in question have been able to participate without coercion. And whereas the 'Reason' of the tradition assumed a pre-established harmony of interests, the new paradigm must eschew this assumption and increase awareness of differences and conflicts.

At one time, Habermas's break with the tradition was so intense that, according to Thomas McCarthy, he believed that at the level of the organization of processes of enlightenment, the appropriate model of interaction should be a 'therapeutic discourse'.[60] However, because he took the model of 'therapeutic discourse' to be the psychoanalytic dialogue between patient and analyst, he subsequently abandoned this position. Justifiably. But if we construe 'therapeutic discourse' more broadly, so that the position becomes an argument for a model of discursive consensus formation which understands and values the communicative interactions as 'moral-transformatory processes', then the position achieves considerable persuasiveness.[61] And indeed, this seems to have been the direction Habermas's subsequent thinking took, for in *Communication and the Evolution of Society*, Habermas writes that

> Whereas Marx localized the learning processes that release epochal developments . . . in the *forces* of production, there are in the meantime good reasons for assuming that learning processes also take place in the dimension of moral insight, practical knowledge, communicative action and the consensual regulation of conflicts – processes which are precipitated into maturer forms of social integration, into *new relations* of production.[62]

Later in this text, where Habermas is exploring the relationship between (1) models of 'processes of Enlightenment' necessary for the continued rational evolution of society and (2) models of the stages of personal growth and development, i.e. the individuating, self-formative processes of moral-practical learning and maturation through which the character of the mature rational individual must pass, he argues more fully for this position:

> Naturally, we cannot draw any precipitous conclusions for the developmental levels of societies from [the stages of individual psychological] ontogenesis. . . . But social systems can, by exploiting the learning capacities of socialized subjects, form new structures in order to solve critical steering problems [e.g. around procedures of legitimation]. To this extent, the evolutionary learning processes of societies are dependent on the competencies of the individuals who belong to them. The latter, in turn, do not acquire their competences as isolated monads, but by growing into the symbolic structures of their life-world.[63]

Between individual and society, then, there is a circular, two-way process of learning and change. But if self-formative processes are dependent on and conditioned by the developmental level achieved by society as a whole, then the individual's experience of suffering and misery, and, in particular, the individual's discovery of social and cultural conditions that limit further self-transformation, could be symptomatic of real inadequacies in the evolutionary processes of society.

In the chapters that follow, we will be giving thought to the function of listening in the reproduction of social life, attending, for example, to the norm-governed role of listening in the achievement of democratic procedures of communication free of domination; the contributions of listening to social harmony, consensus formation, and integration; the significance of a developed listening capacity for the reversibility of roles and the schematization of reciprocity; and the way a developed capacity for listening decentres the ego and promotes a more enlightened intersubjectivity.

It is my belief that a critical consciousness is the outcome of self-formative processes – *Bildungsprozesse*. Here, then, in this study, we shall be thinking about the development of our capacity for hearing as a self-formative process, and about how this development can guide and inform critical consciousness. Thus, in effect, we shall also be giving thought to the practical cultivation of listening as a new 'organizational principle' of society.[64]

Part VI
Social Change: The Potential in Perception and Sensibility

Observing that 'the existing society is reproduced not only in the mind . . . but also in the senses',[65] Marcuse undertakes, in *Counter-Revolution and Revolt*, a lengthy meditation on Marx's dream of the 'emancipation' and 'spiritualization' of the senses, a dream first expounded in the 'Economic and philosophical manuscripts of 1844':

> 'Emancipation of the senses' implies that the senses become 'practical' in the reconstruction of society, that they generate new (socialist) relationships between man and man, man and things, man and nature. But the senses would also become the

> 'sources' of a new (socialist) rationality: freed from that of exploitation. The emancipated senses would repel the instrumental rationality of capitalism, while preserving and developing its achievements.[66]

Returning to the early writings of Marx in which the practice of a revolutionary humanism is outlined, Marcuse argues that

> Human freedom is . . . rooted in human sensibility: the senses do not only 'receive' what is given to them . . . rather, they discover, or *can* discover by themselves, in their 'practice', new (more gratifying) possibilities and capabilities, forms and qualities of things, and can urge and guide their realization.[67]

And then he immediately adds that 'the emancipation of the senses would make freedom what it is not yet: a sensuous need': a need, in other words, that would be authentically generated by our human sensibility, since authentic need interpretation depends on our ability to overcome our alienation from the body of felt experience and make contact with our own unique experiential processes – our own uncommonly good sense.[68] This is an extremely important point, and we shall be returning to it later. For I want to argue that the cultivation of listening is a practice of the Self which enables us to listen to our own body of felt needs and hear what they are calling for.

I welcome Marcuse's work because, as he points out, after Marx,

> Marxist emphasis on the development of political consciousness shows little concern for the roots of liberation in individuals, i.e., for the roots of social relationships there where individuals most directly and profoundly experience their world and themselves: in their sensibility, in their instinctual needs.[69]

Recalling his thinking in *An Essay on Liberation*, Marcuse writes:

> I suggested that without a change in this dimension, the old Adam would be reproduced in the new

> society, and that the construction of a free society *presupposes* a break with the familiar experience of the world: with the mutilated sensibility. Conditioned and 'contained' by the rationality of the established system, sense experience tends to 'immunize' man against the very unfamiliar experience of the possibilities of human freedom. The development of a radical, non-conformist sensibility assumes a vital political importance in view of the unprecedented extent of social control perfected by advanced capitalism: a control which reaches down to the instinctual and physiological level of existence. By the same token, resistance and rebellion, too, tend to activate and operate at this level.[70]

I concur, and hope that this study will bear out Marcuse's faith in the radical potential, not only subversive but also constructive, that awaits realization in practices of the Self which can turn felt needs into social change. In this regard, it is, I think, unfortunate that Marcuse concentrated so much on the libidinal character of the body and on its fulfilment through aesthetic experience. This study shifts the subject of the developmental work. This shift is very much needed – particularly in light of the recent shift within critical theory itself: the shift, that is, toward a theory of communicative praxis and communicative rationality.

Part VII
Developing our Capacities: Listening as a Practice of the Self

> The [Aristotelian] Principle states that, other things being equal, human beings *enjoy* the exercise of their realised capacities (their innate or trained abilities), and that this enjoyment increases the more the capacity is realised, or the greater its complexity.
>
> Rawls, *A Theory of Justice*[71]

> [When] the limited bourgeois form is stripped away, what is *wealth* other than the universality of

> individual needs, capacities and pleasures, productive forces, etc. . . .? The absolute working out of Man's creative potentialities, with no presuppositions other than previous historical development, which makes this totality of development, i.e. the development of all human powers as such, the end in itself, not as measured on a *predetermined* yardstick.
>
> Marx, *Grundrisse*[72]

> The potential immanent in capitalist civil society is to allow self-actualization through the unfolding of human capacities and powers.
>
> Benhabib, *Critique, Norm and Utopia*[73]

> Radical change in consciousness is the beginning, the first step in changing social existence: the emergence of a new Subject.
>
> Marcuse, *An Essay on Liberation*[74]

> We must promote new forms of subjectivity.
>
> Foucault, 'Why study power? The question of the subject'[75]

> If one wants to analyse the genealogy of the subject in Western societies, one has to take into account not only the techniques of domination but also techniques of the self.
>
> Foucault, Howison Lecture on 'Truth and subjectivity'[76]

Foucault tends to assume that all practices of the Self are 'techniques', that techniques are instrumentalizing, and that all practices of the Self therefore involve the imposition of socially derived forms. The Howison Lecture betrays this tendency. But when he speaks of promoting new forms of subjectivity, this tendency is being checked, for we may presume that these 'new forms' do not merely reproduce the operations of domination. I take the promoting of new forms of subjectivity to be the work of 'practices of the Self' that involve the individual in processes of personal growth which have the effect of making the person less susceptible to social control – especially the imposition of experiential meaning – and more capable of authentic social living.

In an essay titled 'What is maturity?', a commentary on the answers Habermas and Foucault have given to the Kantian question, 'What is enlightenment?', Hubert Dreyfus and Paul Rabinow quote Foucault with approval:

> The critical ontology of ourselves has to be considered not, certainly, as a theory, a doctrine, nor even as a permanent body of knowledge that is accumulating; it has to be conceived as an attitude, an ethos, a philosophical life in which the critique of what we are is at one and the same time the historical analysis of the limits that are imposed on us and an experiment with the possibility of going beyond them.[77]

Following the quotation, the commentators observe that 'this critical ontology has two separate but related components: work on oneself and responding to one's time'.[78] I trust it is already clear that this present study is intended to contribute to the realization of precisely this project.

Given Dreyfus's admiration for Foucault's project, it is very strange that, in a private communication regarding my work, he should have written that 'healing nihilism has nothing to do with getting individuals to see or hear better (although recognizing the problem of nihilism may have some such sensitivity as its prerequisite)'.[79] What makes this assertion so extremely curious is that the remark put within parentheses is in fact such a major concession that it virtually negates the preceding statement, which is made with a very self-assured gesture of dismissal. Despite his smugness, Dreyfus is obviously wrong. Even if this present study accomplished nothing more than the sharpening and heightening of our 'sensitivity', this in itself would be a significant contribution to our collective response to the needs of our time – particularly if understanding the phenomenon of nihilism 'may have' such 'sensitivity' as 'its prerequisite'.

Heidegger clearly says, in a passage Dreyfus has ignored, 'But we do not yet hear, we whose hearing and seeing are perishing through radio and film under the rule of technology'.[80] And, in *Being and Time*, written about twenty years earlier, Heidegger argued that the human being (*Dasein*) has an inveterate tendency to lose itself in 'publicness and idle talk', and consequently

> fails to hear its own Self in listening to the they-self [i.e. the Self socialized into a condition of conformity and self-alienation, out of touch with itself]. If *Dasein* is to be able to get brought back from this lostness of failing to hear itself, and if this is to be done through itself, then it must first be able to find itself – to experience itself as something which has *failed* to hear itself, and which fails to hear in that it listens away to the 'they' [i.e. to what 'others' hear, say and think]. . . . This listening-away must get broken off; in other words, the possibility of another kind of hearing which will interrupt it must be retrieved by *Dasein* itelf.[81]

After distinguishing hearing as 'obedience', hearing as 'conformity', from hearing that is 'authentic', hearing that listens to itself and is rooted in *Dasein*'s ownmost sense of itself, Heidegger indicates a task for the Self: work on oneself that involves a critical examination of one's experience with hearing.

'Indeed', says Heidegger, 'hearing constitutes the primary and authentic way in which *Dasein* is open for its ownmost potentiality for being [*sein eigenstes Seinkönnen*].[82] Here he connects the work we need to do in order to achieve authentic living with the inherent nature of listening: 'Listening [*das Hören auf*] is *Dasein*'s existential way of being-open in its being-with-others for others [*das existenziale Offensein des Daseins als Mitsein für den Anderen*].' This 'initial' openness, however, is open to different processes and ways of living, different ways in which the *Dasein* may choose to live it. This openness lays the ground for an openness to others in which we are tempted to fall into obedience and conformity. But there is always also another existential possibility, whereby the openness lays the ground for an authentic existence.

In *What Is Called Thinking?*, Heidegger reflects on this task and writes:

> What we can do in our present case, or anyway can learn, is to listen closely. To learn listening, too, is the common concern of student and teacher. No-one is to be blamed, then, if he is not yet capable of listening.[83]

Thus, if we turn to an older Heidegger for an answer to the

question, 'What might the *Vollzugsein*, the fulfilment, of our hearing potential be?', words that he spoke in 1921 would probably still work: 'The meaning is found in the actual living-out of existence.'[84]

Medard Boss, a psychiatrist influenced by Heidegger, has given a useful exposition of the implications of Heidegger's thinking for a practice of the Self concerned with the development of our perceptual endowments:

> the meaning of human being inheres in responding, with all our inborn possibilities, to what we encounter, thereby allowing what is encountered to unfold itself in our open realm of perception.[85]

Elaborating this responding, Boss suggests that

> The openness of human existence consists in the capacity for perceiving the presence and meaningfulness of whatever appears, the capacity for responding meaningfully to the perceived significance of these phenomena in a way that corresponds to their significance.[86]

'Put another way', he says, 'the worldwide perceiving openness, which is the essential ontological trait of our being, bodies itself forth in the distinct ontic modes in which we see, hear, smell, taste, and touch things.'[87] And these 'ontic modes', though given by nature and always subjected to processes of socialization before we are old enough to realize this, can always be taken up by us in our maturity, taken over as a question of our response-ability, and taken into a practice of the Self: what Seyla Benhabib refers to as 'moral-transformatory processes', an 'ethics of practical transformation'.[88] Our listening is a competence which is not just cognitive; it is always also affective and motivational as well.

In developing our listening as a practice of the Self, there are many existential possibilities for us to work on – and many different ways of working with them. One matter, to which we must ultimately give our attention, is the formation of the auditory *Gestalt*. In a late manuscript, Merleau-Ponty wrote: 'The *Gestalt* is a spontaneous organisation of the sensuous field which makes the alleged 'elements' depend on 'wholes' which are themselves articulated into extended wholes.'[89] In his late work, Merleau-Ponty gave a good deal of thought to *Gestalt* formations, which he boldly, and astutely, connected with the problematization of ontology and epistemology.[90] Since the *Gestalt* is a structure that takes place when a figure differentiates itself from its background field, i.e. when a figure-ground difference emerges, the question of the character of the *Gestalt* process becomes a question of paramount concern in a case study that attempts to bring the Question of Being – and therefore the ontological difference – to bear on our capacity for listening.

If we want to 'overcome' metaphysics, and that means avoiding its closure to (of) Being, then we need to work on balancing and integrating the metaphysical privileging of focus over diffusion and dissemination, centre over periphery, figure over ground, object over context, substance over process. 'Overcoming metaphysics' means ending its privileging of permanence over perishing, totality over whole, and cognitive control over letting-be; it means changing our epistemological attitudes and our ontological commitments.

These attitudes and commitments are not separable from the lifeworld they have constellated under distinctive social, cultural, historical influences. It is significant, I think, that our metaphysics, and the *Gestalt* it has privileged throughout its history, belong to the patriarchal archetypes. For these are the archetypes that have privileged easily graspable figures and denied any value in the elusive, ever-changing, incommensurable ground. It is very much to the point that, as Mary Daly has observed,

> the Background is the realm of the wild reality of women's Selves. Objectification and alienation take place when we are locked into the male-centred, monodimensional foreground.[91]

Accordingly, we shall be engaged, in this study, in a practice of the Self that will involve working with our listening capacity under the influence of those archetypes which traditionally have belonged to the feminine spirit. The imbalance between the masculine and the feminine must be corrected – even in our ways of channelling attention and structuring the auditory situation.

Part VIII
The Listening Self: Four Stages of Self-Development

The ear is the most spiritually determined of the senses.

Kierkegaard, *Either/Or*[92]

It is now time to run through, very briefly, the logic of the process I shall be laying out in the chapters to follow.

Stage I

The first stage is one I am calling our *Zugehörigkeit*. Taken from Heidegger, this word will refer to the fact of our inherence in, belonging to, and attunement by the dimensions of the auditory field as a whole. Since this field, an utterly open, incommensurable matrix of sonorous energies, is how the Being of beings primordially manifests itself for the organs of our hearing, *Zugehörigkeit* is a pre-ontological understanding (or an ontological pre-understanding) of Being. Heidegger never recognized in this *Zugehörigkeit* a pre-ontological understanding of Being. Although he introduced this term into his texts because he wanted the auditory significations it carries (*hörig, gehörig*) to resonate within the discourse he was setting in motion, he did not in fact use the term as we shall here, namely, to describe the hearing modality distinctive of our earliest infancy, when our hearing is minimally complex and is functioning with relatively little figure-ground articulation and little differentiation of the positional being of the listener from the encompassing being of the auditory field (the sonorous topology of Being) as a whole.

In this 'first' phase, our hearing may be said to inhere in, and be attuned by, the field of sonorous Being as a whole: the infant lives in a bodily felt inherence in the openness of the sonorous matrix and hears with – hears through – the entire body. The infant's ears are the body as a whole. Hearing in this rudimentary phase is global, holistic, syncretic, synergic, ek-static; it is an elementary hearing, deeply, symbiotically embedded in the elemental ecology of nature. Our experiences during this phase are constellated under the influence of familiar feminine archetypes: the 'uroborus', roundness, wholeness, openness, receptiveness, embodiment, feeling, communion with the matrix of soundings. During this earliest phase of our lives, our hearing is pre-personal and pre-egological: since no selfconsciously continuous centre of experience has yet coalesced and no strong-boundaried ego-logical identity has yet emerged, the auditory situation is not yet structured as subject with object.

By grace of this initial state, the gift of a primordial openness to the sonorous dimensionality of Being, the infant may be said to 'enjoy' the gift of a pre-ontological understanding of the Being of beings. Naturally, the infant is not (much) conscious of this relationship with Being; nevertheless, this experience of being so related, with which, as a hearing being, the infant is always and already graced, is at work in all motivations, movements, and gestures: it is an understanding borne entirely by the auditory body as a whole.

In the next chapter, I shall tell this story – about the embodiment of our pre-ontological understanding and the development of this initial gift – in more detail. Heidegger tells us only that there is a pre-ontological understanding of Being always assigned to us, and that we have an inveterate tendency to 'forget' it, to conceal it from ourselves. He gives no account of our self-development in this regard; nor does he explicitly *embody* this pre-ontological understanding, although he writes of the fact that *Dasein* is always embodied.

In the process of socialization, we inevitably lose touch with this pre-ontological relationship to, and understanding of, Being; and as we mature, the utterly open dimensionality of our hearing is increasingly repressed – sometimes getting psychotically split off. This 'renunciation' of our primordial ecstasy is in fact a *necessary* condition for the further development of our auditory capacity. What is unfortunate is not its *Aufhebung*, its sublimation, in stage II, but our continued abandonment of Being, and our unwillingness to retrieve it, later in life, in the time of our maturity.

Stage II

In the second phase, extending from later infancy to adolescence or adulthood, our hearing is gradually developed. In the course of our socialization, the biological potential naturally manifests; by the time the infant is a year old, there is already, in fact, a well-developed auditory competence: the child can discriminate between and recognize many different sounds and sources of sound; can recognize many different patterns of sound; can accurately imitate, or echo; can understand the significance of different tones of voice. Stage II culminates in a hearing that is personal, adequately skilful in meeting the normal demands of interpersonal living, and ruled over by the ego, which habitually structures all the auditory situations in which it finds itself in terms of subject and object. In the modern age, this structuring has become peculiarly wilful and oppositional: the auditory *Gestalt*, manifesting the distinctive character of our present historical situation, accordingly becomes enframing – a *Gestell*, obliterating the ontological dimensionality of the field.

Stage III

As adults, we are capable of assuming responsibility for our hearing: hearing is a skilfulness we can develop beyond what normal living, normal socialization, minimally requires of us. In stage III, the individual is committed to further training, a practice of self-discipline. By virtue of this commitment, this work on oneself, the self-responsible individual grows beyond an ego-logical identification and begins to live the more creative becoming of a Self. Recognition of the difference between (the being of) the ego and (the being of) the Self is crucial. Whereas the ego is a defensively adaptive structure identified with an essentially fixed, socially conforming content, the identity which begins to form in the work of stage III, the way of living I am calling the 'Self', is an ongoing process of self-development, a structure of individuation creatively open to change, a structure organized by, and identified with, processes that *carry forward* learning and growth.

There are many different goals that can motivate such work on oneself. We shall be considering four specific fields of self-disciplinary practice: in Chapter Four, the ecology of nature, the art of music, and the interactions of psychiatry; and in Chapter Five, the discourse of politics. In Chapter Four, I will argue that, in the third stage of listening, we are essentially involved in developing our listening as a practice of compassion, increasing our capacity, as listeners, to be aware of, and responsive to, the interrelatedness and commonality of all sonorous beings. (Although distinct from this compassion practice, the development of hearing as an aesthetic skill both contributes to, and is in turn advanced by, the development of hearing as an organ of compassion. For the aesthetic is precisely the cultivation of sensibility, a deepening of our capacity for sensuous and affective appreciation.) In Chapter Five, then, I will argue that the development of a deeper awareness of the reversibility dynamics inherent in all auditory situations – an awareness necessary for the emergence of a sense of justice, an understanding of reciprocity principles, and participation in rational processes of consensus formation – is a third-stage development; and, moreover, that it is a development which *must* take place, if our capacity for hearing is to be fulfilled in the good life of a just and democratic society.

Stage IV

Borrowing a term from Heidegger, we will be calling this stage 'hearkening' (*das Horchen*). Very few people ever attempt to continue the development of their hearing beyond the kinds of skill belonging to stage III. Even fewer attempt to do the kind of work necessary for the achievement of 'hearkening'. Hearkening requires the disciplined practice of *Gelassenheit*, i.e. letting-go and letting-be, as a mode or style of listening. In learning *Gelassenheit*, the art of 'just listening', listening without getting entangled in the ego's stories and preoccupations, one learns a different way of channelling, focusing, attending. There is a restructuring of the figure-ground difference, with an awareness that it manifests the appropriation of the auditory field by the double tonality of the *ontological* difference. Hearkening makes, or lets, this ontological difference – the difference between beings and Being – be manifest, be audible, within the *Gestalt* of the auditory situation.

The *Gestaltung* of stage IV is a distinctively *spiritual* accomplishment. The work of this stage begins with the practice of *Gelassenheit* and gradually performs an ontological recollection, a recollection of the utterly open dimensionality of the auditory field, as which the sonorous Being of beings manifests for our (properly) listening ears. Though never finished, this recollection realizes and fulfils our potential as human beings in relation to the Question of Being. With the achievement of this ongoing recollection, not as a cognitive operation separate from our listening, but precisely in and as the character of our listening, we may enjoy an authentically ontological relationship to, and an existentially meaningful understanding of, the Being of beings: in particular, (1) Being as such and (2) the dimensionality, the radical alterity, of other human beings. The pre-ontological relationship and understandimg that we once inhabited (during our infancy), and that we subsequently lost touch with in the course of our socialization (our ego-logical development), we begin to retrieve in stage IV, getting it back, this time, in a highly conscious, thoughtful, and articulate experience, meaningfully integrated into the auditory situations of our daily lives.

Our practice at stage IV is a practice that needs to take place under the influence of the feminine archetypes: there must be an appreciation and a recovery of experiencing modalities that, in our culture, have been traditionally constellated through these archetypes.

By virtue of our existential work, our channelling is opened up. In this state, it 'invites' a gathering of all sonorous, audible beings from all sonorous dimensions, bringing them into a *Gestalt* that we will call, again borrowing from Heidegger, *das Geviert* – the Fourfold. Whereas, in stage II, the auditory *Gestalt* is enframing, is a *Gestell*, here the structure becomes a *gathering* of sonorous Being: a gathering mindful of its utterly open dimensionality, attentive to the primordial difference by grace of which all auditory structures are possible, and respectful of the incommensurability of the Being of sonorous beings, letting the inaudible be inaudible.

The four stages are laid out, together with characterizations along seven different axes, in Table 1.1.

Let me briefly explain the seven axes: A–G. The first axis, *Axis A*, describes our hearing as an experience in relation to the Question of Being. In stage I, there *is* a relationship with Being, but it is for the most part unconscious and, in any case, undeveloped. In stage II, we are preoccupied with beings (the ontical dimension) and forgetful of Being (the ontological). In stage III, there is a recollection of Being by way of a 'return' to our still preserved, pre-ontological sense of Being. In stage IV, we achieve an authentic ontological understanding. ('Achieve' does not mean 'finish' once and for all.)

Axis B outlines the emergence of the ego and, in stage IV, its transformation, or sublimation, within the constellation of a Self. In distinction from the ego, the Self does not reductively and exclusively identify itself with the structure of subject and object. It is a process of centring open to change and growth; it values a wholeness that cannot be totalized;

TABLE 1.1

The Four Stages of Listening

	I *Zugehörigkeit*: primordial attunement	II Everyday listening (*Jederman*)	III Skilfully developed listening	IV *Hearkening*: listening as recollection
A	Pre-ontological	Ontical everydayness	Ontical skilfulness developed	Ontological authenticity
B	Pre-egological	Ego-logical	Ego-logical maturity	Constellation of the Self (beyond ego)
C	Pre-personal	Personal and interpersonal	Personal and interpersonal	Transpersonal
D	Aesthetic immediacy (conformity)	Ethical mediation (individuation)		Religious immediacy
E	Stage I Infancy	Stages II–VII: childhood to adulthood	Stages VII–VIII: existential maturity	Stage VIII: mature wisdom
F		Pre-conventional (stages 1–2), conventional (stages 3–4), post-conventional (stage 5)	Post-conventional (stage 6: 'Universal ethical principles')	
			Communicatively achieved understanding (stage 7 in Habermas)	
G	Unstable, very fluid, minimal complexity	*das Gestell*	Skilfully developed *Gestalt* attunements	*das Geviert*: gathering of the Fourfold

and its perceptual responsiveness is fresh, alive to whatever may be present, not mediated by representations that have been accumulated from earlier experiences or that conform to the prevailing social construction of 'reality'.

Axis C outlines the structural development of 'personality', beginning with a stage that we will be calling the 'pre-personal', taking a term from Merleau-Ponty's *Phenomenology of Perception*. In stage IV, there is a 'return' to the pre-personal sense of experience that we still carry with us by grace of our embodiment. Making contact with our bodily felt sense of this pre-personal way of inhabiting the world, we can 'retrieve' it, bring it 'back', and integrate that sense of ourselves – that sense of ek-static living – into our daily lives. Achieving the transpersonal stage does *not* mean the obliteration of personal and interpersonal ways of experiencing and living, some psychotic depersonalization or disintegration of personality, but rather that our personal and interpersonal existence is *rooted* in a deep sense of our connectedness with (the Being of) all sonorous beings: a moral and spiritual sense, then, that there is an infrastructure of interdependencies, whose law (*nomos*) is one which governs our existence long before it must give way to the rule of the ego, and to which, by working on ourselves, we can always turn for its guardian wisdom. (We shall explore this dimension of our experience in a later chapter, when we go into what Merleau-Ponty calls 'the intertwining'.)

Axis D attempts to map Kierkegaard's three stages of existence on to our four-stage process of self-development. This mapping, like the mappings on axis E and axis F, are only rough approximations, suggestive homologies.

Axis E, then, attempts to correlate our schema with Erik Erikson's.[93] I am suggesting a (rough) correlation between Erikson's stage i (infancy) and our stage I. For Erikson, the principal psychological issue at this stage is the question of trust and mistrust. In terms of psychosexual development, this stage mainly involves what Erikson calls 'incorporative modes' of being: oral-respiratory and sensory-kinaesthetic. Erikson's stages ii–vii (early childhood into adulthood) seem to correlate with our stage II. Erikson's stage ii involves opportunities for individual initiative, together with the corresponding possibility that these opportunities will constellate as psychological difficulties and crises (shame, guilt, self-doubt). The principal 'psychosocial modality' at this stage is to do with holding (on) and letting go. (In psychosexual terms, this stage is concerned with retentive-eliminative processes.) If satisfactory experiences during Erikson's *first* stage are critical for our subsequent willingness to trust in openness, rather than listen to our anxiety and adopt an attitude of closure, satisfactory passage through Erikson's *second* stage is critical for the subsequent development of our capacity for *Gelassenheit*, the letting-go and letting-be of hearkening (stage IV in our scheme). Erikson's stages vii and viii (adulthood and mature age) may perhaps be correlated suggestively with our stage III. For Erikson, the psychological crises of these stages are: generativity vs. self-absorption (stage vii) and integrity vs. despair (stage viii). In our stages III and IV, and particularly in the latter, questions in these two categories are very much to the point. Also, I would note that, in Erikson's stage viii (mature age), the 'radius of significant relations' is extended to embrace all of humanity, and a wisdom of acceptance is achieved, perhaps drawing strength from a compelling sense of mortality. Thus, Erikson's stage viii could be a propaedeutic step on the way to hearkening, an openness that gathers the sounds of what Heidegger calls the Fourfold – earth and sky, gods and mortals – into its embrace. (I suggest that the term 'gods' could be used to refer to our normatively projected ideals, our role models, our archetypes, rather than a divine personality.)

Axis F attempts to correlate our scheme with one proposed by Lawrence Kohlberg.[94] (As Carol Gilligan and others have pointed out, however, there are serious problems with Kohlberg's hierarchical and cognitivist model. We cannot examine these problems here, but I want it understood that my correlations do not imply an endorsement of his model in regard to these problems.) Kohlberg discerns *six* universally recognized stages in moral development, and groups them into three levels: 'pre-conventional', 'conventional', and 'post-conventional'. The first stage centres on obedience and punishment: extreme dependency and heteronomy. (Note that 'obedience' means 'listening from below', so that Kohlberg's first stage of morality implicates a distinctive way of listening. But Kohlberg does not research how this listening itself evolves in correlation with the development of moral character.) The second stage centres on instrumental relationships: the pragmatism of an emerging ego. The third and fourth stages, constitutive of the 'conventional level', involve the child in relationships that progress from conformity to independence, that abandon selfishness for role reversibility and reciprocity, and that stimulate the development of conscience and public awareness. The fifth and sixth stages, belonging to the 'post-conventional level', involve an increasing understanding of social interdependence and the discourse of rights and social contracts (stage 5), and a deepening commitment to universal ethical principles (stage 6). For Kohlberg, this sixth stage is identified with the achievement of the mature, socially responsible, genuinely autonomous moral person, a moral agent modelled after the Kantian paradigm.

It is, I think, worth considering here, if only briefly, how this model could be mapped on to the model with which we shall, in this book, be working. Kohlberg seems to offer no interpretation of the stage that is first in our model and first in Erikson's. I would put his first five stages, or at least the first four, in our stage II. His 'final' stage is one I would put in our stage III, for its seems to me that the universalizable, reversible standpoint of Kohlberg's stage 6 is not achievable to any significant degree without the kind of maturing that takes place in our stage III. Needless to say, the moral capacity exercised in Kohlberg's stage 6 is greatly enhanced by the kind of work distinctive of our stage IV. In Chapter Five, we shall explore the experiential grounding of the procedural principles that are at the heart of our moral and political life, relating the justificatory grounding, which always needs to be worked out within the framework of a discursive rationality, to the character of a reflectively and communicatively developed capacity for listening. It should then be apparent (1) how listening can contribute to the development of Kohlberg's stage 6 capacity for principled moral judgement and action (a capacity resting on the practice of role reversibility and a commitment to reciprocity), and (2) why our listening inherently calls for a *seventh* stage – the communicatively achieved understanding for which Habermas has long argued.

Finally, we come to *axis G*, in which I attempt to correlate, with each of the four stages, a quite distinctive organization (*Gestaltung*) of the sonorous energies constitutive of our auditory situations. To each stage of self-development, there corresponds (co-responds) a different type of *Gestalt* character. For the (historical) character of the *Gestalt* always echoes the (historically shaped) *character* of the one who is listening.

The development model I am proposing in this study – and not only the model, but also the design of the table, which cannot accommodate a hermeneutical time-dimension – will be open to some very destructive misunderstandings unless, anticipating them here, I can successfully ward them off by clarification. That is what I shall now try to do.

First of all, it is essential to understand that the developmental process is not a straightforwardly linear progression, but rather a dialectic of sublimations or sublations: a dialectic for the evolution of which Hegel introduced the word *Aufhebung*. In other words, each phase in the process is carried forward: not only transformed, but also preserved, *as* transformed, by the subsequent stage. Thus the first stage, *Zugehörigkeit*, is never entirely left behind, nor is it ever totally split off, when the infant undergoes a process of socialization. To be sure, socialization gradually installs an ego-logically boundaried centre in the 'place' where an ecstatically *open* centre once functioned; but the auditory body always continues to bear within it some 'traces', or an echo, of this primal experience with the sonorous dimensionality of Being.

In this regard, it is crucial to keep in mind that the 'primordial relationship with Being' attributed to infancy is a past that has never really been present – a past that never *was* what it *now*, i.e. from the vantage point of stage IV, presents itself as having been. *Zugehörigkeit* is a projection, a reconstruction, an understanding constituted after the fact, redeeming an experience that 'from the very beginning' fell short of itself: fell short, I mean, of being 'the beginning', a primordial experience of the pure and total *presence* of Being.

Nevertheless, in order for us to grow out of infancy, the structural openness of *Zugehörigkeit must* give way to an increasingly ego-centred and normalized channelling of our listening capacity. (When interpersonal conditions, especially relationships within the family, are hostile to such growth, a psychotic closure – autism or schizophrenia – will ensue.) The formation and stabilization of an ego-logical identity is a normal, healthy, necessary stage in the development of the human being. Thus, when social conditions are 'normal', our biologically *given* nature will *ensure* a maturation of our listening capacity that brings it within the functional controls identified with the ego-logical stage – stage II in our model. But, even though there never *was* an 'original' experience with Being as absolutely pure and total presence in the first place, the advances of stage II are not achieved without a loss: a loss that we may call, using Heidegger's phrase, a 'loss of Being', or a loss of *contact* with the ecstasy (*ek-stasis*) of Being – 'Being' understood, here, as the utterly open ek-static dimensionality of the auditory field, the sonorous field. And yet, this loss of contact (which, as noted, never *was* an experience of pure presence) is not total, and therefore not irrevocable or irremediable: by grace of our embodiment, echoes of our earliest experience with the Being of the sonorous field are preserved and continue to resonate, so that, later in life, *after* the ego is firmly established, it becomes possible to 'return' to these echoes, not only making contact with our bodily felt sense of that pre-ontological openness – whatever sense of that 'primordial ecstasy' we may now, by virtue of some directed exertion, be able to feel – but also 'retrieving' it and freeing it for an ongoing integration into present living.

In principle, then, the infant's experience of *Zugehörigkeit*, a 'primordial' inherence in the openness and wholeness of Being, is always to some degree retrievable. And when it *is* retrieved, it is always also *more* than retrieved, as well as less, since it is only *nachträglich*, after the fact and belatedly (as Freud would perhaps have wanted to suggest), that this experience, which the infant lived through without (much) consciousness, gets to be recognized for what it was (is) and accordingly comes to be understood as an *ontological* relationship. The 'retrieval' therefore retrieves in *two* senses: it brings back what was 'forgotten'; but it also *redeems* it by 'making' it what it never was.

The recollection of Being – the very same movement by which we grow beyond our ego-logical identifications – is a *hermeneutical* movement: we must first 'go back' to *Zugehörigkeit*, 'back', as it were, to 'the beginning', in order to develop beyond the ego-logical stage of ontological forgetfulness in listening. Or rather, to state this point more accurately, since in truth this 'beginning', this 'origin', can never be retrieved *now* as it actually was *then*, we must first generate within ourselves *a presently felt sense* of our 'pre-ontological beginning'. This movement forward, this growth, requires a hermeneutical movement backward: a movement, however, that must not be confused with an infantile or psychotic regression. It is essential to understand the difference between this hermeneutical 'return' and a pathological regression. Regression is a movement in *one* direction only; it *repeats* what came earlier instead of redeeming it; and it is always a movement, therefore, that *closes* the process of personal growth.

We are always free, of course, to continue living in the stage II reality of anyone-and-everyone (*das Man*), virtually deaf to the dimensionality of Being that resounds all around us. But after we have *achieved* the maturity of stage II, we *can* still continue to grow, committing ourselves to a practice of the Self by virtue of which we begin to grow *beyond* the ontologically alienated condition of being-an-ego to find ourselves more opened up to this dimensionality of Being and enjoying a spiritual wholeness not otherwise possible. The hearkening of stage IV, a gathering embrace of whatever may be given to our ears for their hearing, is an achievement that brings with it a self-fulfilment altogether different from that which comes in stage III: a self-fulfilment that is not possible at all in stage II.

It is essential to understand, at this point, that the ways of the Self are never secured once and for all, and that stage IV listening can always – and for much of the time it does – fall back into stage III or stage II: back, that is, into the ego's old inveterate habits. Just as, in principle, our listening can *at any moment* effortlessly shift from ego-centred ways of structuring into the Self's more 'spacious' ways of hearkening simply by a spontaneous 'recollection' that attunes us to the ground, the open dimensionality of the ontological difference, so our hearkening can at any moment *forget* this field of difference and *fall back* into ego-logical modalities of ontological indifference, momentarily distracted, momentarily entangled once again in the old patterns of desire, or totally immersed in instrumental relations. The difference between these two ways of listening is a difference in their grounding, their dimensionality. But *this* difference can make all the difference in the world: the difference, for example, between deafness to cries of injustice and a listening which resists prevailing social representations and is more responsive.

The difference between stage II and stage IV is never, then, a finished achievement – something absolute. This is another point concerning which Table 1.1 can be misleading, for it suggests a linear passage from II to IV: a 'horizontal' movement in one direction, irreversible, final. But the passage from II to IV can be as simple, and yet also as difficult, as a shift in the channelling of attention: a shift, say, from a listening tightly controlled by expectations and preconceptions to a listening that is more spacious. And conversely, the passage from IV to II can be as simple, and as easy, as the shift from a listening which is relaxed and calm to a listening which is troubled by anxiety and needing to be very defensive. In the passage from II to IV, the listening ego is *not* dissolved or obliterated once and for all. Since it never *was* a substantial being in the first place, but only a relatively unified and coherent way of organizing and structuring auditory situations, the 'disappearance' of the so-called 'ego' in stage IV 'merely' signifies a radical reorganizing and restructuring of the perceptual *Gestalt* in accordance with a different constellation of principles – principles concerned with grounding and centring, to name only two, in a constellation I am calling, all too conscious that it is nothing but a convenient abbreviation, 'the Self'. (*A fortiori*, the model of psychotic process, which can hear, in the 'disappearance of the ego', nothing but symptoms of extreme psychopathology, should not be applied to the developmental process at stake in this study. The ego's 'disappearance' can signify the constellation of a post-egological Self as well as a regression to pre-egological states of fusion.)

Before proceeding to examine the conception of human nature presupposed by this account of self-development, I want to emphasize that the four successive 'stages' must also be read as four functionally contemporaneous 'centres'. The table I have presented here, conceived of course from the standpoint of an individual who has achieved the consummate listening characterized as 'stage IV', is *not* only a diachronic model of self-development, showing the four developmental stages laid out horizontally in their temporal, biographical succession – laid out, that is, to be read as forming one after the other in a lifetime process of self-formation. The table is also to be read synchronically, vertically, i.e. as a vertical cross-section that shows, for each achieved developmental stage, and for any time, any moment during which one is principally situated, or centred, *within* that stage, what other dimensions of listening are contemporaneously co-operative, always simultaneously co-functioning, implicitly, interdependently, and as potential modalities into which, or at least toward which, the centre of listening may shift at any moment, at any time.

This is of course implied by the point I made earlier, viz. that in the developmental process, the preceding stages are transformed: they do not simply disappear, but continue to function in sublimation, *aufgehoben*, as implicit possibilities. What this means is that a listener in the first stage of development – normally an infant – is initially capable only of *Zugehörigkeit*, but becomes increasingly capable of the differentiations characteristic of stage II; and that a listener who has achieved the second or third stage can at any time (but normally not before adolescence, at least) awaken to the stage IV sense of the open dimensionality and begin to appreciate this openness as that by grace of which we are enabled to hear. In other words, the listener in stage II or III, normally an adult, may at any time undertake a recollection of Being by retrieving, to begin with, his or her presently felt sense of *Zugehörigkeit*. The vertical reading also tells us that people of consummate achievement, people who have to some degree achieved the fourth developmental stage, can at any time *fall back* into the habitual, ego-logical ways of structuring auditory situations that are characteristic of stage II development, and may even, in extreme cases of psychopathology, regress (temporarily or permanently) into a modality similar to the modality of the first stage. No one is ever exempt from this terrible possibility. It is essential to understand this, because otherwise we will miss both the character of listening as it is actually experienced within the different stages and the character of the various shifts as actually experienced processes.

For the purposes of cognitive and moral psychology, theories of education, and critical social theory, a developmental chronology, or biography, defining the successive stages of a lifetime process of self-development, would perhaps have been sufficient. But an exclusively diachronic, horizontal reading of the table proposed here – and *a fortiori*, of the entire text in which it is embedded – would altogether miss the hermeneutical phenomenology: the actual experience of the moment, with all its latencies, its potential, its implicate order; and also the ways in which processes of change, processes of development and regression, take place.

As I have already indicated, I believe that the development of our capacity for hearing is something worth undertaking for its own sake, i.e. in order that we fulfil ourselves, and be able to enjoy our self-fulfilment, as auditory beings. But I also believe that we can respond to the historical advent of nihilism, and realize the social dream of humanism, only if we develop our capacity for listening. Thus, I am attempting (1) to lay out, in terms of our experience with hearing, the successive stages of a lifetime process of self-development and (2) to correlate these stages with processes of social evolution, processes realizing the 'Enlightenment potential' within our present society.

But I am also attempting to take our thinking into the lived character of our listening experience at the moment. This is not its horizontal, biographical extension, surveyed, as it were, from outside, but rather its vertical dimensionality, its structural complexity and developmental tensions (its latencies, potentialities, and implicate order), during the time it is determined by its location *within* one of the four stages. Consequently, when I want to concentrate on individual self-development, on the biographical, I shall refer to 'stages'; but when I want to emphasize the vertical dimensionality, i.e. the dimensions, the structures and tensions co-operating in various ways at every moment *within* one of those stages – what it is like, in short, to be listening and hearing within a stage – I shall refer to the four stages as 'centres'.

Now, our concept of 'development', here, presupposes that there *is* such a thing as 'human nature' – that it makes sense to think in these terms. I believe that human beings do have an 'innate' nature. But I am not at all confident that I *know* what it is – and can become. I am quite sure, however, that it is not the 'nature' conceived by Judaeo-Christian theology and western metaphysics. (1) We cannot 'know' our nature a priori. (2) We cannot know it, so to speak, 'as it is in itself', e.g. apart from its historical conditions. (3) All our knowledge about human nature is historically conditioned, irremediably uncertain, and always defeasible. (4) Moreover, although there is a pregiven biophysical confluence of conditions, laying down within this ecology a complex of tendencies, predispositions, and intentionalities, and setting down parameters on possibilities and impossibilities, likely and unlikely ends, what we are calling 'human nature' is neither totally predetermined (in or by itself) nor totally unchangeable (i.e. non-interactional).

Which constituents of human nature are actualized and which remain in latency as mere potential will always be a function of particular interactions between the givenness of our nature and the prevailing conditions of the world. To a considerable but unknown extent, human nature is determinately indeterminate. And the world in which it has flourished, and apart from which it cannot be conceived, is no less indeterminate and changeable. Thus, the course of our self-development as human beings is not completely (pre)determined: neither by the state of the world nor by its own inherent predispositions. The pregiven in our 'nature', and in the world into which we are cast, provides only the setting for new and still indeterminate interactions.

To appreciate how this analysis bears on our project, we need to recall the 'Aristotelian Principle' that John Rawls formulates in *A Theory of Justice*: 'other things being equal, human beings *enjoy* the exercise of their realised capacities (their innate or trained abilities), and . . . this enjoyment increases the more the capacity is realised'. (See the beginning of Part VII.) I agree with Aristotle; and I think Rawls's decision to write this wisdom into his theory of justice attests its importance. The interpretation of self-development with which we shall be working here *depends* on the understanding of human nature expounded in this 'principle'.

Broadly speaking, at each stage of our development there are basically two possible directions for further change: one of these is discordant and alienating, and causes inner conflict, or inner splitting; the other is (more) harmonious and (more) integrating, and contributes a sense of coherent, meaningful growth. When a capacity is realized, exercised, and developed, when there is a process of harmonious change, a process of real growth, the human being experiences rich pleasure and self-fulfilment. Erikson's model of developmental stages shows that he understands the point I am making here. According to Erikson, each of his seven stages involves a 'psychological crisis', two possible directions – two opposite directions – for further change: in infancy, for example, it is a question of trust or mistrust; at play age, it is a question of initiative or self-defeating guilt; at school age, the child is challenged by demands that it be industrious, and if it should fail to meet these demands, its sense of who it is may be badly damaged by feelings of inferiority; in adolescence, the crisis involves a choice between going along with peers or suffering rejection and isolation on a path of authentic individuation; and in 'mature age', it is a question of achieving wisdom and integrity or falling into despair.

The social, political, and cultural conditions that surround our development either encourage or discourage the more harmonious, more integrating, more organismically fulfilling 'next step'. If, in infancy, for example, a child must contend with an erratic, undependable, or abusive parent, this child will develop a deep-seated, generalized, self-perpetuating attitude of mistrust, not easily changed by subsequent life-experience. Conversely, if the infant is handled in a way that encourages a basic sense of trust, this trust will generalize, becoming the generative, self-confirming basis for further growth and more self-confidence.

What most encourages harmonious, self-integrating, self-developing, and self-fulfilling processes are conditions of interaction, within the family, the larger society, and the life of the culture, that *respect* the inherent needs and norms of individual 'human nature' and work *in harmony and attunement* with them. This respect is all the more imperative in light of our ignorance and uncertainty regarding the 'givenness' and 'essence' of 'human nature'. I acknowledge this ignorance and uncertainty; but I am also convinced that harmony and consonance are crucial here: first, that the 'pleasure' about which Aristotle wrote is an experience of the harmony between a capacity and its exercise, a potential and its realization; second, that the possibility of *this* harmony is dependent on the harmony and consonance of the *interactions* people experience in regard to the developmental needs and norms of their 'nature'; and third, that these interactions are themselves dependent on the harmonies achieved by our social, political, and cultural orders.

As for the third point, I would argue that, when the interactions manifest or echo forms of social injustice, sexual and racial prejudice, authoritarian indoctrination, or hate and brutality, the potential for harmonious self-development is seriously threatened. Since nature gives us a potential that includes opposing existential possibilities and tendencies, our self-development in any particular direction is never automatic, never guaranteed. Thus, society must be prepared to take part in the formative process. And if the formative process is to achieve the ends that a social system prescribes for it, then the participation of society must be *consonant* with those ends. The Aristotelian Principle, which I have elaborated in terms of the three points stated above, becomes particularly consequential when the ends of the self-formative process are the ideals of the Enlightenment. Only interventions *consonant* with the autonomy of the individual will contribute to the formation of the *capacity* for autonomy, for the character of the self-formative process will always tend to echo the character of the interactions within which it takes place. It follows from what I have been arguing that the lifeworld needs to be changed in some very fundamental ways before *all* people can hope to enjoy the self-formative processes encouraged by harmonious interactions.

Taking place within the family, the neighbourhood, the school, places of work, and in all the other contexts of daily life, these interactions – communicative interactions – are ultimately *dependent* on a finely tuned sense of harmony and consonance: a respectful sense of what is needed, what is called for, what is appropriate. Good mothers are familiar with this 'sense'. So are good teachers and good psychotherapists. The forming of this sense is connected with the cultivation of our hearing: listening through the inner and outer ears. The outer ears we understand a little; the inner ears – that is to say, listening as a capacity of the body in its ontological wholeness – we understand virtually not at all.

And yet, as I hope to demonstrate in this study, the future of humanism depends on our listening.

Part IX
Humanism Today

Many philosophers, today, have attacked the tradition of humanism and strongly repudiated its vision. Horkheimer, Adorno, Heidegger, and Foucault are undoubtedly the most outstanding of these philosophers. Unfortunately, they all make it difficult to find much in common among their different critiques. But they have also made it difficult – for me at least – to discern in these critiques more than a quarrel still taking place within, and therefore also continuing, the discourse, the spirit, of humanism. As I read them, the attacks on humanism never seem to effect its destruction, but only, rather, to purify it of corruption, clarify ambiguities and obscurities that only its more recent historical roles have brought to light, and correct current misunderstandings and misrepresentations, appealing to principles and values that have always been in the preserve of the spirit of humanism.

Adorno's quarrel with humanism seems mainly to consist in (1) a rejection of its static, deterministic, and dogmatic definitions of 'human nature' and (2) a rejection of its anthropocentric elevation of 'Man' to a position of domination over all domains of nature.[95] Foucault's quarrel seems to be directed toward a different problematic. According to Foucault, 'humanism is based on the desire to change the ideological system without altering institutions', while 'reformers wish to change the institutions without touching the ideological system'.[96]

In his 'Letter on humanism', Heidegger points out – quite rightly, I believe – that 'if one understands humanism in general as a concern that man become free for his humanity and find his worth in it, then humanism differs according to one's conception of the "freedom" and "nature" of "Man". So too there are various paths towards the realisation of such conceptions.'[97] Now, Heidegger's own quarrel with humanism seems to *include* Adorno's two points of attack; but it also adds, in regard to (1), that if our interpretation of 'human nature' is to recognize and care for the true 'dignity' of Man, it must understand the being of *Dasein* ontologically, i.e. as a radical openness to (the questioning of) Being; and, in regard to (2), that it is not sufficient to refrain from elevating Man to a position of domination over nature, while we continue to make 'Man' the measure of Being.

Heidegger argues that

> However different these traditional forms of humanism may be in purpose and principle, in the mode and means of their respective realisations, and in the form of their teaching, they nonetheless all agree in this, that the *humanitas* of *homo humanus* is determined with regard to *an already established* interpretation of nature, history, world, and the ground of the world, that is, of beings as a whole.[98]

Moreover – and on this point Heidegger is particularly emphatic –

> Every [version of] humanism [in our tradition so far] is either grounded in a metaphysics or is itself made to be one. Every determination of the essence of Man which *already presupposes an interpretation of beings* without asking about the truth of Being . . . is metaphysical. . . . Accordingly, every [conception of] humanism [coming out of our tradition] remains metaphysical. In defining the humanity of 'Man', humanism not only does not ask about the relation of Being to the essence of 'Man'; but, because of its metaphysical origin,

> humanism even impedes the question by neither recognising nor understanding it.[99]

For Heidegger, we must break away from the self-centredness of our tradition, a humanism which, since the beginning of modernity, has conceived the 'Self' of this centredness in terms of egoity; and we must begin to question ourselves in terms of a 'Self' centred, instead, by its (decentring) openness to Being.

Some philosophers contend that attention to the *Seinsfrage*, the Question of Being, is, in effect, a gesture of contempt for the human – that it is, at the very least, to disregard the distinctive concerns of human beings, and that this disregard makes ontological thinking the enemy of humanism. Nothing could be farther from the truth. It is the Question of Being which contests the reduction of human being, the distinctive being we humans are, to mere objects and instruments of power: *Zuhandensein*, being ready-to-hand. It is the Question of Being which holds open the dimensionality of our being – our own being and the being of others. Since the work of Lévinas has recently begun to command the attention of many philosophers, I would like to emphasize, before we proceed any further, that the Question of Being keeps us alert to the dangers presently threatening the *being* of human beings, and that, among other things, it serves to remind each one of us of the radical alterity, the dimensionality and profound otherness, which is the very essence of 'other people'. To experience other human beings *as beings* is to acknowledge, to recognize, the irreducible, unpossessable dimensionality they are; it is to see and hear them as radically and essentially other; it is to grant them an ontological difference that one cannot overcome – and should not want to attempt.

I can only hope that the 'humanism' I have embraced in the present study does not err in the ways Adorno, Foucault, and Heidegger have subjected to their criticism, and that, on the contrary, this study will succeed in restoring our faith in the spirit of humanism, critical and emancipatory. I think our future desperately needs its guardian wisdom.

Since the formation of the individual is at the heart of our project, I would like to conclude this chapter by listening to Kierkegaard's conception of the individual. In his *Concluding Unscientific Postscript*, he says: 'An existing individual is constantly in process of becoming . . . and translates all his thinking into terms of process.'[100] It is perhaps our close attention to the processes of actual experiencing which, more than anything else, will enable us to maintain the distinctive critical vigilance that our humanism of the past always struggled, despite its always falling short, to keep.[101]

Humanism has always defended Reason, for it has always been moved by the conviction that to care for the being of human beings requires that we speak out with the voice of Reason. But history suggests that this 'voice of Reason', which grounds our actions in principled argumentation, must not be *cut off* from its originary *experiential* grounding. We must certainly accept no substitute for the *justificatory* grounding contributed by a discursive rationality. By the same token, however, we must never tolerate the ideological, institutionally promoted denial of our body of experience. The authority of its experiential grounding is our closest philosophical touchstone.

In his Introduction to the first volume of *The Theory of Communicative Action*, Habermas observes that 'philosophical thought originates in reflection on the reason embodied in cognition, speech, [and] action'.[102] In this study, I want to demonstrate that philosophical thought also originates in reflection on the distinctive contributions of a reason that is embodied in our capacity for listening.

CHAPTER 2

Zugehörigkeit: Our Primordial Attunement

Opening Conversation

By taking the question of Being as our clue, we are to destroy [*Destruktion*] the traditional content of ancient ontology until we arrive at those primordial experiences in which we achieved our first ways of determining the nature of Being – the ways which have guided us ever since.

Heidegger, *Being and Time*[1]

When I turn toward perception, [I] find at work in my organs of perception a thought older than myself, of which those organs are merely a trace.

Merleau-Ponty, *Phenomenology of Perception*[2]

The symbols of the Self arise in the depths of the body.

Jung, 'The psychology of the child archetype'[3]

I echo the vibration of the sound with my whole sensory being.

Merleau-Ponty, *Phenomenology of Perception*[4]

To be consciousness is here nothing but 'to belong to'.

Merleau-Ponty, *Phenomenology of Perception*[5]

Zugehörigkeit, a word meaning, basically, 'belongingness', comes from Heidegger's discourse. Because of its root, *hörig*, which pertains to hearing, it is particularly fitting as a word to describe the primordial nature of our listening. In the context of our study, it refers to our inherence in, belonging to, and attunement by the sonorous field as a whole.

In his *Sonnets to Orpheus*, Rilke speaks of 'an ear of the earth', *ein Ohr der Erde*, an ear that is *of* the earth in that it comes from the earth, belongs to it, and is made open to the earth's song.

Our hearing is a gift of nature. Enfolded, encoded within it, there is an ontological gift – and, inseparable from it, a claim, an assignment, a task: a *Seinsgeschick*. By grace of our primordial situation, our *Zugehörigkeit*, we always enjoy a pre-ontological experience with, and a pre-ontological understanding of, Being as a whole. For it is *as* an auditory field, a field of sonorous energies, a 'tremendous ocean of energy' (to borrow a phrase from David Bohm), that the Being of (sonorous) beings initially and primordially manifests in relation to our listening organs.[6]

By grace of this *Zugehörigkeit*, we begin our lives in infancy *already* attuned to Being, already attuned *by* its tonality. *Zugehörigkeit* thus constitutes an 'organismic a priori', the receiving of a primordial, initial *disclosure* of Being: an opening up of the auditory field and a primal articulation (*legein*, *logos*) of the ontological difference. Merleau-Ponty observed that 'when I perceive, I belong to the world as a whole'.[7] By grace of this originary belonging, a bodily felt inherence and attunement, everyone not born physically deaf begins life *already* bearing the response-ability implicit in a pre-ontological relationship to the Being of beings. (Heidegger asserts, in *Being and Time*, that the *Dasein* is 'always and already' gifted with an 'implicit pre-understanding' of Being. But he does not give thought to the body's sensori-motor capacities and their channels of perception to learn more about how this 'pre-understanding' is borne and carried.) Because the *Zugehörigkeit* relationship to Being is primal, an 'implicate order' encoded in the flesh, Heidegger's phrase, 'always and already', must be qualified: the *gift* of understanding is *already* inscribed; but this gift is *not yet* understanding.[8] The experience with the Being of beings that we inhabit by grace of our *Zugehörigkeit*, our bodily felt belonging to the sonorous field as a whole, is *not yet* an ontological understanding. That understanding does not come naturally; nor does it come easily. A good deal of experiential work with our hearing – work I have called a 'practice of the Self' – must first take place. But it is one of the weaknesses of Heidegger's thinking – a deficiency he *shares* with the metaphysical tradition he wants to 'destroy' – that it totally separates itself from questions of practice, questions concerned with our *experiencing* of the processes of self-development. (This criticism applies, to some extent, even to his work before the *Kehre*.)

In *Being and Time*, Heidegger attempts an existential 'analytic of *Dasein*', boldly breaking away from traditional accounts of 'human being' by thinking through what he calls our 'moodedness' (*Stimmung*): the primordial condition (*Befindlichkeit*) in which we find ourselves.[9] This moodedness constitutes the most fundamental structure of our being-in-the-world. This structure is our *ek-stasis*, an opening openness that attunes us to Being as a whole. This primal experience of the openness and its wholeness is not only a necessary condition of the very possibility of hearing in the first place; it is also a crucial experience for our psychological development.

John Welwood hears psychopathology in our losing touch with 'a holistic mode of organizing experience, a mode of relationship which transcends the normal workings of focal attention by grasping multiple connections as a whole without serial differentiations'.[10] We all suffer the pressures of everyday life: the restriction of experience. According to Welwood, what are suppressed and unconscious are, as he puts it,

> the holistic ways in which the organism structures situations, without having to articulate them in discrete focal units. These unconscious modes of relationship always occur as the background of an experiential field whose foreground consists of discrete objects or figures of focal attention.[11]

Judging by our everyday comportment, it would seem that we are fragmented souls, inevitably torn between *holistic experiencing*, without any figure-ground differentiation, and *entitative experiencing*, with a total suppression of background awareness.[12] But the truth is that these are not the only perceptual modalities open to us. We do not need to empty the background of all meaning and value in order to attend to objects; nor do we need to think of maintaining an *awareness* of the background by taking entitative experiencing – the modes of our attention to objects – as our paradigm of intentionality (perceptual directedness) in general. We do not need to *suppress* entitative intentionality in order to enjoy an awareness of the background, the field as a whole, the open dimensionality. There is another possibility, which we can *work* to develop, namely an awareness of the ground that lets it be ground. Instead of suffering between unconsciousness (suppression of the ground) and entitative intentionality (reduction of ground to figure), we are capable of developing this other modality.

In this regard, what Freud would have called 'primary process' symbols can make an important contribution, guiding us by their hermeneutical wisdom. Of particular value, here, are the metaphors, symbols, and myths that belong to the realm of plants, the spacious sanctuary of the Great Earth Mother, guardian deity of the plants.[13] Within this realm, we find powerfully transformative metaphors. We have noted that *Zugehörigkeit* is a corporeal intentionality: anonymous, pre-personal, pre-egological. But, from the realm of plants, we can learn more about it. The intentionality of *Zugehörigkeit*, the nature of our listening in its primordial moment, is suggested by the vegetative tendril, the plant's system of roots. Both words, *intentionality* and *tendril*, stem from the same etymological root.

If we want to retrieve our primordial experience, the initiatory moment of listening, we need to learn the ways of the plants; we need to heed the teachings in their simple presence: rootedness, openness to the ground, bending with the winds, obedience to earth and sky, silence. . . .

Perhaps it is worth recalling Aristotle's discussion of the 'vegetative soul' in his *Nicomachean Ethics*:

> The soul is represented as consisting of two parts, a rational and an irrational. As regards the irrational part, there is one subdivision of it which appears to be common to all living things, and this we may designate as having a 'vegetative' nature, by which I mean that it is the cause of nutrition and growth.[14]

But Aristotle, of course, split off the vegetative soul, denying it a function in the constitution of the human character. I am suggesting that we need to integrate the vegetative soul and the rational soul, and that the wisdom of the vegetative, too, has a function in the formation of moral character.

Zugehörigkeit is an experience within which is encoded an understanding of the Being of beings that is radically, subversively different from the understanding we learn through our socialization. Socialization teaches us *Zuhandensein*, and later we learn *Vorhandensein*; but by grace of *Zugehörigkeit*, we are acquainted with the ecstasy (*écart*) of Being, and with its wholeness. Heidegger's *Being and Time* makes ready-to-hand being – instrumentalized being – the primary experience of the Being of beings: a forest is *for* timber, a river *for* water power, mountains *for* the quarrying of rock.[15] Heidegger later realized that the ontology projected by *Being and Time* is totally controlled by a technological viewpoint, and he attempted to open his thinking to a different experience with Being. So far as I can tell, however, he did not give thought to the task whose possibility is proposed here: in retrieving our sense of *Zugehörigkeit*, perhaps we can begin to recollect an experience of Being in relation to which we could find our way out of the technologically reductive determination of Being.

This task will become clearer as our narrative unfolds. For the moment, let us enter the narrative where it opens. Our narrative, an *experientially generated* reconstruction of our primordial experience with hearing in its initial stage, i.e. during the earliest phase of infancy, opens upon an event of almost inconceivable beauty: an ocean of sonorous energies, an immeasurable dimension of soundings-and-silences, a vast symphonic atmosphere. And there, where an infant is born, there is (*es gibt*) an opening. The infant's being there also makes a difference: in the opening, an in-gathering organization of the auditory field begins to take place. And out of its long communion with the matrix of its birth, the infant's hearing suddenly emerges, the entire body an organ of fresh responsiveness, vibrantly alive.

The infant's hearing is primarily, at first, an aesthetic, bodily generalized feeling, a bodily felt attunement by and to the whole of the field. The infant turns to hear, moved by some passing enchantment. Its listening wanders and drifts. It listens to whatever is given. It lets the noises of life, the music of life, penetrate deeply and reverberate within, organizing its moods, orchestrating its gestures, calling forth its voice. As differentiation continues, the hearing selectively channels itself through the changing articulations of the tonal world. As the infant's needs and desires begin to assert themselves, the primal diffusion of hearing, a libidinal dissemination, gives way to greater intensity and concentration: an intentionality whose formation is inseparable from the awakening of a sense of self-centredness. This is the moment when hints of the ego-logical subject and its simultaneously coemergent object first appear in the auditory field. Gradually, a pattern-recognizing competence, a more discriminating, object-orientated listening, initially unsure of itself, begins to take over, whilst the hearing of bodily generalized feeling slowly disappears, commonly for ever, in the natural transformation.

As the structure of subject and object takes hold, however, the infant's awareness of the ground, the field as a whole, slowly withdraws, and the ground as such silently recedes, giving way to the objects of attraction and aversion that now make claims upon the infant's listening. More and more, the child's hearing is restricted to the ears, and the ears become organs of the ego. Without a word, the infant's initial experience of Being, a preliminary but essential understanding of Being, sinks into the silence, the 'unconscious', of the body. Recalling this moment, Mallarmé wrote: 'L'enfant abdique son exstase.'

Even in its concealment, however, this initiatory experience with Being always continues to influence, to affect, to structure our listening. Sublimated, *aufgehoben*, even more recessive, it nevertheless continues to be the structuring principle which keeps our ears open: it *is* our listening openness, the opening without which there would be no hearing, no hearing at all. Most of the time, we are listening to the beings of our world without any awareness of their sonorous dimensionality and without any understanding of the opening that Being is and gives – the opening that, as Heidegger says, *es gibt*. (*Es gibt*, in German, means both 'there is' and 'it gives'.) But it would be utterly impossible for us to hear anything at all unless, despite our ignorance or indifference, our ears remained open and attuned by the openness of Being, the sonorous field as a whole. That is why I have described this experience with Being as both 'initial' and 'primordial'. 'Initial' says that it is an experience and understanding that we are simply given right at the beginning; we are already initiated into its wisdom with the gift of a healthy body. But 'primordial' says that, however deeply concealed, however deeply forgotten, no hearing can take place except by grace of the ontological difference, the structural opening up of the sonorous field as such, and that it is only through our continuing relationship to this primordial event (*Ereignis*) that we are enabled to hear the callings of beings. 'Primordial' says that an implicit understanding of the ontological difference is always necessarily with us. It says that, with every 'act' of listening, we have *always and already* let ourselves be attuned by the Being of beings, manifesting, in relation to our hearing, as the opening-up and in-gathering of a sonorous field.

Always and already. And yet, not yet. For the difference between a pre-ontological understanding and an ontological understanding, the difference between unconsciousness of Being and the recollection of Being, makes all the difference in the world.

Nature, however, has its own ways, ways that will always be hidden from us, beyond our understanding. The process of self-development, obeying nature's laws, demands of the infant an ultimately returnable sacrifice in return for the original gift: the infant is required to renounce, and is expected to forget, the ecstatic experience of the opening moment.

In Figure 2.1, the diagram below, the significance of *Zugehörigkeit* for the recollection of Being is clarified by a mapping which puts the process of recollection into the body of auditory being.

In case the possibility, or even the very intelligibility, of the recollection for which I am arguing should seem to call for an immediate repudiation, I would like to quote from a letter that Descartes, of all people, wrote to Mersenne in April 1640: recognizing a remembering taking place in, by, and through the body, he declared: 'I think that all the nerves and muscles can serve [memory], so that a lute player, for example, has a part of his memory in his hands: for the ease of bending and disposing his fingers in various ways, which he has acquired by practice, helps him to remember the passages which need these dispositions when they are played.' The process on which we are working is different, but not radically so.

Figure 2.1 illustrates recollection as a bodily carried process. In *The Basic Problems of Phenomenology*, Heidegger tells us that 'The distinction between Being and beings exists *pre-ontologically*, without an explicit concept of Being, *latent in Dasein's existence*. As such, it can become an *explicitly under-*

Figure 2.1 The performance of recollection as a bodily process

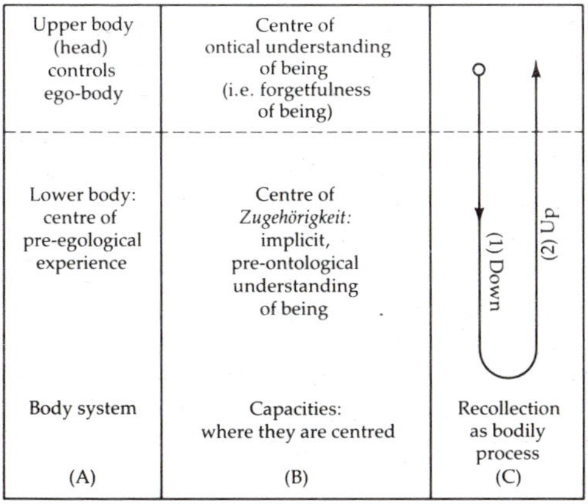

Upper body (head) controls ego-body	Centre of ontical understanding of being (i.e. forgetfulness of being)	
Lower body: centre of pre-egological experience	Centre of *Zugehörigkeit*: implicit, pre-ontological understanding of being	(1) Down (2) Up
Body system (A)	Capacities: where they are centred (B)	Recollection as bodily process (C)

Notes

Column A shows the body system: the upper and lower parts of the body, i.e. the head and the trunk.

Column B shows our ontical understanding, forgetful of Being, centred in the upper body; and it shows our implicit, pre-ontological understanding of Being, constitutive of our auditory *Zugehörigkeit*, centred in the lower body, the chest and belly.

Column C shows the two phases of the recollection process as a movement down into the lower body (phase 1) and a movement back up (phase 2), making contact with the lower-body sense, raising it up into an upper-body awareness, and integrating the understandings of the two body centres.

Phase 1 is the hermeneutical return, *Erinnerung*: down into.

Phase 2 is the hermeneutical retrieval, *Wiederholung:* back up.

stood difference.'[16] This gift, a pre-ontological understanding of Being, and of the ontological difference between Being and beings, is given to the auditory body, which carries it from birth to death. It is carried as an experience of *Zugehörigkeit*, a bodily felt sense of our inherence in, our belonging to, and our attunement by, the auditory field as a whole.

Although the difference between beings and Being remains forgotten and concealed, not only by the individual, but also by the history of Being that is constitutive of our culture, Heidegger firmly believes that 'it has left a trace which remains preserved in the language to which Being comes'.[17] Thus, Derrida writes, in 'Sending: on representation', that the trace is pre-ontological, 'pointing to Being, which remains concealed'.[18] And because of the character of this pre-ontological relationship to Being, i.e. because our *Zugehörigkeit* is an inherence in the primordial intertwinings of the auditory field, Merleau-Ponty speaks of an 'anonymous existence of which my body is the ever-renewed trace' and argues that this existence 'inhabits both bodies [mine and the other's] simultaneously'.[19] *Zugehörigkeit*, our pre-ontological understanding of Being, is that 'thought older than myself', of which Merleau-Ponty says that my perceptual organs are 'merely a trace'.[20]

By grace of our *Zugehörigkeit*, we belong to the laying-down and gathering-collecting (*Legein*) of an auditory ground (*Logos*), and we are accordingly attuned by its tonality. But this relationship to Being (*Logos*), into which we are gathered and collected, is initially unconscious: Being, therefore, never *was* really present. However, through our efforts at recollection, we *can* recover a presently felt sense of that 'origin', that 'ground of silence' which opened the field; and when we realize this bodily felt sense of our relation to Being, we find that it carries the sense of 'always already', i.e. it tells us that we have *always* been living in that relation, and that consequently we were *already*, albeit unconsciously, *in* that relation. Thus, recollection makes possible a new beginning – both for the individual and for the history of Being.

But we must be careful here, in thinking this 'recollection of Being'. For the beginning is not identical with the origin. Like an echo which makes it difficult to hear what is being said, concealing the very words that originated it, the beginning is, in fact, as Heidegger says, the 'veil' that *conceals* the origin, revealing it *as* concealed: concealed from the very beginning, concealed precisely *by* the revealing at the beginning.[21] 'We have forgotten the unifying rhythm,' as Lukacher says, 'but we have not forgotten that we have forgotten *something*.'[22] Recollection is both necessary and impossible – impossible, that is, as a total retrieval of 'the origin' as such. Recollection, as Merleau-Ponty would undoubtedly have wanted to argue, is 'a movement toward what could not in any event be present to us in the original and whose irremediable absence would thus count among our originating experiences'.[23]

In Joan Stambaugh's translation of 'Overcoming metaphysics', Heidegger writes of 'the primal incorporation of the oblivion of Being'.[24] By grace of our *Zugehörigkeit*, a pre-ontological understanding of Being, and of the ontological difference between Being and beings, is deeply incorporated.

But childhood is a beginning that conceals the 'origin': the incorporation guarantees the preservation and protection of the ontological difference; but it is, inevitably, an irrevocable forgetting – a forgetting which happens not only *as soon as* the trace is inscribed into the flesh, but in the very *enactment* of incorporation. Such forgetting, therefore, is ontologically prescribed: our way of preserving and protecting. Paradoxically, the incorporation is a forgetting which makes a belated (*nachträglich*) recollection possible; it is a preserving that forgets, but carries a *trace* of that which, from the very beginning and *as* that beginning, has always already been concealed, keeping itself in the preserve of the inaudible.

Recollection has two phases. In the first, *Erinnerung*, we go down, down *into* the lower, chthonic body: we go down into our body's presently felt sense of auditory being; into the heart of our body's implicit, pre-ontological understanding of Being. We make contact with the lower body's auditory sense of Being as such. Then, in the second phase, *Wiederholung*, we retrieve this sense of Being, already carried in our natural *Zugehörigkeit;* we bring it *up* into an authentically ontological awareness – and make it explicit, audible, by virtue of our way of listening, within the world audible to others.

This recollection is in fact a re-collecting, a mimetic gathering-up (*legein*) of the auditory field, whose primordial gathering (*Legein*) was already laid down (*Legein*) as a law, a *nomos,* for our hearing. In recollecting, we re-collect, we gather up the primordial collection, the primordial in-gathering of Being, the ingathering field of sound by grace of which we are enabled to hear. In the final phase of recollecting, we return to the world, carrying within us, like a song, the vibrancy of Being. And to the extent that we can make this song audible to others, we gather them, too, into the vitality of the primordial recollection, a gathering of 'the Fourfold'.

CHAPTER 3

Everydayness: The Ego's World

Opening Conversation

The Eye of Man a little narrow orb, clos'd up and dark, Scarcely beholding the great light, conversing with the Void; the Ear a little shell, in small volutions shutting out All melodies & comprehending only Discord and Harmony.

Blake, *Milton*[1]

I think white people are so afraid of the world they have created that they don't want to see, feel, smell or hear it.

Lame Deer[2]

The ego is a complex that does not comprise the total human being; it has forgotten infinitely more than it knows. It has heard and seen an infinite amount of which it has never [or not yet] become conscious.

Jung, 'Spirit and Life'[3]

Self-understanding should not be formally equated with a reflected ego-experience.

Heidegger, *The Basic Problems of Phenomenology*[4]

At fifteen, I set my heart on learning; at thirty I took

> my stand; at forty I came to be free of doubts; at fifty I understood the Law of Heaven; at sixty my ear was attuned; and at seventy I followed my heart's desire without overstepping the line.
>
> Confucius, *The Analects*[5]

For many people today, including many philosophers, questions concerning our capacity for hearing are questions about the physics of sound, auditory neurophysiology, tissue structures and biochemistry – the body's 'audio equipment'. The objective sciences have colonized the everyday world and secured the hegemony of physicalism, a reductive interpretation, in contradiction to the self-understanding which centuries of everyday life-experiences generated and supported. While I do not deny the validity claims our sciences of hearing may justifiably make, I want to contest their assumption that they can tell the whole truth, the whole story. It may be extreme to say, as Heidegger says in his *Introduction to Metaphysics*, that 'true hearing has nothing to do with ear and mouth', 'nothing to do with the lobes of our ears'.[6] But I certainly concur in his argument that 'the ears are more than acoustic receivers and transmitters. These technical terms do truly explain certain dimensions of the experiential process; but they do not, and cannot, exhaustively define it'.[7] We should certainly not reject the accounts of science; but we must at all costs resist the discrediting and invalidating of our so-called 'merely subjective' experience.

Of course, Heidegger does not challenge the hegemony of the scientific account of hearing in order to defend the everyday understanding of common sense. He is no less critical of the common-sense understanding; and he subjects our everyday habits of listening, which this understanding 'grounds', to an examination as harsh as it is honest. 'Mere hearing', he says, 'scatters and diffuses itself in what is commonly believed and said.'[8] Most of our listening, directed by the ego, obeys and conforms. We hear only what everyone else hears. We can hear only the prevailing discourse. We don't often take the time to hear ourselves.

This is not incompatible with the fact that our listening is channelled most of the time by desire, for most of our desires are socially conditioned, socially imposed: our desires themselves are attuned to conformity.

Very soon after birth, the infant manifests a *desire to hear*. What Heidegger says about sight, in *Being and Time*, holds true also of our hearing: its character shows itself 'in a peculiar tendency of being which belongs to everydayness'.[9] This tendency, which he calls 'curiosity' (*Neugier*), constitutes 'a peculiar way of letting the world be encountered by us in perception'.[10] First, then, there is the openness of enchantment. Then, fascination and curiosity. But these states also evolve, taking on the character of passion: 'the passion [*Ohrenlust*] of the ears'.[11] Very early in life, the child's listening becomes a channel of and for desire, an intentionality of attractions and aversions, entangled in the ego's will to power – its aggressions and defences.

The listening ego inhabits a structure polarized into an ego-subject and its object. 'Objectification, however', as Heidegger observes, 'blocks us off against the Open. The more venturesome daring does not produce a defence.'[12] That the ego-logical structure functions as much as a system of defence as a system for the fulfilment of desire is a truth that Heidegger takes pains to formulate in his interpretation of Rilke. It is an observation Nietzsche put into words many times, convinced that such thoughts fall mostly on deaf ears.

Reflecting on his experience in clinical psychology, John Welwood notes that

> What is most threatening to the ego . . . is not the instinctual demands, but rather the groundless, open quality of our basic being-in-the-world. We find that we cannot establish our ego securely, our self-identity keeps slipping away, we are subject to little deaths from moment to moment, and there is nothing to hold on to. Thus anxiety signals a threat, not so much from instinctual demands, but rather from the insubstantial nature of the basic ground of our existence. Guilt can be interpreted in this light as arising from a commitment to 'small mind', as opposed to 'big mind'. We may feel guilty when we choose our small version of the world, at the expense of the larger, expansive version that arises from the basic relatedness of self and world. Resistance, repression, and defenses can be recast here as ways of armoring ourselves against this relatedness that undercuts our notion of a separate self.[13]

Our listening often functions defensively: as a way of coping with anxiety; as a way of protecting our small version of the world; as a way of avoiding moral claims and their call for an appropriate response.

Writing about a mother of eight children who, in desperation, committed infanticide and spoke, after her arrest, of 'a sacrifice', Adrienne Rich argues that 'if we assume that any word of hers is simply the ravings of a "paranoid-schizophrenic", we shall not hear what she was saying'.[14] In a patriarchal culture, there is a certain 'deafness' which makes it very difficult for us to hear this mother's cry. This deafness is the avoidance of a moral claim.

There is also a deafness which shields us against a deep-seated ontological anxiety – little deaths from moment to moment; and this is a deafness to silence, a listening which constantly insists on making noise, or surrounding itself with other people or audio equipment, in order to fight off the horror of a 'deathly silence'. For many people, silence is the sound of death; its open quality, a clearing where there is nothing for hearing to hold on to, is an experience of unbearable anxiety, and not the gift of a resting-place, an *Aufenthalt*, for the quiet recovery of the weary soul.

Writing about himself, about his own ways of using hearing defensively, Carl Rogers says:

> But what I really dislike in myself is when I cannot hear the other person because I am so sure in advance of what he is about to say that I don't listen. It is only afterward that I realise that I have heard only what I have already decided he is saying: I have failed really to listen. Or even worse are those times when I can't hear because what he is saying is too threatening, and might even make me change my views or my behaviour. Still worse are those times when I catch myself trying to twist his message to make it say what I want him to say, and then hearing only that.[15]

In *Religion within the Limits of Reason Alone*, Kant argues that our 'natural inclinations' should, and need to be, 'brought into harmony in a wholeness which is called happiness'.[16] For Kant, here, 'happiness', personal fulfilment, consists in the harmony of wholeness. But what is wholeness? What is harmony? How are we to recognize and understand this harmony? How are we to achieve it with others?

Does it not call for an exertion of listening – open listening to others, and the quiet, inner-directed listening we must do in order to hear ourselves? How else can we be attentive to the 'call of conscience', which reverberates through the medium of our own body of experience? How else can we achieve harmony with others?

In 'Laches', Plato characterizes Socrates as 'harmonious', *mousikos*, meaning that there is a true harmony, in his way of life, between the words (*logoi*) he speaks and the deeds (*erga*) which embody them.[17] But if we say that, in Socrates, *logos* and *bios*, word and life, are in harmony, attuned to and by one another, must we not assume that Socrates is skilful in the practice of listening? When I read Plato's *Dialogues*, I find myself in the company of a man who is exceptionally skilful in listening both to himself and to others. I submit that the harmony we admire is a virtue achieved, in part, through good listening. The harmony in question is a harmony we should be able to hear: it reverberates in the words themselves, as well as in the actions. Listening for it, we move toward its achievement.

In Chapter Five, we will give thought to the achievement of consensus: a different harmony, of course, but one for the achievement of which good listening is no less decisive.

CHAPTER 4

Skilful Listening

In *Being and Time*, Heidegger observes that

> It requires a very artful [*künstlich*] and complicated modification of attitude [*Einstellung*] in order to 'hear' a 'pure noise' [*reines Gerausch*]. However, that we *first* hear motorbikes and cars is experiential confirmation [*Beleg*] that the human being [*Dasein*], as a being always already in the world, holds itself open to [*sich aufhalt bei*] that which solicits its worldly concerns [*das Zuhandene*], and not at all to [mere] 'sensations' [*Empfindungen*].[1]

The 'artful modification' to which Heidegger is referring here first becomes possible in the third stage of hearing, i.e. only *after* our capacity for hearing has achieved the normal degree of ego-logical control: the ability to recognize common patterns of sound within the normal range of hearing; the ability to locate sounds in relation to their sources; the ability to imitate and accurately repeat a normal range of sounds, particularly sounds involved in speech; the ability to objectify and recall sounds and configurations of sound. Only after such basic achievements can we begin practices of self-discipline enabling us to hear what the philosophical tradition calls 'pure sounds', i.e. discrete, atomic, acoustic sensations – simple acoustic 'essences'.

This 'artful modification' is a process which Samuel Todes

calls 'sensuous abstraction'.[2] According to Todes, there is a process of abstraction which can discriminate, separate and isolate a *sensuous* 'essence'. This is a peculiar kind of object, not at all like Plato's 'forms' or Husserl's 'eidetic' entities, for it is neither purely mental, purely 'intelligible', nor immediately sensuous: while it continues to be sensuous, sensuously contacted, it has also been worked over, produced, modified by idealization. Sensuous abstraction *produces* its object – an 'intentional object' that is constituted entirely *within* the experiencing process. It is therefore an *Erlebnis,* not an *Erfahrung*.)

The process of sensuous abstraction is an extension of an ability which, to some degree, we all develop and enjoy, without much effort or thought, in the course of everyday living. We *sniff* the air to identify or locate what we are smelling. We *savour* a fine wine or sauce so that we can enjoy its flavourful taste. We gently *caress* a wooden table so that we can feel its grain and texture. We stand still and *focus* our eyes so that we can see the graceful motion of the eagle soaring in the sky above us. The sniffing enables us to abstract an aroma, a fragrance. The savouring enables us to abstract the flavour. The tactful caress enables us to abstract the 'feel' of the wood. The focusing gives us a better 'look'.

As an 'artful modification' of the everyday habit, the 'natural attitude', sensuous abstraction effectuates a kind of *epochē*: refraining from our habitual involvement with the object and its world, we slow down and shift our attention to the experience itself. We don't lose, reject, or even suspend belief in the object; but we consciously redirect our attention – away from the (existence of the) object *as such* and toward something in our *experience* with it. Sometimes, e.g. for the sake of aesthetic appreciation, we may temporarily suspend our interest in the (existence of the) object itself in order to concentrate all the more on the intrinsic qualities of the sensuous abstraction it enables us to produce; but most of the time, we constitute a sensuous abstraction in order to acquire a better knowledge *of the object*. Attention to the sensuous abstraction for its own sake is typically a procedure necessary for aesthetic appreciation. Even in this case, however, the (existence of the) object that inspired the abstraction does not lose all importance or meaning.

Sensuous abstraction, however, in the sense of a disclosure skilfully produced, as Todes puts it, 'by inhibition of the perceptual consummation in which our intelligible sense of reality is founded', is not the only way we can 'artfully modify' our perceptual relationships.[3] Sometimes, instead of subjecting our everyday perception to a skilful inhibition alien to its habits, we develop our perceptual capacities by learning how to let go, how to *undo* the inhibitions we learned unconsciously. These other inhibitions are ego-logical defences generated by deep anxieties. And since the anxieties are so widespread, they are transmitted in – and as – the 'normal' mode of perception. Whereas the skilful inhibition produces a sensuous *abstraction*, the skilful *undoing* of inhibition – the unconscious inhibition constitutive of everyday perception – produces a sensuous *intimacy* and *communion*, a perception *without* defence.[4] This, too, requires exertion, practice, and skill. This, too, is productive of knowledge and understanding.

Sensuous abstraction, inhibiting the natural attitude in perception, constitutes an *abstract* entity: atomic, discrete, isolated, separated from all contextual distractions. Sensuous intimacy and communion, undoing the inhibitions already at work, unconsciously, in the natural attitude of everyday perception, constitutes a *contextual* entity: by cultivating the potential in our sensibility for a mode of perception that is comparatively more global, more synaesthetic, more holistic, and more deeply rooted in bodily feeling, we can constitute an object which is more fully, more comprehensively situated in its relational field, so that, at the same time that it becomes *more concrete*, it also becomes *more comprehensible* as an entity of differentiation. The first procedure skilfully *abstracts* from the elemental background, whereas the second skilfully *integrates* the object into the differential interplay of its perceptual field. Both of these procedures can develop our perceptual capacities beyond what is normally required of them in the course of everyday living. Both, therefore, are stage III skills.

Let us now think more specifically about hearing. As Todes points out, perception normally 'begins' with a preparatory phase, in which the percipient subject favourably postures and positions herself in readiness to perceive. Thus, for example, she prepares herself to hear what is to be heard by listening for it. This *listening-for* is a kind of openness-to-the-field-as-a-whole. It is alert, vigilant, receptive, attuned. In the second phase, the process is completed, the perception either fulfilled or annulled: that which one expects from the perceived either is or is not perceived. Thus, for example, the listener is satisfied: she *hears* whatever it may be that she was listening for. But a third phase is also, as Todes demonstrates, an option. In this third phase, equivalent to our stage III, there is a skilful cultivation of our perceptual capacities – practices that bring out the inherent skilfulness of our perceptual gifts and increase our enjoyment of life as well as our knowledge and understanding of the world. Thus, for example, when our imaginary listener hears a bird in the tree overhead, she may stop to listen to it. This *listening-to* is a concentrated attention, silent, patient, willing to *take the time* to listen carefully. It is a listening that requires some discipline – to avoid being distracted, to fine-tune one's hearing, to *stay with* what is sounding long enough to achieve a real familiarity, or perhaps a certain intimacy.

Going out into nature, the naturalist works to improve his skilfulness as a listener. He listens for animals, birds, winds, and waters, and when he hears them, he listens to the sounds they make. He learns to make differences; he learns how to recognize different patterns of sound and to associate these patterns with different sources and different situations. Being quiet, inwardly as well as outwardly, cultivating silence, the naturalist listens to the sounds of nature. Being quiet, alert, and attuned, he listens with such care that even the different winds become familiar in their differences.

The musician cultivates a different dimension of our listening skilfulness. Listening to sounds, chords, melodic lines, and the different instruments of sound, the musician cultivates her ear for pitch and timbre, tonal register, harmonies and discords, changes in key, subtle inversions and quotations. Allowing her body to become, itself, a medium, an instrument, for the resonance of sound, the musician can hear sounds, fields of sound, choirs of sound, that the rest of us will never hear.[5] Listening with well-trained ears, the musician breathes in an atmosphere that is filled with music: each thing, each being, has its own distinctive sound – even the heavenly spheres. The skilled listening of the musician also requires an inner and outer silence: without that silence, more silent than the silences to which everyday living accustoms us, the musicality of beings, and the voices of our man-made instruments, will not give themselves to be heard. 'Like crystal, like metal and many other substances, I am', says Merleau-Ponty, 'a sonorous being.'[6] The musician listens to the sounds of things with a listening that comes from a bodily felt understanding of what this means. . . .

Michael Taussig observes that there is a 'look that, in

reflecting, passes into the cause of what is reflected'.[7] I would point out that there is also a listening which works in this way: a listening that is responsible for creating what it hears – a listening, for example, with the power to cause or to alleviate the very suffering it is hearing.

In 'Andenken', Heidegger says that 'the authentic greeting recognises [*anerkennt*] the one being greeted with respect for his ownmost being [*in seinem Eigenen*]'.[8] And he adds that

> The authentic greeting accords to the one who is greeted the resonance of his ownmost being [*den Anklang seines Wesens*]. The authentic greeting occasionally is able to let the one being greeted shine in the light of his ownmost being, so that he might lose his false way of being-a-Self [*die falschen Selbstigkeit verliert*].[9]

How many opportunities for friendship, for peace, for a deeply meaningful intimacy, have we missed and lost, because we failed to lend an ear? How often, and how well, do we listen to other people? Do we in fact *know how* to listen to others in an open, welcoming, receptive way? Are we able to hear, to greet, what others tell us, no matter how painful it may be, no matter how threatening to our ego, no matter how demanding on our capacity to care and be compassionate? How well do sons listen to, and hear, their father's counsel? How well do fathers listen to their sons? Do white people really hear what the long-suffering Indians and blacks have to tell them about racial hatreds, colonial exploitation, and bureaucratic indifference? To what extent has our collective deafness itself been responsible for this misery and suffering?

What did Goethe hear? On 7 October 1786, while on his Italian journey, he wrote about 'the cry of some lonely human being sent into the wide world till it reaches the ears of another lonely human being who is moved to answer it'.[10] But loneliness is only one form of suffering: only one of the many sufferings that cry out to be heard. The blacks and native Americans, and people all around the world who have lived under colonial rule, know other forms of suffering. Can we hear their cries and their speech? There is also the suffering of people living with the daily violence of totalitarian states. Do we listen? What do we hear? Do we realize that, sometimes, just listening can be helpful, all by itself?[11]

'If the protests of children were heard in kindergarten, if their questions were attended to, it would be enough to explode the entire educational system.'[12] Gilles Deleuze is right. Why do we not listen to our children? Why do we not hear what they are telling us? Do we not need, all of us, to learn what it means to listen, really listen, to our children? If we practised the art of listening, of welcoming their experience, we might learn something. And what if they can *hear* our deafness?

Carl Rogers has learned, from many years of listening to people classified as 'mentally ill', that the continued experience of not being heard, really heard, 'makes some individuals psychotic'.[13] Listening to other people is a skill we all need to work on. Like the naturalist and the musician, the psychotherapist is one who has cultivated to an exceptional degree the skilfulness inherent in listening. The therapist is one who listens to *others* with exceptional attention. She is a woman who greets the other with an unconditional receptiveness. He is a man who can hear meanings inaudible to others and, sometimes, meanings inaudible to the person who is speaking. She is a woman who can hear repressed pain, concealed anguish, the suffering that the patient himself cannot yet hear or speak. He is a man whose very act of listening can enable the other to hear herself, hear the sound (*Anklang*) of her ownmost needs and desires.

'I find it very precious', says Rogers, 'when, for some moment in time, I have felt really close to, fully in touch with, another person.'[14] Rogers freely shares with us the deep satisfaction he feels when, as he puts it, 'I can really hear someone.' He writes:

> I think perhaps this has been a longstanding characteristic of mine. I can remember this in my early grammar school days. A child would ask the teacher a question and the teacher would give a perfectly good answer to a completely different question. A feeling of pain and distress would always strike me. My reaction was, 'But you didn't hear him!' I felt a sort of childish despair at the lack of communication which was (and is) so common.
>
> I believe I know why it is so satisfying to me to hear someone. When I can really hear someone, it puts me in touch with him. It enriches my life. It is

> through hearing people that I have learned all that I know about individuals, about personality, about psychotherapy, and about interpersonal relationships. There is also another peculiar satisfaction in it. When I really hear someone, it is like listening to the music of the spheres, because, beyond the immediate message of the person, no matter what that might be, there is the universal, the general. Hidden in all the personal communications which I really hear there seem to be orderly psychological laws, aspects of the awesome order which we find in the universe as a whole. So there is both the satisfaction of hearing this particular person and also the satisfaction of feeling oneself in some sort of touch with what is universally true.

He goes on to emphasize that,

> When I say that I enjoy hearing someone, I mean, of course, hearing deeply. I mean that I hear the words, the thoughts, the feeling tones, the personal meaning, even the meaning that is below the conscious intent of the speaker. Sometimes, too, in a message which superficially is not very important, I can hear a deep human cry, a 'silent scream', that lies buried and unknown far below the surface of the person.
>
> So I have learned to ask myself, can I hear the sounds and sense, the shape, of this other person's inner world? Can I resonate to what he is saying, can I let it echo back and forth in me, so deeply that I sense the meanings he is afraid of yet would like to communicate, as well as those meanings he knows?

Rogers argues that both listening and not listening have 'consequences':

> When I do truly hear a person and the meanings that are important to him at that moment, hearing not simply his words, but *him*, and when I let him know that I have heard his own private meanings, many things happen. There is first of all a grateful

> look. He feels released. He wants to tell me more about his world. He surges forth in a new sense of freedom. I think he becomes more open to the process of change.
>
> I have often noticed . . . that the more deeply I can hear the meanings of this person, the more there is that happens. One thing I have come to look upon as almost universal is that when a person realises he has been deeply heard . . . in some real sense he is weeping for joy. It is as though he were saying, 'Thank God, somebody has heard me. Someone knows what it's like to be me.' In such moments I have had the fantasy of a prisoner in a dungeon, tapping out day after day a Morse code message, 'Does anybody hear me? Is there anybody there? Can anyone hear me?' And finally, one day, he hears some faint tappings which spell out 'Yes'. By that one simple response he is released from his loneliness; he has become a human being again.

And Rogers observes, with a sadness that we may hear, that

> There are many, many people living in private dungeons today, people who give no evidence of it whatever on the outside, where you have to listen very sharply to hear the faint messages from the dungeon.

In listening to others, accepting them in their irreducible difference, we help them to listen to themselves, to heed the speech of their own body of experience, and to become, each one, the human being he or she most deeply wants to be.[15] Moreover, by listening well to ourselves and to others, we can resist false, ideological interpretations of 'need' and steer public life towards the fulfilment of more authentic needs. Thus, in the next chapter, which concerns listening in relation to our political life, we will give thought to the proposition that the development of our listening – that is, our achievement of the third stage and, in particular, our realization of the capacity *as* a communicative praxis – is at the same time the development of a utopian-emancipatory potential. I will argue that to understand the role of communicative praxis in our political life, to understand our capacity for listening *as* a communicative praxis and exercise it accordingly, is therefore a *consummation* of the third stage of our self-development as auditory beings.

In listening to others, we are gathered into compassion.[16] How far into the world of radical alterity is it possible for our hearing to reach out with compassion? If the reach and range of our compassion is dependent on the reach and range of our hearing, can we extend the compass of our listening?

In listening to the soundings of nature, listening to the music of sounds, and listening to the speech of others, we learn, we grow, we help others to learn and grow, and we realize that hearing is a gift to be valued and enjoyed. Developing our skills in listening, learning ways to channel our hearing and modify the structures we habitually impose on auditory situations, we can make the world a happier, more beautiful place in which to dwell. Thus, as Heidegger says, in his study on the 'Logos' fragment of Herakleitos: 'It concerns the hearing of mortals.'[17]

But how capable are we, each one, of becoming, in Rilke's words, 'a being with no shell, open to pain . . . shaken by every sound'?[18]

CHAPTER 5

Communicative Praxis

There can be no beauty if it is paid for by human injustice, nor truth that passes over injustice in silence, nor moral virtue that condones it.
Borowski, *This Way for the Gas, Ladies and Gentlemen*

Part I
The Body Politic

Opening Conversation

You open wide the portals [*pavillons*] of your ears to admit the State.
Derrida, *The Ear of the Other*[1]

Every form of the reality principle must be embodied in a system of societal institutions and relations, laws and values which transmit and enforce the required 'modification' of the instincts. This 'body' of the reality principle is different at the different stages of civilisation.
Marcuse, *Eros and Civilization*[2]

In the dance of peace, what we have to consider is

whether a man bears himself naturally and gracefully, and after the manner of men who duly conform to the law.

Plato, *Laws*[3]

Song duels are used to work off grudges and disputes of all orders, save murder. . . . Singing skill among the Eskimos equals or outranks gross physical prowess.

Adamson Hoebel, *The Law of Primitive Man*[4]

What mode of investment of the body is necessary and adequate for the functioning of a capitalistic society like ours? . . . One needs to study what kind of body the current society needs. . . . It's as though 'revolutionary' discourses were still steeped in the ritualistic themes derived from Marxist analyses. And while there are some very interesting things about the body in Marx's writings, Marxism considered as an historical reality has had a terrible tendency to occlude the question of the body, in favour of consciousness and ideology.

Foucault, *Power/Knowledge*[5]

Let us ask . . . how things work at the level of on-going subjugation, at the level of those continuous and uninterrupted processes which subject our bodies, govern our gestures, dictate our behaviours.

ibid., 97

Culture [*Bildung*] begins with obedience [*Gehorsam*].

Nietzsche, *Ecce Homo*[6]

What I want to show is how power relations can materially penetrate the body in depth, without depending even on the mediation of the subject's own representations.

Foucault, *Power/Knowledge*[7]

[There are] social contradictions that sink into the very bowels of the individual.

Jacoby, *Social Amnesia: A Critique of Conformist Psychology from Adler to Laing*[8]

> [T]he economic changes of the eighteenth century made it necessary to ensure the circulation of effects of power through progressively finer channels, gaining access to individuals themselves, to their bodies, their gestures and all their daily actions.
>
> Foucault, *Power/Knowledge*[9]

> The ego is first and foremost a bodily ego; it is not merely a surface entity, but is itself the projection of a surface.
>
> Freud, *The Ego and the Id*[10]

> The body is the inscribed surface of events.
>
> Foucault, 'Nietzsche, genealogy, history'[11]

> [The task of genealogy is to expose] a body totally imprinted by history and the process of history's destruction of the body.
>
> ibid.

> [T]he revolution is or is not being prepared in every minute particular of daily existence: the way babies are held or love made or speech spoken or work conducted.
>
> Kovel, *The Age of Desire*[12]

If Foucault's understanding of the historicity of the body is correct, then Kovel must be mistaken; conversely, if Kovel is right, then Foucault has to be wrong. They cannot both be right: if the body is *totally* imprinted by history, or if it *can* be totally imprinted, then revolution, and even gestures of resistance and gestures that refuse to conform, cannot be considered possible. I am going to side, here, with Kovel; but I want to elaborate my disagreement with Foucault.

I have nothing but praise for Foucault's attempt to embody critical social theory: his recognition of the significance of the body for political theory continues the thinking which Marx began and which Marcuse revived after a long history of interruption; and his critical analyses of the body as the construct of power and the material substratum for its application are major contributions to our contemporary understanding of the political economy and culture in which we live. But the two conceptions of 'body' that figure in his thinking are ultimately self-defeating. And the one conception that would have enabled him to articulate both oppression and resistance, and perhaps even to schematize a new body politic, namely, the conception worked out by Merleau-Ponty, is totally missing.

The 'lived body', the 'body of felt experience', an active body endowed with intelligence and sensibility, a body of skills, competences, and capacities, a body capable of critical thinking, learning, and self-development, does not appear in Foucault's work – not even between the lines or in the margins. In Foucault, this body is reduced either to (1) the condition of a passive, docile object (medium or substratum for the application and reproduction of power) or to (2) the subjectivity of a body whose agency is essentially a deaf-and-blind activity, turbulent gestures issuing from a chaos of Dionysiac drives and capable of expressing only wildness, irrationality, and anarchy. In Foucault, the body figures only as a metaphor for power in a 'rhetoric of bodies and pleasures', a 'history of political technologies of the body'.[13] To be sure, Foucault's understanding of the body enables him to demonstrate the application and reproduction of power technologies and to display the body as a product of these technologies; but it also precludes the possibility of conceptualizing any purposive, organized, intelligent resistance, and even the possibility of any coherent understanding, coming *from* the subjugated body.

In 'Foucault on freedom and truth', Charles Taylor observes that, for Foucault,

> there is no order of human life, or way we are, or human nature, that one can appeal to in order to judge or evaluate between ways of life. There are only different orders imposed by men on primal chaos, following their will-to-power.[14]

Conceptualizing the body as a passive object, as a substratum for the imposition of power, or as a surface upon which social order is inscribed, does certainly contribute to the analysis of domination and oppression. But how could the body, conceived in this way, ever speak and act with intelligence? How could it ever talk back to history? How could it ever become the source of situationally appropriate resistance to oppressive regimes of power? In order to take up the question of resistance, or the question of emancipatory praxis, we need to recognize a body-subject capable of assuming the functions of an intelligent historical agent. But, in so far as Foucault conceptualizes the body as active, he fails to recognize that the human body has any order of its own. Under the spell of Nietzsche's Dionysiac body and Freud's libidinal body, 'a chaos, a cauldron of seething excitement',[15] Foucault cannot conceptualize a body with any organization of purposes, any order, of its own. For him, the body is inherently autistic; order and interaction must therefore be socially imposed. Like Freud, he assumes that the libidinal body is inherently cut off from the world, and that the ego which emerges on the 'surface' of this body is an order entirely imposed by society.

To be sure, we must sharpen our alertness to the internalization of socially imposed meanings, often virtually invisible and inaudible. And we must understand that, as Marx observed, 'Nature as it comes into being in human history – in the act of creation of human society – is the *true* nature of man'.[16] But it does not follow from this that our nature is *totally* determined by its social history. It cannot seriously be doubted today that there *is* a *given* biological nature. Thus, although we cannot know the nature of this givenness in its totality and in the full determinateness of its contents, we do know the facticity of its givenness, *as* that which provides the possibilities for, and sets the limits on, the social reworking of 'human nature'. The realization of our 'true nature' certainly cannot happen automatically, i.e. in a spontaneous unfolding of innate potentialities. There are, in any event, various, even conflicting, possibilities and tendencies that society will either encourage or restrain. However, the work of society is never totally free or totally arbitrary, because it is compelled to recognize the givenness of a pre-civil nature, a transhistorical nature, a nature never *outside* social history, yet not *reducible* to social determination.

In his 'Notes on Kafka', Adorno asserts that 'the social origin of the individual ultimately reveals itself as the power to annihilate him'.[17] This is a point that needs to be heard; but our attention to the social origin of the individual must not prevent us from recognizing a biological, transhistorical origin as well; nor should it be allowed to obscure the fact that, however much the mature individual may owe to society, the individual is always more than the sum of factors actually contributed by society. Thus I also take issue with a passage in *Minima Moralia*, where Adorno writes:

> Not only is the self entwined in society; it owes society its existence in the most literal sense. All its content comes from society, or at any rate from its relation to the object. It grows richer the more freely it develops and reflects this relation, while it is limited, impoverished, and reduced by the separation and hardening that it lays claim to as an origin.[18]

Without arguing, against Adorno, that the self is a monad, self-originating and self-producing, we may nevertheless dispute his contention that all the 'content' we may attribute to the self comes from society. As a matter of fact, if this were so, individuals like Adorno would not be possible. We should agree that the self is not a self-contained substance or a transcendental subject outside history; we should agree that the self is always entwined in society, formed in a nexus of social interactions. But we must not agree to his extreme historicization of nature any more than we should agree to the reactionary naturalization of the social, the cultural, and the historically contingent.

In *Critique, Norm and Utopia*, Seyla Benhabib notes that 'the repression of internal and external nature has grown to such an unprecedented proportion that the rebellion *against* this repression itself becomes the object of new exploitation and manipulation'.[19] Ironically, Adorno's rejection of an 'inner self', his insistence on the totally social origin and socially filled identity of the self, ultimately serves the very forces of repression that he wants to defeat. How can the self fight back, if its identity is nothing but a product of social control? Perhaps it is now clear that the 'body' from which resistance would have to come, according to Foucault's theory, is also the body which incarnates the totally socialized 'self' that figures in Adorno's account.

Kovel locates this problematic in the writings of Marx:

> Men make their history, Marx wrote, but they do not make it as they please; they make it under conditions handed down from the past. And our body is paramount among those conditions handed down from the past, i.e., from nature, which always has the quality of 'that which comes before'.[20]

There is a transhistorical dimension to the body-self produced in social history: 'a dimension in which the penetration of the administered world of political economy is only partial'.[21] Moreover, as Kovel says,

> The body is not clay to be molded by history any more than workers are clay to be molded by capital: it makes an active input, a demand upon history, that occurs across all historical situations. It is neither above history nor below it, but somehow pressed into history and transformed by it – in other words, it is transhistorical.[22]

Later, when we reflect, with Merleau-Ponty, on the body's dimensionality as 'flesh', we shall return to this question of our transhistorical nature, and I will attempt to articulate the deep structural order constitutive of this corporeal nature. For the time being, it may perhaps suffice that we understand the sense in which I am claiming, in agreement with Kovel, that the body-self is both historical and transhistorical. Let us then understand that the body is not transhistorical *in itself*, and that, as Kovel notes, 'to posit such a thing means we have already named it, i.e., drawn it into history'.[23] The transhistorical never appears, and is never to be known, except in and through our history; in this sense, it is historically relative and dependent, and is not a transcendental condition or a metaphysical origin. However, to the extent that the nature of the body-self cannot be reduced to the ontology of an historical production; to the extent that it constitutes contingent conditions of possibility and contingent limitations, relative to history, that history can neither create nor totally reorganize, it must be recognized as bringing into history a transhistorical otherness – history's unconquerable alterity, of which, in fact, the historical body-self itself always carries at least a trace.

How we conceptualize the human body, the *being* of the body-self, is a matter of the gravest consequence. Foucault himself tacitly acknowledges this, since, as we have already noted, he deliberately positions the body in the centre of his discourse: *The Birth of the Clinic, Discipline and Punish, The History of Sexuality*, and many of his lectures and interviews take the body as their principal concern, their object of discourse. The two conceptualizations of which Foucault makes use are certainly valuable in focusing critical attention on the operations of power that circulate throughout our lifeworld. But they cannot easily sustain a discourse of resistance – and even less easily, the discourses of emancipation or redemption.

Foucault denies us all substantive and procedural *grounds* for resistance; all ethical grounds, such as 'rights' and 'objective interests'; all epistemological grounds, such as transcendental conditions, objectivity, and a non-relative standard of truth; and finally, all practical grounds, because power is pervasive and defines even the gestures of resistance.[24] We have no choice but to throw our energies into what Nancy Fraser calls 'multiple local resistances carried out in the name of no articulatable positive ideals'.[25] Given such a situation, it becomes all the more imperative that we be able to conceptualize, for the use of social and political theory, the body of felt experience. For if we must renounce abstract grounds, principles, and ideals, we might still realize the possibility of drafting political theory and praxis on the basis of needs and concerns schematized within the depths, the flesh, of this body-self. In any case, this is what I shall attempt to argue in the course of the present chapter.

As I read Foucault, it seems that he forces us to choose between the horns of a tragic dilemma: either we must consent to the standards of the tradition, or we must resist oppression *without* any standards of rationality and justice to guide and support us. Either the same old bankrupt standards – or no standards at all. If we adopt the first alternative, our resistance is compromised and defeated from the very beginning. If we adopt the second, however, our resistance becomes a mere exercise of power, praxis without reason. Is there a way out of this corner?

Foucault, of course, chooses resistance without grounds, principles, reason. And he assigns this resistance to the body subject to intolerable regimes of power. Foucault's way out, however, will not work, for neither of his two conceptions of the body enables us to conceive a body-self capable of purposive, reflectively critical action. Despite the presence of Merleau-Ponty at the Collège de France, Foucault seems to have learned nothing at all from his phenomenology of the body: Foucault's work shows no awareness of the body of experience for which Merleau-Ponty argued so eloquently; in fact, it seems to recognize no conception of phenomenology other than Husserl's transcendental version, although both Sartre and Merleau-Ponty had already, for many years, been advocating its existential alternatives. Be this as it may, we clearly need to think the political questions Foucault presses us to consider in terms of the 'body' conceptualized in the phenomenological work of Merleau-Ponty. When we begin thinking Foucault's problematic in terms of the 'lived body', the body of felt experiencing, then his difficulties with questions of praxis, and in particular his difficulties thinking the oppressed body as a source of resistance, can be taken over and overcome within the framework of a more promising analysis. Foucault's commitment to a Nietzschean, Freudian body of drives makes freedom the victory of impulse over reason. We need a conception of 'body' that enables us to 'ground' resistance to oppressive power in the needs and concerns, reasons and motives that are constitutive of, and constituted by, the body-self's lived experience. Resistance is connected to the interpretation of needs; but need interpretation must be rooted in the body of felt experience: an intelligent body capable of self-reflection, a body capable of articulating its motives and reasons for action.

I shall accordingly argue that it is not true that the body-self's only order is an internalized order, socially imposed. I shall argue against the widespread opinion that the body-self, 'in itself', is a body of primitive drives, totally disorganized, chaotic, and without any immanent structures of meaning. Moreover, I want to argue against the view that the immanent organization of meaning constitutive of our so-called 'inner' or 'subjective' experience is somehow less 'real' than the order that belongs to, and originates in, our collective life. We need to understand, here, that the very distinction between 'inner' and 'outer', and between 'subjective' and 'objective', can be, and in fact often is, an instrument of social domination, in so far as this duality is used ideologically as a way to discredit, privatize, and derealize the potentially subversive authority of individual experience. (The political meaning of this dualism cannot be determined apart from its functional context; the dualism itself is politically ambiguous. Insistence on 'inner' experience can, for example, be a way of protecting individual experience from engulfment, total incorporation into the field of social power, total reduction to socially imposed meaning; in other words, it is a culturally available way for individuals to conceptualize their ability to resist domination or annihilation.

I want to argue that, if we pay close attention to our actual experiencing, we will discern the fact of its immanent organization of meaning, its own organismic order. Such order needs to be examined, because it bears within itself an immanent normative direction: the process orientation which formulates needs and concerns, and which schematizes the body's dream of a body politic. Such attention and 'inwardness' must not be confused, however, with 'freedom'. Liberation which is merely 'inner' is an ideological delusion.

In a recent paper, Reiner Schürmann noted that, for Foucault, 'there is no deep originative self'.[26] This position has found many advocates, and is now expounded as if it were an incontrovertible fact, or else an assumption essential to the possibility of New Left politics.[27] I submit, however, that the concept of a 'deep self', together with its companion concept of a 'body of depths', cannot be properly evaluated with regard to their critical, emancipatory, and redemptive potential without considering their discursive contexts and how they are functioning *within* these contexts. Apart from context and function, these concepts are ambiguous, and their political implications undecidable. Apart from context and function, we cannot tell whether the 'deep self' and the 'body of depths' are concepts referring to something authentic or whether, instead, they are referring to something false – the constructs and projections of an oppressive ideology.

Conceptualizing the self and the body as 'deep' may indeed be a way of capturing them for social domination: creating a depth of which the individual is unconscious and then filling it with a content (of meanings, motives, reasons, intentions, beliefs) that conforms to the dominant ideology and is taken, therefore, to confirm it. (Psychoanalytic explanations for social problems often function this way.) But conceptualizing the self and the body as 'deep' may also be a way of recognizing an irreducible individuality and protecting self and body from social domination and totalization. If, as Freud claimed, the ego forms at, and as, the surface of the libidinal body, and if this ego is a product of socialization, i.e. of social interaction, then conceptualizing the body and the self as 'deep' may be a way of denying their reduction to a socially imposed, socially imprinted surface; it is a way of representing their withdrawal from, and their resistance to, a surface-being that is totally determined by the prevailing social prescriptions. Let us not forget that the *persona* is a mask that conceals even as it reveals, and that the human *face* is not a surface, but rather a depth, a dimensionality, the presence of an unrepresentable alterity and a very radical ethical demand for recognition.

I am arguing that the body-self has – is – an order of its own, an order that is not socially imposed. This order is not only a structuring structure; it is also need and demand. The tired body-self *orders* sleep: that is to say, it structures, needs, demands, and organizes itself for, the coming of sleep. Similarly, the hungry body-self orders food: that is to say, it organismically structures-in needs, and demands something to eat. These are examples of very basic, organismically organized structures, needs, and demands. But the human being, a body-self, has – is – many other kinds of needs and demands; there are emotional needs, spiritual needs, and many needs whose realization, recognition, or satisfaction directly bear on social and political policy.

Later in this chapter, I will make use of the texts in which Merleau-Ponty sketches a hermeneutical phenomenology of the flesh, in order to show the nature of the order that is deeply inscribed into the flesh of the body-self. More specifically, I will show that this order, which Merleau-Ponty describes, in dynamic terms, as an 'intertwining', implicitly schematizes a new body politic, a political order radically different from the prevailing orders of past and present. This schematism is an inherent need, a demand, structured by the very character of the flesh; it is a corporeal image, a utopian image, borne in, and by, the body of depths. And the body-self is capable of *speaking* from out of these depths; it is capable of addressing history and making claims on society, speaking with eloquence of its deepest needs, concerns, and dreams.

Foucault urges us to consider what kind of body our current society needs, what kind of body our society has invested in, what kind of body our society refuses to tolerate, and what kind of body it abuses, exploits, shapes, disciplines, punishes, and dreams of. I think it is significant that he nowhere considers what kind of future society our *bodies* need – and what kind of society would fulfil that need and dream.

In *Language, Counter-Memory, Practice,* Foucault states that 'if the fight is directed against power, then all those on whom power is exercised to their detriment, all who find it intolerable, can begin the struggle on their own terrain and on the basis of their proper activity (or passivity) . . . fighting in those places where they find themselves oppressed'.[28] Now,

Foucault is, I think, saying something very important here. But it is unfortunate that, when he wrote the words 'all who find it intolerable', 'struggle on their own terrain', and 'the basis of their proper activity (or passivity)', he did not attempt to understand how the body to which he gives so much importance must be conceived in order to make it possible for the body itself to speak, struggle, and organize the direction of resistance. Nor did he critically examine his own way of conceptualizing 'the body', to discover why the resistance to power that he advocated so well could not be adequately understood as a resistance articulated and directed by the 'body' subject to this power. Given the two conceptualizations of 'body' with which he was working, it should not be surprising that there is no acknowledgement of a *body* capable of finding power intolerable, articulating from out of its own experience a struggle on its own terrain, and drawing on itself, on the wisdom of its own experience, to constitute the 'basis' of an intelligent and effective political praxis.

Eventually, it seems, Foucault worked his way to an abstract *theoretical* understanding of this point, for, in one of the texts published in *Power/Knowledge*, he said: 'Power, after investing itself in the body, finds itself exposed to a counter-attack in that same body.'[29] Although he explicates this counter-attack in reference to non-legalized cohabitation (*l'union libre*) and abortion, it should be understood, here, that there are many other situations where power could be, should be, and in fact has been, subject to intelligent counter-attacks coming from the body, and that there are many different ways in which the body is *capable* of talking back, expressing needs, formulating demands, and generating, from within its own order, its own immanent organization of meaning, the most appropriate 'next steps' in the experiencing process – steps, that is, through which these needs and demands would be recognized, achieved, fulfilled. (In his writings on the experiencing process he calls 'focusing',[30] Eugene Gendlin examines, and articulates in detail, the 'logic', that is, a movement at once phenomenological and hermeneutical, of these bodily organized steps.)

In this regard, it is noteworthy that Adorno sometimes described his style of critique as a method of listening for 'dissonance': the dissonance between thought and action, word and deed, project and reality, concept and actuality, means and ends. Thus, for Adorno, the task of the social critic is to listen for sounds of disharmony, to catch the moments of discord and discrepancy, and to make audible, in as articulate a formulation as possible, the contradictions, the untruths, toward which the dissonance is calling our attention.[31] The critic needs a good ear for this work. Such listening does not come naturally or easily; it needs to be developed, sharpened, directed. And it is only through the critical power of political theory that this skilfulness can be developed. Theory alone is not enough; but neither is a listening untutored by theoretical understanding.

The Lakotas know *in their bodies* that their sweat lodges, their vision quests, and their seven pipe ceremonies are not instances of 'savagery', 'ignorance', and 'superstition'; listening to their bodies, they can talk back, speaking of their health, sanity, healing, well-being, and wisdom; they can speak out with the authority, the wisdom, of their own bodies. Women know *in their bodies* that menstruation and giving birth are not 'sicknesses', and that their moments of rage are not due to their 'hysterical nature', but to the frustrations of living in a male-dominated society. They know this, listening to the dissonance that the prevailing ideology sets in motion. Blacks know *in their bodies* that their non-standard idioms of speech are not evidence of any intrinsic intellectual inferiority afflicting their race, but the evidence, instead, that accuses their oppressors. They know this, listening to the dissonance that the prevailing ideology sets in motion. Similarly, the poor know *in their bodies,* as they stand in court before the judge, whether or not the judicial system is treating them with democratic respect and fairness; whether or not their abject poverty makes a difference to the just and equal application of the law. They, too, will know this – by listening to the dissonance that takes over their alienated and humiliated bodies.

In a chapter titled 'Universal pragmatics', John Thompson holds that, for Habermas, a crucial task for rational reconstruction is 'to investigate the general competencies required for the successful performance of speech-acts, and thereby "to reconstruct the universal validity-basis" of speech'.[32] I would like to broaden the field of investigation, so that it includes other competencies: our capacity to listen and hear, for example.

Communication requires more than the successful performance of speech-acts; it requires, among other things, the capacity to be touched and moved by what one sees, and the capacity to listen carefully and with an open mind.

Perhaps, then, the most consequential deficiency in Foucault's analysis of the body in relation to power is that it ignores the body as a complex of capacities and competencies. Had Foucault conceptualized the body in *these* terms, I believe he would have been able to offer, not only a negative analysis, displaying the body as an object (or docile subject) of power, but also a more constructive project, drawing on the capacities and competencies of the body in order to articulate sound motives and reasons for courses of action concerned with the oppressiveness of power.

The advantage of conceptualizing the body in terms of its capacities and competencies is that we can critically examine the oppressiveness of power (for power is oppressive when it neglects, blocks, or denies the developmental *needs* of our capacities and competencies), whilst we can also, at the same time, elicit and formulate, beyond spontaneous anger and rebellion, even beyond mere strategies for local and intermittent resistance, some of the possibilities for constructive, systematic praxis that are implicitly schematized, i.e. already projected and motivated, by these very same capacities and competencies. Because he ignores the capacities and competencies constitutive of the body of experience, Foucault misses an opportunity to work with an ideality whose normative 'axis' is latent in the flesh: the dream of a new body politic, already announced through the felt needs and demands of our capacities and competencies: a dream already calling us to its vocation through the channels of our capacity to listen.

Part II
States of Deafness: Listening for the Excluded Voices

Opening Conversation

Nec audiendi, qui solent dicere: Vox populi, vox Dei. Cum tumultuositas vulgi semper insaniae proxima sit: And one should not listen to those who say the voice of the people is the voice of God. For the noisiness of the masses is always very close to madness.

Alcuin, in a letter to Charlemagne[33]

That the millions of virtuous citizens, whose agents the government are, have no place to interpose, and must shut their eyes until the last howl and wailing of these tormented villages and tribes, shall afflict the ear of the world.

Emerson, in a letter to President Van Buren[34]

Under a government which imprisons any unjustly, the true place for a just man is also a prison. . . . On that separate, but more free and honorable ground, where the State places those who are not *with* her but *against* her. . . . If any think that their influence would be lost there, and their voices no longer afflict the ear of the State . . . they do not know by how much truth is stronger than error, nor how much more eloquently and effectively he can combat injustice who has experienced a little in his own person.

Thoreau, 'On the duty of civil disobedience'[35]

The concrete other is a critical concept that designates the *ideological* limits of universalistic discourse. It signifies the *unthought*, the *unseen*, and the *unheard* in such theories.

Benhabib, 'The generalized and the concrete other: toward a feminist critique of substitutionality universalism'[36]

[We must recognize] the need for an effective communication of the goals of liberation and the indictment of the established reality. It is the effort to find forms of communication that may break the oppressive rule of the established language and images over the mind and body of every human being.

Marcuse, *Counter-Revolution and Revolt*[37]

Our standards of reflective acceptability, and the social and cultural ideals in terms of which we criticize societies and ideologies, are 'just' part of our tradition and have no absolute foundation or transcendental warrant. For Adorno, therefore, we must start from where we happen to be historically and culturally, from a particular kind of frustration

> or suffering experienced by human agents in their attempt to realize some historically specific project of the 'good life'.
>
> Geuss, *The Idea of a Critical Theory*[38]

> Critical theory . . . must plumb the psychic depths for sounds of sadness and revolt.
>
> Jacoby, *Social Amnesia: A Critique of Conformist Psychology from Adler to Laing*[39]

> Only when philosophy discovers in the dialectical course of history the traces of violence that deform repeated attempts at dialogue and recurrently close off the path to unconstrained communication does it further the process whose suspension it otherwise legitimated: mankind's evolution towards 'maturity' [*Mündigkeit*].
>
> Habermas, *Knowledge and Human Interests*[40]

> There were no voices [heard] from the outside to arouse his conscience.
>
> Arendt, *Eichmann in Jerusalem: A Report on the Banality of Evil*[41]

> There can be no beauty if it is paid for by human injustice, nor truth that passes over injustice in silence, nor moral virtue that condones it.
>
> Borowski, *This Way for the Gas, Ladies and Gentlemen*[42]

When 'the' people speak, Alcuin hears only noise and frenzy – and yet, it should be noted, only a *single* voice, a *univocal* communication, 'always very close to madness'. Let me first of all pluralize the 'voice' of the people, recognizing their solidarity, but also acknowledging their differences. Now I want to ask: are these voices close to madness because that is the 'nature' of 'the masses'? Or are they close to madness because they have not been heard? Alcuin argues that, *because* they are close to madness, the people should not be heard. I would argue that his justification for not listening is a very poor attempt at rationalization: the truth is that his causal sequence should be reversed. Nothing can be more effective in driving people crazy than not listening to their efforts to communicate distress. Moreover, since we human beings are essentially social, and our sense of ourselves is constituted through our interactions with others, not being *heard* by others diminishes our capacity to hear ourselves, and may sometimes so *deprive* us of the possibility of listening to ourselves that it even becomes difficult for us to know our real needs and concerns: in sum, to know ourselves and form an authentic personal or collective identity.

In 'Ideology, social science, and revolution', Alasdair MacIntyre maintains, against the possibility of social critiques grounded in, or appealing to, universal principles (e.g. the projects of Kant, Rawls, and Habermas), that 'to identify ideological distortion one must not be a victim of it oneself'.[43] This objection strikes me as quite mistaken. My own position is the one represented by Thoreau, Adorno, and Geuss, in the textual passages of the 'opening conversation', which I have used in order to introduce the subject of my reflections in this part of the chapter.

To be sure, the judgment of the victim of ideological distortion cannot be entirely free of its distortion. But this does not at all prevent the victim from experiencing the distortion *as* distortion and from speaking out against it with words this experience brings forth. MacIntyre's argument seems to make sense, and seems to catch the political critic in the corner of an inescapable dilemma, until we realize that it depends on the assumption that resistance to ideology is never merely a question of *cognitive* positions. We can imagine cognitivism generating an analysis in terms of which there is *no* position from which criticism of society would be reasonable, for if the victims of ideological distortion are to be disqualified because they are 'inside' and their judgment will be correspondingly distorted, those who are *not* in the position of victims are 'outside' and therefore not in a position to know or understand. Under the spell of cognitivism, MacIntyre does not seem to understand that critical positions are always rooted in the victim's experience, the victim's body of evidence. Consequently, he fails to appreciate the fact that when a victim is experiencing the distortions caused by pain, misery, and suffering, this bodily felt distortion can be sufficient ground for his realizing the distorted nature of the ideological situation. In other words, the victim is often able to form a very clear sense of the distortion *as* distortion precisely because he or she is able to *experience* the intense distortion manifesting in the facticity of the pain, misery, and suffering.

MacIntyre's argument also depends on two other questionable assumptions that I want to challenge here: (1) the assumption that the possibility of identifying ideological distortion requires *total* exemption from its effects, i.e. the error of totalism, and (2) the assumption that critique requires an exclusive appeal to absolutely unquestionable, absolutely objective standards of judgment, i.e. the error of cognitivism, or logocentrism. One can *begin* social critique, as Thoreau, Adorno, and Geuss have suggested, by speaking very directly – that is to say, phenomenologically – from out of one's own experience. And if the experience is an experience *of* distortion, the distortion borne within the experience itself will be an eloquent beginning for the task of critique. The experience of not being heard, of being excluded from discourse and its consensus, is a very strong beginning, as feminist thinking already has argued, for the criticism of social institutions and their ideologies.

But it is not only as ideological regimes that modern societies victimize; as Habermas points out, in his *Theory of Communicative Action*, even the increasing 'juridification' (*Verrechtlichung*) of society, though designed to extend the justice of formal law to everyone, can institute numerous 'pathological deformations' in the communicative infrastructures of the lifeworld, ultimately creating or tolerating ideological distortions that threaten the individual's sense of identity, self-esteem, and meaningful living.[44] Excessive juridification, a consequence of the technocratic 'rationalization' of democratic justice, works *against* the principles of justice and equality inherent in the logic of the communicative situation, and consequently blocks and distorts the communicative process. Nevertheless, there are, in every situation, infrastructural spaces where good listening can at least be demanded, if not exercised, and where its demand and its exercise could make a difference.

Foucault's analysis of power is ambiguous, and different thinkers have therefore been able to draw from it opposite practical conclusions. If power is everywhere, omnipresent, then it cannot be escaped and we are condemned to suffer its oppression: the conclusion of despair. But if power really is everywhere, present in every situation, then at every moment and in every setting there are opportunities to resist oppression and change the functioning of power: the conclusion of the pragmatist. The pragmatist takes strategic advantage of the theoretical insight that power is pervasive; Foucault's analysis suggests that every structure, every institution, creates within itself certain infrastructures, certain interstices or indeterminate spaces, where the freedom of difference can sometimes take hold. Good listening, something essential for good communication, is always a struggle; but it *can* make a significant difference in the places where it happens.

Habermas is therefore formulating an important criticism of Marx's conception of alienation when he argues that at 'the stage of post-traditional forms of life, the pain that the separation of culture, society, and personality causes in those who grow into modern societies, and who form their identities within them, counts as a process of individuation and not alienation'.[45] As he points out, in 'an extensively rationalized lifeworld, reification can be measured only against the conditions of communicative sociation, and not against the nostalgically loaded, frequently romanticized past of premodern forms of life'.[46] Habermas thus attempts to redefine the Marxian conception of alienation by shifting the focus to breakdowns and injustices – internal contradictions – in the modes and institutions of communication. In other words, he is arguing that there is, in our contemporary world, a significant and unnecessary curtailment of the conditions favourable to individuation and autonomy, and that this is a consequence, in part, of 'a systematically induced reification of communicatively structured domains of action'.[47]

I would accordingly emphasize, here, that the individual and collective development of our capacity for listening inherently constitutes some *resistance* to this reification and that this resistance would generate some possibilities for *changing* the 'communicative infrastructures' within which we live. More specifically, I would point out that when our listening has achieved the self-awareness, conscience, and skilfulness of stage III as a way of taking part in the communicative processes of social and political life, it is bound to resist, and if possible deconstruct, any power relations that are (audibly) coercive and not symmetrical or egalitarian.

My reason for saying this is that listening which has achieved stage III *as a communicative practice* will be a listening (1) that has experienced, and consequently knows, what it is like to listen to others carefully and openly, resonating, as if with the attunement of an echo, to the claim on our respect that is constitutive of their communication; (2) that accordingly has experienced, and thereby knows, what it is like to be really listened to and be accurately, deeply, fully heard; and (3) that, in virtue of (1) and (2), is sensitively attuned to breaches in the communicative process, and especially vigilant when it is (audibly) abused, distorted, and blocked by the conditions of power – power relations (audibly) organized around assumptions of domination and subordination, for example – or by assumptions of procedure and substance that cannot be shared. (It should be recalled that, in my discussion of Table 1.1 in the first chapter, I correlated Kohlberg's 'stage 6', where relationships are constituted in terms of a recognition of universal ethical principles, with my third stage of hearing.)

Two further points should be considered here, as we reflect on the skilfulness of stage III listening in relation to the questions of power – especially coercive power – that are involved in all communicative situations. Note that, at stage III, listening is developed *as a capacity of the body* – the body of intersubjective, intercorporeal life, the body of auditorily felt experience, the body as an auditory whole. Thus, in stage III, the listening skill one brings to the communicative situation will be a listening-to-the-other which *also* listens to the body and hears its needs, the speech of its needs. It will be a listening that *knows* when what it needs the other to hear has been both communicated adequately and heard with openness and accuracy. Note also that coercion and ideological indoctrination can certainly operate in extremely subtle ways – ways so subtle that, for the listening developed only into stage II, they are not really audible. But they will be audible – not all of the time, but certifiably much more of the time – for listening that has achieved a stage III development. Stage III hearing can *hear the difference* between speech with the 'ring' of truth and speech with the 'hollow' sound of the lie. It can hear the difference between sincerity and deception. It can hear the difference between the tones of coercion and the tones of respectful suggestion. It can hear the difference between speech that is listening attunedly to the other and speech that is indifferent to the other and refuses to listen.

In his *Critique of Instrumental Reason*, Horkheimer, often sounding the tones of pessimism and despair, writes these surprising words of hope: 'As long as there are hunger and misery on earth, he who can see will have no peace.'[48] Is this true? Is this, in any case, a firm ground for hope? Most human beings have eyes; most of us therefore can see. But what do we see? Since hunger and misery exist, since in truth they are widespread, though so many people seem to be 'at peace' (the 'peace', I would say, of complacency), it must be concluded that many people do not see: do not really *see* this hunger and misery, even when the suffering is there to be seen, right before their eyes.

When I last had occasion to read Horkheimer's words, I was thinking about our capacity for listening. So I immediately thought of substituting the word 'listen' for the word 'see'. The problem, of course, remains. I am *tempted* to think, and certainly would like to *believe*, that as long as there are hunger and misery in the world, those who can hear will have no peace. But I am compelled by the facticity of hunger and misery to conclude that many people simply do not hear, that somehow they turn a deaf ear. This book would not have been written, however, if I did not have the faith, the hope, that we are capable of listening to, capable of hearing, what it is now difficult for us to hear, and that, because this capability is so intimately, so essentially bound up with our self-development, our fulfilment as human beings, the necessary motivation for this work – an ethical task – can be encouraged. As our (stage III) listening develops, it can change local communicative structures, and thereby make possible the further development of our listening capacity. Conversely, we can undertake changes in the communicative structures, making local spaces for the further development of listening. We can respond to the problem taking either as our point of departure. We can respond wherever we are. This is the sort of thing, I think, that Foucault had in mind when he conceptualized an array of micro-practices and micro-processes, and called attention, by documenting the omnipresence of power, to very specific, localized possibilities for strategically resisting intolerable power, increasing participation, and reorganizing power relations, particularly within administrative decision structures.

But I want to conclude this meditation on 'states of deafness' by tempering my expressions of faith and hope. The stage III possibility of achieving a satisfactory approximation to the ideal communicative process, a situation in which there would be a shared sense that each of the different positions has been really listened to and heard without distortion, sometimes can seem quite hopeless. When Alejandro Bendaña, currently the Foreign Minister for Nicaragua, was interviewed for television by Sam Donaldson, two listeners, senators bringing with them opposing political dispositions, somehow heard two totally different meanings, two absolutely irreconcilable messages. What could have been done here? Were both people listening to the minister's tone of voice and attending to the 'body language'? Were they listening with equal openness, equal effort to hear freshly, as if for the first time? Were they listening with equal attention? If the answers to these questions are negative, what is to be done? Would more time for listening, more time for conversation, make a difference? If so, why is that need not heard – or, if it is heard, why does it not motivate the necessary accommodations? What stands in the way?

This question cannot be answered solely in terms of individual psychology. It can only be answered after we include a more theoretical analysis of power and its institutions. For the participants in the conversation are never merely individuals; they are always also representatives of institutional power, bringing with them a multiplicity of vested interests – and many virtually inaudible agendas. Habermas's account of communicative interaction unwittingly postulates an unproblematic hearing: a listener who always hears all there is to be heard; a listening which is invariably accurate and complete. There is no theoretical recognition of auditory distortion, ideological deafness, institutional noise, the specific ways in which power channels hearing and listening channels power. It is as if, when it comes to listening, a metaphysics of presence still governed his thinking.

Part III
The Conscience of Listening: The Self as Intersubjectivity

> We are without culture, more, we are ruined for living, for right and simple seeing and hearing.
>
> Nietzsche, 'On the uses and disadvantages of history for life'[49]

> As *you* are, so are even the best nowadays: you are content to let yourselves be deceived! You come with coarse and lustful ears; you no longer bring the conscience of the art of hearing with you; on

the way here you have thrown away *the finest part of your honesty*!

Nietzsche, *Daybreak: Thoughts on the Prejudices of Morality*[50]

Man appropriates his manifold being in an all-inclusive way, and thus as a whole man. All his *human* relations to the world – seeing, hearing, smelling, tasting, touching, thinking, observing, feeling, desiring, acting, loving – in short, all the *organs* of his individuality, like the organs which are directly communal in form, are, in their objective action . . . the appropriation [i.e. the essential coming-into-its-own] of our human reality.

Marx, *Economic and Philosophical Manuscripts of 1844*[51]

The world of social action and event, the world of time and process, has a particularly close association with the ear. The ear listens, and the ear translates what it hears into practical conduct.

Northrop Frye, *The Anatomy of Criticism*[52]

We are thus in a position to assess the radical, i.e., transcendent, quality of particular praxes. Clearly, a radical act need not be an explicitly political one, even though its universalizing quality can be consummated only at the level of all society, indeed, for the entire globe. However, as history has yielded a fragmented society, so it may be undone, i.e., transcended, at the level of a fragment. As personal life is a principal one of these fragments, the question of transcendence may validly be asked of it.

Kovel, *The Age of Desire*[53]

We have to promote new forms of subjectivity through the refusal of the kind of individuality imposed on us for several centuries.

Foucault, 'The subject and power'[54]

Under circumstances that prohibit the thought of revolution and give one reason to expect revolutionary processes of long duration, the idea

> of the revolution as the process of forming a new subjectivity must also be transformed.
>
> Habermas, *Philosophical-Political Profiles*[55]

In *Dawn and Decline*, Horkheimer advances the argument that as 'their telescopes and microscopes, their tapes and radios become more sensitive, individuals become blinder, more hard of hearing, less responsive, and society becomes more opaque, more hopeless, its misdeeds . . . larger and more superhuman than ever'.[56] There is a certain irony implicit in what we call technological 'progress', an irony which, to a degree, Plato already intuited: as we invent a technology to extend and amplify our powers of perception, the technology assumes a 'life' of its own, and our natural powers begin to atrophy or change, altered by the conditions of technologization. Plato's argument against writing rests on the claim that, since it makes memory unnecessary, writing contributes to its delinquency. In *The Opening of Vision*, I questioned the relationship between technology and vision, and pointed to evidence that the technology of cameras and television has contributed to the predatory character of the gaze. Here I would suggest that the increasing technocratic 'rationalization' of our society, and what Habermas calls the 'systematic colonization' of the lifeworld, may be significant factors in the deterioration of our ability to listen and hear one another. But I think we should also bear in mind that there are other factors, some of them generated by technology itself, which work against this tendency, actually increasing and refining our communicative possibilities. In any case, I do not regard the degeneration to which Horkheimer has called our attention to be an inevitable or irreversible process.

Vigilance, however, must be maintained. In 'What is enlightenment?', Foucault asks: 'How can the growth of capabilities be disconnected from the intensification of power relations?'[57] Habermas formulates a closely related question in 'Moral development and ego identity', when he asks: 'How do the . . . basic institutions of a society interfere with an ontogenetic developmental pattern?'[58] These are not easy questions to answer, but they are questions we should continually ask ourselves. Thus, the task they formulate is one of the principal concerns of the project to which this present study is a contribution.

If Foucault's analysis of power is basically accurate, then we should not expect any theoretical answer, any answer formulated in abstraction from the specifics of particular power relations, to be adequate. Nevertheless, I would like, here, to make some very general remarks on the subject. Foucault has persuaded me that the growth of capabilities cannot be disconnected from power relations. But it seems to me that, if we can agree (1) that our capabilities – to perceive, to listen, for example – are not totally determined by socially organized modes and relations of power, (2) that there are latent *developmental needs, ontogenetic needs,* inherent in such capacities, and (3) that these needs implicitly bear within them, as a legitimate moral claim, a felt sense, a corporeally constellated dream, of their realization and fulfilment in 'the good life', then we may suppose (4) that, when these developmental needs are *not* being realized and, in particular, when they (or their claims) are intolerably frustrated and painfully unfulfilled by the conditions of life, they will spontaneously begin to constitute, at *some* level of awareness and understanding, an initial working basis not only for resistance to oppression, but also for the formulation and effectuation of the social, political, and cultural changes that are needed. In other words, even when our developmental needs encounter conditions of power that frustrate, block, distort, or deny them, and perhaps especially then, they always bear within themselves, however inarticulately, a contrary sense, a certain message, regarding what needs to be changed in the organization of the lifeworld, *if* their legitimate moral claims to developmental realization and fulfilment are to be respected and encouraged.

To be sure, we must recognize the problem of 'false consciousness', the ideological distortion and concealment of needs and their interpretations. However, *genuine* needs always *do* know, at some level of awareness and understanding, what it is that they need. Consequently, if there is a lively, critical, public discourse that encourages our capacities to develop by stimulating reflection on the character of their developmental needs and provoking thought concerning their moral claims, the 'logic' or 'dynamics' of the developmental process can itself become an increasingly articulate source of emancipatory praxis.

Let us listen, then, wherever we are positioned in the actual contexts of daily life, for those dissonant points of contact between the growth of our capabilities and the networks of power, where a critical public discourse, focusing on natural capacities, personal growth, and developmental needs, and articulating their points of contact with power in terms of a theoretical understanding of power, can decisively contribute to emancipatory and self-fulfilling 'processes of enlightenment'. A critical, theoretical systems-analysis is of course indispensable, but we must also trust in ourselves; we must ultimately put some trust in the innate wisdom of our natural capacities, trusting that, through critical discourse, we can elicit from them their *own* sound sense regarding what they need in order to continue developing – and what they need to change *in the world* to make their continued development possible. The participatory reform of administrative decision-making structures is a necessary condition for emancipation, but it is not sufficient for individual fulfilment and the 'good life'. We must also change ourselves. As we change and develop, however, in the freedom of 'private' or 'domestic' spaces, we also learn more about what administrative structures we need to change – and how, concretely, to accomplish that.

Who we are, and how and why we fall short of happiness and the 'good life', echo prevailing social conditions – conditions that need to be changed. It is equally true, however, that what is wrong with society is an echo of who we are – and an indictment of the *character* of our listening. Our limited development of listening, a capacity whose potential we have only begun, as individuals and collectivities, to appropriate, contributes to social conditions that perpetuate, even intensify, the forms of dissatisfaction, suffering, and misery that reverberate throughout our world. The forms of our distress are distinctive manifestations of our historical situation, the age in which we live.

The distress we experience as auditory beings, and the ills of society that are audible to us, urgently call for a transformation of the character of our hearing through our capacity for further self-development. In order to change the social ills we hear, we need to change our habits of listening; we need to change ourselves. But society itself needs to be changed. It is not enough simply to give voice to the pain, the suffering, and the need – and let that all be heard. The experience of the individual must be *connected* to a critical theoretical interpretation of society and culture – and to appropriate social praxes. 'Inner' changes are no substitute for necessary changes in our social-political reality. The pain, the suffering, and the genuine unmet needs, are not only 'inner', not only 'subjective'; and they cannot be overcome, or transformed, by only 'inner', only 'subjective' changes. They are, and need to be understood as, essentially connected to social, political, material, and cultural conditions. We need to hear the different forms of human pain, suffering, and need as the 'effects', the consequences, of changeable social arrangements. Once our self-development has reached a certain stage of maturity, the needs inherent in our various capacities will *themselves* begin to indicate what social conditions must be changed before further individuation, further maturation, is possible.

Self and society are not separate systems. The stage III development of the human capacity for listening is needed equally by the self and by society, and any real advances in the listening function of the one encourage corresponding advances in the other. I would like this chapter to make the point that stage III listening is uniquely important for this evolutionary circuit, because the self is essentially social and society is no less essentially dependent on mature processes of communication.

In a text published in *Langugage, Counter-Memory, Practice,* Foucault opined that it 'is possible that the rough outline of a future society is supplied by the recent experiences with [psychedelic] drugs, sex, communes, other forms of consciousness and other forms of individuality'. And he conjectured that 'if scientific socialism emerged from the *Utopias* of the nineteenth century, it is possible that a real socialization will emerge, in the twentieth century, from *experiences*' (op. cit., 231). I think we may infer from this that, at least in the late 1960s and early 1970s, Foucault would not have *equated* subjectivity with subjugation. Subjectivity certainly *can* be a form of subjugation; but the point is that it can *also* be a ground of struggle and resistance, a challenge to oppressive power, a source of utopian-emancipatory energies. Foucault's statements, here, tell us that he perceived the significance of the Awareness Movement that began in the mid-1960s. I think that he accurately measured its potential.

Has 'the Movement' totally failed? Has it ended? What Foucault thought is not clear. He may have changed his mind; or perhaps he wavered, sometimes thinking one thing, sometimes another. In some of his public statements made in the late 1970s and early 1980s, he seems to recognize that the 'experiences' in question may have changed the lives of many individuals, but that, despite their status as 'subversive' and 'excluded', and despite their utopian potential, these 'experiences' remained, for the most part, privatized, and did not bring about any significant transformation of society. I think, however, that such a verdict would be premature, for there is much evidence, which Foucault's impatiently sweeping glance overlooks, to suggest that the genuinely emancipatory, consciousness-raising processes begun in the 1960s have in fact continued, though assuming, in the 1980s, much less visible, less eye-catching, less media-ready forms. Foucault's categorizing glance sometimes moves much too quickly. It was easy to see the utopian potential in the 'experiences' of the 1960s. Today, it takes a more discerning, more patient eye – and in fact a carefully listening ear – to recognize the *continuation* of the 'experiences' that shaped the world of the 1960s. For the 'continuation' has also been their evolution and transformation.

In any case, in an interview recorded by Dreyfus and Rabinow shortly before his death, Foucault was asked: 'Isn't the Greek concern with the self just an early version of our self-absorption, which many people consider a central problem in our society?'[59] Foucault answered as follows:

> in a culture to which we owe a certain number of our most important constant moral elements, there was a practice of the self, a conception of the self, very different from our present culture of the self. In the California cult of the self, one is supposed to discover one's 'true' self, to separate it from that which might obscure or alienate it, to decipher its truth thanks to psychology or psychoanalytic science, which is supposed to be able to tell you what your 'true' self is. Therefore, not only do I not identify the ancient culture of the self with what you might call the California cult of the self, but I think they are diametrically opposed. (ibid.)

We need to think about 'practices of the self' that are *not* forms of self-absorption and self-indulgence, i.e. forms of narcissism. We need to think about 'practices of the self' that do *not* separate the self from society and withdraw it from social responsiblity. We need to think about 'practices of the self' that *understand* the essential intertwining of self and other, self and society, that are aware of the subtle complexities in this intertwining, and that conceptualize self-development as a process of 'enlightenment', mediated by social learning. We need to think about 'practices of the self' that understand how the self *grows* by virtue of its participation in, and its assumption of responsibility for, the processes of power constitutive of democratic societies. Finally, we need to think about 'practices of the self' that are critical and emancipatory: *not* mere 'functions of bio-power', *not* mere 'technologies' applied to the control of the self and dictating a fixed content or 'true' essence.

I share Foucault's contempt for 'practices of the self' which are nothing more than forms of self-absorption, the symptoms of an epidemic cultural narcissism. But I cannot permit him to identify the diversity of movements making up the 'Awareness Movement' as a whole – all the different consciousness-raising and emancipatory movements that began in the 1960s – with the practices and ideologies of a few misguided sub-groups. Foucault's sweeping denunciation equates the whole with some of its parts. This is an extremely serious error, since it fails to recognize and legitimate the existence of some authentic practices, processes, and projects: I am thinking, here, of the women's movement, the black movement, the gay rights movement, and the native American movement. All four of these movements essentially involve consciousness-raising and emancipatory practices of the self – practices in which a newly emerging self, an historically new individual and social identity, is being 'cared for'.

Russell Jacoby is certainly right to insist, in *Social Amnesia*, that to forget that, today, social relationships are inhuman 'is to indulge in the ideology of sensitivity groups which work to desensitize by cutting off human relations from the social roots that have made them brutal'.[60] Thus I am inclined to agree with his conclusion: 'More sensitivity today means revolution or madness. The rest is chatter.'[61] The ills of society, the body politic, cannot be cured by curing (only) the individual; nor can individuals authentically develop without the corresponding transformation of society. The possibilities for authentic subjectivity – for its emergence – are certainly threatened and blocked today, in many ways; but the 'cults of subjectivity', glorifying a false, narcissistic individualism and hedonism and ignoring forms of social domination and oppression, are not in fact responding to authentic needs. Foucault's analysis makes no distinction between true and false subjectivities. He also fails to perceive that the liberation movements at the heart of the 'Awareness

Movement' have all repudiated 'practices of the Self' that conceptualize the 'self' as a fixed content, structure, or essence. In his paper, 'A philosophical critique of the concept of narcissism: the significance of the Awareness Movement', Eugene Gendlin examines in experiential detail his very radical conception of the self: a self which is constellated within the 'practice' he calls 'focusing', and which, radically breaking with the ego-logical 'self' of the Cartesian and Kantian traditions, cannot be defined in terms of a fixed content, structure, or essence; a self, in short, which can only be defined in terms of experiential process.[62]

Only near the end of his life did Foucault return to the discourse of subjectivity (the subject, the self) and take part in its project. Obviously, he found that he could not do without it, and that, instead of renouncing it altogether, he needed to transform it. Thus, when he examined the practice of truth-telling (*parrhēsia*) in relation to moral character, he conceptualized this practice as a 'practice of the self'. In 'What is enlightenment?', he states, as we already noted in Chapter One (Part VII, p. 41), that 'the critical ontology of ourselves has to be considered not, certainly, as a theory, a doctrine, nor even as a permanent body of knowledge that is accumulating; it has to be conceived as an attitude, an ethos, a philosophical life in which the critique of what we are is at one and the same time the historical analysis of the limits that are imposed upon us and an experiment with the possibility of going beyond them'.[63] This 'critical ontology' requires more than theoretical, systemic, and abstractly historical analysis; it requires practices of the self, rigorously phenomenological and hermeneutical; it requires, as Foucault puts it, 'work carried out by ourselves upon ourselves as free beings'.[64]

I conceive the project of this book as an experiment of the kind Foucault is proposing. In the third stage of listening, then, we are working toward a critical ontology of ourselves, taking as our starting-point, not a 'permanent body of knowledge', but rather our embodied capacity for listening. And we are 'working on ourselves' by taking up the body of auditory experiences as a critical-emancipatory practice of the self.

Now, it seems to me that, in this regard, we need to twist the 'self' free of the traditional discourses of modernity: in particular, the discourse of ego psychology and the 'transcendental' discourses of Descartes, Kant, and Husserl. For

Freud, the 'ego' is essentially the 'face' projected by society on to the 'surface' of the body.[65] The ego is therefore a product of social work: the face prescribed by society, an organ that is inscribed with the norms of our society and that reproduces its order. But Freud is unable – unwilling – to conceive a mature life that has outgrown its fixed ego-logical identity. At the level of theory, therefore, he condemns us to lives of social conformity: the most we can wish for, the most we should want and hope for, is a well-adapted life kept within the bounds of an identity determined by the socially constituted ego.

For me, then, the concept of 'self' is a way of thinking out the possibility of growing beyond our normal ego-logical identity. This is not only essential for the developmental process, which needs to be understood in a way that recognizes continued growth; it is also a necessity from the standpoint of autonomy, which calls for freedom from social domination. Strengthening the ego does not achieve either one of these two objectives. As Adorno observes, in *Negative Dialectics*, 'freedom is really delimited by society. . . . Even where men are most likely to feel free from society, in the strength of their ego, they are society's agents at the same time.'[66]

A first step, therefore, must be experimentation with practices that enable us (in Anthony Giddens's words) to 'overcome traditional dualisms of subject and object in the analysis of social reproduction'.[67] Pursuing the argument Giddens proposes, Hugh Willmott asserts that 'dissolving the illusion of security based upon a dualistic, egoistic mode of awareness is as much a condition for realizing fully human relations as is the removal of structured social inequality'.[68] He accordingly maintains that a 'critical theory of the subject must recall the primacy of the non-dualistic mode of awareness. Specifically, it must explore how it both conditions the emergence of dualistic awareness and offers the possibility of its transcendence. To this end, a critical theory of the subject must attend to the social organization of the openness of human nature and reveal alternative possibilities for its expression.[69] The dualism in the subject-object structure is not an immutable transhistorical and transcendental reality: it is a product of our socialization in the modern world. Thus, it is not our fate. Quite the contrary.

Conceived as a 'practice of the self', the stage III development of our capacity for listening calls for the formation of identities no longer restricted to the structure of subject and object; and it essentially involves a 'retrieval' of the non-dualistic mode of awareness characteristic of *Zugehörigkeit*. Later in this chapter, I will formulate this exercise of retrieval in terms of the auditory body, within whose flesh there is, as a dimension concealed by the ego-logical structure of subject and object, a chiasmic openness to others – and the possibility of a new identity formation, grounded in the communicative realization of our intersubjectivity: our intersubjectivity as an originary intercorporeality. The listening of the *self* differs from the listening of the *ego* in that it is attuned, through self-awareness, by the actual and ideal communicativeness of this intercorporeality.

In his *Theory of Communicative Action*, Habermas writes that 'we have to suppose that the concept of ego identity will increasingly fit the self-understanding that accompanies [a changing] everyday communicative practice. In this case, we face the serious question of whether, with a new stage of identity formation, the conditions and criteria of identity do not also have to change.'[70] What kind of changes in ego identity are called for by the self-understanding that accompanies a listening practice which is contactfully grounded in a vibrant sense of its intercorporeality, and which brings this groundedness into the communicative processes of daily life? Perhaps the changes are such that we should no longer speak of the ego.

Although he projects an identity formation radically different from the one that traditional discourses, whether Freudian, Cartesian, or Kantian, have defined in terms of the ego, Habermas continues to use the old vocabulary. The familiarity of this vocabulary, however, should not deafen us to the boldness of his thinking. In a passage located near the text we just read, Habermas makes the point that the 'ego-identity of the adult proves its worth in the ability to build up new identities from shattered or superseded identities, and to integrate them with the old identities in such a way that the fabric of one's interactions is organized into the unity of a life-history which is both unmistakable and accountable'.[71] This ability to form new identities is precisely what the older ego-logical subject cannot do; for, as Gendlin has shown, such an ability makes experiential process more important than structure or content in constellating strong identity. It is in order to mark this difference and think experimentally with it that I have distinguished 'self' and 'ego'.

The passage from ego to self needs to be specified, needs

to be detailed, as a stage III developmental learning process, a *Bildungsprozess*, involving our capacity for listening. There is, inherent in this capacity, a character potential: enlightenment possibilities whose social-emancipatory implications have yet to be recognized and thought through.

In ways, and for reasons, that are reminiscent of Merleau-Ponty, Habermas attempts to leave behind him the modern 'philosophy of consciousness', a standpoint in which, despite himself, even Marx was caught up. Drawing on Hegel's insight, later at work in Durkheim and Mead, that, as Benhabib puts it, 'the relation between self and other, I and thou, is *constitutive* of the structure of human self-consciousness' – an insight which leads empirically, as she notes, 'to a conception of the human personality as developing only in interaction with other selves', and which 'implies a model of autonomy according to which the relation between self and other is not external to the ego's striving for autonomy', Habermas sets in motion a profound rethinking of the Kantian tradition of moral and political theory.[72] This rethinking accurately targets, therefore, a metaphysical self: the 'self' that is assumed by the narratives which this tradition, still under the spell of Cartesianism, has written and reproduced. The 'Kantian tradition' is one that includes, for Habermas, the research programmes of Piaget, Rawls, and Kohlberg.

The 'self' of this tradition is essential monadic, essentially rational, and not essentially embodied and situated. Its moral deliberations are solitary, monological, and strictly cognitive or logocentric: feelings and needs are excluded from the process of reasoning, together with questions of custom, history, and tradition itself. Even the 'rationality' of this 'self' is conceived very narrowly: it recognizes a cognitive-instrumental function and a moral-practical function; but it totally excludes the aesthetic-expressive. The 'self' of this tradition is, moreover, a fixed nature, an entity endowed with an object-like essence, common to all selves.

Habermas is now contesting this egocentric, ego-logical self. Joined by Carol Gilligan and Seyla Benhabib, whose positions are embedded in the women's movement, Habermas has undertaken to work out a different theoretical paradigm. For want of any better term, I shall call this alternative 'the new critical paradigm'. As I read it, the new paradigm attempts to incorporate and integrate some of the concepts and concerns that have frequently been associated with the Aristotelian tradition. I am thinking, in particular, of the concern, in that tradition, for questions centred on the definition of 'the good life', and for questions centred on moral character: questions about virtue, self-realization and self-fulfilment, the human potential for self-transformation, moral sensibility and its formation, and the normative weight that we should ascribe to custom, history, and culture.

The women's movement, functioning simultaneously as consciousness-raising and redemptive, critical and emancipatory, normative and utopian, has contributed significantly to the new critical paradigm. Without subtracting from the importance of procedural justice and fairness, without ceasing to appeal to principles and rules, and without renouncing the struggles that must continue to move within an ethics of rights and duties, the women's movement has insisted on the importance of love, friendship, and solidarity, reminded us that sympathy and compassion are necessary not only for the flourishing of a civilized society, but also for our fulfilment as individuals endowed with moral sensibility, and argued with great eloquence for an ethics of care and responsibility, to support and carry further the ethics of rights and duties. In these ways, then, the women's movement has led the struggle to release the 'self' from its self-destroying identification with a basically masculine egoity and to break through the enframing historically sedimented in the structure of subject and object.

Since the ego-logical subject and its object are constituted interdependently and contemporaneously, and exist only in their intertwining, the new critical paradigm contributed by the women's movement articulates a radical transfiguration of the reified 'object' at the same time that it frees the self from an egocentric and ego-logical subjectivity.

This transfiguration of things – of situations and landscapes too – is of course extremely important. But equally important is the release of 'the other', which, since the time of Descartes, the discourse of modernity has forced into the position of 'object'. The ethics of care and responsibility radically changes this position. The new critical paradigm does not deny the value of the Kantian universalizability procedure, which constructs an 'other' by abstraction and generalization; but it insists on the necessity of recognizing 'the other' as *also* a concrete other, an absolutely unique individual different from all others. The new paradigm insists on the ethical importance of recognizing and respecting the differences that make others 'other'. Sameness, the sharing of a sense of our common humanity, must of course always play a role in determining our moral comportment toward the other; but respect for our differences is no less important. Whilst insisting on these differences, however, the women's movement vehemently contests the traditional, and basically androcentric, interpretation of difference, according to which differences are necessarily competitive and exclusionary, rather than possibly complementary and mutually enhancing. This introduces, in turn, a different interpretation of the Kantian reversibility test, which, for him, is at the very heart of the self's moral relationships to others.

Meanwhile, Habermas has concentrated on another dimension of the same problematic. He regards the self as an essentially social achievement: a being whose subjectivity is already from the very beginning an inter-subjectivity. The self's moral life is therefore not most appropriately conceptualized by a monological model. For Habermas, the moral self thinks, judges, and acts within situations that are discursively structured: processes of reflection and deliberation are dialogues with implicit and explicit, concrete and generalized others; and the ground of moral life is in communicative practices orientated toward the achievement of shared understandings. Thus, to the traditional conception of rationality, Habermas adds a crucial function: the social-communicative. And this finally enables him to develop his argument that rationality can be more than critical – that, in short, it can also be emancipatory and redemptive, taking up for thought and action the utopian images and dreams that circulate within the life-forms of our society.

Habermas's formulation of a communicative ethics has led him far away from the philosophy of consciousness. It has also compelled him to recognize some very serious problems and deficiencies in a research programme that he had, because of its Kantian affinities, for a long time found very attractive: Lawrence Kohlberg's moral-developmental psychology.[73]

Now, according to Kohlberg's theory (see my discussion of Table 1.1 in Chapter One), the ego-self has achieved the highest, most mature stage of moral development when it has mastered the cognitive capacity to reason from principles (rather than norms), is demonstrably an autonomous agent in the Kantian sense (i.e. the will is determined solely by its unconditional respect for the moral law), and is capable of *abstract reversibility*, i.e. assuming the hypothetical, counterfactual standpoint of the generalized other. This theory is vulnerable to many criticisms, many of which have been articulated by Carol Gilligan in her 1982 book, *In a Different Voice: Psychological Theory and Women's Development*.[74] Since I have already spelled out some of the main objections she raises, at least with regard to the cognitivism and universalism central to the conception of the 'self' in the Kantian tradition that Kohlberg continued, I shall not say more about them here, except to take note of the fact that Habermas, though more or less in agreement, or at least comfortable, with most of what Gilligan argues, has recently deemed it necessary to abandon the Kohlbergian model. Before altogether abandoning it, however, he added a *seventh* stage of moral development, believing that this addition would overcome the major objections to the theory. What he added was a stage of 'communicative ethics', a stage of 'universalizable need interpretations': in other words, a stage in which the self would finally be able to participate in open and unconstrained public discourse, in which our individual and collective needs, and the various cultural traditions informing them, together with questions concerned with happiness and the good life, are brought forth for rational examination and reasoned consensus formation. Only at this stage, then, could we speak of a genuine self, a self whose self-determination (i.e. autonomous action orientated by universal principles) and self-actualization (i.e. fulfilment as a unique potential for individuation) are not only attuned to its own constellation of needs, but also responsive to the specific needs and concerns – as well as the rights and entitlements – of concrete others. This point enables us to clarify a difference between the ego and the self. Unlike the self, whose form of identity consists precisely in its openness to processes of change, the ego is an essentially *fixed* identity structure which does not have a developed capacity for this kind of responsiveness. It is important to realize that the responsiveness in question, here, will often call for personal growth, a willingness to change.

Habermas's addition of a seventh stage was certainly a significant step in the right direction. However, to the extent that it did not fundamentally recast the six preceding stages, but left them, for the most part, intact, and to the extent that it still preserved too much of the Kantian tradition (its logocentrism, its subordination of sensibility to reason, the subordination of relatedness to the achievement of autonomy, the subordination of the concrete other to the other of abstract reversibility), it did not resolve the problems brought to light by recent critics of Kohlberg's model.[75]

We shall return to the matter of reversibility later in this chapter, when we take up for thought the corporeal schematism that 'prescribes' our intersubjectivity. All that I want to say here, then, by way of bringing this part of the chapter to a conclusion, is, *first*, that, as the root meaning of the word 'obedience', namely, 'listening from below', implies, careful listening (or, in the case of the physically deaf, its attentional equivalent) is crucial for the early stage(s) of moral development. Thus we may assume some developmental changes in the character of our listening which are correlative to the maturational changes in moral character Kohlberg has discerned. But the stage of communicative ethics requires a *character* of listening (or, with the deaf, its equivalent) which is very highly developed: developed, I mean, far beyond the obedient listening of the child and even the adult listening typical of our stage II, i.e. the listening ability which happens (in the case of people who are not deaf) more or less by grace of nature. Thus, whereas Kohlberg's first *five* stages of moral development are achievable *within* the *Gestaltung* of our second stage of hearing development, the sixth ethical stage, and the seventh stage even more so, cannot be achieved without the skilful *work* with listening – work I would subsume under the category 'practices of the self' – that distinguishes listening in its *third and fourth* stages of development. Indeed, I would like to argue that the listening for which communicative ethics calls, namely, a listening fully capable of participating in the discourses of need interpretation, is a listening whose character exemplifies the ontological attitude of *Gelassenheit*. *Gelassenheit* is an enlightened listening: its ontological attitude, i.e. its mindful attitude toward beings *as* beings, demonstrates an auditory *Gestalt* that can only be the singular achievement of an enlightening *Bildungsprozess*.

The *second* point I want to make in concluding this part of the chapter is that competence in the stage of moral development defined by the concept of communicative ethics is an achivement which deeply *fulfils* our listening potential as a whole. What I mean by this is (1) that communicativeness, openness-to-others, is deeply inscribed into the very flesh of our listening capacity; (2) that this deep 'inscription' functions accordingly as an initial corporeal prescription, or schematism, for the further development of our listening, and (3) that the 'communicative ethics' achieved in the moral development Habermas once defined as 'stage seven' *realizes and fulfils* the normativity inherent in the schematism. Later in this chapter, when we go into the experience of intercorporeality, a dimension of human experience to whose soundings Merleau-Ponty opened himself, we shall return to the articulation of this schematism. Here it may suffice to add that, since this communicative potential inherent in our capacity for hearing is a *normative* potential, and it can be realized and fulfilled *only* in the third and fourth stages of our auditory development, it follows that our gift of a capacity for listening innately summons us to take it up as a practice of the self. The work on ourselves that is called for by a communicative ethics is always already called for by the conscience schematized in the listening body.

Part IV
Needs and their Interpretation: Listening to Inner Nature

> Ego identity requires not only cognitive mastery of general levels of communication but also the ability to give one's own needs [and the needs of others] their due in these communicative structures; as long as the ego is cut off from its internal nature and disavows the dependency on needs that still await suitable interpretations, freedom, no matter how much it is guided by principles, remains in truth unfree in relation to existing systems of norms.
> Habermas, 'Moral development and ego identity'[76]

> An emancipated society and a fulfilled individuality imply one another. . . . [Thus,] the project of the future begins by revolutionizing our needs and wants.
> Benhabib, *Critique, Norm and Utopia*[77]

In responding to Foucault, I argued, earlier in this chapter, that it is self-defeating to ask what kind of body our capital economy needs and demands without *also* asking what kind of society our bodies want and need. I want to argue, here, that listening is a capacity the development of which not only facilitates the process whereby we get in touch with existing and already recognized needs, both our own needs and the needs of others, and including the needs inherent in listening itself, but also makes possible the constellation of genuinely new or different needs and wants. Listening to needs, and listening to their communication, are not simple processes of discovery, processes merely 'noticing' wants and needs that are already fully formed; rather, they are processes of learning, growth, and self-creation.[78] Need interpretation, and the listening this entails, must be understood as a hermeneutical process: a process, therefore, to which the communicative dialectic can make a distinctive and often decisive contribution.

Whenever we philosophers visualize moral discourse, it seems that we are tempted to see the self in silent monologue, reasoning from universal principles and forming well-grounded judgments. And it seems to make sense, when we are thinking this way, to suppose that moral judgments and decisions can be made, more or less, according to the reflexivity of the Kantian model: that is to say, by hypothesizing an abstract reversibility of position and role, substituting a generalized other for myself and myself for this other. This picture may be tempting, but we must at all costs resist it. When we find ourselves actually involved in dialogue, face to face with concrete others, we are compelled to broaden, expand, and enrich the Kantian discourse of rights and duties, taking into account the specific, concrete needs and concerns, feelings and intentions, that we and the others bring with us to the communicative situation. And we are compelled by the moral claims, the audible demands of the face-to-face situation, to explore, together, ways of reasoning and arguing that derive from this recognition of needs, as well as from general moral principles.

Kant would have us ignore, silence, even suppress our real needs and feelings: all our desires, anxieties, motives, and intentions. He assumes that, since these states of mind and body do not/should not constitute the strictly moral identity, we must abstract moral discourse from the narratives they press us to hear. For Kant, then, the attempt to comprehend and accommodate the needs of the other, taking into account their motivations, their goals, their anxieties, their dreams and aspirations, can only be a temptation to lose sight of the moral law that binds us in universality and grounds the possibility of our reciprocal understanding. Benhabib puts the matter well:

> As is evidenced by Kantian moral theory, a public ethics of principles entails a repressive attitude toward 'inner nature'. Our needs and affective nature are excluded from the realm of moral theory. This results in a corresponding inability to treat human needs, desires, and emotions in any other way than by abstracting away from them and by condemning them to silence. Institutional justice is thus seen as representing a higher stage of moral development than interpersonal responsibility, care, love and solidarity; the respect for rights and duties is regarded as prior to care and concern about another's needs; moral cognition precedes moral affect; the mind . . . is the sovereign of the body, and reason the judge of inner nature.[79]

Habermas's communicative ethics has been steadily moving away from a Kantian rationalism. Today, therefore, it is clear that he has in fact embraced the very conception for which Benhabib was arguing when she wrote that

> By allowing need interpretations to move to the centre of moral discourse and by insisting that 'inner nature' must be 'placed in a utopian perspective' [cf. the chapter on 'Moral development and ego identity', op. cit., 93], Habermas comes close to subverting this bias of traditional normative philosophy: but his insistence that the standpoint of the 'generalised other' alone represents the moral point of view [ultimately] prevents this move. It is also inadequate to claim that aesthetic-expressive discourse can accommodate the perspective of the 'concrete other', for relations of solidarity, friendship, and love are not aesthetic but profoundly moral ones. The acknowledgement of the *specificity* of the concrete other is just as essential as the recognition of the *human dignity* of the generalised other. Whereas the perspective of the generalised other

> promises justice, it is in the relation to the concrete other than those ephemeral moments of happiness and solidarity are recovered.[80]

Benhabib astutely traces many of the problems surrounding the recognition and interpretation of needs in the theory of communicative ethics to Habermas's incomplete, or at least insufficient, renunciation of the Kantian conception of autonomy. (Unlike Habermas, Kohlberg does not even begin to subject the Kantian conception to any serious criticism. His uncritical assumptions have been sharply attacked by Gilligan and others in the women's movement.) One of the problems with the conception of autonomy that Habermas used to advocate, then, is that 'autonomy is not only *self-determination* in accordance with just norms, but the capacity to assume the standpoint of the *concrete other* as well'.[81] This is a capacity for which the skilful development of the listening potential is of the greatest importance. The emphasis on autonomy, typically an androcentric narrative, fits together all too tightly with the strong intellectualism of the tradition, for, as we know, the solitary, self-contained, self-sufficient *cogito*, essentially disembodied, and therefore not capable of listening, dominates the discursive field of rationalism.

Commenting on Habermas's conception of the self as embedded in and constituted by the communicative forms of intersubjectivity, Benhabib notes that 'normatively, this conception of identity implies a model of autonomy according to which the relation between self and other is not *external* to the ego's striving for autonomy'.[82] But, in interpreting this 'not external', she is pointing beyond the Kantian position where Habermas once wanted to rest his case. She writes: 'In requiring that need interpretations become the subject matter of practical discourses, Habermas is underscoring both points [namely, that the self develops and matures only in interaction with other selves, and that such interaction is not external to the achieving of autonomy]' (ibid.). But this means, as she then says, making a point that Foucault, and even (to some degree) Habermas himself, did not adequately appreciate: 'From the standpoint of socialization theory, individual nature, while being "private", is not immutable; individual need interpretations and motives carry with them the marks of societal processes by participating in which alone an individual learns to become an

"I" ' (ibid.). Foucault tends to historicize and socialize the individual so deeply, so totally, that he is compelled, in the final analysis, to deny the possibility of *any* individual transformation not initiated and effectuated entirely by society.[83] This I think, is not only wrong, but extremely self-defeating.

With these various points, then, Benhabib was challenging the last remnants of Cartesian and Kantian rationalism jeopardizing Habermas's original project: its persistent theoretical abstraction from real-life situations, its consequent adoption of the standpoint of the 'generalized' other when testing for the reversibility at the heart of our concepts of justice and fairness and, finally, its tacit disembodiment of the self, an ultimately fatal repression, which deprives the self of its primary contact with the reality of needs, desires, and motivations, and which excludes from moral discourse this essential speech of the body.

As Benhabib understood the matter,

> Kohlberg and Habermas have had to admit that the hypothetical moral capacity tested by cognitive-developmental theories does not translate into a corresponding capacity to form the right, correct, appropriate judgement in *real* life-contexts.[84]

To be sure, as she says, 'they insist that the *moral justification* of principles must be distinguished from their *contextualization* – their appropriate and skilful embodiment in right actions as well as the exercise of perspicacious judgment' (ibid.). Nevertheless, I think Benhabib is making a valid point when she replies that the 'distinction between *justification* and *contextualization* shows once again the limits of a rationalistic interpretation of communicative ethics and creates a number of thorny questions both for the methodology of moral-developmental psychology and, philosophically, for a universalist-ethical theory' (ibid.). Justification and contextualization certainly can, and must, be analytically distinguished; but this is not the same thing as keeping them functionally separated. And, in point of fact, the listening body-self that enters into the communicative process of moral discourse is positioned precisely at the intersection of justification and contextualization; it is, we might say, the narrative organ of their intertwining. When it is a question of need interpretations, the discourse of justification refers back to the contextual body of needs: it must address this metaphorical body and listen well to its words.

Habermas does, of course, attempt to correct the excesses of the tradition by introducing a dialogical model to replace the monologue on which rationalism would have us depend. For him, need constitution is an essentially intersubjective process:

> Internal nature is thereby moved into a utopian perspective; that is, at this stage, internal nature may no longer be merely examined within an interpretive framework *fixed* by the cultural tradition in a nature-like [i.e. totally deterministic] way. . . . Inner nature is rendered communicatively fluid and transparent to the extent that needs can, through aesthetic forms of expression, be kept articulable or be released from their paleosymbolic prelinguisticality.[85]

Habermas makes an important advance here, although we should not let him restrict the articulation of needs to 'aesthetic forms of expression' (a locution which suggests that this articulation cannot be a 'reasonable' contribution to the argumentative dialectic), nor let him, as the word 'paleosymbolic' suggests, consign our body of needs to a Freudian-Dionysiac body, a body without any organismic order, any experiential 'logic' of its own.

Be that as it may, Benhabib's commentary on this passage is focused on the creative or transformative power inherent in discourses which are open to need interpretation. In particular, she focuses on what the articulation of needs, and more generally, the articulation of our affective and emotional constitutions (not only our own, of course, but also those represented by concrete others), can contribute to the further development of autonomy:

> Ego autonomy is characterized by a two-fold capacity: first, the individual's *reflexive* ability to question the interpretive framework fixed by the cultural tradition – to loosen, if you wish, those sedimented and frozen images of the good and of happiness in the light of which we formulate needs and motives; second, such reflexive questioning is accompanied by an ability to *articulate* one's needs

> linguistically, by an ability to communicate with others about them.[86]

This leads her to formulate a point of the utmost consequence – a point whose significance cannot possibly be exaggerated: our discourses – the discourses of need interpretation, for example – must be understood as 'moral-transformatory processes', as constitutive of 'an ethics of practical transformation'.[87] She says:

> If Habermas assumes that in their discourses, individuals preserve the *same* need and interest interpretations as they had in ordinary, everyday contexts, then a consensual acceptance of norms reflecting the general interests of each can hardly follow. For this to be the case, either one must assume that a pre-established harmony of interests exists – clearly an unacceptable premise for a critical social theory – or one must interpret this process minimalistically as aiming at the establishment of the lowest common interest, while leaving substantive conflict of interest untouched. . . . But, if neither of these alternatives is acceptable, then we must assume that discourses are processes through which *new* needs and interests, such as can lead to a consensus among the participants, emerge.[88]

Habermas has now moved very close to this conception; but until recently, he was not articulating it with sufficient clarity. Misunderstandings were easy. Nancy Fraser, however, like Foucault, still seems to be to be limited by the horns of a false dilemma: either, in her words, a totally, 'thoroughly cultural and historicized conception of need' (social determinism), or else an essentialism of 'needs as they really are in themselves, apart from any human vocabulary used to describe them' (transcendental determinism).[89] Neither conception gives us any concrete reasons for hope; neither opens up the possibility of an ethics organized around 'moral-transformatory processes'. There *is* a *given* human nature, a nature whose givenness we must accept: we cannot totally change this nature. But we must also recognize that, in many ways, the 'nature' we are given is given (determined) as indeterminate – capable of further determination, further development. Society plays a crucial and decisive role in this further determination, for our given nature can and will evolve only so far 'on its own'. Since socialization is always at work on our 'nature' from the very beginning, we never can encounter 'our nature' as it 'is' in and for itself: we always encounter an 'it' already inscribed by social processes. And yet, these processes can no more determine the totality of our character than can nature itself. What *society* contributes to the individual's formation can always be taken up and reworked, just as both individual and society can always take up the constitution given by *nature* and rework it.

This leads me to another point. The term 'socialization' suggests a false simplicity. There are many different *kinds* of socialization processes, and we must take the time to differentiate them. No one has attempted this with more care for detail and more sensitivity to the subtleties and complexities, especially in regard to manipulation, coercion, and ideological distortion, than has Eugene Gendlin, whose recent work – for example, 'Process ethics and the political question' and 'A philosophical critique of the concept of narcissism' – enables us to tell the difference, in concrete and experiential terms, between processes of socialization that constitute, for the individual, an emancipatory-transformative space and processes of socialization that cut off the individual from 'inner nature' and its enlightenment potential.[90]

There are potentials in us which cannot emerge or develop except in (specific kinds of) communicative interactions with others – and there are some potentials which can be brought to fulfilment only in specific types of communities or societies.

In the writings of Harold Searles, an extraordinary psychiatrist with many years of experience working therapeutically with schizophrenics, there are some remarkable accounts of discursive interactions enabling new needs and interests to emerge. These accounts exemplify 'moral-transformatory processes' and model paradigmatically the possibility of an 'ethics of practical transformation'. I shall record Searles's account of two such transformative interactions. The first takes place through the insight and compassion of the gaze, whilst the second takes place through the echoing and responsive resonance of good, friendly listening:

(1) Among the most significant steps in the

> maturation which occurs in successful psychotherapy are those moments when the therapist suddenly *sees* the patient in a new light. His image of the patient suddenly changes, because of the entry into his awareness of some potentiality in the patient which had not shown itself before. From now on, his response to the patient is a response to this new, enriched view, and *through such responding he fosters the emergence, and further differentiation, of this new personality area.* [It is a process of] seeing in the other person potentialities of which even he is not aware, and helping him, *by responding to these potentialities,* to realize them.[91]
>
> (2) The therapist, through hearing the new emotional connotation, the new meaning, in the stereotyped utterance, and responding in accordance with the new connotation, fosters the [patient's] emerging differentiation. Over the course of months, in therapy, he may find the same verbal stereotype employed in the expression of a whole gamut of newly emerged feelings.[92]

The processes that Searles has described here, processes in which interpersonal mediations have enabled new feelings, new self-understandings, and new meanings to emerge, should not be restricted to good psychotherapy. They could also occur, and certainly ought to occur, in all our political debates. In a group or community where all people are committed to the reciprocity of good listening, each participant develops a clearer, more individual *sense* of the matter in question by helping each of the others to do the same. Where there really is such reciprocated listening, what is facilitated is not only the *sharing* of an *existing* understanding, but also the *emergence and formation* of *new* understanding. When a debate is organized around such listening, each participant is helped to constellate an individual sense of their collective intercorporeality. Such intercorporeality is a consonance-in-difference: a good ground, I think, for the emergence of a new *sensus communis*, a new *consensus*.

In making the 'linguistic turn', Habermas has initiated a new theoretical programme for political praxis. Useful though his 'transcendental conditions' for rational discourse and consensus formation unquestionably are, I submit that they need to be supplemented by an interpretation that specifies in phenomenological terms the reciprocity norms for listening which must underlie all rational discourse among equals.

What kind of society does our listening need? What kind of society do we need in order to feel that we have been adequately and fairly heard? What kind of dialogical process does the process of listening itself need? What moral claims can be made, if any, on the listening capacities of others? What moral duties, if any, attend the *capacity* to listen? If there *is* a utopian dream nurtured by the listening body, do we know what that is?

Part V
Sounds of Truth

> [We need to reflect on] our experience . . . of inhabiting the world by our body, inhabiting the truth by our whole selves.
>
> Merleau-Ponty, *The Visible and the Invisible*[93]

Unlike the philosophers of antiquity – Herakleitos, Socrates and Plato, for example – the philosophers of modernity have been satisfied with formal theories of truth: spelling out, for example, the necessary procedural conditions for the adequate or correct representation of the world. They think of correspondence, but not of co-responsiveness. They think of truth in terms of a visual paradigm, and not in terms of an experience with listening. Their conception of 'correspondence' cuts truth off from our experiences with consonance and dissonance, harmony and discord, resonance and emptiness, voices and silence. For the good of our political life, we must break the ideological spell of this tradition. We must begin to think of truth as an experience with listening. The listening body bears an understanding of truth that the philosophical discourse on politics needs to hear.

In *Land or Death: The Peasant Struggle in Peru*, Hugo Blanco, at one time a principal organizer of the peasant movement in Peru, describes the special significance of the peasant gatherings in Cuzco and Quillabamba, places where I have been:

> A concentration of *ponchos* in the main plaza, the heart of the city. At the court on the cathedral portico, which dominates the plaza. . . . The odor

> of *coca* and Quechua [the indigenous language], permeating the air. Quechua, out loud from the throat; Quechua shouted, threatening, tearing away the centuries of oppression. A march down the main streets, before and after the meeting. Windows and doors of the powerful fearfully slammed shut at the advance of the multitudes . . . shouting in Quechua truths silenced by centuries of Castillian Spanish. The Indian, master of plazas and streets, of the entire street and the sidewalk.[94]

We are called into question by our listening; we are tested by what we hear; we can be accused by what we do not hear. There are ways in which we are responsible to others, responsible to humanity, for the character of our responsiveness as beings capable of listening and hearing. We are responsible for creating social spaces in which the voices of truth can be heard; we are responsible for opening up social spaces in which the truth can be spoken: spoken and not shouted, spoken without fear of punishment or reprisal, spoken without shame.

Listening is a question of character. Its development is a practice of the self. In this practice, one works on oneself. It is a moral struggle to *become* someone who can always listen and hear the truth – to become a person who *seeks* the truth, who *values* the truth more than ease, more than gain. It sometimes requires enormous courage to listen and hear the truth. This is the work of listening at stage III.

The text from *Land or Death* is 'out of place' in a philosophical discourse. I should not have introduced it. Aside from the fact that its presence is a mark of 'bad manners' or is in 'poor taste', a formal theory of truth would exclude this kind of passage – intensely passionate, extremely partisan, more evocative than informative – and the truth it speaks would not be recognized. Its truth would be passed over in silence. For centuries, then, the discourse of truth has actually sided with the forces of oppression.

In 'Questions and counterquestions', Habermas argues that

> Instead of following Nietzsche's path of a totalizing and self-referential critique of reason . . . it is more promising to seek this end through the analysis of

> the already operative potential for rationality contained in the everyday practices of communication. Here the validity dimensions of propositional truth, normative rightness, and subjective truthfulness or authenticity, are intertwined with one another. From this network of *a bodily and interactively shaped, historically situated reason*, our philosophical tradition selected out only the single thread of propositional truth and theoretical reason, and styled it into the monopoly of humanity.[95]

With these words reverberating, I can now say that our stage III concentration on listening as a capacity that needs to be taken up by us in an ethical 'practice of the self' is intended as a contribution to 'the analysis of the already operative potential for rationality contained in the everyday practices of communication'. Since 'reason' is an embodied reason, interactively shaped, we need to understand it as an 'operative potential' always already immanent within our capacity for listening. In other words, there is a 'rationality need' implicit in the communicative nature of our capacity: rationality is an 'implicate order' (David Bohm's phrase) organizing the deep nature of our hearing and calling for its fulfilment, its realization, through the individual and collective development of our capacities. I will give this claim further clarification and support later in the chapter, when we go into the corporeal schematism that Merleau-Ponty has enabled us to articulate.

Since Habermas refers, in the text we just read, to the problematic of 'validity dimensions', I also want to argue, here, that the difference between truth and ideology has to be understood at a concrete level: for example, in terms of our experience with hearing. We need to (be able to) *hear* that difference with our ears. If there *is* a difference, it should be audible. And if the difference makes a decisive difference in the life of the body politic, then it is a difference the learning of which should be of paramount concern to us. In stage III, we are committed to this learning.

In *The Culture of Narcissism*, Lasch observes that, in our contemporary world, truth 'has given way to credibility, facts to statements that sound authoritative without conveying any authoritative information'.[96] I want to take these words to be suggesting an interpretive history of the politics of truth. Thought in this way, his words suggest the possibility that there is a correspondence, a correlation, between such a narrative about truth and the narrative about our capacity for listening that I have projected in the chapters of this book. If truth, today, has given way to statements that *sound* authoritative even though they are false, then the political history of truth must somehow be related to the history of the ways in which we hear, and fail to hear, its sound.

Too many, today, do not know the soundings of truth; too many of us do not know how to sound it, how to sound out what we hear, how to test what we hear, for its truth. As auditory beings gifted with the capacity to hear, we need to learn the difference, the audible difference, between sincerity and deception, ideology and truth, sophistry and truth. According to Socrates, knowing the truth is not merely a question of cognitive competence; it is also, always, a question of character. And, just as it takes character to hold to the truth and avoid the temptations of sophistry and deception, so too it takes character to listen for the truth, to care enough about it to be open to hearing it and willing to learn its sounds.

Skilfulness in hearing the distinction between truth and lie does not come naturally or easily: it presupposes, it requires, caring for the truth, caring enough to listen. But if the capacity to hear implicates competence in distinguishing the truth from deception, then this capacity must be one which carries within it an immanent demand for its actualization as moral character. In 'Discourse and truth: the problematisation of parrhēsia', Foucault returns the philosophical discourse *about* truth to the concern of the ancient Greeks for truth *in* discourse. Instead of perpetuating the increasing formalization of truth, its increasing abstraction from the experiences and practices of our lifeworld, Foucault invites us to think about truth as a discursive practice – the practice, that is, of truth-telling. And he connects this practice with moral character. What I want to add to this is the point that *listening for* truth and *listening to* truth can no more be separated from *speaking* the truth than listening can be separated, as such, from speaking and telling, and that, as it takes character to *tell* the truth, so it takes character to *hear* it.

Whenever we speak, our speaking makes a prima facie claim to truth. Conversely, truth makes a moral claim on our speaking. When we speak, our character is at stake. Analogously, whenever we listen, truth makes a moral claim on the character of our listening. Socrates, loitering in the *agora*, was as renowned for his capacity to listen as he was for his eloquence – his stammering eloquence – in speaking.

We are responsible for listening and hearing. We are responsible for responding to what we hear. It is said, in Plato's 'Laches', that Socrates was a 'musical' man because his life was a harmony between words and deeds. What the text implies, but does not actually say, is that his life was also a harmony between what he heard and how he responded: how, because of what he could hear, he acted. Listening in this way becomes a critical and emancipatory praxis, a praxis involving us, among other things, in an ethics of self-transformative processes.

In a time when both the public and the private spheres of our lifeworld are increasingly subject to domination by the administrations of powerful technocracies, the ability to hear the difference between truth and lie, truth and ideological distortion, becomes a problem of the utmost consequence. At the beginning of Part Three, we noted Horkheimer's attempt to connect our epidemic deafness to the increasingly powerful technologies we possess for recording and transmitting patterns of sound. And we heard, with his words, his deep concern. If we, too, hear the truth of the problem, then I would argue that a truth claim on our hearing has indeed been sounded and echoed. In stage III, our hearing is responsive to this claim.

Part VI
In the Depth of the Flesh: the Body Politic as Corporeal Image

> Put briefly: perhaps the entire evolution of the spirit is a question of the body; it is the history of the development of a higher body that emerges into our sensibility . . . the body desires to perfect itself.
>
> Nietzsche, *The Will to Power*.[97]

> It is not merely a question here of confronting ideas but of incarnating them and making them live, and in this respect we cannot know what they are capable of except by trying them out. This attempt involves a taking of sides and a struggle.
>
> Merleau-Ponty, *In Praise of Philosophy*.[98]

[Critical theory is] the self-clarification of the struggles and wishes of the age.

Marx, in a letter to A. Ruge.[99]

In order to live a fully human life, we [women] require not only *control* of our bodies (though control is a prerequisite); we must also touch the unity and resonance of our physicality, our bond with the natural order, the *corporeal ground* of our intelligence.

Rich, *Of Woman Born*.[100]

[We must undertake] a return which . . . actualizes a superior potential latent in the origin to begin with.

Wolin, *Walter Benjamin: An Aesthetic of Redemption*[101]

The individual who listens to the secondary process and brings it across into this world will . . . change his immediate environment and the world around him, too.

Mindell, *Working with the Dreaming Body*[102]

1 The Narcissism of the Flesh

Narcissism means, in [traditional] psychoanalysis: libidinally cathecting one's own ego instead of love for other people. The mechanism of this shift is to be found in society, which puts a premium on the hardening of each individual – the naked will to self-preservation.

Adorno, *Kritik*[103]

Make not [only] an existential psychoanalysis, but [going beyond this] an ontological psychoanalysis.

Merleau-Ponty, 'Working notes'[104]

Do a psychoanalysis of Nature: it is the flesh, the mother.

Merleau-Ponty, 'Working notes'[105]

According to Merleau-Ponty, 'there is a fundamental narcissism in all vision'.[106] In the years that immediately preceded his death, it seems that he was attempting to work out a new, more radical phenomenology of perception, grounded in an ontology that only his hermeneutics of the flesh could sound out. Convinced, as he wrote in his 'Working notes',[107] that 'a philosophy of the flesh is the condition without which psychoanalysis remains anthropology', he began a ground-breaking enquiry into vision, and perceptual experience in general, and he connected what he was learning to the psychoanalytic theory of narcissism. The account that he left to us is a post-metaphysical account which leads us into the dimensionality of being he called the flesh, and into the depth of its intertwinings, its intersubjective tangle of roots.

I submit, however, that if 'narcissism' is understood in terms of the theory expounded by Freud, i.e. the traditional theory that Adorno explains, then (1) the character of the flesh is not 'narcissistic' and (2) Merleau-Ponty's attempt to make this connection between the phenomenology of narcissism and the character of the flesh is extremely misleading. Misleading, but nevertheless instructive. I want to argue that the narcissism of our visionary and auditory flesh, the self-mirroring and self-echoing process that Merleau-Ponty brings out, is *essentially different* from the narcissism defined by Freud; that it differs significantly from the phenomenon described by Jacques Lacan; and that, if Descartes' *Meditations on First Philosophy* may be read as a work of narcissism, then the experience disclosed by the hermeneutics of the flesh is certainly *not* narcissism, but rather its post-metaphysical deconstruction: a phenomenology of perception that shows the impossibility of Cartesian subjectivity. Considered in relation to the historical discourse of reflection, a discourse inaugurated by Descartes and continued, not only by Freud, but also, despite all protestations, in the work of Lacan, and, much more surprisingly, even in the Freudian psychologies of critical theory, the 'narcissism' which appears in the reflections and resonances of the flesh can only be thought ironic. Whereas some have seen in narcissism a withdrawal and self-absorption that isolates the self from the social world, others have seen in narcissism a self-constitution and self-recognition that ultimately alienate the self from itself in a relentlessly hostile world, and still others have seen in narcissism a socially disruptive self-aggrandizement and will to power, Merleau-Ponty perceived a 'narcissism' of ecstatic intertwinings, consonances, and reversibilities, in which the self can see and hear itself being 'completed' through social relationships of communion and reciprocity. Thus, given the history of the word, it is misleading, if not perhaps wrong, for Merleau-Ponty to describe the reversibilities of the flesh in terms of the concept of 'narcissism'. However, it is not this problem with terminology, but his radical phenomenology of the flesh – that experiential process to which his use of the word is meant to point – which shall henceforth occupy our thought.

This chapter is a chapter in the story of the post-metaphysical revolt against Descartes – a revolt that Merleau-Ponty helped set in motion. In section 2, I shall sketch Freud's vision of narcissism. In section 3, I shall outline the critical points in Lacan's theory of ego formation as a narcissistic process. In section 4, I shall examine some of the texts assembled in *The Visible and the Invisible*, so that we can begin to understand why Merleau-Ponty wants to claim that there is a 'narcissism' of the flesh and get a feeling for what this disclosure signifies. Finally, in section 5, I will argue that, in the narcissism of the flesh, the 'narcissism' of the monadic metaphysical subject is reversed: turned, in fact, into its opposite, intersubjectivity. In the 'narcissism' of the flesh, there is, in effect, a double-crossing, and this dialectic *deconstructs* the narcissistic structure of the self, redeeming for subjectivity its primordial sociality, its inherence in the reciprocities of a social world – a 'moral community' – from the very beginning. Thus ends subject-centred reason.

2 Freud: Primary and Secondary Narcissism

Freud's first sustained analysis of narcissism appeared in 1914 with the publication of 'Zur Einführung des Narzissmus'. Subsequently, this analysis figured prominently in his theory of sexuality. It also shaped his theory of self-development. In the second theory, however, Freud's concept functioned in an especially self-defeating way, since it prevented us for a long time from distinguishing conditions of regressive psychopathology – lives that are less than egologically mature – from stages of self-development that transcend the limits of the ego and manifest a healthy capacity for continuing growth.

Freud did use his model of self-development to distinguish two forms of narcissism: there is, he thought, a healthy form of narcissism, typical of all human beings in early infancy; but there is also a more pathological narcissism that can occur in later life, but most often begins in childhood or early adolescence. The first form, which he called 'primary narcissism', characterizes the normal conditions of the healthy infant prior to the emergence of a stable ego formation: for Freud, it is an auto-erotic, but vulnerable, state of relatively undifferentiated symbiotic awareness, in which the differences between self and world, self and other, subject and object are not yet stabilized in a dialectic of structured oppositions. Because of this primal fusion, this ontological 'confusion', the dimensions of the infant's ego are virtually coextensive with the dimensions of the world. The infant accordingly experiences itself as an eternal, immortal being, omnipotent and omniscient – very much, in fact, like a god.

Whereas primary narcissism is unproblematic, the phase of human development that Freud called 'secondary narcissism' is much more complex, ambiguous, and problematic. It *can* be perfectly normal; but it may also be pathological. In *secondary* narcissism, the erotic libido of the id is withdrawn from the object(s) to which it had been cathected and is given, or returned, to the ego itself. (For this reason, there was a time when Freud called the narcissistic libido an 'ego-libido'.) Now, according to Freud's theory, if this withdrawal is part of a process in which the child's cathected object is being internalized – introjected as an ego-ideal constituted within the ego – then it is a necessary transitional phase in the normal and healthy maturation of the ego: a phase making possible, and culminating in, the formation of a stable and civilized superego structure. If, however, this withdrawal does not take place only temporarily, or as part of such a process, taking place, for example, much later, i.e. in adulthood, or in a way that blocks a 'return' to object-cathexes (i.e. 'love-objects' other than oneself), then it is to be treated as avoidable, abnormal, and pathological.

As we go through the vicissitudes of life, it is both natural and normal for us to change, or abandon, love-objects, and to mourn the loss or abandonment of a loved other; but when the loss moves the ego to withdraw totally from the world into the solipsism of a long-term or permanent self-absorption – the condition that Freud once called 'melancholia' – then what is currently termed a 'narcissistic pathology' has emerged. In the most serious cases, the ego, totally absorbed in its identification with the internalized 'lost object', becomes paralysed, imprisoned within its own fantasies, attached only to itself, or to objects conceived in its own (inadequately reflected) image. Narcissism is one of the ways for an ego, wounded in its interactions with others, to protect itself against subsequent loss and hurt. In the long run, however, it is a defence that becomes self-destructive. Only when it is temporary, e.g. as a process of mourning real loss, or as a phase in the formation of an adult ego, can it be, for Freud, a healthy state of mind.

Harry Stack Sullivan, Jacques Lacan, and Heinz Kohut significantly enriched Freud's original interpretation of narcissism by contributing analyses of its psychogenesis that (1) focused clinical attention on disturbances and inadequacies in the 'mirroring' which infants and children receive from their interactions with others during the early years of life, and that (2) broke away from the Freudian commitment to an ego psychology, locating secondary narcissism in the character of the *self* and letting it be seen and heard as a pathology in the self's sense of *identity*. (All three have pointed to some defensive need for the self to block the continuation of its process of individuation and self-development.)

The third edition of the *Diagnostic and Statistical Manual of Mental Disorders*, which was published in 1980 to report the official consensus of the American Psychiatric Association, describes the 'narcissistic character' as a disorder 'in which there are a grandiose sense of self-importance or uniqueness; preoccupation with fantasies of unlimited success; exhibitionistic need for constant attention and admiration; characteristic responses to threats to self-esteem; and characteristic disturbances in interpersonal relationships that alternate between the extremes of overidealisation and devaluation, and lack of empathy'.[108] The *Manual* adds that the 'exaggerated sense of self-importance may be manifested as extreme self-centredness and self-absorption. Abilities and achievements tend to be unrealistically overestimated. Frequently the sense of self-importance alternates with feelings of special unworthiness.'[109] Narcissistic disorders frequently involve extreme mood-swings, states of depression, and profound disturbances, ruptures, or instabilities in the person's sense of identity – his sense of being, for example, a firm, independent centre of initiative. Self-esteem is often extremely fragile, and often entails, correspondingly, that there is a very weak sense of reciprocity: 'interpersonal exploitativeness, in which others are taken advantage of in order to indulge one's own desires or for self-aggrandisement, is common; and the personal integrity and rights of others are disregarded'.[110]

Reading the *Meditations* of Descartes after reading the *Manual*, one cannot easily avoid seeing a sequence of feigned attitudes and positions that seem to mimic very closely the attitudes and positions of the narcissistic character disorder, the epidemic psychopathology most distinctive of our present age. What are we to make of the startling appearance, in a text which inaugurated the discourse of modernity, of virtually the entire spread of narcissistic symptomatology? Most strikingly, I have noticed the cogito's withdrawal from the world, its extreme self-centredness and self-absorption, a disturbed sense of identity, alienated affect, fantasies of omnipotence and omniscience, and disturbances in interpersonal relationships.[111] (As for the last of these, I would remind the reader of Descartes' chilling reflection, whilst looking out of the window, that, for all he knows, the hats and coats he sees could be covering robots instead of people.) It is difficult not to postulate some sociological connection between this paradigmatic text, written at the very beginning of modernity, and the equally paradigmatic disorder of our present time, the 'end' of modernity, the moment, in any event, when what was already implicit in the very beginning, concealed within its glory, finally becomes explicit, manifesting its more problematic implications.[112]

Be this as it may, Merleau-Ponty's 'narcissism of the flesh' is not only a radical break with the epistemology and metaphysics of Cartesianism; it is also a decisive break with the psychology of narcissism that has shaped modernity from the very beginning. How it breaks with Cartesianism it is not difficult to surmise; but how it breaks with the psychology of narcissism is a story with some surprising twists and turns. The first twist to be considered will appear when we locate the point of difference between Merleau-Ponty and Jacques Lacan.

3 Lacan: The Mirror and the Self

For Lacan, as, later, for Heinz Kohut, the American psychoanalyst, 'secondary' narcissism is seen as constituting a necessary phase in the process of self-development.[113] The phase in question is called 'narcissism' because it involves the infant and child, initially sunk (or so the story goes) in a primary, 'autistic' narcissism, in a dialectic of interpersonal relationships structured by a process of 'mirroring' that eventuates in the emergence of a coherent body-self image. In a paper entitled 'The mirror stage as formative of the function of the "I" as revealed in psychoanalytic experience' (1949), Lacan attempted to argue for a theory of ego formation on which he had been working for many years and which he first put into writing in a 1932 paper – already anticipating some of his later criticisms of Freud's ego psychology and the theory of narcissism.[114]

Lacan figures in our story for a number of reasons. One of these is that he played an important role in Merleau-Ponty's thinking about child development (see Merleau-Ponty's study on 'The child's relations with others') and that his paper on the mirror stage undoubtedly encouraged Merleau-Ponty to make use of the images and concepts of narcissism in articulating the dimension of the flesh in *The Visible and the Invisible*.

Lacan drew on the research of Wolfgang Köhler, who reported in 1925 on chimpanzee reactions to their mirrored images, and on the work of Henri Wallon, who reported in 1931 on the mirror experiences of children. Although the American psychiatrist, Harry Stack Sullivan, devoted many years of clinical research to the mirroring process in mother-child relationships, and was already writing and lecturing on this subject in 1945, I know of no evidence to the effect that Lacan was aware of Sullivan's work. But I very much like the fact that Sullivan conceptualizes the problems in mirroring in interpersonal terms, rather than, as the Freudians did, in essentially intrapsychic terms, or as Lacan did, in terms of an objective mirror.[115] This difference between them is important, because Lacan's analysis leads only to a negativity, whereas Sullivan's, like Merleau-Ponty's, leads us to see the beginning schematization of social perceptions basic to our ethical and political life.

In summarizing Lacan's theory, I am going to rely on *Lacan and Language*, the excellent guide to his *Ecrits* written by John Muller and William Richardson.[116] According to these authors, Lacan's 1949 paper on mirroring is an attempt to exhibit 'the role of the image in the development of the subject and the manner in which social experience evolves'.[117] Lacan argues that 'the newborn is marked by a prematurity specific to humans, an anatomical incompleteness evidenced in motor turbulence and lack of coordination. This state of fragmentation becomes camouflaged through the infant's jubilant identification with its reflection, experienced as a powerful gestalt promising mastery, unity, and substantive stature.'[118]

On their reading, then,

> Lacan's principal thesis is that the newly born human infant, initially sunk in motor incapacity, turbulent movements, and fragmentation, first experiences itself as a unity through experiencing some kind of reflection of itself, the paradigm for which would be self-reflection in a mirror. This normally occurs between the ages of six and eighteen months. This mirror-like reflection, then, serves as the form that in-forms the subject and guides its development. So it happens that there is an 'identification' between infant and its reflection 'in the full sense that analysis gives to the term: namely, the transformation that takes place in the subject when he assumes an image'. It is this reflected image of itself, with which the infant identifies, that Lacan understands by the 'I'. The consequences of this conception are manifold.[119]

But there is a problem, a danger, latent within this process as Lacan sees it: 'Since this reflection (whose prototypical image is as seen in a mirror) is an external form, to identify with it as ego means to install a radical alienation and distortion in the very foundation of one's identity.'[120] As we shall see in the next section, Merleau-Ponty also discerns an 'alienation' in this process, and therefore admits the possibility, or danger, of a 'distortion' in one's identity; but his unique contribution to the discourse, a contribution of the utmost significance, is his argument that this alienation effect is not *essentially* a 'distortion' – that, on the contrary, it can be, and for the most part is, a way of awakening and eliciting the social, and indeed pro-social, foundations of the child's identity.

Now, to be sure, the essential here is, as Muller and Richardson emphasize, that 'the external image in which the infant discovers both himself and the "reality" around him' will be a 'human form', and that, 'in the concrete', it is 'likely' to be the 'mothering figure'.[121] Nevertheless, the infant's identification with his image poses, for Lacan, a serious developmental danger:

> What, more precisely, does the infant discover in experiencing his form reflected in the mirror? First of all, a total unity that replaces his prior experience of fragmentation. This totality becomes idealized into a model for all eventual integration and, as such, is the infant's primary identification – the basis for all subsequent 'secondary' identifications. This model, however, although it 'fixes' the subject in a certain permanence that contrasts with the 'turbulent movements that the subject feels are animating him', does so through a form that initially (i.e., before the subject's assumption of it through identification) is 'other' than the subject, exterior to it, hence an 'alienation' of it.[122]

Since Lacan believes, as Muller and Richardson point out, that identification 'with a constellation of images leads to a behavioural pattern that reflects the social structures within which those images first emerge',[123] he looks at the mirroring process with suspicion: it con-forms the infant body and soul to an alienated identity at the same time that it first makes it possible for him to experience any distinct identity at all.

The child's ego, in fact, undergoes a *double* alienation from itself: (1) first of all, the child confusedly identifies itself with the reflected *image* of itself; then (2) the child confusedly identifies its own reflected image with the image, or representation, of the *other*. Here we can see the significance of Sullivan's analysis. Sullivan assumes that the primary mirroring will be interpersonal, and he shows in great detail how it works and how its working can be disturbed. I think it much to his credit that he makes this crucial assumption. Lacan, by contrast, assumes that the primary mirroring involves the mediation of real mirrors. His 'realism', here, is unfortunate. Thus, for example, he argues that, whenever the mirroring involves a real mirror, rather than another person, e.g. the mothering one functioning in a mirroring way, there is also a 'primitive distortion' in the ego's experience of reality, 'for the reflection in the mirror is an inversion of what stands before the mirror'.[124] For Lacan, these alienations and distortions are extremely significant, because their operation within the process through which the structure of the ego is constituted means that the ego will always be predisposed to experience and relate to others in a pathologically narcissistic way, i.e. with a certain paranoia, exaggerated defensiveness, and unprovoked aggressivity – in short, with an attitude of closure, rather than an attitude of trust and openness.[125]

I submit that we should *reject* the inversion argument, since it assumes, contrary to fact, and indeed rather perversely, that the mirroring process is mostly and primarily an experience with real mirrors, whereas it is, mostly and primarily, an experience of interpersonal relationships. But I think we should *heed* the alienation argument – although, as I shall argue in the next section, this second argument must be corrected, for it sees only the moment of negative sociality in the dialectics of narcissism and overlooks the genuinely transfigurative moment, the moment of recognition, that Merleau-Ponty brings to light in his hermeneutical phenomenology of reciprocating gazes and motor echoes, perceptions gathered, through their intertwinings and reciprocities, into the communicativeness – the communion – of the flesh. In the dimension of the flesh, there is a radical deconstruction of the ego, the metaphysical subjectivity of our historical culture. Here, then, contrary to what Lacan is constrained, given his assumptions, to believe, the alienations of the mirroring process – in particular, the peculiar 'paranoia' and defensiveness Lacan sees it producing – can be redeemed. Merleau-Ponty shows us a possibility that Lacan does not conceive: how narcissism itself can be transformed.

4 Merleau-Ponty: Narcissism as Self-Deconstruction

The principal concern of Merleau-Ponty's essay on 'The child's relations with others' is the argument that human beings are not self-contained, self-sufficient subjects contingently and externally related to one another, but beings who are formed, from the very beginning, in and through their social interactions. The principal antagonist in this essay is, therefore Descartes, whose thinking gave shape not only to the discourse of modern philosophy, but also to the discourses of all the sciences.[126] Merleau-Ponty contends that an unexamined commitment to Cartesianism makes it impossible for psychology to understand the child's relations with others, and even the child's capacity to learn and develop, since Cartesian psychology presupposes a subjectivity so solitary, so essentially isolated by its (temporary and contingent) embodiment, that the developmentally essential consciousness of another – any other – is rendered logically inaccessible.

Without any 'direct access' to the 'mind' of another, 'I cannot know what you are thinking, but I can suppose it, guess at it from your facial expressions, your gestures, and your words'.[127] Mind and body are, for Descartes, distinct and separable substances, related to one another in such a way that the skin of the body imprisons and hides the mind within it. Since, however, all my efforts to experience the consciousness of another are based upon a faulty analogy, it is uncertain, in the final analysis, whether I am ever justified in making even a probabilistic inference. In any event, I am now at least an adult, and therefore capable of reasoning. How would children too young for such reasoning ever take part in a social world? Descartes' intellectualism cannot explain the sociality of the infant too young to reason through chains of self-evident propositions.

'I live in the facial expressions of the other, as I feel him living in mine.'[128] When, in a nursery, one infant starts to cry, the crying spreads to the other infants. Within seconds, they are all crying. At an extremely young age, long before the perceptual field is completely stabilized (as early as two weeks, according to some recent research by Meltzoff and Moore), an infant will respond to the mother's smile by smiling back in return.[129] Between mother and infant, there is an 'empathic flow', a 'synchrony' of looking and listening, a 'symphony of choreographed movements duplicated in each other's experience', a 'shared state of experiencing' and 'mutual felt sensing'.[130] These intercorporeal synchronizations are, in fact, so deeply ingrained, so deeply constitutive of our embodiment, that they persist into adulthood and continue to govern behaviour that is regarded as perfectly normal. Thus, as Nancy Henley observes, in *Body Politics*: 'Participants in an interaction often show synchronized nonverbal behavior with such postures as legs crossed in the same manner, similar standing positions, hand to chin or hip, or arms similarly folded (and maybe mirror-image style). Several researchers have studied this interactional synchrony and have noted that even fast-passing motions, of which most of us are unaware, exhibit this synchrony.'[131]

For the child still living in symbiotic relationships (the first of which is an intrauterine one),[132] there is no stable, continuous, and coherent sense of separateness differentiating the child from the parenting one; that is, sociality is already constitutive, forming and informing, long before the emergence of a social, personal ego. Thus, in the pre-personal state Freud called 'primary narcissism', there is already, as Merleau-Ponty says, an 'anonymous collectivity', an 'initial community', social interactions already articulating the experience and comportment of the infant.[133] Contrary to the Cartesianism of Freud's psychology, it is evident that the body is from the very beginning interactional, not monadic – and not only proto-social, but also even pro-social, or proto-moral.

Summing up his research on mother-infant relationships, Michael Coyle asserts that 'the early infant possesses capacities for interpersonal interactions on a level that was previously believed unattainable'.[134] Infants are neither passive nor autistic, i.e. non-relational. Nor is their experiencing ever totally undifferentiated and unstructured. Indeed, he found that healthy infants already enjoy, at a very early age, a strong organismic sense of self-centredness *in relation to others*.[135] Observing cycles of 'attention and withdrawal behavior on the part of the infant that was mirrored by the mother's behavior', Coyle found himself witnessing 'a self-process [that] is implicitly functioning from the interaction of the infant's subjective, bodily felt sensing with his own regulatory functioning': a process of self-formation, therefore, which essentially requires, and depends on, extremely sensitive interpersonal interactions.[136]

Sociality – responsiveness to others – is so primordially inherent in the infant's existence that adults commonly catch them 'attributing to others what belongs to the subject himself'.[137] Normally, of course, processes of differentiation progressively structure the child's experiential field: 'my body' takes shape as a substantial, objectified, coherently bounded presence, and 'I' become identified with, and assume my identity as, 'this body'. But this development, culminating in my individuation, my sense of being a separate existence, is essentially dependent upon *appropriate* social interactions: 'there must be a consciousness of the reciprocity of points of view in order that the word "I" may be learned and used'.[138] Children sometimes do not have the benefit of interactions that encourage such reciprocity. Not all adults can mirror and echo the child in ways that enable him or her to form a strong sense of self – a sense of self, I mean, as a social, interactive being.

Because of the 'syncretic sociality' of infantile experience (the stage Freudians call 'primary narcissism'), the child is especially susceptible to mimetic transfer influences – postural 'impregnations' and 'transgressions' by the other. Close or intimate interactions with others involve the child in processes of *mirroring* (the child sees itself reflected in and through the gaze, the gestures and postures, of the other, whilst the other, whom it sees, sees this child and always in some manner reflects back how he or she is being seen) and *resonating* (the child hears itself echoed in and by the other, and hears, through the other, how it is being heard). By virtue of such mirrorings and echoings, the bodily presence of the parent symbolizes, or carries, the felt sense of the infant's own bodily functioning. This mimetic symbolizing mediates and carries forward (metaphors) the infant's subjective feeling process – until it can do it by itself.[139] (I draw my use of the verb 'metaphor' from the original Greek: to translate, to transport, to transfer, to carry.) This, in turn, helps the infant to develop the inborn capacity for self-awareness.[140] (See my reading of Plato's *Republic* and *Laws*, spelled out in *The Body's Recollection of Being*. I argue that Plato's extraordinary attention to child-rearing practices, such as cradling, holding, and rocking, and his deep concern for the proper teaching of dance, music, and gymnastics, let us know that he understood the social and political implications of the symbolizing processes, and that, in particular, he understood how they make use of the body's spontaneous mimetic predispositions to symbolize and metaphor, for the infant, a knowledge the body initially carries without knowing it.) On the basis of his extensive research, Coyle writes: 'The infant's bodily responsiveness indicates that from the start the infant is "interacting" felt experience with [the mother's] spoken symbols.'[141] Consequently, the mother's 'soft and comforting voice' can echo the infant's processing of emotions and translate his or her bodily rhythms into a temporal integration, the necessary ground of the infant's sense of identity.[142]

Gradually, if the mirroring and resonating are not for some reason distorted or disturbed (e.g. because the parent is schizophrenic or does not really love the child), the child will develop a firm sense of its body as a coherent, bounded whole and an originating centre of action: it will develop an appropriate 'corporeal schema', a clear sense of itself as a body-self. But the character and quality of the interaction processes may be decisive, perhaps even fateful, for the infant. One cannot exaggerate the infant's need for mirroring and resonating: interaction processes that are accurate, reliable, trustworthy, loving, and caring. Since the infant learns these qualities of character by intercorporeal mimesis, the adults with whom it interacts (initially, for the most part, the mothering one) must model them in their own corporeal behaviour.

In *Identity, Youth and Crisis*, Erikson points out that 'the infant's sense of trust is a reflection of parental faith; similarly, the sense of autonomy is a reflection of the parents' dignity as autonomous beings. For no matter what we do in detail, the child will primarily feel what it is we live by as loving, co-operative, and firm beings, and what makes us hateful, anxious, and divided in ourselves.'[143] Good parents, then, are parents who, by virtue of their own bodily presence and comportment, consistently model, or schematize, the character of autonomous bodies. The modelling in question, however, is not a self-contained, monadological demonstration, but rather a character and quality of interaction, a demonstration-in-action, engaging the child. For the child's intercorporeal mimesis depends, here, on parental love and care. Without love and care, embodying a deep respect for the child's own abilities and capacities, and for the corporeal schematism, already encoded in the flesh, that informs them, the child's movements toward autonomy will be thwarted and the achievement made difficult or precarious. Good listening draws out, educes, the child's readiness for autonomy; and it succeeds because it is a means that is consistent with, in harmony with, its intended end. In the education of children, such consonance is absolutely essential. One can *hear* its presence and its absence.

We learn what it is to give others respectful recognition by receiving it ourselves from people who model (embody) it and who, by virtue of giving us that kind of attention, enable us to develop the capacity ourselves. The child who is mirrored and echoed with respectful recognition learns much more, in fact, than how to show respect for others. It learns also to value and respect itself. And this, in turn, guides and facilitates its achievement of autonomy. But autonomy is *not* merely an achievement in self-development; it is also an experience that teaches us the importance of according others a respectful recognition.

In his *Critique of Instrumental Reason*, Horkheimer therefore insists on connecting the future of social freedom to our historical potential for self-development; and he makes a point of arguing that the historical possibilities before us are already encoded in the earliest mother-child dynamics.[144] Considered in this light, the testimony of Harold Searles, an eminent psychiatrist with years of experience helping schizophrenics, assumes particular significance: 'I am convinced, from daily-life observations of infants and young children, and from psychoanalytic and psychotherapeutic work with neurotic and psychotic adults, that lovingness is the basic stuff of human personality, and that it is with a wholehearted openness to loving relatedness that the newborn infant responds to the outside world, with an inevitable admixture of cruelty and destructiveness ensuing only later – being deposited on top of the basic bedrock of lovingness – as a result of hurtful and anxiety-arousing interpersonal experience.'[145] Searles's experience agrees with Erikson's, and both bear out the connections that Horkheimer wants to make.

Children need the accurate and empathic mirroring-and-listening of close interpersonal relationships.[146] As Coyle says, the 'empathic relating of a primary caretaker (mother) is a necessary factor for completion of the subjective experiencing process'.[147] In other words, it is by grace of the empathic medium of a 'good' intercorporeality, an interaction process formed, for example, by good listening, that the child enjoys an opportunity to get a feel for the wholeness and fulfilment of processes of bodily sensing, and is enabled accordingly to constitute a firm, self-integrating sense of identity.[148]

Lacking, at first, any 'inner self-experience', lacking, at first, any reflectively constituted sense of self, children need (to see and hear) what reactions they bring out in others. For it is through interacting with others, through experiencing their empathically accurate mirroring and resonance, that children begin to constitute for themselves a private, characterological 'interiority' of feelings, thoughts, sensations, and motivating intentions: experiences with public names about which they may be confident, even though there is a sense in which the referents will never be altogether publicly observable. Our sense of self is formed through difference: difference in interactions with others, but also difference in interactions with the objective world.[149]

In his discussion of Habermas on ego identity and moral development, Thomas McCarthy resumes the argument, which I fully support, that since 'personal identity can be achieved only on the basis of mutual recognition, individuation can be understood only as a process of socialisation'.[150] The institutionalization of this mutual recognition – the incorporation of such recognition into the processes and procedures of political debate, our public discourse on social policies, for example – remains, however, an extremely difficult problem. The formation of personal identities based on childhood experiences of mutual recognition does not translate automatically into mutually satisfying communicative processes and procedures later on – that is to say, in the political discourse carried on by adults who may be presumed to have achieved their identity on the basis of some earlier experience with mutual recognition.

In any case, the processes of interpersonal mirroring and echoing are profoundly ambiguous, because, at the same time that they enable the child to sense itself, and constitute itself as an ego-logical centre, they also subject it to alienation, forming the child in conformity to the images of the Other. (Since these images have traditionally been constellated in a society over which men have ruled, girls have suffered a particularly traumatic alienation in passing through these processes. So, too, *a fortiori*, have boys in whom the spirit of the feminine archetypes strongly manifested.) In 'The intertwining – the chiasm', Merleau-Ponty takes note of this problem, pointing to the fact that 'Narcissus was the mythical being who, after looking at his image in the water, was drawn as if by vertigo to rejoin his image in the mirror of the water'.[151]

Soon I will argue that Merleau-Ponty's phenomenology of the flesh implicitly *challenges* the Lacanian analysis, which can see in the identity formed by mirroring only the inevitable alienation. I contend that, in the 'narcissism' of the flesh which his hermeneutical phenomenology discloses, we see and hear the constitution of a form of subjectivity radically different from the forms our systems of metaphysics and psychology have made familiar: a subjectivity which is not ego-logical; a subjectivity which the mirroring-and-listening process has decentred.

Merleau-Ponty's 'narcissism' of the flesh in fact schematizes a form of subjectivity which the texts of Descartes, Freud, and Lacan conceal: a subjectivity that finds itself, that gets to know itself as an inherently social being, through the mediation of sociality – social processes of identity formation. Thus, whereas the three can see in the mirroring of narcissism only the shaping of an ego-logical, egocentric identity, Merleau-Ponty sees in it the limning of a non-ego-logical identity, radically decentred by its dialectical experiencing of the intertwining of self and other. And, whereas Lacan can see in this mirroring only a process of alienation that imposes social conformity as the price for a coherent embodied identity, Merleau-Ponty sees in its deeper dimensions a compelling disclosure of our primordial sociality: a disclosure that enables the ego it has produced to *overcome* its narcissistic impulses, and that consequently *frees* it to continue its individuation, beyond socially imposed roles, by taking part in the communicativeness and reciprocity of a social existence.

Commenting on Descartes' *Dioptrics*, Merleau-Ponty draws our attention to the 'ghost in the machine' his epistemological narcissism implies:

> *who* will see the image painted in the eyes or in the brain? Therefore, finally, a *thought* of this image is needed – Descartes already sees that we always put a 'little man' inside man, that our objectifying view of our own body always obliges us to seek still further inside that seeing man we thought we had under our eyes.[152]

In Descartes, the narcissism consists in the character of inward turning, the looking inside – and in the presumption of a power to be self-grounding. True vision is really, therefore, *thought* of vision, a vision which has abandoned the objects of its worldly involvement for the sake of the security it imagines it can find in the self-evidence of its own operations.

As we noted, in 'The intertwining – the chiasm', Merleau-Ponty asserts that 'there is a fundamental narcissism in all vision'.[153] What *is* this 'narcissism' he attributes to vision, and to the flesh? The answer, stated very succinctly, is that he speaks of narcissism because of the phenomenon of reflexivity, or mirroring. But he locates this phenomenon in the flesh of the world, not in the privacy of the mind. So, as we shall see, and also hear, instead of postulating, like Descartes, what is, in effect, a 'ghost in the machine', he uses hermeneutical phenomenology to disclose a dialectic of reflexivity taking place in the 'intertwinings' of subjectivity and world: 'my eyes which see, my hands which touch, can also be seen and touched', and 'therefore, in this sense, they see and touch the visible, the tangible, from within'.[154]

But this 'from within' is altogether different from the Cartesian thought 'inside'. In contrast to the epistemological narcissism of Descartes, a narcissism in which, for the sake of achieving absolute certainty, there is a decisive withdrawal into the solipsism of the *ego cogito*, the 'narcissism' we find in Merleau-Ponty is an experience of existence which shows me that I am inseparably intertwined with the 'presence' of the Other, and which accordingly requires a thoroughgoing deconstruction of the Cartesian egology – its self-certainty, its self-absorption, its withdrawal, its monadic state, its cognitive construction of the world.

For Merleau-Ponty, the 'essential notion for such philosophy is that of the flesh, which is not the objective body, nor the body thought by the soul as its own (Descartes), [but rather] . . . the sensible in the two-fold sense of what one senses and what senses'.[155] But now, the 'flesh is a mirror phenomenon', the medium of a subject-object mirroring.[156] The flesh is 'the formative medium of the object and the subject'.[157] It is the elemental matrix, the texture, the field or dimensionality of our being: that 'medium' in the depths of which subject and object, simultaneously coemergent, are forever unified, and through which they are continually mirroring, echoing, one another.

Although mirroring plays a crucial role in psychoanalytic accounts of the secondary narcissism process, the mirroring that figures in the 'narcissism' Merleau-Ponty locates in the flesh functions to *deconstruct*, rather than to reinforce, the withdrawal into solipsism and autism. In Descartes, the method of withdrawal and self-absorption is an attempt to achieve a state of self-sufficiency or self-containedness that would make it possible for the ego to claim absolute epistemic self-evidence for the immanent *cogito*. But, for such self-evidence, such epistemological unquestionableness, to be possible, there would have to be a perfect temporal *coincidence* between the conditions of knowledge and the circumstances of being, a coincidence between the existence of the knower and the presence of the known. Although Merleau-Ponty sees a kind of 'narcissism' in the phenomenon of mirroring, he displays the fact that *his* mirroring, *his* reflexivity, is a dialectic that double-crosses the possibility of a Cartesian narcissism – a narcissism of total coincidence.

There is, in fact, in the mirroring and echoing narcissism

of the flesh, 'a sort of dehiscence', an ecstasy (*écart*) which 'opens my body in two'.[158] There is, then, no possibility of fusion: the Cartesian 'return to immediacy', the Cartesian 'search for an original integrity', can only be regarded as the philosopher's 'narcissistic delusion'.[159] According to Merleau-Ponty, 'the immediate is at the horizon and must be thought as such'.[160]

In his later work, Merleau-Ponty showed that he was as much the sworn enemy of the 'metaphysics of presence' as Derrida has been. We must not be misled by his mythopoetic references to a 'narcissism' of the flesh and jump to the conclusion that, since the narcissistic position of the Cartesian ego is used to justify the claims of a 'metaphysics of presence', the 'narcissism' which Merleau-Ponty espouses in the texts of *The Visible and the Invisible* is likewise bound up with an argument for this metaphysics.

In his 'Working notes', Merleau-Ponty suggested that

> To touch *oneself*, to see *oneself* . . . is not to apprehend oneself as an ob-ject; it is to be open to oneself, destined to oneself (narcissism) – Nor, therefore, is it to reach oneself; it is, on the contrary, to escape oneself, to be ignorant of oneself. The 'self' in question is by divergence (*d'écart*), is [an] *Unverborgenheit* of the *Verborgen* as such, which consequently does not cease to be hidden or latent.[161]

It is essential to note, here, that the 'narcissism' which Merleau-Ponty brings out in this passage is *not* the immediate narcissism of Cartesian self-absorption and epistemic coincidence, but rather the *mediated* narcissism of a passage through the *écarts*, the ecstatic disseminations, of the flesh: I see myself mirrored in my alterity: I hear myself echoed; I am disclosed to myself only in the course of a relationship; my encounter with myself is not an 'origin' but a 'destiny'.

'In fact', he argues,

> I do not entirely succeed in touching myself touching, in seeing myself seeing; the experience I have of myself does not go beyond a sort of immanence; it terminates in the invisible. . . . The self-perception is still a perception, i.e., it gives me a *nicht urpräsentierbar* (a non-visible, myself.[162]

In brief, and in words that are reminiscent, for me, of Montaigne, he draws the conclusion that 'I am a self-presence that is an absence from self'.[163] Thus, the 'narcissism' about which Merleau-Ponty is writing is a mediated experience of oneself: a 'return' to oneself, a 'retrieval' of oneself, that must *pass through* the otherness, the *différance*, of the flesh. Moreover, there is never a total recovery, a return to 'the same'. My touching, he says, 'takes place in the untouchable'.[164] Likewise, in gazing at people and things in the world, I can see myself: not *only* myself, which would of course be solipsism, but rather myself *as well*. And yet, both the beings I am looking at and the 'me', the 'self' I encounter in the dialectic of the mirroring, are rooted in the depths of the flesh, the depths of an element at no time totally visible. Indeed, I can encounter myself only because I am always partially invisible: the 'narcissism' that Merleau-Ponty espouses is therefore an experience of oneself that is made possible only because our bodily mode of being-in-the-world makes the Cartesian self-absorption and coincidence *not* possible.

In 'The intertwining – the chiasm', Merleau-Ponty contends that 'he who sees cannot possess the visible unless he is possessed by it'.[165] But to be 'possessed by' the visible is to be a *cogito* dispossessed: an ego not in total possession of itself; an ego not totally present to (for) itself. Now, we might call this fact an 'alienation'. Lacan does. But there are different kinds of alienation, and the 'alienation' for which Merleau-Ponty wants to argue is not the Lacanian. What Lacan calls to our attention is an incipient pathology in the visual channel of self-development. According to his analysis of visual mirroring, the dialectic is one which enables the child to acquire a coherent, well-ordered body and, therewith, a coherent sense of self. In brief, the mirroring bestows an egocentric identity. But, for Lacan, this identity is really an illusion, a sham, because in truth it represents the child's unconscious conformity to an alien image. The 'self' acquired in this process is nothing but a pattern of socially imposed roles: an ego, rather than an authentic self. Thus, for Lacan, the dialectic of mirroring is always a disguised form of social violence: the child gains an ego but loses its 'self'.

Now, I do not want to deny, or even to underestimate, the possibility, the danger, against which Lacan wants to warn us. He has certainly called attention to a phenomenon that Freudian psychoanalysis did not consider: a phenomenon, I would add, the very existence of which it could not acknowledge without radically calling into question its tacit normative commitment to an egocentric psychology. But the point I want to make, here, is that the 'alienation' which Merleau-Ponty brings to light is an alienation through which we are radically decentred, drawn out of our egocentric selves, and projected into a social existence with many possibilities for non-egological individuation. Lacan sees only the negative moment of the dialectic. Merleau-Ponty acknowledges the negative, but also sees a field of more positive existential possibilities: authentic alternatives, inscribed in the very ambiguity of the dialectic, to the social imposition of identity.

It is true that, in the dimension of the flesh, 'things pass into us as well as we into the things'.[166] We should not be blind to the violations that take place in the name of 'necessary' or 'inevitable' social interactions. But we also need to see and hear how the 'narcissism' Merleau-Ponty discloses – the encounter with myself in the mirroring and echoing resonance of the other – makes possible a self-identity based on my self-recognition as an essentially social being, a being, moreover, whose self-development *beyond* the limits of a socially imposed egocentric identity is inherently dependent on its capacity to contribute to the transformation of social existence – and do this, moreover, on the basis of, and in concordance with, the 'idealities' already adumbrated and schematized in the very nature of the flesh. Let us take note of his observation, in 'The intertwining – the chiasm', that we will 'have to recognise an ideality that is not alien to the flesh, that gives it its axes, its depth, its dimensions'.[167] The point of this quotation is that, in the 'narcissism' of the flesh, my encounter with myself becomes an encounter in which, in addition to seeing myself and hearing myself, i.e. *only* myself, I also see and hear myself in and as the other. In other words, I get to see and hear myself as inherently social. But seeing and hearing myself in *this* way guides and furthers my self-development as a social being whose deepest identity is in the making, inextricably bound up with the collective realization of specific possibilities already implicit in the organization of all social life. What makes Merleau-Ponty call our experience 'narcissistic' is the fact that, whilst perceiving others, we are always also seeing, touching, hearing ourselves. But this 'narcissism' is not Freud's, is not Lacan's, is not Descartes'. It is, rather, an implication encoded in the fact that we inhere, with all others, in the communicativeness of an elemental flesh.

In 'Interrogation and intuition', there is a passing but important reference to narcissism.[168] The 'narcissistic' is described, there, as 'eroticised, endowed with a natural magic that attracts the other significations into its web, as the body feels the world in feeling itself'.[169] We should pause to reflect on the clause that ends this sentence, because it shows very clearly how the 'narcissism' of the flesh is different from the 'narcissism' of interest to Freud and Lacan – and how it is also different from the epistemological position of the Cartesian ego (the *ego cogito*). Freud and Lacan see the narcissistic ego feeling *only* itself. Descartes sees the self-possessed, self-evident ego knowing *only* itself. Merleau-Ponty, however, sees and hears a dialectic, an ongoing process, in which the body-self suddenly begins to 'feel the world': feeling the world, we feel ourselves.

He writes, in his 'Working notes', that

> One feels oneself looked at (burning neck) not because something passes from the look to our body, to burn it at the point seen, but because to feel one's body is also to feel its aspect for the other.[170]

The sense of 'narcissism' implicit here is so different from the senses we have been eliciting from our readings of Descartes, Freud, and Lacan that I cannot refrain from questioning the wisdom in Merleau-Ponty's appropriation of this term. Why use the term 'narcissism' to describe the character of an experiential process in which the self-aggrandizing self-absorption widely and commonly regarded as definitive of narcissism is double-crossed by the body, and in which the discovery of oneself in the mirror, in the resonance-field, of the others – an encounter compelling self-recognition as both same and different, familiar and strange – irrevocably shatters the ego's narcissistic self-enclosure, opening it for ever to the facticity of its inseparable coexistence, and its inherent kinship, with the other? Merleau-Ponty's thinking is ahead of his vocabulary. But the vocabulary obscures the radicality of his thinking. We must, therefore, be extremely careful in reading him.

Let us return to a point in the text of 'The intertwining – the chiasm' which we have already read, picking up, this time, some of the words that precede it.[171] Merleau-Ponty argues, here, that since 'the seer is caught up in what he sees, it is still himself he sees: there is a fundamental narcissism in all vision'. This argument then continues:

> And thus, for the same reason, the vision he exercises he also undergoes from the things, such that, as many painters have said, I feel myself looked at by the things, my activity is equally passivity – which is the second and more profound sense of the narcissism: not to see in the outside, as the others see it, the contour of the body one inhabits, but especially to be seen by the outside, to exist within it, to emigrate into it, to be seduced, captivated, alienated by the phantom, so that the seer and the visible reciprocate one another and we no longer know which sees and which is seen.[172]

Now, what makes the visionary experience Merleau-Ponty is displaying a form of 'narcissism' is the fact that, in seeing the other, I am (still) (also) seeing myself: seeing myself as the other sees me, i.e. from that other's point of view. (Martin Dillon's interpretation is, I think, correct here: Merleau-Ponty is not saying that, when I look at a tree or a mountain, these things look back at me, returning my gaze in this 'symmetrical' sense, but rather that, in so far as my gaze goes out to things and inhabits them, it locates itself where those things are and gets a sense of seeing from their location.[173]

Clearly, this narcissism of the flesh is not Cartesian: it is not self-absorption, not a disconnection from the world. On the contrary, it is a movement toward the other: to see is to go outside myself, to live in and with the other. Merleau-Ponty describes our vision as a 'seduction', a 'captivation', an 'alienation'. But the 'alienation' in question is not of the Lacanian type, because here, in the dimensionality of the flesh, the alienation *becomes* reciprocity, an occasion for the recognition of concrete others, an occasion to acknowledge our kinship and affinity. It does not involve – as Foucault seems to think – the social imposition of ego-logical structures on a totally docile, passive body; nor does it entail, as Nietzsche and Freud would probably have said, the imposition of order on a turbulent, chaotic body of drives, but, on the contrary, it is, rather, an alienation which gives rise to a moment of self-transcendence and self-redefinition, a moment when the ego-logical seer-listener begins to see and hear himself or herself as essentially intertwined with others in relationships that are capable of a developing and deepening reciprocity. Therefore, 'We no longer know which sees and which is seen' does not mean a Cartesian coincidence; even less, a confusion of identities. What it describes is our *anagnōrisis*, our self-recognition, as inherently social beings. And, more than this, it suggests a deep perception of our belonging-together within the 'universal flesh' of a moral community.[174] Thus, ironically, in the 'narcissism' of the flesh, the narcissism of *egos* is challenged, and we get a feeling for the idea that the channels of an intercorporeality essential for the building of community are waiting to be awakened.

Now, the principal concept Merleau-Ponty uses to interpret the nature of the flesh is 'reversibility'. It is the 'reversibility' of the flesh, he says, 'which is the ultimate truth'.[175] 'Reversibility' names very precisely the experience about which we have been thinking: 'We no longer know which sees and which is seen.' It names an experience that can serve as our ground for the cultivation of those reciprocities so necessary for ethical life. In his 'Working notes', Merleau-Ponty tells us that 'the chiasm, reversibility, is the idea that every perception is doubled with a counter-perception . . . is an act with two faces; one no longer knows who speaks and who listens'.[176]

This reversibility manifests 'the intertwining of my life with the other lives, of my body with the visible things, by the intersection of my perceptual field with that of the others'.[177] Beause of this 'intertwining', my body 'discovers in that other body a miraculous prolongation of my intentions'.[178] Here, then, we learn that the 'narcissism' of the flesh, as Merleau-Ponty is wont to call it, can eventuate in a deeper awareness of our essential coexistence, our essential involvement with others, and does not inevitably lead, as in narcissistic character disorders, psychotic states of fusion (total identification with the other), and the autism or solipsism (total separation from the other) of the Cartesian *cogito*, to a breakdown of sociality and a loss of 'self'.

Whereas Lacan sees in the mirroring process and its narcissism only an alienation and distortion of one's identity, Merleau-Ponty can see an alienation that is *self*-developing: socializing in the best sense. That is, he can see in the 'narcissism' of the mirroring a double-crossing (chiasm) which is stretching, decentring, and opening, taking the ego out of itself – taking the 'self' out of its identification with the structure of the monadic ego.

What I call 'my body' is not an extended material substance; it is, rather, a texture, a field – 'a field open', as he says, 'for other Narcissus'.[179] Belonging to the intertwinings of a 'universal flesh',[180] 'my body' both is and is not (identical to) itself. Rooted in this dimension of the flesh, I *am* 'my body'; but I am also 'intercorporeality'.[181] This elemental intercorporeality, however, enables each of us to enter into the dialectics of narcissism and grow beyond it, learning from our recognition of ourselves in the face of the other not only the basic truth of our primordial sociality, but also, and more specifically, that, from the very beginning, social coexistence is a dialectic of transposition and reversibility.

As a reflective moment in deeply felt experience, this 'narcissism' of the flesh leads to a self-understanding that *reverses* what others have called 'narcissism', namely, an inveterate tendency of the ego to inflate itself at the expense of its response-ability in relation to others. Because of the peculiar 'narcissism' of the flesh, we are entwined with others, seduced into a vision, a sounding of ourselves as already orchestrated by a dialectic of reversibility. In the moment of recognition, we see and hear ourselves in reversibility: mirrored by others, we see ourselves from where they are; echoed by others, we listen to ourselves with their ears. We find ourselves seduced into an equivocation, and, in the final analysis, a reversal of positions: captivated, just as Merleau-Ponty says, but captivated less by otherness in general than by the *position* of the other. Reversibility teaches us the root meaning of reciprocity: a basic sense, as Merleau-Ponty put it so well, of 'an ideal community of embodied subjects, of an intercorporeality'.[182] Stating this point in a formulation for which I shall argue in the next section of this chapter, I want to say that reversibility *schematizes* reciprocity. It is a corporeal schema encoded in the flesh, an implicate order that anticipates, calls for, and is carried forward to completion by, the achievement of reciprocity in social and political life.

When I first read Horkheimer's argument for the utopian, emancipatory significance of *mimesis*, I was taken aback. I could think of imitation only as a reactionary process. But when I returned to *The Eclipse of Reason* many years later, my work with the texts of Merleau-Ponty's last phase enabled me to appreciate the utopian, emancipatory potential for which Horkheimer was pleading. Moreover, I realized that, by giving *mimesis* an interpretation which locates it in the reversibilities of the flesh, I could connect it to the corporeal schematism of reciprocity, a fundamental process in the life of the body politic we are struggling to achieve.

Pointing out that imitation is one of the primary forms of interaction, and therefore of learning, during the years of early childhood, and that later socialization teaches the child to renounce the 'mimetic impulse' for the sake of 'rational', goal-directed behaviour – in other words, instrumental reason and its postures of domination – Horkheimer pleaded for a 'restitution' of this impulse, arguing that its 'transformation' into 'the universal medium of language . . . means that potentially nihilistic energies work for reconciliation'.[183]

It seems to me that, if we accept Merleau-Ponty's account of perception, and then graft on to it Horkheimer's analysis of *mimesis*, we can advance the projects in both discourses. *Mimesis* is an intercorporeal process in which (to take the simplest case) one corporeal presence (a child, for example) responds to another corporeal presence (a parent, for example) by 'incorporation', developing its own corporeal schematism (its latent potential) in consonance with the body its other schematizes. Infant-parent interactions, and indeed all interpersonal interactions, are therefore opportunities for the progressive schematization of a utopian intercorporeality, concretely structured by forms of reciprocity generated from within the shared body of experience.

5 The Intertwining and Its Reversibilities: A Radical Political Order

> We continue to unweave the prevailing dis-order,
> weaving our way deeper into the labyrinth.
>
> Daly, *Gyn/Ecology*[184]

> The roots of the term *order* are from the Latin *ordiri*,
> which means 'to lay the warp, begin to weave'. Since
> the prevailing order is warped, dis-ordered, we
> unweave it as we begin to weave. Since it is a
> source of our known dis-ease, we unweave it with
> increasing ease, uncovering its previously
> unknown causes.
>
> ibid., 415.

Integrating the dreambody into your life . . . is bound to take you to the edge of your personality and bring you into conflict with the world around you.

Mindell, *Working with the Dreaming Body*[185]

The dawning sense of freedom feeds upon the memory of the archaic impulse not yet steered by any solid I. . . . Without an *anamnesis* of the untamed impulse that precedes the ego – an impulse later banished to the zone of our unfree bondage to nature – it would be impossible to derive the idea of freedom, although that idea in turn ends up reinforcing the ego.

Adorno, *Negative Dialectics*[186]

In the semantic heritage of a cultural tradition are contained the *images and anticipations* of a fulfilled life-history and of a collective life-form in which justice does not exclude solidarity, and freedom is not realized at the expense of happiness.

Benhabib, 'The utopian dimension in communicative ethics'[187]

[Individuation] requires not only cognitive mastery of general levels of communication, but also the ability to give one's own needs their due in these communicative structures; as long as the ego [the self] is *cut off from its internal nature* and disavows the dependency on needs that still await suitable interpretations, freedom, no matter how much it is guided by principles, remains in truth unfree in relation to existing systems of norms'.

Habermas, 'Moral development and ego identity'[188]

Basic psychological and sociological concepts can be interwoven because the perspectives projected in them of an autonomous ego [self] and an emancipated society reciprocally require one another.

ibid., p. 71

Inner nature is 'moved into a utopian perspective',

in the sense that its contents, our needs and affects, become communicatively accessible.

Benhabib, *Critique, Norm and Utopia*.[189]

Ego autonomy [as Habermas conceives it] is characterized by a twofold capacity: first, the individual's *reflexive* ability to question the interpretive framework fixed by the cultural tradition – to loosen, if you wish, those sedimented and frozen *images* of the good and happiness in the light of which we formulate needs and motives; second, such reflexive questioning is accompanied by an ability to *articulate* one's needs linguistically, by an ability to communicate with others about them.

ibid., 333.

The problem is not so much that of defining a political 'position' (which is to choose from a pre-existing set of possibilities) but to imagine and bring into being *new schemas* of politicization.

Foucault, *Power/Knowledge*.[190]

[Current research documents the fact that] the infant is born with a wide range of *organizational schemas* previously unheard of.

Coyle, 'An experiential perspective on the mother-infant relationship'[191]

To the extent that I can elaborate and extend my *corporeal schema*, to the extent that I can acquire a better organized experience of my own body, to that very extent will my consciousness of my own body cease being a chaos in which I am submerged and lend itself to a transfer to others.

Merleau-Ponty, 'The child's relations with others'[192]

My body . . . discovers in that other body a miraculous prolongation of my intentions, a familiar way of dealing with the world. Henceforth, as the parts of my body together comprise a system, so my body and the other person's are one whole, two sides of one and the same phenomenon, and the *anonymous existence* of which

> my body is the ever-renewed trace henceforth inhabits both bodies simultaneously.
>
> Merleau-Ponty, *Phenomenology of Perception*[193]

> The communication or comprehension of gestures comes about though the *reciprocity* of my intentions and the gestures of the other, of my gestures and the intentions discernible in the conduct of other people. It is as if the other person's intention inhabited my body and mine his.
>
> Merleau-Ponty, *Phenomenology of Perception*[194]

> [We need to retrieve] the *intertwining* of my life with the other lives, of my body with the visible things, by the intersection of my perceptual field with that of the others.
>
> Merleau-Ponty, 'Reflection and interrogation'[195]

> The chiasm, *reversibility*, is the idea that every perception is doubled with a counter-perception . . . one no longer knows who speaks and who listens.
>
> Merleau-Ponty, 'Working notes'[196]

> Ego psychology, by identifying the biological sources of the ego, actually locates some of the *biological roots* of sociation.
>
> Whitebook, 'Reason and happiness: some psychoanalytic themes in critical theory'[197]

In 'The subject and power', Foucault said: 'We need to promote new forms of subjectivity through the refusal of the kind of individuality which has been imposed on us for several centuries.'[198] I concur. From the outset, I have been directing our reflections on narcissism (which, for ego psychology, is a necessary stage in the process of personal growth and maturation), and in particular, here, our reflections on Merleau-Ponty's 'narcissism' of the flesh, toward the very difficult project that Foucault was proposing. I am attempting to point to the fact that our self-recognition, a self-understanding based on our auditory experience of ourselves as rooted in the elemental intertwinings and reversibilities of a 'universal flesh' (Merleau-Ponty's term), can *decentre* the egocentric subject honoured by the traditional discourses of epistemology and psychoanalysis, and can *deconstruct* the traditional sense of individuality. (Joel Whitebook's defence of ego psychology and psychoanalytic theory is a strong one, and I am persuaded by his critique of drive psychology as a radical ground for critical theory. But the adequacy and radicality of ego psychology cannot be demonstrated simply by arguing for its superiority in relation to the psychology of drives. Despite all the points that Whitebook can make on behalf of the ego, I submit that we need to conceive, and practise, a new form of subjectivity. The ego is not a structure which allows the kinds of individuation and socialization processes toward the achievement of which this book is directed. To emphasize this point, I have formulated a distinction between *ego* and *self*. Habermas does not make this distinction, so he speaks of 'ego identity'. But it is clear from what he has to say about this identity that the *subject* of his discourse is really a *self*, and not the traditional *ego*.)

For the most part, Merleau-Ponty fleshes out his new interpretation of subjectivity in terms of our visionary experience. He introduces us to this new subjectivity by way of the process of mirroring, hermeneutically articulating the intertwinings and reversibilities that are constitutive of our subjectivity and its identity formation. The use of experience drawn from vision perpetuates, of course, the hegemony of the traditional paradigm – the very same paradigm that accompanied, and to some extent generated, the power of the modern form of subjectivity. Thus his use of vision makes it peculiarly difficult for him to bring forth a *new* form of subjectivity, profoundly different from the modern. There is, however, an important text where he specifies the problematic in terms of our auditory experience: instead of mirroring, it is a question of listening, echoing, resonating. The text alerts us to a 'motor echo', an experience of intertwining and reversibility, in the auditory field, organized around the intercorporeality of two subjects:

> But if I am close enough to the other who speaks to hear his breath and feel his effervescence and his fatigue [a closeness typical of the mother-infant relationship], I almost witness, in him as in myself, the awesome birth of vociferation. As there is a reflexivity of the touch, of sight, and of the touch-vision system, there is a reflexivity of the

> movements of phonation and hearing: they have their sonorous inscription; the vociferations have in me their motor echo.[199]

This motor echoing is of enormous importance for the self-developmental processes of the young child. By virtue of the adult's accurate, well-tempered, well-timed resonating and echoing, the child gets to hear and recognize itself. The motor echo gives the child an experience of reflexivity; but it grants this experience in, and as, a form of intersubjectivity – a process of self-formation mediated by the communicative listening of the other. And, just as there are 'good' ways of mirroring and 'bad' ways of mirroring – a question of rhythm, timing, consistency, reliability, accuracy, and the quality of its character, so there are 'good' and 'bad' ways of listening, echoing, resonating. The 'good' facilitate a reflexivity which helps the other (not necessarily a child) to form a better sense of self. The 'bad' can be, for an infant, extremely disintegrating, traumatic. But 'good' and 'bad' listening, echoing and resonating with the other(s), can also make a decisive difference in the formation and achievement of consensus, the task of political discourse.

In the audible reversibilities of the flesh, a new form of subjectivity, a self which recognizes itself as essentially constituted through social relationships of reciprocity, and even, correspondingly, a new body politic, are in fact *already* being schematized. This hitherto unrealized dimension of the corporeal schema is what, on my interpretation, the text of 'the intertwining – the chiasm' is on the verge of disclosing. What accounts for the fact that the text does not explicitly articulate this schematization? Only, I think, or mainly, this: that Merleau-Ponty confined his attention to questions of epistemology and metaphysics. Although he touched on moral education, and on the connection between perceptual rigidity and the authoritarian personality type, in 'The child's relations with others', the various texts assembled in *The Visible and the Invisible*, wherein he explores the dimension of the flesh, restrict themselves to questions of ontology and epistemology. My reading carries forward the project he began, eliciting from his texts their meaning, their treasury of implications, for ethics, social theory, and politics.

Intercorporeality already schematizes, although of course only in a rudimentary and preliminary way that *needs* to be appropriately cultivated, the embodiment of a self deeply rooted in an ethics of care and open to the kind of communication necessary for the building of a society truly organized by principles of justice. Another way to say this – a way I take to be extremely consequential, when we consider the *Zugehörigkeit* which grounds all our listening – is to say that, by grace of the corporeal reversibilities we inevitably live, we already belong to an 'initial community',[200] and already have, in the dimension of the flesh, an empathic, preconceptual understanding of the reciprocity necessary for the kind of communication a rational and just society, an 'ideal community of embodied subjects', requires.[201] Reversibility is the initial form of what later could *become* a genuine reciprocity.[202] In stage III, then, we attempt to develop our capacity to hear, and hear *with*, this reversibility.

In 'Moral development and ego identity', the text we read at the beginning of this section, Habermas laments the fact that the modern self is a self which is deeply 'cut off' from its own 'internal nature', and he argues that we must create a society which can 'give our needs their due'. I agree, but contend that the self is more deeply cut off than he thinks, because his conception of our 'internal nature' is ontologically shallow. And, since there is a dimension he misses, there are needs he does not recognize, needs whose claims he does not hear. If our capacity to hear, for example, is rooted in *Zugehörigkeit*, a dimension of our auditory being-in-the-world which the processes of socialization tend to conceal, then the truth is that we are cut off from the wisdom, the pre-ontological understanding, borne in the auditory experience of this dimension, and that there still is a body of needs which must be recognized and enabled. I am arguing not only that there *is* such a dimension, and that we are cut off from it, but also that, in the dimension from which we are cut off, the normative character of an historically new subjectivity, and correlatively, the principles of a new body politic, a new political order, are always already schematized, initially inscribed in the auditory flesh as a corporeal schema implicitly orchestrating the conduct of our lives *despite* a form of society that even today suppresses and distorts its functioning.

Joel Whitebook tries to defend ego psychology against the claims, made by Horkheimer, Adorno, and Marcuse, to the effect that the wild libidinal energies recognized by *drive* psychology are potentially much more emancipatory, subversive, and revolutionary than all the 'rational strengths' at the disposal of the ego. The defence Whitebook proposes is that ego psychology recognizes, and is committed to nurturing, the 'biological roots of sociation'. Now, I do not want to take up the cause of drive psychology, which, for many reasons – some of them formulated very eloquently in Whitebook's essay – I reject as a touchstone for critical theory; but I also do not want, for all its commitment to the 'biological roots of sociation', a psychology that can neither conceive nor imagine any forms of subjectivity different from the mature ego and any forms of intersubjectivity not structured on the model of a subject and its object.

Be this as it may, I nevertheless welcome Whitebook's affirmation of the 'biological roots of sociation'. This is an extremely important point. However, we lose touch with the truth in this point, and miss its normative, intensely transformative significance, unless we are prepared to recognize the experiential equivalent, the phenomenological correlate, of these biological roots. I want to argue that the experiential equivalent is a corporeal schema, a schema which can be bodily felt, bodily sensed, and that the nature and character of this schema has been hermeneutically articulated by Merleau-Ponty's phenomenology of the flesh. What this phenomenology lets us, or enables us, to hear are the roots of sociation, always already intertwining us in the lives of others: an intercorporeality which is audible, even though it remains an unrealized potential, by grace of the *Zugehörigkeit* into which every one of us is initially cast.

We can always, as Merleau-Ponty says in 'The child's relations with others', quoted at the beginning of this section, 'elaborate and extend' the corporeal schema with which we find ourselves. That is to say, we can always work to make contact with the intercorporeality, the intertwinings and reversibilities, schematized in the depths of our fleshly being, our fleshly presence. And we can always work to retrieve this dimension of our embodiment. But, more than this, we can raise it into consciousness and then work with it – work on ourselves, I mean, by developing ourselves in the wisdom of its image. This would be a significant 'practice of the self', because there is a utopian-emancipatory potential in the corporeal schematism Merleau-Ponty discloses, and it is a potential which can be heard – if we listen with skill and care. This is stage III work.

Benhabib evokes 'sedimented and frozen images': images long suppressed and perhaps forgotten, images that can be awakened and recovered. This is a promising movement of thought, but its significance is diminished by the fact that she *disembodies* the images she evokes. This fact is not apparent in the passage I quote from *Critique, Norm and Utopia*; but it cannot be denied when we read the passage I quote from 'The utopian dimension in communicative ethics'. Here she unequivocally locates the 'images and anticipations' in 'the semantic heritage of a cultural tradition'. I am not disputing the fact that there are utopian-emancipatory 'images and anticipations' which have been formed in, and transmitted by, our 'semantic heritage'. But I do want to contest her excessive linguistification: quietly, implicitly abstracting these 'images and anticipations' from their crucial body of meaning. I am *not* arguing against languaging: we *need* processes of articulation. But we need to learn *new* processes of languaging – processes rooted in, and channelled through, the body of our experience. Thus, we must not let these semantic processes get cut off from our bodily nature. By abstracting 'images and anticipations' from the body and locating them exclusively in a 'semantic heritage', Benhabib *cuts them off* from the roots of their meaning. If these 'images and anticipations' are significant in the way she presumes, then they should be representations of our needs and dreams. But needs and dreams always implicate the body of experienced meaning.

Horkheimer, Adorno, and Marcuse were, then, justified in being suspicious of ego psychology as a touchstone for critical theory and revolutionary praxis. But they should not have been so easily seduced into embracing drive psychology and espousing its biological body. For, without a phenomenology of the lived body, a hermeneutical phenomenology of experienced perception, there can be no 'grounding' of theory and praxis in experienced meaning. The 'body' conceived by drive psychology is a body *without* any felt, sensed, experienced meaning. If it is essential that we not be cut off from our 'internal nature', then it is imperative that our thinking and living maintain their rootedness in the body of experienced meaning.

In the passage we read from *Negative Dialectics* (see the beginning of this section), Adorno writes about a 'sense of freedom' that is nourished by a 'memory', an *anamnēsis*, of the 'archaic impulse', the 'untamed impulse', which 'precedes the ego': an impulse, he says, 'not yet steered by any solid I'. I would argue, in response, that the mature ego, the 'solid' and therefore reified 'I', is a product of socialization, i.e. an assimilation of, and an accommodation to, socially imposed meanings, and that what 'precedes the ego', the *archē* sought by Adorno's *anamnēsis,* is an embodied experience of ourselves in our wholeness: an experience, for example, of our primordial *Zugehörigkeit* as auditory beings. But bringing this wholeness into our recollection would not end up, as Adorno supposes, merely 'reinforcing the ego'. Quite the contrary. Since what precedes the formation of the ego is a wholeness free of ontological dualisms (subject and object, ego and other), the recollection which reconnects us with our wholeness of being and retrieves it for present living promises to contest and resist the empire of the ego. But the recollection of the wholeness which graces our auditory initiation is much more than a critical deconstruction of the social control inherent in the ego's rule; more constructively, it also grounds and motivates a principled reciprocity, a respectful recognition of the other, in the intertwinings and reversibilities of an intercorporeal auditory field.

In his critique of the discourse of subjectivity and, in particular, in his objections to Horkheimer's conception of the subject of critical theory, Habermas discerns an undetected, but very treacherous, equation, which entails, in the final analysis, a reduction of the achievements of the 'anonymous subject' – in Marxian terminology, the 'species' – to the experience of an historically constituted, specific human group.[203] This reductive equation certainly serves the interests of the prevailing institutions of power. Consequently, Habermas attempts (as Benhabib states it) a 'reconstruction of the species competencies of an anonymous subject': a project which, in effect, brings him back to the discourse of subjectivity.[204] (In this respect, Foucault's thinking followed a strikingly similar trajectory. Although in his earliest work he embraced the 'transcendental subject' of phenomenology, he subsequently repudiated it in the name of structuralism. But in the period just before his death, the period marked by his work on *The History of Sexuality,* Foucault found himself deeply embedded, once again, in the discourse of subjectivity.) Now, to be sure, we must be wary of a fictional collective 'we', an assumed, but in fact unachieved, universality. Benhabib is right to engender questions about a 'philosophical narrative of the formative history of the *subject* of history' which attempts to reconstruct the 'species competencies' of an anonymous subject.[205] However, it can hardly be denied that males and females belong to the same species, and that, in this sense, there *is* an 'anonymous subject' endowed with species competencies. Furthermore, when we turn from biology to ethics and politics, it is clear, I think, that both men and women want for themselves, above and beyond forms of equality, a recognition of some shared humanity. Determining the 'content' of this universality is, of course, a difficult matter, partly empirical, partly normative – and in any case, therefore, a matter for social policy debate and political consensus formation.

What draws me into the discussion Habermas set in motion is my conviction that there are 'evolutionary potentials', utopian-emancipatory potentials, which are already schematized, for our species, in the very nature and character of the medium Merleau-Ponty calls 'the flesh'. In 'The child's relations with others', for example, Merleau-Ponty pointed to 'an anonymous collectivity, an undifferentiated group life'.[206] Many years before this, however, he had already brought out, by virtue of his hermeneutical phenomenology, a 'pre-personal existence', an 'anonymous perception', a mode of relatedness, a mode of intercorporeal channelling, that operates, as he later put it, 'beneath the relation of the knowing subject to the known object'.[207]

Our task in this chapter is to retrieve for present living our sense of that dimension of our embodiment wherein we are both universal and particular, both generalized and individualized: a dimension where there is an unrealized developmental and evolutionary potential, and in the recognition of which it becomes clear that our individuality is – consists in – how we develop, how we achieve, how we redeem, the universality in our relations with others. The character of our individuality *is* this project. But the body which figures in this process is not 'an extra-historical residue, invariant and mute'.[208]

Drive psychology assumes, with Hobbes, our constitutional unsociability; it assumes a body that is anti-social, totally disorganized; it assumes, in Whitebook's words, that 'social norms must be brought in from the outside, "grafted [to quote from David Rappaport] upon the genetically asocial individual" by "discipline and socialization".'[209] Although committed to the ego as the highest possible stage of human development, and therefore, in this sense, tacitly counter-revolutionary, ego psychology has at least the virtue of attempting to explain the social development of the individual by 'tracing the unfolding of the genetically social character of the human individual in the course of his encounter with the social environment'.[210]

Even in its 'original condition', its hypothetical 'state of nature', the infant body is in fact always already informed by an operative schema of the ideal body politic: a schema of organismic principles woven into its tissues, its musculature, its organs and limbs of perception and action: an incarnate dream, born of the flesh. This schema is a programme, an organismic grammar, and it calls for a collective political achievement. At the same time, however, it also calls for a process of individuation, a process the stages of which are not only contributory to the collective achievement, but also essentially dependent on them. Thus, the schema dreams the 'body politic' in both a collective sense and an individual sense. The intention of this chapter is to argue that we must endeavour to retrieve the auditory body's initial schematization of a body politic which would meet its deepest needs and fulfil its oldest dreams. This is work for stage III listening.

We have already had occasion to consider Kohlberg's model of moral self-development, as well as Habermas's argument for an additional stage, beyond Kohlberg's sixth, where 'the principle of the justification of norms is no longer the monologically applicable principle of generalizability, but a communally followed procedure for the discursive redemption of normative validity claims'.[211] At this point, what I want to say is that a listening which retrieves, and thereby grounds itself in, a bodily felt sense of its elemental, field-embedded intertwinings and reversibilities – the intercorporeality of its *Zugehörigkeit*, is exceptionally well qualified to facilitate the achievement of the seventh stage of moral development – and, correspondingly, the social reproduction of a more rational, more reciprocity-governed process of consensus formation.

It is necessary to understand, however, that there are, as Harold Searles states it, 'cultural undercurrents in our present-day society, even in politically democratic countries, [which contribute to the] thwarting of ego-development and the undermining of ego-functioning',[212] and that these undercurrents would be even more intense in their opposition to the stage of self-development we are attempting to flesh out here.

So we come, now, inevitably, to the question of education.

What kind of developmental process, what kind of *Bildungsprozess*, does the corporeal schema we have been articulating call for?

Are all pedagogical processes, processes of self-formation, 'technologies of power'? Is all moral education merely the imposition of social control? Foucault can see no real differences. For him, all teaching is subjugation and domination.[213] I am prepared to concede that moral education is always a form of social control; but I am not willing to ignore extreme differences among the different processes in regard to questions of coercion and control. Neither is the French historian, G. Snyders, whose *Pédagogie en France aux dix-septième et dix-huitième Siècles* documents a significant difference between a 'pedagogy of surveillance' (in the sixteenth and seventeenth centuries) and the more 'natural' teaching and learning advocated, for example, by Rousseau and Pestalozzi (in the century of the Enlightenment).[214]

I shall give only a very brief answer to my questions, but I think it will be sufficient to indicate at least the general direction in which my conception of teaching and learning is moving. What I will say here builds on what I said in *The Body's Recollection of Being*. In a chapter entitled 'Moral education: the body's felt sense of value', I took over the work of Rousseau, Piaget, Erikson, Dewey, Rogers, and Gendlin, and argued for a moral education that develops the body's own implicit sense of value. My principal source of inspiration, however, was Plato. Despite his contempt for the body, *The Republic* and *Laws* chronicle a body-centred, body-respecting conception of child-rearing and education which is extremely suggestive – and quite revolutionary, even by today's standards.

The formative process I have in mind does not coercively *impose* a socially prescribed image on the child's docile body. Instead, it begins with the assumption that the child's body is already informed by ideality, already shaped by a proto-social, and indeed pro-social, schematism: an organismic a priori gracing the child with an implicit sense of normativity. Consequently, the educational process can avoid imposing an external schema – the authoritarian solution. We can work, instead, with the schema already functioning; drawing it out, encouraging its development, supporting the child's initiation of trials and errors. Without making the child conform to an image of the body that alienates him from himself, her from herself, we can model or schematize it, letting it 'transfer' without pressure, simply by virtue of our own bodily presence and 'contagious' comportment. And if we can retrieve our bodily felt sense of the 'ideal body' we ourselves are carrying within us, then we can by its means help the child to make contact with its *own* felt sense of the corporeal image sleeping within it, guiding its retrieval and incorporation. Education works best when it works in harmony with the child's native gifts. Skilful listening is therefore essential, otherwise the social control will be insensitive and alienating, and will not support the child's need for autonomy as the way to bring out the full potential.

But learning is not just for children. Adults also learn – and need to learn. If we adults will really listen to one another, learning can be greatly facilitated, because when we experience being well listened to and really well heard, it becomes easier for us to make felt contact with a sense of our intercorporeality. When we each give the gift of good listening, we help one another to achieve stage III listening: to *hear* the intertwinings and reversibilities which silently function within the echoes, the undercurrents of resonance, set in motion by our listening. And hearing this, we are helped to experience a new *sense* of ourselves, of who, most deeply, we are: not only individuals, different from all others, but human beings, sharing in the flesh, the anonymous intercorporeal subjectivity, of the world.

Now, developing the deeper body, the body schematized by the intertwinings and reversibilities in which we always find ourselves already taking part, is decidedly, at best, an extremely difficult process. But the difficulties we have touched upon are amplified by the fact that the process is one which invariably puts us in conflict with the prevailing social order, since the order, the body politic, which is schematized in the depths of the flesh is radically *different*, and therefore reveals the fact that the prevailing order is historically contingent, historically changeable. Far from giving its support to the dominant body politic, the transhistorical nature of the flesh – especially its communicative intersubjectivity and reversibility – continually contests it, resisting its reifications and evoking ever-new possibilities for progressive social change. (Marx understood this.)

The existence of a schematism deeply engrained in the flesh does not mean that one and only one political system is possible. The schematism is of course determinate, but only partially, and not totally; it is not a totally fixed order.

Moreover, the way in which the schema unfolds or develops is not pre-ordained or automatic: what it becomes is very much a function of prevailing social, political, and cultural conditions, filtered through parents and family. The schematism both limits and enables, both resists and reinforces social conditioning; but it is itself correspondingly *modified* by the particular social conditions – the socialization processes – into which it is cast.

We must avoid both biologism and historicism when we conceptualize the body and its capacity for listening. Foucault's thinking confusedly shifts back and forth between a conception of the body caught in biologism (the body is reduced to a riot of drives) and a conception of the body caught in historicism (the body is assumed to be nothing but a carbon copy reproduction of the prevailing social body). Whilst the second conception may at least empower us with a critical understanding of the operations and effects of power – and with a sense of how our listening, readily alienated, can be used to secure our obedience, the first is also self-defeating: it assumes a body totally bereft of *logos*; consequently, it catastrophically incapacitates us.

There *is* a biological order, a transhistorical order not reducible to social conditioning. But this order is not a totally determinate, totally pre-determined mechanism. Much depends on the character of socialization: it is not a transcendental order; it never appears outside historical conditions. We may also say, here, that there is a *logos*, a certain rationality, deeply inscribed in the flesh. This *logos* is a rudimentary, preliminary schematism that orders, that calls for, its fulfilment: although more than one social arrangement can develop and fulfil what it calls for, what it needs, not all arrangements are equally consonant with, and equally accommodating to, its call. Only some forms of social organization, only some bodies politic, represent genuinely harmonious developments of the reversibility-structure already schematized in and by the flesh. Since this reversibility-structure inherently deconstructs and contests the ultimacy of an ego-logical identity, and since bourgeois capitalism, more than any other social system, honours and promotes the rule of the ego (the ego-centred body), it may fairly be concluded that capitalism cannot be counted among those ideal bodies politic most favourable to the harmonious development of the sociability and rationality-potential inherent in our initial corporeal schematism.

Writing about the 'dreambody' as touchstone for deeply needed changes, Mindell records his conviction

> that the individual of the future, like the individual of today, faces the lonely task of transforming himself, with or without the agreement and understanding of those around him. He needs only to know that transforming himself means coming up against interiorized cultural edges. If this transformation is to occur, he will have to disturb the status quo of the world around him as well. The person in the midst of an individuation process must know that when his symptoms disappear, a new kind of pain is likely to arise: conflict with the history of the world, of which he has been an integral part. How he deals with this conflict is a creative task which no one can predict. But one thing is certain. Becoming an individual means stepping over cultural edges and therefore, paradoxically, also freeing the public to communicate more freely.[215]

In ideal circumstances, the communicativeness of listening is no less important than the communicativeness of speaking – and not merely because, for every speaker, there must be at least one listener, but also because the process of listening *can* be, for both sides, a sense-constituting, thought-forming, need-forming, need-interpreting movement.

Recalling what Harold Searles wrote, in a passage we read earlier, near the end of the section titled 'Needs and their interpretation: listening to inner nature', I want to emphasize just how crucial being listened to and really well heard can be in facilitating the formation, recognition, and interpretation of our feelings, our thoughts, our needs, our motivations. When listening really echoes and resonates, when it allows the communication to reverberate between the communicants, and to constitute, there, a space free of pressure and constraint, it actively contributes, quite apart from the speaking, to the intersubjective constellation of new meanings, meanings actually born within this intercorporeality; and it promises, because of this, the achievement of mutual understanding – if not also consensus.

When all the communicants are listening well to one another, and are also, therefore, being well heard, they are made more aware of the pressures and constraints, the desires and avoidances, the interests and intentions that are blocking the achievement of free communication. And when, moreover, the communicants are actually willing to work at the deepening of their shared sense of a communicatively satisfying listening-space, there is a good chance that they might find themselves *freed* from some of their separateness and oppositeness. The better the listening, the deeper the field of echoes and resonances, informative medium of the intertwinings, transpositions, and reversibilities that already gather us before the trials of reason.

6 A Sense of Justice

In his 'Introduction' to Jürgen Habermas's *Lectures on the Philosophical Discourse of Modernity,* Thomas McCarthy observes that 'the critique of subject-centred reason is a prologue to the critique of a bankrupt culture'.[216] Looking at this same culture, Christopher Lasch pointed out its destructive narcissism, an epidemic social psychopathology distinctive of our modernity.[217] But the critical discourse on modernity has many voices and registers. Here, in this chapter, I have tried to outline how Merleau-Ponty's late work in hermeneutical phenomenology contributes a new sense of subjectivity to the contemporary paradigms of epistemology, ethics, and political theory. What he brings out is the fact that, in the dimensionality of the flesh, in the intertwinings, reversibilities, and communications of its depths, there is already at work a 'miraculous' dialectic, one that suggests the possibility – but of course no more than a possibility – of an alternative cultural direction.

I can hear myself when I listen to the other: I can hear myself *in* the other, or in the position of the other. But the reverse is also true. I can hear the other when I listen to myself; I can hear the other, or the position of the other, *in* myself. Between myself and the other, there are echoes and resonances: extremely deep reverberations that carry enough energy, when they become audible, to deconstruct the boundaries, the armour, fabricated by our ego-logical subjectivities: reverberations that will mix, blend, even reverse our role identifications. We do not 'normally' hear this dialectic of reversibility: it calls for effort – and method. For the most part, in fact, it is not something we would *want* to hear. Too disquieting, too unsettling. Moreover, even if we do hear it, or were to hear it, it would often not be at all sufficient to resolve conflicts of interest and power, forms of dissonance which are generated within larger structural and institutional dimensions.

Nevertheless, it would be a mistake to underestimate the significance of this dialectic, which Merleau-Ponty unfortunately borrowed the word 'narcissism' to describe, because it articulates the normativity of a corporeal schema in which a new form of subjectivity is already in operation: a form of subjectivity in which, and for which, interdependence, a sense of shared humanity, and a basic familiarity with reciprocity are of the very essence.

Just as, for Habermas, the 'ideal speech situation' is necesssarily implied in the competency structure of speech itself, so the reciprocity that is necessary in the constitution of a rational and just social order is an organismic 'fulfilment' implied in the structural reversibilities that already organize and predispose the flesh. (I am using the term 'fulfilment', here, in its Husserlian sense, according to which it describes, for example, the perception of a crow anticcipated by our hearing of its raucous calls.)

The subject of a society organized in consonance with the body-self that is deeply schematized in the reversibilities of intercorporeality must await, however, another time to be examined further. Suffice it to say here, perhaps, that the corporeal schema laid out in our intercorporeality constitutes a very difficult social task. The task it projects is certainly feasible; but it requires the most careful cultivation, particularly consequential in early childhood socialization, of a potential, a moral capacity, latent in the flesh. (Here we connect with the problematic Habermas works on in 'Moral development and ego identity'.) The task also requires, I believe, a cultural critique of the hegemony of the visual paradigm in the life of western civilization. For, if Merleau-Ponty should be right, and 'there is', as he words it, 'a fundamental narcissism in all vision', then the dominance of vision in our social and political life cannot be without disturbing consequences. In my book, *The Opening of Vision*, I have wrestled with this problematic. But it is by no means evident that we know, both individually and as a society, how to respond to the gift, the suppressed utopian dream, of the human flesh.

For this reason, I try to keep in mind what Merleau-Ponty once wrote about the contribution of philosophical enquiry to the discourse on modernity: 'Philosophy is not a particular body of knowledge; it is the vigilance which does not let us forget the source of all knowledge.'[218] And if we hear the *literal* body brought to speech here, what is said, as it were, in excess gives us much to think about.

The moral values, social ideals, and political principles of Enlightenment humanism did not suddenly appear *ex nihilo* in the modern world. Many people would say, I think, that they formed, rather, in response to historical conditions. I agree. But I would like to add that they carried forward, life-affirmingly, values that are inherent in, and constitutive of, our most universal organismic capacities.

In 'The idea of equality', Bernard Williams argued that some of the capacities with which we are endowed as human beings – for example, our capacity to feel pain and our capacity to perceive suffering and misery in others, give rise to moral claims, claims on ourselves and on others, that we should not disregard or neglect.[219] According to John Rawls, 'a sense of justice' is one of these 'capacities'.[220] And there is, he thinks, a 'higher-order interest' in the exercise and development of this capacity. (Such an interest seems, in fact, to be constitutive of *all* our capacities. Sullivan describes 'the child's pleasure in manifesting any ability he has achieved', and Rawls codifies the point in his 'Aristotelian Principle': 'other things being equal, human beings enjoy the exercise of their realised capacities . . . and this enjoyment increases the more the capacity is realised'.)[221] I agree with Rawls that the 'sense of justice' is a capacity, and that, wherever this capacity manifests, it 'calls' for recognition, exercise, and development. I would say that it constellates a distinctive 'need', and what Williams defines as a 'moral claim'. But, whereas Rawls construes the 'sense' in our 'sense of justice' to be a cognitive disposition or endowment, a form of understanding, I want to root it in our bodily sensibility. More specifically, I want to ground it experientially in the communicative reversibilities of the *auditory* body. Since (1) the capacity to hear binds us to others in a dialectic of reversibilities, and (2) justice involves a reciprocity that *depends* on reversibility, the stage III development of our capacity for listening exercises and develops our (bodily felt) sense of justice. The primary *sense* of justice is not seeing, but hearing. The sense of justice is channelled through the most communicative, most sensitively attuned of senses: our capacity for listening.

Children begin life expected to listen with simple, unquestioning obedience. As they mature, they are expected to listen and question, substituting reflection for obedience and conformity. But there is a listening, a highly developed capacity, which is obedient to justice: obedient by virtue of its deeply cultivated sense of the reversibilities that are always silently attuning it.

In this chapter, we have brought out a 'source' of moral and political 'knowlege', and we have traced our 'sense of justice' to our capacity for listening. We have found, in the reversibilities of an auditory flesh, an organismic basis for the principle of reciprocity. We have also explored why reciprocity, a necessary condition of social justice, may be said to 'carry forward' and 'fulfil' that need which an organismic reversibility, audible even in narcissism, primarily inaugurates – and for which it demands the most vigilant, most enduring recognition.

The auditory body's primal schematization of reciprocity, grace though it is, nevertheless leaves to us a very difficult historical task. In a recent essay on 'The return of values', sociologist Alan Wolfe observed that the 'major question facing a revival of moral sociology is whether it is possible to posit ties that can hold people together without subjecting them to historical traditions or political decisions over which they have no control'.[222] My project for this chapter has been to suggest how the auditory nature of the human body holds the beginning of an unexplored answer to this question.

Against Nietzsche, against Freud, against Lacan, against Marcuse, and against Foucault, I have argued for the following propositions. (1) It is not true that the only order in the human body is an order totally imposed by society, and that its order is nothing but the accumulated historical effect of political controls. (2) The human body has – is – an order of its own. (3) This order is not inherently aggressive. On the contrary, it is already pro-social: in other words, the body's pro-social behaviour is not, and does not need to be, totally introduced by the work of society. (4) It is of course basic, and needs to be socialized. Society's work of socialization, and its conception of moral development, should respect, and be responsive to, the primal, transhistorical order already inherent in the child's auditory body. If pro-social behavioural tendencies are already present in the biological endowment of the child, constituting, in effect, an implicate moral order, then education can indeed be a process of bringing out and drawing out; but if human beings are innately 'nasty and brutish', aggressive and hostile, then education must be a process of imposing constraints. My commitment to the first of these two conceptions implies a faith in enlightened education – education directed by the ideal of autonomy.

(5) Reciprocity is a socially produced discursive order; it is also the only order we know of that adequately carries forward the surprising reversibilties in which the body's own order is manifest. In stage III listening, we need to develop our awareness of these reversibilities. (6) In the phenomenology of 'narcissism' that Merleau-Ponty articulates, we can hear our awakening to the ethics of reciprocity: we can hear it taking form in the character of the body's primal order. (7) Working for social justice today calls for 'promoting new forms of subjectivity', as Foucault finally argued. And this means collaborating with the inherently pro-social order of our auditory bodies to achieve in society at large a level of moral development in which questions of social justice, and the communicative procedures that reflection on these questions requires, are of paramount concern: a possibility we cannot recognize, I believe, without understanding that neither the monadic ego (in the discourse of Cartesian metaphysics) nor the chaotic body of drives (in the discourse of Freudian psychoanalysis) should continue to represent for us the distinctive social character, the distinctive communicativeness, of the human self.

When we are thinking about how we can retrieve for present living the *sense* of justice that is deeply inscribed in the auditory flesh of our being, it is well to bear in mind that the story of Narcissus is, after all, a story of *lost* self-recognition.

Part VII
Consensus and Difference

Opening Conversation

'Of these faculties, for the mere necessities of life and in itself, sight is the more important; but for the mind [*nous*] and indirectly [*kata symbebēkos*], hearing is the more important . . . because it makes the largest contribution to wisdom. For discourse, which is the cause of learning, is so because it is audible; but it is audible not in itself, but indirectly, because speech is composed of words.' [Aristotle, *On Sense and Sensible Objects*, 437a4–17] The point of the matter is that he [Aristotle] seems never to have remembered this observation when he wrote philosophy.

Arendt, *The Life of the Mind*[223]

The occasion, the company, the very sound of my voice, draws more from my mind than I find in it when I sound it and use it by myself.

Montaigne, *Essays*[224]

It is characteristic of cultural gestures to awaken in all others at least an echo, if not a consonance.

Merleau-Ponty, 'The indirect language'[225]

Diversity is a sign of wholeness in individuals and in civilization. But wholeness, too, must have defined boundaries. In the present state of our civilization, it is not yet possible to foresee whether or not a more *universal identity* promises to embrace all the diversities and dissonances, relativities and mortal dangers which emerge with technological and scientific progress.

Erikson, *Identity, Youth and Crisis*[226]

We can only say 'the same' [in contrast to 'the equal' or 'the identical'] if we think difference. It is in the carrying out and settling of differences that the gathering nature of sameness comes to light. . . . The same gathers what is distinct into an original being-at-one. The equal, on the contrary, disperses them into the dull unity of mere uniformity.

Heidegger, 'Poetically man dwells'[227]

An emancipated society . . . would not be a unitary state, but the realization of universality in the reconciliation of differences. Politics that are still seriously concerned with such a society ought not, therefore, to propound the abstract equality of men even as an idea. Instead, they should point to the bad equality today . . . and conceive the better state

> as one in which people could be different without fear.
>
> Adorno, *Minima Moralia*[228]

> Discourse ethics . . . requires that controversies over the validity of contested norms be settled through an argumentative process in which the *consensus of all concerned* decides upon the legitimacy of the controversial norm. Participation precedes universalizability. The old adage, 'no taxation without representation', is now reformulated as 'no universalizability without participation'.
>
> Benhabib, *Critique, Norm and Utopia*[229]

> Communicative ethics proceeds from the Kantian insight that the validity of specific norms is to be established in light of a procedure which first defines the ground of all normative validity, and this is the rational consensus of all concerned.
>
> Benhabib, *Critique, Norm and Utopia*[230]

> Discourses about needs and motives unfold in this space created by commonality and uniqueness, general societal processes, and the contingency of individual life histories.
>
> Benhabib, *Critique, Norm and Utopia*[231]

> We must assume that discourses are processes through which *new* needs and interests, such as can lead to a consensus among the participants, emerge.
>
> Benhabib, *Critique, Norm and Utopia*[232]

The traditional conception of rationality, the paradigm which has dominated the lifeworld of modernity, is oculocentric, monological, and authoritarian. And it privileges the rationality of a speculative thinker, a man of theoretical vision, a man whose time, however, will ultimately be justified on instrumental grounds.

In the 'Preface' he wrote for *The Phenomenology of Perception*, Merleau-Ponty distanced himself from this conception: 'But the meditating Ego, the "impartial spectator" (*uninteressierter Zuschauer*), do not rediscover *an already given rationality* [to which they conform in blind obedience]; they establish themselves, and establish it, by an act of initiative which has no guarantee in being, its justification resting entirely on the effective power which it confers on us of taking our own history upon ourselves.'[233] His steps were needed – are needed. But they are only a beginning. What is a satisfying alternative to the traditional conception? If we adopt a rationality always 'in the making', are we compelled to let its truth, its processes of justification, rest entirely on pragmatism? What, in any case, does 'pragmatism' mean? And when we take the settling of rationality claims out of the traditional monologue and locate it in dialogues and debates, how do we work with the differences, the sometimes irreconcilable conflicts in position, that the picture of the monologue invariably conceals?

There is, to be sure, a long history of contractual rationality, and we, readers and author, have all, directly or indirectly, enjoyed some of its benefits. But it must be understood that, because of the extreme inequalities and injustices, the marginalizations and exclusions structured into our social order, some people have benefited much more than others, whilst some have been disadvantaged by it and some even miserably destroyed.

Today, we are obliged to acknowledge that the 'universalistic promise' of bourgeois consent theories has not been fulfilled.[234] Today, in fact, there is a real crisis in the consensual basis of our social world. The traditional forms of integration and consensus no longer work, but new forms of integration and legitimation, non-authoritarian forms more consonant with individual and collective autonomies, have not as yet emerged.[235] What has happened?

Our steady progress toward democratic pluralism, glorious, certainly, in principle, makes the old institutions of consensus unworkable: there seem to be no collectively shared understandings, no sufficiently shared contexts of life, from which the consensual process can begin. Even the consensus model requires *some* presuppositions. Today, this is extremely problematic. Progress toward ending social injustices and inequalities, and changing the conditions which produce them, has created almost as much social conflict and, correlatively, almost as much cynicism, despair, and distrust, as it has consensus, a spirit of hope, and popular faith in the possibility of a genuinely rational and humane society. Paradoxically, our progress in addressing social ills by constitutional means, or by means validated by long-standing, normatively secured institutions, has been accompanied by an increasing *delegitimation* of the entire system. It seems that our progress only makes us ever more conscious of the inadequacies, the limits and the failures of the system – and even of rationality itself. Thus it seems that progress only *increases* our demands on the processes of legitimation, weighting them with the task of achieving a genuinely new form of moral and cultural integration – much more, in short, than the already substantial task of accomplishing a rational consensus.

Moreover, as Habermas has argued, the increasingly technocratic organization of our society, establishing the hegemony of an economic and administrative, essentially cognitive-instrumental rationality, has seriously disturbed the 'communicative infrastructure of everyday life', subordinating, and to some extent even suppressing, long-standing forms and channels of communicative rationality, and jeopardizing the cognitive and utopian-emancipatory 'potentials' inherent in the moral-practical sphere.[236] This, I think, is the point at stake in Merleau-Ponty's condensed and rather cryptic assertion that we should begin to think of the world 'as primary embodiment of rationality'.[237]

One of Habermas's major contributions to the philosophical discourse on society and politics is his formulation of a communicative or discursive concept of reason. As Benhabib notes: 'Habermas maintains that it is not the mind's cogitative relation to an object or to a state of affairs which defines truth, nor is it some unique, undefinable quality of actions and affairs, incommunicable to others, that defines the validity of norms. Both truth claims and normative validity claims are public assertions that can only be tested and contested argumentatively.'[238] For Habermas, then, this new concept of reason forms the basis for a consensus theory of legitimation, but also lays the ground for a consensus theory of *truth*, proposing a conception of 'universality' which, unlike the conception that has governed all progressive social movements since the beginning of the Enlightenment, understands in the principle of recognizing different points of view and models a way of working with them: a conception, therefore, which does not suppress, deny, or exclude dissonant voices, but encourages us, and helps us, to listen and hear them.

In 'Kantian constructivism in moral theory', Rawls claims

that, according to his conception, 'the search for reasonable grounds for reaching agreement rooted in our conception of ourselves and in our relation to society replaces the search for moral truth. . . . What justifies a conception of justice is . . . its congruence with our deeper understanding of ourselves and our aspirations.'[239] This is appealing – though it depends on the 'deeper understanding'. In this case, however, there is no deeper understanding of the auditory body and of our self-development as beings endowed with a capacity for listening communicatively.

Rawls's constructivism formulates a significant amendment of the 'rational universality' advocated – but not without self-contradiction – by philosophers committed to the ideals of the bourgeois Enlightenment. Nevertheless, his revision falls short of an interactive, communicatively achieved universalism, and is rooted in a conception of ourselves which abstracts from our identity as social, historical, embodied beings. And, because of this abstraction, Rawls cannot root his universalism in the emancipatory potential of a self-understanding that is deepened through the communicative process – deepened by participation in discursive processes free of coercion and governed by reciprocity. In other words, Rawls not only stops short of a genuinely discursive universality, but, because of *this* shortcoming, he also misses an opportunity to conceptualize a self whose self-understanding is developed, is deepened, by the experience of taking part in such communicative processes. And this, in turn, means that, conversely, he misses an opportunity to relate the achievement of a progressively more rational consensus to the deepening of our self-understanding as a consequence of our learning more evolved communicative processes.

In a paper calling for the recognition of the concrete other, Benhabib writes, very much to the point, that

> While agreeing that normative disputes can be rationally settled, and that fairness, reciprocity, and some procedures of universalizability are constituents, that is, necessary conditions of the moral standpoint, *interactive universalism* regards difference as a starting point for reflection and action. In this sense, 'universality' is a regulative ideal that does not deny our embodied and embedded identity, but aims at developing moral attitudes and encouraging political transformations

> that can yield a point of view acceptable to all. Universality is not the ideal consensus of fictitiously defined selves, but the concrete process, in politics and morals, of the struggle of concrete, embodied selves, striving for autonomy.[240]

I submit that we cannot form an adequate conception of 'interactive universalism' as a concrete process of embodied selves without understanding, and taking into account, our capacity for listening, our potential for self-development as auditory beings, and the two-way causality between the realization of *this* potential and the realization of the 'rational consensus' potential implicit in discursive situations.

Now, we have noted that Habermas proposed a consensus theory of truth as part of his consensus universalism. According to Benhabib, 'this leads [him] to claim that *truth*, interpreted as the attainment of rational consensus, involves the norms of *freedom* (the right to concede to the force of the better argument alone) and *justice* (the reciprocal and symmetrical distribution of rights among participants)'.[241] These three concepts are tightly woven together in his model of the 'ideal speech situation'. Benhabib concisely summarizes the four conditions of the 'ideal speech situation' as follows:

> first, each participant must have an equal chance to initiate and to continue communication; second, each must have an equal chance to make assertions, recommendations, and explanations, and to challenge justifications. Together we can call these the 'symmetry condition'. Third, all must have equal chances as actors to express their wishes, feelings, and intentions; and fourth, the speakers must act *as if* in contexts of action there is an equal distribution of chances 'to order and resist orders, to promise and to refuse, to be accountable for one's conduct, and to demand accountability from others'.[242]

The latter two she calls 'the reciprocity condition', remarking that while 'the symmetry stipulation of the ideal speech situation refers to *speech acts* alone, and to conditions governing their employment, the reciprocity condition refers to existing *action contexts*, and requires a suspension of situations of untruthfulness and duplicity on the one hand, and of inequality and subordination on the other' (ibid.). In other words,

> 'The ideal speech situation' describes a set of *rules* which participants in a discourse would have to follow (the symmetry condition), and a set of *relationships* (the reciprocity condition) which would have to obtain between them, if we were to say of the agreement they reach that it was rationally motivated, dependent on the force of the better argument alone. (ibid).

Now, about this reciprocity as a condition necessary for consensus, Habermas says:

> competent agents will – independently of accidental commonalities of social origin, tradition, basic attitude, and so on – be in agreement about such a fundamental point of view only if it arises from the very structures of possible interaction. The reciprocity between acting subjects is such a point of view.[243]

Merleau-Ponty's phenomenology confirms this analysis. It brings out a reciprocity structure always implicit in the speech situation: 'the acquisition of language is itself a phenomenon of identification. To learn to speak is to learn to play a series of roles, to assume a series of conducts or linguistic gestures.'[244] Thus, in the very process of learning to speak, we learn the reversibility of positions and roles that is necessary for the demanding practice of reciprocity. But listening, too, teaches us reversibility: to listen to another is to learn what the world is like from a position that is not one's own; to listen is to reverse position, role, and experience. To refuse this reversibility is to refuse to listen.

For Habermas, there is an *ideal* speech situation; and that means that our speech is governed by critical norms. But in stage III listening, we exercise our understanding of the fact that there is also an ideal *listening* situation: an entire problematic which Habermas does not acknowledge. However, it should be clear by now that listening is also governed, at least tacitly, by norms and standards; and furthermore, that listening is a capacity the developmental stages of which are normatively related to our self-development as moral agents.

Habermas tries to establish the norm of reciprocity by demonstrating its implicit operation in the reversibilities of the speech situation. But our work in this book has brought out the fact that, in the *Zugehörigkeit* of our listening, we are always already 'obedient' to intercorporeal reversibilities: processes which, in effect, implicitly constitute a corporeal schematization of the ideal reciprocity relations in which, and as which, they would be genuinely fulfilled.

Although Habermas recognizes a significant correlation between ego identity and moral development, he does not give thought to the fact that listening is a developmental capacity, and that its developmental stages are normatively related to our self-development as moral agents. We have already noted that the word 'obedience' means 'listening from below'. Now if, as Erikson and Kohlberg have demonstrated, obedience manifests a very early stage of moral development, should we not suppose that the obedience-listening correlation continues, and that, as obedience gives way to an ethics of autonomy, responsibility and care for others, the capacity for listening would not only undergo corresponding maturational changes, but would also, by virtue of these very changes, contribute to, and facilitate, the further development of moral character as a whole? This is the kind of thing I have in mind when I say that Habermas ignores our embodiment. His neglect is unfortunate: because of it, he misses the normative, moral-political *groundwork* already performed by our perceptual experience.

Just as one can derive the normative conditions of an 'ideal' speech situation 'from the very structure' of speech situations as such, so, correlatively, one can derive the normative conditions of an 'ideal' listening situation 'from the very structure' of the listening process as such. (The phrase 'from the very structure' comes from the Habermas text last quoted.) Moreover, one can even derive a partial formulation of the normative conditions of an 'ideal' *speech* situation from the very structure of listening interactions as such. The practical implication, here, is that one way – indeed, an extremely important and perhaps extremely effective way – for us, both as individuals and as a society, to approximate the conditions of the 'ideal speech situation' is for us to work on developing our capacity for listening – and, in particular, to work on rooting our listening in the intertwinings and reversibilities manifest through a bodily felt sense of the intercorporeal echoes and resonances, consonances and dissonances constitutive of our auditory relations with others.

By virtue of such practised listening, we can reach a generalized other mediated and enriched by our experiencing of concrete others. Moreover, whereas the thought experiment of the monological ego is fulfilled once it achieves a clear determination of the position of a *generalized* other, the phenomenology of listening always brings us back to others in their concrete individuality. This process accordingly *reverses* the Kantian procedure for learning and achieving a shared understanding, for in the Kantian, our ethical movement toward the other is always mediated, first, by a *generalization* of the concrete other.

In 'The intertwining – the chiasm', Merleau-Ponty says that 'like crystal, like metal and many other substances, I am a sonorous being'.[245] This is true. But, as he knows, we are beings distinguished from all other sonorous species by the grace of our capacity for language. The extent of our sonorous capacity, however, is not sufficiently recognized by the rules and practices which govern the 'normal' consensus-forming situation. And it follows from this, moreover, that the full register of our sonorous nature cannot be fulfilled within the conditions established for speech by our cognitive-instrumental rationality.

There is a dimensionality of our sonorous nature not contained by, and not channelled through, the structures of language. There is more to communication than language. There is more to language than its cognitive-instrumental content. In every discursive situation, there are consonances and dissonances, echoes and resonances which remain unspoken – and which perhaps cannot be spoken. There are consonances and dissonances, echoes and resonances, tones and undercurrents of meaning, of sense, of feeling, communicated only through the listening-space *around* language and *between* language, or *by* it, but not *in* it.

The point is that a theory of rationally motivated consensus cannot limit itself to the formulation of conditions pertaining only to speech; it must also take into account what hearing hears, and what our listening is capable of hearing. Our hearing can hear what has not been said; we can hear the communication of matters that speech denies it wants to say – or that speech is afraid to say. If ideology involves the systematic distortion of communicative processes, the rational consensus model depends as much on skilful listening as on truthful speaking. Skilful stage III listening can often detect ideological distortions, lies, deceptions, and empty words, words with a hollow ring: long before research, long before critical, theoretical analysis, listening can catch the dissonance, the contradiction.

The older, more Kantian model of rational consensus assumes a conception of rationality which our experience as listeners contests. As listeners, we know that rationality can be aesthetic and expressive, as well as cognitive and instrumental: our listening is not fooled by formal procedures and technical vocabularies. Sometimes, there is an audible violence in the measured speech of cognitive-instrumental rationality.

The older, more Kantian model of consensus defines its universality in terms of a *generalized* other. This may seem plausible in so far as we think of consensus as an approximation to an ideal speech situation. But as soon as we attempt to take the process of listening into account – that is, as soon as we realize the *necessity* of taking it into account, this conception manifests its deficiencies. Listening reminds us that consensus depends on *concrete* others, and that universality cannot be legitimate unless it is achieved by the talking and listening of flesh-and-blood people.

Each human being enters the public discourse, the debates of the body politic, in a different register. Can we hear the individual differences? Can their different registers of dissonance be gathered with equal respect into the harmony of a body politic? And must their consonance mean an obedience in which all differences are silenced? What kind of harmony do we need to hear?

In his most recent work, Habermas makes it clear that his notion of the generalized other is different from the Kantian: that his notion is only a way of conceptualizing the fairness conditions established by a group of concrete individuals, each one 'other' for the others. And he emphasizes his conviction that respecting irreconcilable differences is more important than forcing agreement or consensus. Thus, he is more concerned about the establishment of a fair procedure, a procedure respecting the differences and ensuring that they will be spoken and heard, than he is about the achievement of consensus. It is this concrete solution to the procedural question which his notion of the generalized other is meant to address.

The theory of cognitive dissonance, influential today in cognitive psychology, and in pedagogies based on this psychology, rationalizes and conceals the experience of dissonance: it legitimates those who do not hear the dissonance. Considered politically, this is a dangerous theory. So I hope that the effect of this book, and of this chapter, in particular, is to facilitate the hearing of dissonance – to make dissonance more audible.

In 'Body/power', Foucault declared: 'I believe that the great fantasy is the idea of a social body constituted by the universality of wills. For the phenomenon of the social body is the effect, not of consensus, but of the materiality of power operating upon the very bodies of individuals.'[246] Foucault's declaration provokes many questions. What is wrong with this 'fantasy' if it channels our energies toward the achievement of such universality? Can there be a universality which is not coercive? Even if our social body is the historical effect of the materiality of power, by what logic are we compelled to suppose that consensus is impossible – that we cannot possibly achieve, and should not even strive to achieve, a social body based on (a more) rational consensus?

Is Foucault attempting to report *what is* (facts, contingent truths), or is he proclaiming *what must be*? We may assume that he is not an advocate of historical determinism. So, then, we are free to *change* our social 'reality'. But if we are going to remake our society, is it not useful, even necessary, to think, to dream, to imagine what a better society would be like? But if imagining a different social body is useful, even necessary, why does Foucault totally reject the utopian-emancipatory images that individuals can create from out of the experience of their own bodies? By rejecting the possibility of a social body based on consensus, Foucault has in fact *betrayed* the very bodies of individuals. Even though the word *consensus* comes from the sense and sensibilities of the body, Foucault would have us *suppress* this dream of the body. Against Foucault, therefore, I want to argue that the intercorporeal nature of the auditory body is rooted in reversibility, and that our bodies accordingly *dream* of a consensus in the reciprocities of which this reversibility would be realized and fulfilled.

But where can we begin? Foucault's analysis of power actually gives us a hint, a powerful strategy. Since power is omnipresent, we need to make use of it to create 'free spaces' for good listening within the infrastructures of existing institutions: places where we can gather, and can begin to give to one another the kind of listening we need in order to build a more just, a more individuating, and also a more harmonious social order.

All around the world, now, wherever injustice cries out and the truth dares to sing, oppressed groups of people are struggling for their freedom. What their diverse efforts, their gestures, their movements, will ultimately bring forth cannot be guessed. The availability of advanced technology is rapidly making the totalitarian authority of the state, both regimes on the 'left' and regimes on the 'right', more pervasive and intrusive. Those of us who are living at a 'comfortable distance' from the daily struggles of the oppressed, and who are tempted into thinking that some, at least, are beyond the reach of corrupted power and the violence it creates, need to be reminded that everyone, without exception, is ultimately gathered into the Great Gathering, the *Logos*, of the Fourfold – the gathering, that is, of earth and sky, gods and mortals – and need, moreover, to be warned: warned not to turn deaf ears when voices in our midst call attention, again and again, to the powerful forms of silencing that even the most democratic of societies continue to impose on their people – but impose, invariably with the most extreme harshness, on the brave guardians of listening.

As a way of summarizing the thought-steps that led us to this point, and indicating also where, in Chapter Six, we are headed, I have prepared a diagram, Table 5.1, which I would like, now, very briefly, to explain.

The Being of beings presences in different ways, different modes of presence, in the economies of different historical epochs. Thus, audible beings present themselves – are present to our hearing – in different auditory *Gestalten*, different structurations of their presencing, in different historical times. At the present time, the presencing (*das Anwesen*) of what is present (*das Anwesende*) has the historical character of a totalized presence (*Anwesenheit*): a closed auditory *Gestalt* fixated by the relation of a 'subject' to its 'object'. Audible entities (*das Seiende*) are reduced to the beingness (*Seiendheit*) of ready-to-hand subjects and objects. And the dimensionality of Being itself (*das Sein*), as the field in its presencing, is submitted to the pressures and violence of an

Table 5.1 Modernity and Our Future: A Model of Two Epistemes

Episteme	*(I) Modernity*	*(II) A Possible Future*
(1) *Gestalt* name	*Gestell*: enframing	*Geviert*: gathering
(2) *Gestalt* character	Totality (closed *Gestalt*)	Whole (open *Gestalt*)
(3) Paradigm	Vision	Listening
(4) Paradigm's culture of origin	Greek	Jewish
(5) Dominant field character	Spatial: constant, total presence	Temporal: presence/absence
(6) Truth character	Representational correctness	*Alētheia* (unconcealment)
(7) Types of normativity	Pre-conventional, Conventional, Post-conventional	Communicative: recognition of concrete others
(8) Political legitimacy	Assumed universality	Universality in the making
(9) Most mature developmental stage	Ego	Self
(10) Epistemological attitude	Grasping and objectifying	Letting be (will to power overcome)
(11) Ontological commitment	Objects (Metaphysics of presence)	Beings as beings (Hermeneutics)

economy of presence ruled by the forces unleashed by a technocratically organized totalization.

The table shows two columns (I and II), the first of which describes the *episteme* I am calling 'modernity', or 'the present', whereas the second describes the *episteme* of a utopian-emancipatory potential, which I am calling a 'future post-modern possibility'. The term 'episteme' comes from Foucault's 'archaeology', and refers to necessary, pervasive, and anonymous forms of thought. An *episteme* is the 'historical a priori' which, 'in a given period, delimits in the totality of experience a field of knowledge, defines the mode of being of the objects that appear in that field, provides man's everyday perception with theoretical powers, and defines the conditions in which he can sustain a discourse about things that is recognised to be true'.[247] To some extent, the *episteme* therefore resembles the Kuhnian paradigm; it is, however, the regime of a paradigm corresponding to different epochs in western thought.[248] In the table shown here, I am projecting the *episteme* of a future, post-modern possibility – a utopian-emancipatory potential toward the realization of which I am suggesting that we ought to work.

On the extreme left side are the eleven factors in terms of which the present, and the future possibility I am schematizing, are described and contrasted. Factor 1 is a specification of the *episteme* as perceptual *Gestalt*. I follow Heidegger in holding that, in the modern epoch, an epoch of closure, a closure of Being, the *Gestalt* is 'enframed' and 'enframing': a fixated structure he terms the *Gestell*. And I hold, with Heidegger, that we can conceptualize the possibility of a radically different *Gestalt*: a *Gestalt*, namely, which is open and gathering: a *Geviert*. More on this in Chapter Six.

Factor 2 indicates, in column I, the character of the *Gestalt* that rules in our modern epoch and, in column II, the possibility of a *Gestalt* of very different character: an open whole, rather than a closed totality. (This difference was first suggested by the work of Erik Erikson. It is a difference that can be fleshed out with the help of Merleau-Ponty's phenomenology of perception and Fritz Perls's *Gestalt* therapy.)

Factor 3 is the mode or channel of perception that predominates in these modern and post-modern *epistemes* and determines in fundamental ways the other 'properties' of the *epistemes*. I am saying (1) that, since ancient times, vision has generated not only our paradigm of knowledge, truth, and reality, but even the normativity peculiar to our ethical and political life, and (2) that, in modern times, the hegemony of vision – oculocentrism – has been particularly determinative and consequential. (In *The Opening of Vision*, I connected the hegemony of vision to the advent of nihilism.)

The guiding thought underlying the project of this book is that we need a new historical paradigm, and that listening would be a much better channel for realizing our utopian-emancipatory potential, both as individuals and as collectivities. This is a thought which first struck me when, many years ago, I noticed Heidegger's shift from a discourse of vision (very important in *Being and Time*) to a discourse of listening (crucial in his texts on the pre-Socratics), and found the key to an explanation for this shift in the work of Hans Jonas, whose historical studies on perception I was reading concurrently. Recently, I located a brief formulation of this critical thought in Hannah Arendt's *The Life of the Mind.*[249] She is more conscious than Jonas of the nihilism at work in the *episteme* of vision, but she thinks of listening only as a missed alternative, a possibility whose time is past. For her, there is no Benjaminian redemption of this past.

Factor 4 is the culture within which the paradigm originated. The paradigm that has dominated western thinking and living is a paradigm which can be traced back to ancient Greece. For the Greeks, to know is to see, or be able to see. Seeing is knowing. Their word for 'know' actually *means* 'see'. In the Jewish tradition, however, it was listening, and not seeing, which generated the paradigm of knowledge, truth, normativity, and reality. For, as Jonas has argued, the Jewish God could be heard but not seen; and the Jewish conception of truth correspondingly relied on listening, rather than seeing. (See Hans Jonas, *The Phenomenon of Life* and *Von der Mythologie zur mystischen Philosophie*, the second volume of *Gnosis und spätantiker Geist*. Arendt refers to these historical analyses in *The Life of the Mind*, 111–112). I am arguing, then, that, in order to overcome the history of nihilism, the will to power, and the metaphysics of presence, we must retrieve the listening paradigm that originated in the ancient culture of the Jewish people. And I am arguing, further, that this retrieval is necessary for the realization of the utopian-emancipatory potential inherent in our personal lives and social forms.

Factor 5 specifies the dominant 'field character' of the two paradigms. In the oculocentric *episteme* of modernity, spatiality prevails over temporality. But this means that what rules ontology is a constant, uniform, continuous presence: vision surveys a spatial totality of contemporaneous coexistences. In the post-modern, post-metaphysical *episteme* projected as the task of this book, temporality would no longer be subordinated. And because of the nature of listening, the traditional metaphysics of presence would give way to a hermeneutics of presence/absence: experiences of impermanence and incompleteness, experiences of arising, staying, and perishing.

Factor 6 is the character of truth. In the *episteme* of modernity, truth is solely a question of correctness: correctness of representation. In the *episteme* whose post-modern possibility we are contemplating here, it would be understood that truth in its *primary* sense is *alētheia*, unconcealment.

Factor 7 is the normativity of ethics: how norms function, or should function, in the sociality of daily life. In modernity, three main types of normativity have evolved: (1) the pre-conventional (obedience, conformity), (2) the conventional (mutual interpersonal expectations, agreements, and contracts), and (3) the post-conventional (rationally argued rights and duties, and procedural applications of universal principles). (See the Kohlberg model outlined in Chapter One.) But in the post-modern society of the future, the society projected in this book, ethics would be understood, and practised, as a communicative, discursive recognition of concrete others, and not only as a matter of abstract principles concerned with the procedural recognition of a generalized other.

Factor 8 is political legitimacy. In the democracies of modernity, there is always an assumed universality. But in the post-modern society that we are grounding in listening, the universality of rational consensus formation would always be in the making – an achievement of communicative processes.

Factor 9 concerns forms of subjectivity. For modernity, the highest, most mature stage of personal development is identified with the vision of the (socially adapted) ego, whereas, in the utopian society whose future we are projecting, this stage would be identified with the listening Self, whose continual openness to dialogue, and to the processes of personal growth this involves, is what defines it and differentiates it from the ego.

Factor 10 is the fundamental epistemological attitude. In our oculocentric modernity, it is grasping and objectifying: in the society which realizes our utopian-emancipatory potential, it would be grounded in the skilfulness of an auditory 'letting-be'.

Finally, we come to factor 11, the question of ontological commitment. Here the contrast between modernity and our more utopian future would be drawn in terms of the difference between objects (persons and things reduced to an ontology of objects) and beings (persons and things recognized for what they are). It is my contention that the epistemological attitude and its correlate, our ontological commitment, which I have projected into a post-modern, utopian future, can only be achieved in so far as we renounce the visual *episteme* and endeavour to work out the historical implications of an *episteme* constellated within the communicativeness of listening.

In *Heidegger on Being and Acting*, an important new book, Reiner Schürmann effectively deploys Foucault's concept of the *episteme* to articulate Heidegger's history of Being in terms of a history of epochal economies of presence: the different ways in which presencing has come to presence, has presented itself, in the different epochs of world history. Drawing on the analyses of Jonas and Arendt, Schürmann suggests that the 'turning' (*Kehre*) toward which Heidegger attempts to gather our thinking calls for a 'retraining of hearing'.[250] He does not attempt, however, to give further direction to the challenge in this call.

In the next chapter, we will begin the fourth stage of such a retraining. We will attempt a recollection of Being channeled through the auditory body. We shall retrieve the sense of Being we enjoy in *Zugehörigkeit*: a sense that is not, and cannot be, totally determined by our prevailing epochal economy. Through this retrieval, we shall move somewhat closer to an experience of the intertwining of all beings. And this, in turn, may help prepare us for the advent of a different economy of presence – the economy, perhaps, in which the presencing of Being brings us together in a 'gathering of the Fourfold'.

The Greek verb *legein* means 'gathering' and 'setting out'. In the next part of the book, I shall argue that there is a *logos* in our capacity to hear, for listening is a gathering and a setting out, laying out a communicative field and gathering together the sounds of the elements – earth and sky – and all forms of life – above all, the voices of our 'gods', who are the projections of our embodied ideals, and the voices of our fellow human beings, who belong to the response-abilities of the communicative field.

We have, in the course of this chapter, explored the contribution of listening to the achievement of a discursive norm of rationality, a communicative ethics, a politics of participation, a critical theory of truth and ideology, and the formation of our ideal of social justice. We have also moved closer to the overcoming of subject-centred reason, for a rationality rooted in listening cannot be subject-centred and narrowly ego-logical. The rationality we have rooted in listening contests a philosophy of consciousness: it is essentially communicative, and inherently geared to the achievement of uncoerced intersubjective understanding. Moreover, we have dispelled some of the mystification surrounding the entanglement of the ego-logical subject in the history of capitalism, and touched on the problematic relationship between capitalism and social justice. Although the ego-body (the ego-centred body) has appeared in many different societies and cultures, our analysis points to the conclusion that, since the ego-centred body is split off from the reversibilities of the flesh – from experiences of reversibility which lay the ground for reciprocity, then to the extent that the capitalist social system privileges the ego-body and promotes its rule, to that same extent capitalism can only be inimical to the experiential grounding of principles of justice. Thus, at the same time that a rationality rooted in listening works for justice by developing discursive reciprocity-potentials, our hermeneutical phenomenology works for justice by developing our experience of the non-egological flesh and its reversals, and by contesting, on the ground of this experience, the historical alliance between capitalism and the bourgeois ego.

With this analysis to attune us, our thinking now gathers around a different field of questions. Can listening overcome the domination of the metaphysics of presence that has been our history? In *Truth and Method*, Gadamer observes that 'the primacy of hearing is the basis of the hermeneutical phenomenon'.[251] Our concerns in this chapter – our concern, in particular, for the achievement of social justice – make this questioning of presence, and the field of problems it opens up, truly imperative, because respect for differences, respect for the other, ultimately requires the delegitimation of our ocularcentric metaphysics of presence. Hermeneutical phenomenology can be a critical weapon for this purpose.

CHAPTER 6

Hearkening: Hearing Moved by Ontological Understanding

A Spirit aerial
Informs the cell of Hearing, dark and blind;
Intricate labyrinth, more dread for thought
To enter than oracular cave.

William Wordsworth, 'The power of sound'

The / song is in your ears.
William Carlos Williams, Paterson[1]

Part I
The Ontological Appropriation of Hearing

When we develop our capacity for listening as an experience deeply rooted in the nature of the flesh, there is the possibility of achieving a fourth stage: not only the intersubjective reversal of supposedly independent subjectivities, which we examined in the preceding chapter, but also an even more exacting, even more demanding and disarming *ontological* reversal: a reversal of figure and ground, a reversal taking place between the listening self and the field of sound, a reverberation-effect which reverses and contests the intentionality assumed by 'consciousness'. In a poem titled 'Gong', Rilke recalls a sound 'Not meant for ears . . .: boom/ that like a deeper ear/ hears us, the seemingly hearing. Reversal of spaces. Draft/ of inner worlds outside. . . .' If we should find ourselves appropriated by such an uncanny experience, hearing ourselves being heard by the field of sound and silence, we may encounter, and may in fact for the first time be hearing, the hollow ring to the entire history of modern philosophy, a discourse which has attempted again and again to ground the possibility of knowledge in the self-certainty of a monadic subjectivity – a subject-centred reason.

In this chapter, we shall finally give some thought to the fourth stage, or centre, in our self-development as hearing beings. In this stage or centre, there is a recollection of Being. This recollection takes place by virtue of the retrieval of our pre-ontological experience with Being. The retrieval transforms this experience into an authentically ontological understanding: the implicit is made explicit; the potential is realized; a rudimentary understanding is developed; and the primordial claim of Being is redeemed by a thoughtful life.

In stage IV, we work on developing an awareness of the fact that our hearing belongs to the sonorous field of Being; that it belongs to the matrix of sonorous energies, in and as which Being manifests. In 'Interrogation and intuition', Merleau-Ponty reflects on the nature of what he calls 'an ontological organ'.[2] The human ear is such an organ. Through its canal pass the sounds of audible beings; through this canal flows the vibrant song of Being, the Being of all sonorous beings. Since it belongs to the sonorous field, our hearing is appropriated by Being: as primordial opening-out and laying-down (*legein*) of a sonorous field, a layout of auditory situations, the Being of beings lays claim to our hearing, calling it to realize its given potential as an organ of the sheer vibrancy of the *Logos*. (*Logos*, the primordial *legein*, is another name for the vibrancy of Being.)

The biology of hearing initiates the developmental process; however, it does not complete the process. Because the unfolding is left incomplete and open, it is up to us to do the experiential work of self-development. Referring to this work, Heidegger says, in *Being and Time*, that

> It is on the basis of this potentiality for hearing, which is existentially primary, that anything like hearkening [*Horchen*] becomes possible. Hearkening is phenomenologically still more primordial than what is defined 'in the first instance' as 'hearing' in psychology – the hearing of tones and the perception of sounds. Hearkening also has the kind of being of the hearing which understands.[3]

According to Heidegger,

> as understanding, *Dasein* projects its being upon possibilities. . . . The projecting of the understanding has its own possibility – that of developing itself [*sich auszubilden*].[4]

This work, he says, is 'the working out of possibilities [already implicitly] projected in understanding'.[5]

The 'appropriation' of our hearing is a claim (*Anspruch*) which calls for its proper or appropriate 'use'. This 'use' is a recollection of Being which retrieves the pre-ontological understanding, the poorly understood relationship with Being always and already implicate in our hearing, and gives back to the primordial *Es gibt* of Being – the ontological difference by grace of which we are enabled to hear – the gift of its audibility in the world of our dwelling. When we lend our ears to such a recollection of Being, our listening becomes properly tuned, properly thoughtful: it becomes an 'authentic hearing' (*eigentliches Hören*). And this is the achievement of 'hearkening'.[6]

The fourth stage is not possible, however, unless we break

our inveterate tendency to listen with ears that belong exclusively to ontical everydayness – the world of experience as interpreted by anyone-and-everyone (*das Man*). For the most part, *Dasein* 'fails to hear' (*überhören*) its own 'Self' because it is tempted always to 'listen away' (*hinhören*) to that part of itself which has been alienated by conformity and which listens only to what all the others hear.[7] In his study on the 'Logos' fragment by Herakleitos, Heidegger asserts that

> Man can hear wrongly [*verhören*] insofar as he does not catch [*überhören*] what is essential. If the ears do not belong [*gehören*] directly to proper hearing [*eigentliches Hören*], in the sense of hearkening [*Horchen*], then hearing and the ears are in a special situation.[8]

In a letter, Heidegger elaborated on these points:

> The responsiveness [of which mankind is capable] must take into account all of this, on the strength of long concentration and in constant testing of its hearing, if it is to hear an appeal of Being [*Anspruch des Seins*].[9]

This 'appeal', this call and claim, is our 'appropriation'. The question accordingly is: will our hearing be developed so that it can respond appropriately, and thereby become what it properly and essentially is, namely, an organ of Being?

Returning to the 'Logos' text, we read that

> Hearing is actually this gathering [*legein*] of oneself which composes itself on hearing the pronouncement and its claim. Hearing is primarily gathered hearkening.[10]

In the recollection of Being, we ourselves, as listening beings, are gathered into the in-gathering of Being. By lending our ears to this appropriation, we open ourselves to being attuned by Being. It is possible – and this is my hope – that, from out of this attunement, we shall learn some new ways to respond to the nihilism of our time.

Part II
Our Natal Bonding

The reasonable man: there are things he does not see which even a child sees; there are things he does not hear which even a child hears, and these things are precisely the most important things.'

Nietzsche, 'On the uses and disadvantages of history for life'[11]

. . . and a little child shall lead them.

Isaiah xi: 6

Within our infant veins are interfused / The gravitation and the filial bond / Of Nature that connect . . . with the world.

Wordsworth, *The Prelude*[12]

Consciousness can develop only where it preserves a living bond with the creative powers of the unconscious.

Neumann, 'Creative man and transformation'[13]

The primordial unconscious would be . . . the undividedness of feeling.

Merleau-Ponty, 'Nature and Logos: the human body'[14]

Befindlichkeit [i.e. our bodily felt sense of how we are faring] has always already disclosed one's being-in-the-world as a whole.

Heidegger, *Being and Time*[15]

I have taken the title for this part of the chapter from Merleau-Ponty, who argues, in 'Reflection and interrogation', that there is a 'natal bonding between me who perceives and what I perceive'.[16] I want to suggest that this 'natal bonding' initiates the first stage of our auditory lives – that it is, in short, another way of naming our *Zugehörigkeit*, the belongingness of hearing in early infancy. Thus, I am arguing a point that supplements the point made by Merleau-Ponty: if there is a natal bonding *between* subject and object, that is because both structural poles are primordially bound to a unified, unifying field, a shared matrix of sheer vibrancy from which they have simultaneously and interdependently emerged. The natal bonding is not only *within* the structure of subject and object, i.e., *between* them; it is also *underlying*:

> We must rediscover, as anterior to the ideas of subject and object, the fact of my subjectivity and the nascent object; that primordial layer at which both things and ideas come into being.[17]

Both subject and object are primordially bonded to the sonorous *ground* of their possibility.

Heidegger asks, in his essay on 'Alētheia':

> Why is it that we stubbornly resist considering even once whether the belonging-together of subject and object does not arise from something that first imparts their nature to both the object and its objectivity, and the subject and its subjectivity, and hence is prior to the realm of their reciprocity?[18]

If we pursue this question, the answer that will emerge directs our attention to the ground of the auditory situation, i.e. the field of sonorous Being as a whole. An abbreviated answer to Heidegger's question is, therefore, that the resistance is a symptom of the closure of metaphysics: this discourse always forgets to think Being *as* Being; it always forgets to acknowledge the ground – and to let it be grounding.

In this regard, metaphysics only echoes a forgetfulness that has already prevailed within the lifeworld – the lifeworld, that is, of most adults. This lifeworld is serious business. There is no time for music, not even – or perhaps least of all – the music of the celestial spheres. Is it possible that the adult's loss of joy is related to the structure of opposition into which subject and object get locked in the course of the child's development, and to the fact that this opposition, which is also their isolation from one another, is also, at the same time, their separation from the ground, the matrix of their belonging-together?

Because we are forgetful of the ground, the vibrant matrix from which we emerged, the hearing subject loses contact with the sonorous object as it passes through the process of differentiation. We lose contact not only because we ourselves are alienated from the matrix, but also because our forgetting of the matrix detaches the object from its ground. This is not without effects, for this detachment separates the object from the dimensionality of its resonance and causes it to lose much of its vibrancy, its atmosphere of music. This is the loss, then, which corresponds to the adult's loss of joy as a being gifted with the capacity to listen and hear.

Being closer to the matrix of sonorous energies, closer to the field of sheer vibrancy in which subject and object belong together, the child experiences a joy that most adults have lost for ever. Can we retrieve the hearing of the child of joy? Can we 'find' within ourselves a child of joy? And can we begin to listen to the world with a hearing that is in touch with that joy? Can we hear, again, with the child's sense of belonging? 'We have heard', Heidegger says, 'when we belong to the matter addressed.'[19]

In that same text, a study on Herakleitos, Heidegger notes that

> Mortals hear the thunder of the heavens, the rustling of woods, the gurgling of fountains, the ringing of plucked strings, the rumbling of motors, the noises of the city – only and only so far as they always already in some way belong to them and yet do not belong to them.[20]

But *are* we mortals? Do we hear what Heidegger says, here, that 'mortals' hear? There are many ways to hear the thunder of the heavens – and many conditions that ensure that, in some sense, we do not. Do we hear the chirping of crickets and the mating calls of the frogs with the ears of a child? Do we, as adults, even hear them at all any more? Until we have learned to listen, once again, with a hearing open to enchantment; until we have learned to let these sonorous beings transport us into the dimensionality from out of which they draw their great resonance, we shall *not* be able to belong. We belong to them when we gather up, into our hearing, our presently felt – bodily felt – sense of the natal bonding we 'once' enjoyed.

Now, if we say that the infant's belongingness is our first moment of binding, the moment when our hearing is bound to the matrix of sound and entwined, by grace of this field, with all other sonorous beings, then the next moment may also be termed a moment of binding, for it is the moment when our hearing is socialized into everydayness and bound to the ego's will; and the third moment, too, will be a moment of binding, for it is the moment when we bind our hearing to practices of self-formation – spiritual practices – that enable us to belong, once again, and yet also for the very first time, to the wholeness of Being.

I have chosen the word 'binding' to describe these three moments, these three stages, in our self-development, because I wanted the third moment, which I have called a 'spiritual' process, to connect with some of the self-disciplinary practices of religion. The word *religion* derives from *re-ligare*, which means 'to restrain', 'to bind back'. In this basic sense, then, the ontological appropriation of our hearing is a calling, and our responsiveness, our commitment to appropriate self-formative practices, is indeed a *re-ligio*.

Part III
Feminine Archetypes: Earth, Plants, Body, Feeling, Intertwining

Opening Conversation

. . . listening to sounds that are / The ghostly language of the ancient earth.

Wordsworth, *The Prelude*[21]

We do not hear because we have ears. . . . We have ears because we are hearkening [*horchsam*], and by way of this heedfulness [*Horchsamkeit*], need to listen to the Song of the Earth. . . . [New paragraph] The need to hear the Song of the Earth requires [*bedingt es*] that our hearing be a sensuous one which involves our sensory organs, the ears.

Heidegger, 'Logik: Heraklits Lehre vom Logos'[22]

We are plants which – whether we like to admit it to ourselves or not – must with our roots rise out of the earth in order to bloom in the aether and bear fruit.

Johann Peter Hebel[23]

The roots of all living things are tied together. When a mighty tree is felled, a star falls from the sky. . . .

There is too much cold in the world now, and it has worked its way into the hearts of all living creatures and down into the roots of the grass and the trees.

Perera and Bruce, *The Last Lords of Palenque: The Lacandon Mayas of the Mexican Rainforest*[24]

[There are] processes of development and transformation which cannot be assigned to the sphere of animal instinct. . . . They belong to the 'matriarchal consciousness' whose nature and symbolism are as intimately bound up with the plant world as with the world of the Feminine. Its psychic processes – which are in large part independent of the ego and consciousness – are, like the fruit, the emergence of a luminous quality of consciousness, specifically related to time and the phenomenon of destiny.

Neumann, *The Great Mother: An Analysis of the Archetype*[25]

For the spirit, as it first emerges from the unconscious, is fed from the primordial underground springs in the realm of the Great Mother.

ibid., 271

Powerful [female] innocence is seeking and naming the deep mysteries of interconnectedness. It is not mere helping, defending, healing, or 'preventive medicine'. It must be nothing less than successive acts of transcendence and Gyn/Ecological creation. In this creation, the beginning is not 'the Word'. The beginning is hearing. Hags hear forth new words and new patterns of relating. Such hearing forth is behind, before, and after the 'phallocratic creation'.

Daly, *Gyn/Ecology: The Meta-ethics of Radical Feminism*[26]

Only in recent times were the ancient mother cults laboriously rediscovered, and it was reserved for an ego versed in depth psychology to excavate the primeval world of the Terrible and Uroboric

Mother. Her repression was understandable and necessary from the point of view of the patriarchate and of a conscious development with strong patriarchal tendencies. Ego consciousness had to consign these aspects to oblivion, because its fear of the abyss [*Abgrund*] was still too uncomfortably close.

Neumann, *The Origins and History of Consciousness*[27]

The secrets of the female adolescent pertain to the silencing of her own voice, a silencing enforced by the wish not to hurt others but also by the fear that, in speaking, her voice will not be heard. [New paragraph] The difficulty experienced by psychologists in listening to women is compounded by women's difficulty in listening to themselves. This difficulty is evident in a young woman's account of her crisis of identity and moral belief – a crisis that centers on her struggle to disentangle her voice from the voices of others and to find a language that represents her experience of relationships and her sense of herself.

Gilligan, *In A Different Voice: Psychological Theory and Women's Development*[28]

As we have listened for centuries to the voices of men and the theories of development that their experience informs, so we have come more recently to notice not only the silence of women but the difficulty in hearing what they say when they speak. Yet in the different voice of women lies the truth of an ethic of care, the tie between relationship and responsibility, and the origins of aggression in the failure of connection.

ibid., 173

Since the bafflers attempt to interpret the Crones' Chorus by the rules of the going logic, they remain baffled. Since they can hear only sounds but cannot hear hearing, they cannot break the code of the Gyn/Ecologists' Un-Convention, whose participants are hearing ever more deeply into the secret chambers of the labyrinth.

Daly, *Gyn/Ecology*[29]

My interest lies in the interaction of experience and thought, in different voices and the dialogues to which they give rise, in the way we listen to ourselves and to others, in the stories we tell about our lives.

Gilligan, *In A Different Voice*[30]

The investigation of the special character of the feminine psyche is one of the most necessary and important tasks of depth psychology in its preoccupation with the creative health and development of the individual. . . . [New paragraph] But this problem of the Feminine has equal importance for the psychology of culture [which must recognize] that the peril of present-day mankind springs in large part from the one-sidedly patriarchal development of the male intellectual consciousness . . . no longer kept in balance by the matriarchal world of the psyche. In this sense the exposition of the archetypal psychical world of the Feminine that we have attempted in our work is also a contribution to a future therapy of culture.

Neumann, *The Great Mother*[31]

To expand the understanding of human development by using the group left out in the construction of theory [so as] to call attention to what is missing in its account.

Gilligan, *In A Different Voice*[32]

Western mankind must arrive at a synthesis that includes the feminine world – which is also one-sided in its isolation. Only then will the individual human being be able to develop the psychic *wholeness* that is urgently needed if Western humanity is to face the dangers that threaten our existence from within and without.

Neumann, *The Great Mother*[33]

'Ontological interpretation' is 'primordial' when it brings out 'the wholeness of the entity'.

Heidegger, *Being and Time*[34]

Development itself comes to be identified with separation, and attachments appear to be developmental impediments, as is repeatedly the case in the assessment of women.

Gilligan, *In A Different Voice*[35]

The spiritual power of Sophia is living and saving; . . . she communicates . . . a life of the spirit and of transformation, not one of earth-bound materiality. As spirit mother, she . . . is rather a goddess of the whole, who governs the transformation from the elementary to the spiritual level; who desires whole persons knowing life in all its breadth, from the elementary phase to the phase of spiritual transformation.

Neumann, *The Great Mother*[36]

The deep hearing of [women] Journeyers in the labyrinth is hearing in the labyrinthine internal ear. It is this hearing which makes it possible to spin, to weave the Network. The Network which Spinsters spin, alone and together, can break our fall at those times when the ground opens up right under us.

Daly, *Gyn/Ecology*[37]

The Great Mother, adorned with the moon and the starry cloak of the night, is the goddess of destiny, weaving life as she weaves fate.

Neumann, *The Great Mother*[38]

I knew I had been experiencing something I had never experienced before. A complete reversal of the going logic in which someone speaks precisely so that more accurate hearing may take place. This woman was saying, and I had experienced, a depth hearing that takes place before the speaking – a hearing that is far more than acute listening. A hearing engaged in by the whole body that evokes speech – a new speech – a new creation. The woman had been heard to her own speech.

Nelle Morton, 'Beloved image'[39]

I begin in the depths of the water / I begin where the primordial sounds forth, where the sacred sounds forth / I feel very good, [it] says. . . . Little woman who resounds, [it] says / Little woman torn up out of the ground, [it] says. . . . Little woman who gathers up the primordial, [it] says./ Little woman who gathers up the sacred, [it] says.

Maria Sabina, shaman[40]

In the beginning was not the word. In the beginning is the hearing. Spinsters spin deeper into the listening deep. We can spin only what we hear, because we hear, and as well as we hear. We can weave and unweave, knot and unknot, only because we hear, what we hear, and as well as we hear. Spinning is celebration/cerebration. . . . Gyn/Ecology is Creation.

Daly, *Gyn/Ecology*[41]

All mother goddesses spin and weave. . . . Everything that is comes out of them: They weave the world tapestry out of genesis and demise, 'threads appearing and disappearing rhythmically'.

Diner, *Mothers and Amazons: The First Feminine History of Culture*[42]

Knitting, knotting, interlacing, and entwining belong to the female realm in Nature, but so does entanglement in a magic plot . . . and the unravelling of anything that is completed.

ibid., 16

The mindbenders and those who remain mindbound do not see the patterns of the cosmic tapestries, nor do they hear the labyrinthine symphony. For their thinking has been crippled and tied to linear tracks. Spiraling/Spinning is visible/audible to them only where it crosses the straight lines of what they call thinking. Hence the integrity of Spinning thought eludes them, and what they perceive is merely a series of fragmented breaks/crosses, which might appear like an irregular series of dots and dashes.

Daly, *Gyn/Ecology*[43]

> Sensitivity to the needs of others and the assumption of responsibility for taking care lead women to attend to voices other than their own and to include in their judgement other points of view.
>
> Gilligan, *In A Different Voice*[44]

> The Samoan language has no terms corresponding to 'personality', 'self', 'character'; instead of our Socratic 'know thyself', Samoans say 'take care of the relationship'.
>
> Marcus and Fischer, *Anthropology as Cultural Critique*[45]

In *Daybreak: Thoughts on the Prejudices of Morality*, Nietzsche expresses his contempt for the gift of hearing:

> The ear, the organ of fear, could have evolved as greatly as it has only in the night and twilight of obscure caves and woods, in accordance with the mode of life of the age of timidity, that is to say, the longest human age there has ever been: in bright daylight the ear is less necessary.[46]

This is the contempt of a patriarchal male, typically privileging vision and bright daylight and putting our capacity for hearing lower down in the hierarchy of perceptual powers. Our perceptual capacities are ranked according to their will to power. It is all too clear that vision, for Nietzsche, is a masculine power and that hearing is a feminine power. Hearing is associated with night and twilight, the female hours, and with caves and woods, the female places. Nietzsche cannot understand the strengths and virtues of the ears, their distinctive contribution to the character of our moral and political life. He can see only their passivity, which he interprets as weakness, and their vigilance, which he interprets as fear. He cannot see their active role in communication, relationship, and co-operation; he cannot see their capacity for responsiveness; he cannot see how they make us susceptible to feelings of compassion and demonstrate to others that we care. He cannot see how these characteristics, traditionally associated with the sensibility of women, are really great strengths and great virtues.

In our patriarchal, male-dominated society, women have had to carry the wisdom in listening and feeling. Despite the fact that our society has traditionally failed to appreciate this wisdom, both listening and feeling, essentially connected, have contributed in absolutely crucial ways to cultural reproduction, social integration, and the processes of self-formation.

Even though hearing is more closely bound to feeling than our other perceptual capacities, the character of our society has encouraged the subordination of hearing to seeing and increasingly alienated listening from the body of feeling. But in feeling, as Heidegger puts it, 'a state opens up, and stays open, in which we stand related to things, to ourselves, and to the people around us. . . . Feeling is the very state, open to itself, in which our being human hovers.'[47] Heidegger even ventures to suggest, in 'The origin of the artwork', that,

> What we call feeling or mood . . . is more reasonable – that is, more intelligently perceptive – because more open to Being, than all that reason which, having meanwhile become [mere] *ratio*, was misinterpreted as being rational.[48]

Since *hearkening*, the fourth stage, or centre, of listening, is a recollection that demands of us the greatest openness to Being of which we are capable, it is a mode of perceptiveness that we can only achieve by cultivating our capacity for feeling and restoring the connection between feeling and listening. This means, in the important terminology that Eugene Gendlin has introduced, not only that we need to *listen to* our body's felt sense of its *Befindlichkeit* (how we are faring in the various situations of life in which we find ourselves), but also that we need to learn a listening which *listens with* this bodily felt sense.[49] In other words, we need to cultivate a listening that is deeply *rooted* in our body's felt sense of situated being.

When our listening really is well rooted in the body's felt sense of being, it makes contact with our primal, opening relationship to Being as a whole and can retrieve the implicate, pre-ontological understanding of Being that the body has always silently borne – always and already, long before we are mature enough to care about its retrieval. When our listening really is deeply rooted in the body's felt sense of being, it is opened out to the sonorous field as a whole and becomes thereby an organ of Being, an organ of recollection, gathering up into itself the soundfulness of the field. And when our listening really is deeply rooted in the body's felt sense of being, it belongs to what Merleau-Ponty called the 'intertwining', the essential co-origination and interdependence of subject and object, self and other: it belongs (*gehört*) to a dimension of our being which is not restricted to the *Gestell*, the ego-logical structuring and enframing of the auditory situation, but lays out, rather, *between* subject and object, self and other, the resonating, co-responsive interdependence of a 'differential interplay'. (Derrida's concept of the 'arche-trace' is, I think, remarkably close to Merleau-Ponty's concept of the 'intertwining'. According to Rodolphe Gasché, the 'arche-trace' is the 'constituting possibility' of a 'differential interplay', and as such, it is the necessary condition of the possibility of all relationships.)[50]

Due to our long history of patriarchal culture, male domination, and ego-logical psychology, this ontological realization of our capacity for listening, embodying it, rooting it well in feeling, grounding it in a sense of the sonorous field as a whole, and reviving its sense of belonging to a matrix of intertwining identities, differences, and destinies, is a realization that can happen only under the influences constellated by the feminine archetypes.

Patriarchy has been brutal to women. Under male domination, women have suffered. Under male domination, the feminine spirit in general – that spirit which Jung called the *anima* – has suffered a long and terrible repression, repeatedly turning its attempts at self-affirmation into symptoms of disease and psychopathology. Nevertheless, these hostile conditions have also given to many women, and to those men in whom the feminine spirit naturally takes root, the gift of a sensibility that opens them to attitudes and values neglected or excluded by the masculinized world and compels them to develop their unacknowledged strengths into virtues that our present world desperately needs.

Considered historically, what has been constitutionally characteristic of males in our society is what has prevailed as the 'universal' and 'rational' norm for people of both genders. It is time that women, and the men in whom the feminine spirit is particularly strong, achieve their liberation from this unnecessary oppression. What this means is that our society *as a whole* must value, respect, and legitimate the sensibility and virtues of the feminine spirit – the sensibility and virtues into which, for too many centuries, women have been locked. When this comes to pass, it will be normal for *men* to value and respect, and cultivate within themselves, the sensibility and virtues that have traditionally been associated only with women; and it will at long last be possible for *women* to develop what Jung would call their *animus*, i.e. those skills and virtues, and those dimensions of their sensibility, that have traditionally been associated with the archetypes constellated by the masculine spirit. Finally, it will also be possible for men in whom the feminine spirit is particularly strong to develop themselves as *whole* beings, free of a symptomatology that has echoed, and reproduced within them, the violent intolerance of a male-dominated society for any manifestations of the feminine spirit, especially among men.

Carol Gilligan reports that, in the course of doing empirical research on questions concerning the stages of moral development, questions generated, in fact, by the work of Piaget, Erikson, and Kohlberg, she began to hear two different voices, two different ways of thinking about moral problems, and two different modes of describing the relationships between self and other that are taken to be paradigmatic for moral character and constitutive of (the invariant stages of) moral development.[51] The two voices are the masculine and the feminine. The two different ways of thinking about moral problems are: (1) a competitive model, which gives primacy to the individual and relies on the supervenience of formal and abstract rules to achieve co-operation and consensus, and (2) a co-operative model which gives primacy to relationships and relies on contextual narratives and dialogue – communication – to resolve moral problems. The two different modes of describing the relationship between self and other are essentially two different ethics, the one an ethics of 'universal' rights and duties and 'universal' rational principles, the other an ethics of care, responsiveness, and responsibility. And, whereas the first ethics emphasizes the values of separation, individuation, autonomy, and a strong affirmation of ego-logical boundaries, the second emphasizes connectedness and interdependence, and a strong affirmation of kinship and solidarity. The first ethics is represented mainly by images of opposing positions and hierarchical orderings, while the second is represented mainly by images of communicative and collaborative positions, and replaces images of hierarchy with images of webs, networks, and weavings.

Corresponding to these two ethics, there are two very different conceptions of the Self, each with its own set of implications for our understanding of self-development. The Self of the patriarchal tradition, the Self reflected in the *ego cogito* of Cartesian metaphysics, is (1) disembodied, (2) nowhere situated, (3) monadic, i.e. essentially isolated and self-contained, (4) essentially and ideally purely cognitive, purely intellectual, (5) identified with its inner states and their 'contents', and (6) defined in structural, i.e. static, terms. By contrast, the Self toward which the feminist critique is pointing is (1) essentially embodied, (2) contextually situated, (3) relational and interactional from the very beginning, (4) essentially affective, motivational, libidinal, and aesthetic, (5) identified to a large extent with the character of its relationships, and (6) defined in terms of process, that is to say, essentially in terms of the dynamics of change and growth. (In 'A philosophical critique of the concept of narcissism: the significance of the Awareness Movement', Gendlin spells out the differences between the old and the new conceptions of the Self.[52] This is a ground-breaking contribution to the discourse on self-development, as well as a radical critique of the metaphysical Self.)

By now it should be clear, I think, that the *second* conception of the Self and its moral self-development, the conception that speaks with a feminine voice, not only recognizes the importance of listening, but also argues the need for its cultivation. This cultivation is imperative if our society is to overcome its traditional system of domination. It is imperative, if an historically new kind of Self is ever to emerge from the traditional dualism. More to the point, however, in the context of this present chapter, is the idea that, since the primordial experience with Being, our primordial attunement (*Stimmung*), is initially an experience constitutive of the infant's listening body-self, and since the pre-ontological understanding of Being we want to retrieve is an implicate order always already encoded in the initial body of auditory experience, the recollection of Being, which Heidegger attempted in his critical interpretation of the history of western metaphysics, needs to be elaborated in, and as, a practice of hearkening guided by the feminine spirit.

I am not saying only that listening is *one* of the ways in which there can be a recollection of Being; I am also saying that the development of our capacity for listening – a development which inherently constitutes a Self different from the Self reproduced by our tradition – is *an essential contribution* to the work of recollection. And I am saying that our listening cannot become a hearkening until we have allowed it to mature under the influence of the elements which constellate the feminine archetypes: earth, plants, body, feeling, wholeness, relatedness, intertwining. Our listening needs to learn receptiveness, responsiveness, and care. Our listening needs to return to the intertwining of self and other, subject and object; for it is there that the roots of its communicativeness take hold and thrive – and it is there that a non-egological listening-self is sleeping, embedded in the matrix of melodious energies.

On its way to hearkening, our listening needs to be initiated into the wisdom of the feminine spirit. This initiation releases it from the power of the patriarchy and the narcissistic delusions of the masculine ego. This initiation enables it to learn, or begin to learn, the practice of *Gelassenheit*, the listening that lets go and lets be.

Part IV
Gelassenheit: Just Listening

> . . . audible. / Most audible, then, when the fleshly ear / O'ercome by grosser prelude of that strain, / Forgot its functions, and slept undisturbed.
>
> Wordsworth, *The Prelude*[53]

> [Commentary. *Gelassenheit* requires a neutralization of the hearing to which we are habituated in the 'natural attitude' of everyday life. Metaphorically speaking, the 'fleshly ear' must 'sleep' . . . undisturbed.]

> When the entire body is the ear, while hearing you do not hear.
>
> Engo, *Hekigan-roku*[54]

> [Commentary. The sense in which we do *not* hear, here, is related to the sense in which the hearing typical of the natural attitude is put to sleep, neutralized, *aufgehoben*.]

> Sound, which, as a deeper ear, / hears us, who appear to be hearing.
>
> Rilke, 'Gong'[55]

[Commentary. In *Gelassenheit*, there is a peculiar reversal, due to the sublimation of the structure of subject and object. Having returned to its field-inherence and renewed its belonging to the auditory matrix, our hearing becomes an organ of Being. Thus we may be surprised to feel that we are more heard than hearing.]

It is the whole that sees, the whole that thinks, the whole that hears.

Xenophanes[56]

I echo the vibration of the sound with my whole sensory being.

Merleau-Ponty, *Phenomenology of Perception*[57]

[Commentary. This is a true phenomenological description, but its truth is not confirmed until the description has provoked us to a reflection that feels so true that it *changes our experience* in keeping with its deeper understanding of the true potential within our hearing. Initially, the description is false – false, however, precisely because it is actually true to a dimension of our experience concealed and falsified by the shallower experience of everyday living.]

. . . as wakeful, even, as waters are / To the sky's motion: in a kindred sense / Of passion, was obedient as a lute / That waits upon the touches of the wind.

Wordsworth, *The Prelude*[58]

[Commentary. This strikes me as a perfect metaphor for the listening that is *Gelassenheit*. 'Obedient as a lute'. . . . This is not an imposed obedience; nor is it the obedience of conformity. It is the obedience of letting, freely, spontaneously, joyfully yielding. In Latin, 'obedience' is *obaudire*, the obedience of 'listening from below'. In German, 'obedience' may be translated by *Horchsamkeit*, a listening that is heedful.]

Many scholars devoted to Heidegger's work assert that Heidegger's concept of *Gelassenheit* demands of us a level of understanding that it is virtually impossible for us to achieve. This they deeply and stubbornly believe, despite the fact that the 'master' himself unequivocally acknowledged that what he was attempting to say through this concept is to be found in the ancient teachings of the Zen masters.

I want to argue that the concept itself is not very difficult to understand, but that what is *extremely* difficult – indeed virtually unattainable, without the most exacting self-discipline imaginable – is living it: putting it into practice in one's daily life. After many years of strenuous practice, I have been able to enjoy passing moments of 'just listening': my term for the *Gelassenheit* of listening. But passing moments, occasional situations, do not add up to a day and a night. Nevertheless, speaking from out of my own experience, I shall attempt, here, to share what I understand.

Since the question of the Zen teachings inevitably arises whenever *Gelassenheit* is discussed, I would like to report, here, some recent empirical research. It should make the sceptics pause in their arguing. The research involved testing the EEG responsiveness of some Zen monks in Japan. The researchers found that Zen monks who have practised many years of meditation, and who have therefore developed a calm and relaxed state of mind, display an exceptionally continuous, well-balanced, open receptivity to all stimuli. When exposed over a long period of time to a single, repeated sound, their EEG responsiveness remained constant throughout: strong, alert, fresh.[59] Whereas most of us would have found ourselves painfully bored, once we had become thoroughly familiar with the sound and habituated to its stimulation, and would eventually have blocked it out, not even hearing it, these monks continued to respond, to greet the sound, with an astonishing freshness and pleasure.

At the other extreme are people suffering from the patterns of experiencing into which they have locked themselves. In writing about different 'neurotic styles', David Shapiro observes that

> The most conspicuous character of the obsessive-compulsive's attention is its intense, sharp focus. These people are not vague in their attention: they concentrate, and particularly do they concentrate on detail . . . [so that they] seem unable to allow

> their attention simply to wander or passively permit it to be 'captured'.[60]

In consequence, he says, such people are 'rarely struck or surprised by anything'. They rarely experience enchantment – the magical quality of the perceptual world. They rarely enjoy the experience of encountering something freshly. They rarely enjoy the meaningfulness inherent in perceptual experience.

Due to their psychological rigidity, and their intolerance of ambiguity, people entangled in 'neurotic' patterns

> will often miss those aspects of a situation that give it its flavour or its impact: thus, these people often seem quite insensitive to the 'tone' of social situations. . . . Certain kinds of subjective experience, affective experiences particularly, require, by their nature, an abandonment or at least a relaxation of the attitude of deliberateness.[61]

Erik Erikson found, as I already reported, that there is a totalitarian personality-type, and that this type typically needs to totalize perceptual experience, structuring it into closed *Gestalten*, static totalities.[62] Taking up the work of *Gestalt* psychologists, Merleau-Ponty wrote suggestively about the connection between *psychological* rigidity and *perceptual* rigidity in the authoritarian personality-type.[63] These types are extremes, of course. But it could be argued that, to the extent that our own perception falls short of *Gelassenheit*, and so long as it does, we ourselves are still entangled in the 'psychopathology' of everyday life.

At every moment, the adult's perception tends to recapitulate the ontogenetic stages of development through which it passed, beginning with uterine awareness. The *Abhidharma*, a fundamental text in Buddhism, differentiates six phases involved in every 'normal' act of adult perception: (1) an initial phase of formlessness, or openness, (2) a phase of sensation, the advent of bodily felt forms, (3) a phase of feeling, when global moods of ontological attunement emerge and predominate, (4) the phase when motivating intentionalities arise and patterns of desire (attraction, aversion, indifference) take hold, (5) the phase when object-orientated, object-conditioned, ego-logical perception arises and prevails, and finally (6) the phase of conceptual articulations (categorial organization) that further shape and structure the perceptual situation.

The question is: can this process be deconstructed? Can the pathology at work here be worked through? In other words, can we cut through the hard and fast patterns into which we tend to fall and return (more or less) to the openness of the beginning, retrieving it for present living? What is at stake, here, is the possibility of a mode of perception which can relate to its 'objects' in terms of a wealth of conceptual articulations, but which preserves, at the same time, a keen guardian awareness (*Wahr-nehmung*) of the openness, the field of sheer vibrancy, that is its ground. Such a perception would still be figural, i.e. focused, discriminating, selective, and concentrated; but its contact with the openness, its continuous awareness of the surrounding field, would organize a different *Gestaltung*. In listening, for example, there would be a continuous felt contact with the sheer vibrancy of the field: a deeply felt sense of the distinctive tonality, the music, of the auditory situation, and a deeply appreciative realization of the always present, always absent silence, inhabiting and encompassing all sonorous beings. And yet, not despite, but in fact precisely because of this field-gathering awareness, there would be a listening-to-things exceptionally attentive, clear, free of inner and outer distortions, accurate, sensitive, and responsive.

In his learned commentary on the *Mumonkan*, Zenkei Shibayama states that the Buddha, i.e. any enlightened being, 'has no attachment to his mind. His eyes see things but he does not become attached to them; his tongue tastes things, but he does not become attached to them.'[64]

The same, of course, is true of the Buddha's hearing:

> Just as it is, in its as-it-is-ness, whatever you see or whatever you hear is for ever blessed. It is neither one nor two.[65]

The attitude described so well in this commentary is precisely, I think, the attitude, the sensibility, that Heidegger is calling *Gelassenheit*. Often translated by scholars as 'releasement', this word could be translated more phenomenologically, and therefore also more helpfully, as 'letting go' and 'letting be'.[66] (The translation of the scholars is indicative of the fact that they are translating a word which refers to an experience they have not themselves enjoyed.) Another way of characterizing this ontological attitude would be to note that there is a sense in which its perception is 'without' an object: 'without' an 'object' *in the sense* that an 'ob-ject' (*Gegenstand*) is the target of a *grasping* mode of perception and, as the target of our attachments (attraction and aversion), it is set up in a fixated structure of op-position.

It is significant that, in *Identity and Difference*, Heidegger remarks that *Besinnung*, a word which may be translated, depending on its context, as 'reflection', 'mindfulness', 'thought', and 'recollection', 'may well remain wholly without an object'.[67] An attitude of *Gelassenheit* is not an attitude of which we are capable, so long as we comport ourselves in the manner, the style, of the ego. *Gelassenheit* first becomes possible only *after* the structure of subject and object is *aufghoben*. Only when our hearing is free of this structure will it be true to say, as Zenkei says, that there is an auditory situation which is 'neither one nor two'. That is to say, *Gelassenheit* in hearing is neither a (con)fusion of subject and object – a state of merging and dedifferentiation – nor the polarized op-position of the two. We must understand it, rather, as an awareness of the *intertwining* of subject and object: their differential interplay. It is by virtue of the subject's playful openness to the matrix of sound, the sheer vibrancy of the field as a whole, that this intertwining, this interplay of identity and difference, oneness and twoness, is realized.

It is essential to understand, here, that *Gelassenheit* does not at all preclude 'negative' or 'critical' judgments, decisions, and moral positions. Rather, it enables us to make such judgments and decisions from positions based on a genuine openness. *Gelassenheit* clears a 'neutral' space for good listening; it situates us in a space of silence that makes it easier to listen well and hear with accuracy; it enables us to hear what calls for hearing with a quieter, more global, and better-informed sense of the situation. Thus, far from precluding the possibility of a response to danger, malevolence, and evil, *Gelassenheit* is an equanimity which enables us to listen and respond with much greater intelligence, much greater situation-appropriateness. If what presents itself is really evil, the vibrations and tones manifesting that evil will be heard all the more keenly and accurately; as a matter of fact, evils that otherwise could not be heard at all would be discerned much more precisely, because the attunement, the silence of the listening, would let them reverberate, and disclose more of their sense, within its echoic space. *Gelassenheit* in listening does not mean quietism or docility. Quite the contrary. It is the most intelligent ground for responsive action.

Now, in the eleventh meeting of the 1966–1967 Heraclitus Seminar he led, Eugen Fink commented that

> A sentry, for instance, listens intensely into the silence without hearing something determinate. When he hears no determinate sound, still he hears. His hearkening is the most intense wakefulness of wanting to hear. Hearkening is the condition of the possibility for hearing. It is being open to the space of the hearable, whereas hearing [i.e. the ontical, ontologically forgetful hearing of everyday life] is meeting the specifically hearable.[68]

What Fink says, here, is confusing. He confuses *Zugehörigkeit* and *Horchen*, the ontological and the pre-ontological, using the word 'hearkening' to describe the phase I am calling *Zugehörigkeit*. Nevertheless, most of the words he uses here *may* be used to describe *both* phases, provided we construe them in different but homologous ways.

Let us get into the specifics. If we think of the listening attitude attributed to the sentry in the first sentence as manifesting his rootedness in an attunement of which he is virtually unconscious, then we should call it the moment of *Zugehörigkeit*. However, if we think of it as an attitude the sentry consciously and deliberately adopts, then we must regard it as an example of the perceptual preparedness, the readiness-to-perceive, that takes place within stage II. But we should also keep in mind, here, that, in hearkening, too, there is a listening which listens into the silence without hearing something determinate. For in hearkening, i.e. hearing with *Gelassenheit*, we let go of our attachments, our object-fixations, and we open ourselves to the field of sound as a whole, understanding that, by virtue of this openness, we are giving thought – returning thought – to the openness of Being as such. This attitude may therefore be described, as in Fink's second sentence, by saying: 'When he hears no determinate sound, still he hears.' As it stands, however, the sentence is systematically confusing, since it is open to three different readings, each one relating it to a different moment, a different phase. Although the infant hears no *determinate* sound, still it hears. Listening carefully for sounds of the enemy, the sentry hears no determinate sounds; nevertheless, but for different reasons, he, too, must be said to hear. And now, what about the Zen master? Relaxed into a global awareness and attuned to the primordial ground from which all sounds arise, the master may also be said to hear no determinate sound, if by 'determinate' we mean to refer to our normal habits of sound fixation. And yet, of course, he, too, hears. With each reading, there is a different sense – and a different story.

Since *Zugehörigkeit* is an openness that *precedes* wanting-to-hear, and hearkening is an achievement that has gone *beyond* wanting-to-hear, Fink's third sentence describes neither the first nor the fourth moments (stages), but only, rather, the second, i.e. the ego-logical. What then, moving on, shall we make of the fourth sentence? This one reads as follows: 'Hearkening is the condition of the possibility for hearing.' Now, if we construe 'the condition of possibility' in the traditional way, then we must replace the word 'hearkening', for it is *Zugehörigkeit*, our primordial inherence in, belonging to, and attunement by the sonorous field as a whole, and not the achievement of hearkening, which constitutes the primordial condition of the possibility for hearing. Nevertheless, hearkening, too, may be described with these same words, provided that we take them to mean that, since hearkening is a listening informed by an achieved ontological understanding, an authentic understanding of Being, its achievement becomes the *normative basis* for all our subsequent auditory experiences. In other words, as a listening which understands itself in relaaion to the sonorous field as a whole and realizes itself as an organ of Being, hearkening may be described as 'setting the tone' for all our hearing. In this sense – a sense different from the sense connected with *Zugehörigkeit* – hearkening may also be called 'the condition of possibility'. Thus, if we say that hearkening is the condition of possibility for hearing, what we mean by this is that 'true' hearing, 'proper' hearing, 'authentic' hearing, is possible only when there is an *understanding* of hearing in relation to Being and when this understanding *informs* our listening. In *Zugehörigkeit*, there is only an implicit, preconceptual, and rudimentary understanding – an as yet unrealized pre-understanding – of our relationship to Being; and while this relationship continuously *structures* our listening, it does so without the gift of our thought.

Fink's fifth sentence, the last one to be quoted here, begins:

'It is being open to the space of the hearable.' This can be read in two ways, for both *Zugehörigkeit*, the first moment, and hearkening, the homologous fourth, may be described with these words. But there is a world of difference between the openness of the first moment, which manifests a 'pre-ontological understanding', i.e. a relationship with Being that is not yet realized, developed, and fulfilled, and the openness of the fourth moment, which manifests an achievement of authentic ontological understanding and a binding commitment to bring this understanding to bear on all the situations of daily life.

Why does Fink conflate the two moments? Why does he slip back and forth between listening as our primordial, opening attunement and listening as an achieved understanding of itself in relation to Being? It is difficult to know for sure, but I conjecture that the problem lies in the fact that his thinking about hearing is more metaphysical than phenomenological, and, as a result, it misses both the development of hearing in the course of a lifetime and the moment-to-moment dialectic of auditory modalities in relation to the figure-ground difference. Fink's neglect of this dialectic is particularly unfortunate, because it is really crucial to appreciate how this 'being open to the space of the hearable' functions – concretely, moment-to-moment – in our everyday hearing.

Hearkening, i.e. hearing with *Gelassenheit*, is achieved by virtue of a retrieval (*Wiederholung*) of the experience of *Zugehörigkeit*, or, more accurately, a retrieval of our presently felt *sense* of inhering in, belonging to, and being attuned by the sonorous field as a whole. This retrieval *informs* our listening, because what is retrieved is a bodily carried *pre-understanding* of our relationship to Being: a preconceptual experience which is not left behind when we grow out of infancy, and which *continues* to function, throughout our lives and at all times, as the *opening* situation of our hearing. This openness happens, whether or not we give it any thought. However, if we do give it our thought and attempt to retrieve our body's presently felt sense of that openness, the sense we retrieve may thereafter *inform* our listening, and the openness we may accordingly practise could effect a profound reorganization of the auditory situation, the auditory *Gestalt*.

At any moment, and perhaps just for a moment, we may become aware of the primordial openness surrounding our ego-logical *Gestalt*. As infants, we inhabited this openness more or less continuously; but as we matured, we increasingly lost touch with it, inhabiting, instead, the structure imposed by the ego. Nevertheless, this openness continues, functioning unconsciously. To retrieve it *in* our listening and *for* our listening is, however, much more than acquiring some self-knowledge; it is to transform our perception, our auditory relationships, giving to the sonorous beings that call upon us the openness of an ontologically caring understanding. Within this more expansive openness, their sounding forth is different, for sounds sound differently when they are let go, released from our perceptual grasping and holding, and are allowed to sound forth in the open dimensionality of their being.

Silence is our listening openness: in order to hear something, we must first *give* it our silence. As Fink says, in the twelfth session of his seminar: 'The original silence is a constitutive element forming the distance of the auditory space of hearing.'[69] We need to cultivate this silence within ourselves. (Lame Deer, a Lakota medicine man, speaks of the holy man 'wrapping it around himself like a blanket'.)[70] It is through the depth of our silence that we become rooted again in the originary openness of the sonorous field.

Cultivating silence, however, is extremely difficult in our time. The more it is needed, the more it withdraws, giving way to the noises of modern living that cut us off from its teachings of wisdom. The authors of *The Last Lords of Palenque*, two anthropologists, point out that 'in the Lacandon (Maya) language, there is no word for silence. *Hum* means noise. *Mäx hum* is the absence of noise.' Their explanation for this fact gives us much to think about. They write that 'the silence these people had been able to take for granted . . . has now disappeared forever from their forest'.[71] We, too, I think, take it for granted – but in a different sense altogether. The Mayans have taken it for granted because of its silent presence: we take it for granted because of its silent absence. The silence should never be taken for granted. It is a gift to which we must respond by giving it, in return, the gift of our own silence. But the conditions of life in the modern world are not hospitable: outside us, there are too many man-made noises; and the pressures of life today make it difficult for us to form, within ourselves, a *sense* of the opening silence.

I bring the plight of the Lacandon into the context of our discourse here, because I want to say that the cultivation of silence is necessary not only for our individual self-development and moment-to-moment fulfilment as listening beings, but also for our historical relationship to nihilism and the Question of Being. Hearkening is in fact a 'fateful skill' (our *Geschick*),[72] because it is a way of experiencing the Being of beings: a way, perhaps, that could help us to reverse our present historical course, which is taking us ever more deeply into the destroying rage of nihilism. Cultivating silence, we do make it easier for this 'fateful skill' to take root in mankind.

But the cultivating of silence ultimately requires a calm, relaxed, well-balanced state, body and mind. The more this state is achieved, the easier it becomes to *neutralize* the polarizing intentionalities of desire, the vectors of attraction and aversion which bind our everyday hearing to the ego- logically constituted structure of subject and object.

Neutralization makes way for a major *Gestalt* shift: a shift to a gentler, looser, more diffused mode of listening, more open to the sheer vibrancy of the field as such. If we can neutralize some of our attractions and aversions, we can overcome attendant anxieties and dissolve unnecessary defences. And as our ego-logical obsessions are given up, a guardian awareness of the ground, the sonorous atmosphere as a whole, slowly begins to grow.

Gelassenheit, 'just listening', is often a *playful* listening, a listening which enjoys itself, a listening whose ultimate purpose is to be *without* a purpose: *ohne Zweck*, cut loose from the incessant reproduction of *zweckrational* life. 'Just listening' is a listening that wanders and drifts, a listening that delights in *releasing* soundful beings from the representations, the spellbinding fixations, which have effectively isolated them from the soundfulness of the sonorous field and denied them the resonance (*Anklang*) of their deeper nature. Moreover, the playfulness in which 'just listening' delights is reciprocated, for the soundful beings that are thus released will correspondingly give themselves to our hearing with an amplitude of resonance, a sensuous fulness of meaning, that they cannot give when the dimensions of their field of resonance are more restricted. Thus, when our hearing lets soundful beings return to the resonance of their ownmost being: when it lets them be and lets them go and lets them sound forth within a dimensionality they themselves open up, we receive, in return, a gift of sound: resonances that sound and measure the dimensionality, the ontological difference, of Being itself and let us hear deeply into the vibrations of its immeasurable openness.

When soundful beings are greeted by a joyful listening, a listening *opened* by joy, a listening playing freely in the presencing of that which sounds forth, the resonances which they set in motion can reverberate freely: freely within the openness we have given them. When these resonances are received, greeted in this openness, they consequently return to us a sound much richer and deeper than under standard ego-logical conditions they would. This, then, is how the enjoyment in 'just listening' is *amplified* by the interplay of 'subject' and 'object', 'self' and 'other'. And this is how 'just listening', no longer structured by the ego, no longer needing to re-present whatever presents itself, releases soundful beings from their reduction to the status of sound-emitting objects.

The playfulness of just listening opens up the ego-logically constituted structure of 'subject' and 'object' to the *infrastructure* of their interplay. In this interplay, the listening self finds itself inseparably *intertwined* with its 'object'. This is a *Gestalt* of co-responding resonances, an echo-play of differences. This is a *Gestalt* in which the function of representation has become subordinate to the interplay of these co-responding resonances: 'subject' and 'object' are finally related by spontaneous, changing, moment-to-moment correspondences, rather than by structure-binding representations.

The playfulness of just listening radically alters our experience of the relationship between sonorous beings and their field. Consequently, it radically changes our experiences of the ontological difference – the difference between beings and Being, a double tonality. When we release soundful beings from our perceptual grasp and hold, letting them go and letting them be in their alterity, the articulation of figure and ground, the familiar dimension of their difference, correspondingly opens up to disclose itself as a display of the ontological difference, a double tonality manifesting in different ways in relation to different realizations of our capacity for hearing.

Released from our grasp and hold, soundful beings stretch the reach and range of our hearing; they carry our listening beyond the limits of the field constructed by the ego; in short, they transport our listening into the dimensionality of their otherness, the sheer vibrancy and openness of the ontological difference. And suddenly we can hear the double tonality of the figure-ground difference as a local manifestation of the ontological. Equally, we can hear the sheer vibrancy of the ontological difference manifesting in, and as, the local dimensions of a figure-ground difference. 'Just listening' takes us into the interplay, where these two dimensions of difference can also sound as one.

Although, when 'just listening', our hearing often turns playful – wild again, untamed again, it is also *gehörsam*: obedient to a law of difference that metaphysics has never heard. Is metaphysics deaf? In modern times, it has heard nothing. What we have been thinking and obeying in the discourse of metaphysics is a Principle of the Ground, a principle supposed to be soundless, that no mortal could ever hear. But listening and thinking, now, with *Gelassenheit*, we break away from this history. In the discourse of modern metaphysics, the Principle of the Ground has always demanded an implicitly totalitarian obedience. Listening with *Gelassenheit*, however, we are drawn into a *different* obedience; our listening plays, obedient as a lute that waits upon the touches of the wind.

Part V
The Echo and the Ego

> I hearken. . . . Slowly I listen . . . and let it die away into its farthest echo.
>
> Rilke[73]

> The clearing, the opening, is not only free for brightness and darkness, but also for resonance and echo, for sounding and the diminishing of sound. The clearing is the open for everything that is present and absent.
>
> Heidegger, 'The end of philosophy and the task of thinking'[74]

> Original thanking [*Danken*] is the echo of Being's favour [echoing the *Es gibt*, the 'It gives'/'There are', of Being], wherein Being clears a space for itself and gives rise to a unique occurrence: [instead of nothing,] there *are* beings. This echo is man's answer to the word of the soundless voice of Being.
>
> Heidegger, 'What is metaphysics?'[75]

Having failed to achieve 'enlightenment' after years of study, self-examination, ascetic practices, and meditative sitting (*zazen*), Kyogen resolved to try a different approach, and he volunteered to serve as custodian for a small temple in the vicinity of his family home. Many more years passed in this way. But, for some reason, despite his exertions, Kyogen still could not experience enlightenment. One day, however, while he was busy sweeping the precincts of the temple, his broom happened to toss up a pebble. The small stone struck the trunk of a nearby bamboo, making a sharp, clear sound. As the sound echoed within the walls of the temple, and within his own body, he suddenly felt himself powerfully moved and shaken. Suddenly, favoured by this passing echo, Kyogen realized the immeasurable meaning of Being.[76]

According to Reichel-Dolmatoff, an eminent anthropologist, the Tukano tribes of the Colombian rain forest define the human being as 'one who sees and hears the echo and thus knows'.[77] The Tukanos, he notes,

> say that everything has an 'echo', but that not all people can hear it, because the person has to have 'stability' and has to 'sit well' upon his little stool. True knowledge is achieved by *pesi keranyeari*, an expression derived from *peri (pesiri)* / 'to hear', 'to understand': *kerapiri* / 'to step securely', and *nyeari*/ 'to grasp', 'to seize'. [The third word carries the sense of 'comprehension' and is not meant in the sense of an aggressive taking-hold.] That is the essence of 'stabilisation', a concept in which the wooden seat comes to stand for introspection on the road to wisdom. Only by being able to 'hear the echo' can one truly *know* what is being seen and what the object symbolises.[78]

The echo (*keori*) is 'the essence of the thing'.[79] Thus, when one really listens well, one can hear the 'echo' of things:

> that which is 'heard' is the 'echo' of things. Hearing this 'echo', one knows what it is that is being perceived, what it is that is being symbolised. The concept of symbolism, of symbolic thought, is expressed, then, in the word *keori*, the echo . . . the essence. Used as a verb, *keori* means to measure or to take the measure of something, and our

> informant explains that 'the echo is the measure of sound'.[80]

(We shall return to this question of measure, recalling Hölderlin's question: 'Is there, on this earth, a measure?') But the Tukanos believe that the capacity to hear the echo, the essence of things, the ability to span and take the true measure of things, is a difficult spiritual achievement:

> often enough, the echo is only vaguely understood; there are many echoes, many possible meanings which reach the untrained ear and which must be decoded and interpreted – a task that in reality belongs [mainly] to the shamans.[81]

The echo has much to teach us. If we listen for echoes, and listen to them, our listening can grow in its wisdom. The echo is a precious gift to hearing.

Consider the ego in the discourse of Cartesian metaphysics. This ego is a *cogito* transparent to itself, who knows with absolute certainty what it thinks, what it means, and what it is saying. This ego, grounding itself, does not need mediation, otherness, to know itself. For this ego, the truth of things, the essence of things, is totally present. Truth, being, and reality: it grasps these in their full presence, totally clear, totally intelligible, totally certain. But in this discourse, there is no acknowledgement, no recognition, of the echo. Just as the vision of western metaphysics has attempted to banish images and shadows, so its discourse, never stopping to listen to itself, never stopping, indeed, to listen well to what is called 'reason', has attempted for centuries to silence and deny the echo. What happens when we let this discourse echo? What happens when our listening lets its echoes ring? Perhaps this discourse unconsciously realized the answer. For the echo is radically deconstructive, subversive, even anarchic: it sets in motion uncountable vibrations of uncertainty; it refuses to be controlled; it cannot be possessed; it makes careful distinctions interpenetrate; it denies the possibility of pure presence; it decentres the ego. When we recall the excluded echo, the tradition of rational, logocentric discourse – the tradition metaphysics exists to validate – suddenly beings to open up. Introducing atonality and tonal instability, the echo is a challenge to the closure of metaphysics.

Whereas metaphysics reifies and totalizes, making all instances of presencing into objects that are permanently present-at-hand and timelessly positioned in Being, the echo sets in motion a hermeneutical deconstruction of this ontology. Moreover, the echo deconstructs the metaphysical projection of an 'original ground', compelling us to recognize this 'permanent ground', a 'constant presence', as the deluded projection of a metaphysical reading of the field of perception.

The echo is a hermeneutical metaphor, because it *carries* us from the ontic world into the ontological field, and there introduces us to the primordial temporality of Being, stretched ecstatically across the field and appearing, within the ontical world, with the arising, the persisting, and the perishing of all sounds. Only the ungraspable, unreachable echo, gathering us into the region of its perishing, a 'place of stillness' which is also the Nothingness where it is finally gathered into the 'ringing of stillness'[82] and absorbed by silence, is consonant with the truth, the ecstatic *alētheia*, of Being. Only the echo teaches our hearing the unconcealment of Being. Only the echo teaches our hearing the presence of absence and the absence of presence.

In hearkening, listening with *Gelassenheit*, we follow the echo, going where it goes, going where it calls us. But where does the echo go? Where does it take us? It carries us back, metaphorically, into the song of the elemental silence; it carries us back into the primordial ecstasy of sound itself: the interplay of silence and melodiousness where the empty sounds of metaphysics gradually die out in the self-concealment of Being. And there, in that dimension where it sounds the depths of Being and reaches into the abyss beyond sounds and silences, it leaves us behind. There, giving us its measure of the immeasurable, it goes into hiding. The echo gives us, in fact, no alternative: we must ultimately let it go and let it be. . . .

> In the same manner as the voices of persons near rocks and mountains are brought back as an echo, so also all that is has nothing substantial about it. Understand it thoroughly to be devoid of any truth principle. [New strophe] Even if you search for the sound of the echo in the without, the within, and the in-between, you will not find it. So also, if you have intellectually (rationally) investigated all that

> is, be this the within or the without – all that presents itself through the working of mind and mental events – be this on the coarse or on the subtle level, you will find nothing of an essence. Everything is open like the sky, without any substantiality, and transparently pure; and if you understand everything in this way, you will not hanker after and hold on to anything. Even the belief in two realities – which states that things are there for all practical purposes, but ultimately they are not found to be so – is a split set up by the intellect [and] . . . has remained in the range that passes the intellect. [New strophe] This network of propositions set up by the intellect is [a projection of] one's own mind. That in which there is no interference by a network of concepts . . . cannot be grasped concretely. When you know it in this way, you go beyond the limitation imposed by propositions. Out of the primordial dimension of experience, which is like the vast sky . . . and out of its immaculate ocean which is the spontaneity of all capabilities, there comes the world of fictions, having as the condition of its presence the loss of pure awareness, with its proliferation of divisive concepts, and like an echo – there being nothing and yet a presence – it persists for a while here. The self-manifestation of Being, as the presence of the six kinds of sentient beings [gods, titans, humans, animals, hungry ghosts, and the denizens of hell], occurs through the power of the inveterate tendencies. One's own mind, sullied by these tendencies, identifies itself with its fictions through the power of the tendency for fixating identifications [and conformity]. [New strophe] Under these circumstances, the presence mistaken for 'sentient beings' and for 'mind' is an actuality that has no foundation as such and no root whatsoever. Ah! How funny is this paradox of there being nothing and yet there being a presence. What is the point of hankering after and holding to a truth principle in what presents itself as a value but is only like the sound of an echo. . . ?[83]

These words, teaching that 'all that is is like an echo',

teaching that all ontologies are ultimately mere fictions, were written down in the fourteenth century by kLong-chen rab-'byams-pa, one of Tibet's greatest scholars and teachers, and an accomplished practitioner of meditative wisdom. His words, however – these words – cannot be accommodated by the texts of western metaphysics, for the truth that the echo recalls cannot be grasped by the correspondence theory of truth.[84] Herein lies my story of the echo and the *ego cogito*.

Part VI
The Principle of the Ground: Setting the Double Tone

Untroubled, in the final analysis, by the most crippling of doubts, philosophers from Plato to Kant calmly affirmed their faith in the possibility of a life of reason. Is the world we are living in today a world that is listening to reason?

When we look into the history of metaphysics, we find the philosophers' faith in reason, their faith in the ultimate rationality of the world – its intelligibility within existing categories, its conformity to the laws of logic, its ultimately sufficient explainability – inscribed in the 'Principle of the Ground'. Heidegger devoted an entire book to this principle, problematizing its sense, long ago taken for granted, by questioning it in terms of a thinking that expressly casts itself into the audible openness of Being.[85]

I have inserted numbers into Heidegger's text, quoted below, because, since he himself begins the problematization of the principle by situating it provocatively in the field of our hearing, I want to follow each of the sentences I quote with a hermeneutical 'translation' of my own, in which an implicit meaning of his thought is more concretely specified in terms of the ontological appropriation of our listening. Here, in part, is what he says:

> (1) in order genuinely to hear what the principle says about Being, we must direct our attention to the 'is' which sets the all-harmonising tone in the principle 'Nothing is without ground'.

Here, then, is my translation of (1):

> (1) in order genuinely to hear what the auditory

> situation presents of soundful Being, i.e. in order to hear what *Es gibt*, we must direct our attention to that which sets the all-harmonizing tone: the encompassing dimension within which, and from out of which, the various beings of our world sound forth.

Heidegger continues:

> (2) If we listen to, that is, if we freely give ourselves to, what is genuinely spoken in the principle, then the principle will suddenly sound differently.

My hermeneutical interpretation is:

> (2) If we listen to, that is, if we, in *Gelassenheit*, freely give ourselves to what is really given, really presented, in the auditory situation, then that situation will suddenly sound differently.

Now Heidegger:

> (3) The principle will no longer read: *Nothing* is *without* ground, but rather: Nothing *is* without *ground*.

And to this I want to reply:

> (3) The auditory situation will no longer sound forth in sounding beings (figures) whose atmosphere of sound is not differentially heard as the ontological difference, but rather will sound forth in soundful beings whose *ground* resonates through them and around them, so that the presencing (*Anwesenheit*) of the ground itself becomes audible, even in its profound reserve of silence.

Having suggested a different way of hearing the principle, Heidegger then observes:

> (4) Being and ground now ring in a harmony. (5) In this ringing there rings out the fact that Being and ground belong together in a oneness.

In my interpretation, this reads:

> (4) Out of their field of Being, soundful beings now ring out in harmony with their sonorous ground, and there is a harmony such that Being itself (re)sounds through the ground it gives. (5) In this ringing, there rings out the fact that, by grace of their field of Being, soundful beings belong together in a oneness with their ground, which correspondingly (re)sounds with a double tonality, the harmony of its togetherness with Being.

Heidegger again:

> (6) The differently sounding principle now says: The ground *belongs* to Being.

And in my interpretation, this says:

> (6) The differently sounding perceptual situation now presents beings which can be heard to belong, in their soundfulness, to the Being that soundfully grounds them.

Heidegger writes:

> (7) The principle of the ground no longer speaks as the supreme principle of all representations of Being; it no longer [merely] says that every being has a ground. (8) The principle of the ground now speaks as a word about Being.

Which I want to render as follows:

> (7) The auditory situation no longer sounds forth in conformity to our prevailing metaphysical representation of Being, which not only reduces Being to the dimensions of an auditory *Gestell*, but reduces this ground to a constant and totally given presence. (8) The auditory situation now presents beings which, in their sounding forth, audibly resonate with the echo of Being, and accordingly *open up* the representational ground to the immeasurable dimensionality of Being. The

> ground thus *opens up* to let the sounds we hear carry us into the openness of Being, the dimensionality of the ontological difference, a double tonality.

According to my reading, Heidegger is trying to change our twofold representational reductionism, re-presenting what presences, what presents itself to our hearing, in a double reduction: of Being (the dimensionality of Being) to our *representation* of the auditory ground, and of the ground itself to our re-presentation of it within the frame of the subject-object encounter, i.e. in terms that satisfy the 'needs' of an ego-logical subjectivity and that consequently reduce the ground itself to a totally present, totally graspable object.

Heidegger's concern, however, is to change our understanding of the principle: his efforts to change our way of hearing are confined to changes in the way we hear the *assertion* of the principle. Our concern here, however, is centred on listening as such. The working hypothesis behind my own efforts, then, is that the changes Heidegger is suggesting can be generalized, and that, when corresponding changes take place in the auditory situations of everyday life, there is a corresponding, or homologous, change in our experiencing of the Being of the sonorous ground, the vibrant field of our hearing as a whole. In this way, every auditory situation becomes a local event (*Ereignis*) of unconcealment, a local event whose melodiousness is made possible by grace of the silent opening articulated in the ontological difference.

When we listen with *Gelassenheit* to the sounding forth of soundful beings, we release them from our ego-logical re-presentations of their sonorous presence, and we hear their sonorous dimensionality in a double tonality. This release lets them be reconnected to their sonorous ground. But listening with *Gelassenheit* also releases the ground itself from our totalizing re-presentations. This double letting-go and letting-be opens our hearing to the dimensionality of Being as a whole. And it is from out of this dimensionality, an immeasurable reserve of silence and sound, the ground concealed by its very unconcealment, that the 'tone' of our auditory situations – all the situations in which we find ourselves, and by which we are attuned – is set.

In order to hear a different ground – a 'ground' and 'origin' of sound unknown to the metaphysical tradition, we must first learn *Gelassenheit* as a way of listening. This point is reinforced when, for example, we read Rodolphe Gasché's recent book on Derrida, entitled *The Tain of the Mirror: Derrida and the Philosophy of Reflection*. Writing about the 'ground' of metaphysics, Gasché says: 'This ground grounds when it is set free in the very act of returning to it. Such a ground, since it can never be given [as a totalized presence], cannot become the end point of a reflection. As one reaches out for it reflectively, it withdraws.'[86] Thus, it is imperative to keep in mind that the 'recollection of Being' which begins with a listening skilled in *Gelassenheit* is a return from forgetfulness to 'something that is not [already] present in any way whatsoever, but that constructs itself in the very process of our stepping back [and letting go]'.[87]

'Just listening' *opens* us to the unconcealment, the primordial 'ecstasy', of the ontological difference between Being and beings – the tonal event which clears a time-space of melodious silence for the in-gathering and presencing of all soundful beings, and by grace of which the figure-ground differences constitutive of all our auditory situations first become possible. Thus, 'just listening' is an experience of truth as *alētheia*: an experience of the truth of Being that has freed itself from the metaphysics of truth expounded in the correspondence theory.

According to the correspondence theory, truth consists in a correspondence between, on the one side, a cognitive state of mind, or the proposition this state of mind is asserting, and, on the other side, the state of affairs referred to. In other words, truth is a matter of conformity: the proposition or state of mind is true if and only if it *conforms* to the existing state of affairs. Although this is but one way of representing (re-presenting) the truth, the discourse of metaphysics has stubbornly resisted recognizing its theory of truth as 'merely' a representation, an interpretation.

Heidegger argued, in *Being and Time*, that truth in the sense of 'correctness', the truth, namely, of the correspondence theory, phenomenologically *presupposes* another sense of truth: *alētheia*, unconcealment. Before it can be a question of correctness, something must be, must appear, must disclose itself, must sound forth. But this unconcealment of beings can happen only when, and only where, there is a hermeneutical opening, a clearing silence, a field of tonality laid out for the disclosure. This essentially prior event of openness and clearing, of ontological difference, is the primordial moment of truth, the hermeneutical *alētheia* without which there can be no experience of truth in the sense of 'correctness' or 'correspondence'. Before we can *hear* the truth, we must be *open* to listening.

In reading Heidegger's *Nietzsche* work, I found some very striking passages that bear on this question. Examining Nietzsche's critique of epistemology, Heidegger makes the following observation: 'The relation that distinguishes knowing is always the one in which we ourselves are related, and this relation *vibrates* throughout our basic posture.'[88] Vibrates? Through the body? Is this metaphor? If metaphor, is it merely ornamental? Before we rush to answer these questions, we should consider what Heidegger himself had to say about metaphor. In any case, the metaphor is used again, much later in the text – a fact that makes it all the more difficult to erase it or paraphrase it, treating it as merely an embellishment. In a later passage, Heidegger calls our attention to 'the still reverberating yet entirely unheeded resonance of the metaphysical essence of truth'.[89] This passage makes it very difficult to insist that Heidegger is *not* writing about how we experience truth as an auditory phenomenon. What, then, is this 'unheeded resonance'? Why have we not been hearing it? How could we prepare ourselves to hear it? And what is the difference, in terms of how and what we hear, between truth in the sense of 'correct representation' and truth in the sense of *alētheia*, the opening unconcealment? Could it be a difference that we would hear as a difference between the univocal and the polyphonic, the monotone and the melodious? Heard in this way, how does our experience with truth as correctness measure up?

For a listening that is paying attention, attuned to its situation through the body's felt sense, truth as *adequatio*, as correct representation, is missing the deep melodiousness, the resonances and reverberations, that can be heard in 'truth' when it is articulated and experienced as *alētheia* – unconcealment, revealing, opening up. According to Heidegger, 'Truth as certitude becomes the monotony that is injected into beings as a whole when they they are served up for man's securing of permanence.'[90] This monotone is also univocity: 'Truth as securing univocity grants machination exclusive pre-eminence.'[91] If truth as correct representation is fixation, securing, permanentizing, holding-to-be-true, positing what is stable, and making something come to a stand in constant presence, how *could* it be receptive to polyphony, resonance, richnesses of melody, and unruly echoes?[92] Where truth is vibrant, resonant, echoing, it cannot be certain, cannot be controlled. Correctness (*Richtigkeit*) always works to reduce the truth of Being, the truth of the ground, a double tonality, to a sound whose dimensionality we can always measure, and know, with absolute certainty. Correctness is directed by the will to power, and its power over the truth of Being consists in its closure of the ontological difference, the field opened up by and for its resonance.

Now, what I want to argue is that the correspondence theory which western metaphysics expounds – and has, since Plato, expounded – conceals within itself its opening genealogy: the fact that every correspondence, every determination of correctness, every *adequatio*, depends on a situational co-responding, an interaction, an interplay. Because metaphysics adopted vision rather than hearing for its paradigm of knowledge, truth, and reality, it easily ignored the experience of consonance, harmony, and attunement that necessarily *underlies* the correspondence. And because it systematically ignored such experience, it easily fell into a deep forgetfulness of Being, concealing, even from itself, the opening up, the melodious ecstasy (ek-stasis), of the ontological difference – that always elusive play of difference whose double tonality is the originary *ground* of truth.

For the 'Reason' of metaphysics, truth is grounded in correspondence: it is 'reasonable' to *see* truth this way. But when we listen to our *experience* with truth instead of 'listening to Reason', we will know that truth is not grounded in correspondence; we will know that it is grounded, rather, in a possibility which attunement, a co-responding, has first opened up. To hear the truth as *alētheia*, as unconcealment, is to hear the opening up of the sonorous field, as which Being manifests, to the possibility of a local attunement, a local consonance.

When our listening lets soundful beings be; when it lets go of their soundings, we are, in fact, opened to the possibility of a recollection of Being. Now, according to Heidegger, Herakleitos used the word 'Logos' as a name for Being: a name which means, in its verb-form, *legein*, 'to lay (down)', 'to articulate a lay-out', and 'to gather'. Making use of Heidegger's interpretive work to continue our own course of thinking, I want to say that in achieving *Gelassenheit*, the wisdom of 'just listening', we are gathered into the dimensionality of the primordial *Logos*, which, as the primordial layout of the field of sound, *sets the tone* for our hearing.

And if we let ourselves be gathered into the melodious silence of its primordial temporality, a ground that is no *metaphysical* ground, we will know, by virtue of our hearing, that the field of being always and already reverberates with the sense of many *other* historical beginnings. The history of metaphysics is not our pre-ordained fate; it is not an irreversible destiny. As the opening field absorbs into itself the univocal, monotone 'Being' proclaimed by our traditional metaphysics, a history that has become very destructive is therefore already receiving a different attunement. This we may hear, if we can *stop* listening to 'Reason'.

In his preface to *The Phenomenology of Perception*, Merleau-Ponty breaks away from this 'Reason', the logocentrism of the tradition, in order to disclose a different ground, a different *logos*:

> The phenomenal world is not the bringing to explicit expression of a pre-existing being, but the laying down of being. Philosophy is not the reflection of a pre-existing truth, but, like art, the act of bringing truth into being. One may well ask how this creation is possible, and if it does not recapture in things a pre-existing Reason. The answer is that the only pre-existent *Logos* is the world itself. (*Preface*, xx)

Merleau-Ponty's phenomenology, like Heidegger's thinking, is inspired by an experiential understanding of the *Logos;* but, again like Heidegger's thinking, it is not 'logocentric', centred on the *Logos* of the tradition. Heidegger's *Logos* is the vibrant *Es gibt* which lays and gathers a field of double tonality, a field of ontological difference. Merleau-Ponty finally incarnates this *Logos* in the flesh of the world. 'Logocentrism' is overcome by virtue of a more primordial, more radical listening. The 'primal ground', corresponding to this mode of listening, is anarchic, by human measure: a labyrinth.

Part VII
The Gathering of the Logos

Listen not to me, but to the *Logos*.

Herakleitos, Fragment 50

The proper way of hearing is determined [*bestimmt*] by the *Logos*.

Heidegger, *Early Greek Thinking*[93]

We are inexperienced at such hearing, and . . . moreover, our ears are full of things that prevent us from hearing properly.

Heidegger, *Introduction to Metaphysics*[94]

While I perceive, and even without having any [objective] knowledge of the organic conditions of my perception, I am aware of *drawing together* somewhat absent-minded and dispersed 'consciousnesses': sight, hearing and touch, with their fields, which are anterior, and remain alien, to my personal life.

Merleau-Ponty, *Phenomenology of Perception*[95]

Since ego-consciousness does not embrace all psychic activities and phenomena . . . the question naturally arises whether there may not be a *cohesion* of all psychic activities similar to that of ego-consciousness. This might be conceived as a higher or wider consciousness in which the ego would be seen as an objective content. . . . Our ego-consciousness might well be enclosed within a more complete consciousness like a smaller circle within a larger.

Jung, 'Spirit and life'[96]

In everyday living we do not expressly comport ourselves toward the whole, and also not when we knowingly penetrate into the distant Milky Way. But a human being has the possibility of letting become explicit that implicit relationship to the whole as which he always already exists. We exist essentially as a relationship to Being, to the whole. For the most part, however, this relationship stagnates. In dealing with the thinker Herakleitos, one can perhaps come to such an experience in which the whole, to which we always already implicitly comport ourselves, suddenly flashes up.

Fink, Heraclitus Seminar[97]

In 'Recollection in metaphysics', there can be no doubt that Heidegger gives the task of recollection to our capacity for listening: 'the listening response which belongs to the claim of Being, as determination attuned by the voice of that claim. . . . Recollection of the history of Being returns to the claim of the soundless voice of Being and to the manner of its attuning.'[98] The process of recollection is a task for our hearing. This assignment is significant. After the *Kehre*, the turn-around in his thinking, Heidegger depends more on hearing than on vision to overcome the closure of metaphysics. In this part of the chapter, I shall attempt to interpret this assignment in terms of the realization of our capacity for listening.

In his short study of the 'Logos' fragment attributed to Herakleitos, Heidegger argues that what he calls 'proper' or 'authentic' hearing is a hearing that belongs to – is appropriated by – the Logos:

> If there is to be proper hearing, mortals must have already heard the *Logos* with an attention [*Gehör*] which implies nothing less than their belonging to the *Logos*.[99]

These two passages give us much to think about. Before proceeding, then, I would like to use them to bring together the elements of our interpretation and rehearse the steps we have already made.

(1) As listening beings, we 'belong' to Being because we inhere in, and are attuned by, a field of sound. Thus, we belong to the *Logos* in that it calls us and we are attuned by its calling: our belonging is attested by the fact that we are beings who can speak, using words (*logoi*) attuned by the *Logos*, that elemental condition which sets the tone for all our listening and speaking. (2) To belong to Being, to belong to the *Logos*, is to be attuned by it: attuned whether or not we will it, whether or not we are conscious of it, and whether or not we understand its significance for our lives. (3) If and when we become conscious of this belonging attunement, conscious of our inherence in an open field of sound, we realize that, as Heidegger says, we 'must have *already* heard' it. This realization is decisive for the development of our hearing, but, so far, there is still no 'proper' hearing. For 'proper' hearing, there must also be understanding: an understanding which *makes a difference* in our hearing and in

the way we comport ourselves as listening beings. (4) To belong to Being (*Logos*) and be attuned by it is to be *claimed* by it. (5) The claim (calling) made by Being (*Logos*) comes from the fact that it has given us (*Es gibt*) the *gift* of its attunement, setting the environmental tone for our hearing. (6) To hear properly, or authentically, is to hear this belonging attunement, this appropriation: hear its claim *as* a claim, and be appropriately responsive in the character of all our listening. (7) To be appropriately responsive to the claim is to realize our given potential for hearing, fulfilling this potential by living a life in which the ontological understanding we achieve makes our inherence in the field of sound, our belonging to it and our being attuned by it, melodiously audible: audible, that is, *as* that by grace of which alone we are enabled to hear, and can use words to speak. (8) The appropriate response accordingly involves a 'return', a hermeneutical movement, because, even if we are not *now* hearing the *Logos*, the resounding claim of Being, consciously and with genuine understanding, nevertheless we must have *already* heard it (in a pre-conceptual, pre-personal, pre-understanding, preliminary or distracted kind of way), since it is only *by grace of* our belonging attunement, our inherence in the openness of the field, that we could now be hearing any of the soundful beings which claim our attention in the course of our daily life. Therefore, we 'return' to the belonging attunement, our body's felt sense of inhering in an open field of sound, in order to retrieve an experience with hearing that has *not yet* been appropriately lived. The 'always already' accordingly lays out for us an assignment: a way of listening that we have *not yet*, or not for this moment, achieved. This assignment is a process of recollection – a recollection, a regathering, of Being, of the vibrant *Logos*.

Now we are ready to move ahead. The next step involves understanding that Being (*Logos*) is a vibrant gathering and laying. As *Logos*, as the primordial *Legein*, audibly inaudible as such, Being is that double tonality which *gathers* subject and object into their structure, laying down for them, at the same time, their elemental field and ground. Mindful of the fact that the Greek words, *logos* and *legein*, may be construed, in accordance with their etymology, as meaning 'gathering' and 'laying', Heidegger writes, in his 'Logos' study, that the *Logos* 'occurs essentially as the pure laying [laying-down, laying-out] which gathers and assembles [*das reine versam-*

melnde lesende Legen]'.[100] The *Logos*, he says, is 'the primordial laying that gathers'.[101] We might think of it, accordingly, as the (silent) laying-down of a primordial, double tonality, as the setting of a tone that gathers all soundful beings into its atmosphere. The *Logos*, then, is 'the essence of unification, which assembles everything in the wholeness of simple presencing [*ins All des einfachen Anwesens versammelt*]'.[102] Proper hearing, i.e. hearing that responds appropriately to its appropriation by the calling tonality of Being (*Logos*), must therefore become 'concerned' with the 'laying that gathers', because this gathering layout – the field of sonorous energies – is a gathering which gathers *us*. In other words, as beings whose listening belongs to and is attuned by Being (*Logos*), we are fatefully *subject* to the primordial laying down and gathering that Being (*Logos*) is, and as which it presences in relation to our hearing.

But if we understand this, then we realize that a *proper* hearing must be a listening that makes itself into an *organ* of the laying-which-gathers: a listening, in short, which *itself becomes* a gathering laying-down. Such a listening is a repetition of Being, a *mimesis*, a *homologein*. Becoming a laying-which-gathers would thus constitute the *Vollzugssinn* of our capacity for hearing: the fulfilment of its ontological potential, the realization of its need for meaning.

In *What Is Called Thinking?*, Heidegger says: 'Since man is the percipient who perceives what is, we can think of him as the *persona*, the mask, of Being.'[103] The ears of our listening fulfil themselves by learning how to go into a deep silence, an abyss of inaudibility, and by becoming the echo-chambers for Being, themselves gathering and laying down an auditory field that makes audible, that *lets be* audible, the field-clearing silence, the melodious silence of Being, audibly inaudible as such, on which all our listening essentially depends. Our ears become what they already essentially are: an organ of Being. But they must also be a centre that organizes concealment; for it is only by giving concealment that they can let Being be heard. Being as *archē*: an anarchy of sound.

This recollection of Being, a *homologein* attempted by the listening Self, is a redemption of the body, the body of pre-ontological understanding, the body which incorporated the oblivion of Being and always carries within it the traces of a thought older than itself. (See the commentary on Figure 1.1 in Chapter One.) Thus, Ned Lukacher is nearing the incorporated trace when he says that 'the voice of the *logos* is the echo within the self of an earlier incarnation'.[104]

In his *Introduction to Metaphysics*, Heidegger maintains that 'to be human means to take gathering upon oneself'.[105] This responsibility (response-ability) calls to us and belongs to us because, as he argues in 'Logik: Heraklits Lehre vom Logos', 'the human *logos* is the [ontic] self-collecting [*Sichsammeln*] on the basis of the original [ontological] In-gathering [*Versammlung*]'.[106] In his shorter 'Logos' study, he comments that we 'are all ears [*ganz Ohr*] when our gathering [*Sammlung*] devotes itself entirely to hearkening [*Horchsamkeit*]', recollecting – and that means re-collecting, i.e. gathering once again, in and through the character of our own listening – the presencing of Being, the primordial *Logos*.[107]

Now, when our listening assumes responsibility for its response-ability and responds to the claim into which we are gathered by grace of the *primordial* gathering-and-laying-down that Being, the *Logos*, gives us as the condition of the possibility of our hearing (anything at all), we set in motion a process that Heidegger calls, using the Greek word introduced by Herakleitos, the *homologein*: 'The human collecting on the basis of the original gathering occurs in the *homologein*.'[108] This *homologein* is a homology, a mimesis, a repetition, a resonant echoing. And it is an essential part of the process of recollection: 'proper hearing occurs essentially in *legein* as a *homologein*'.[109] For it is by virtue of this *homologein* that the essential nature of our hearing, its fulfilment as a perceptive capacity, is realized, 'gathered in the self-sameness of its [always] already lying-before'.[110]

But what *is* this *homologein*, phenomenologically considered? In 'Logik: Heraklits Lehre vom Logos', Heidegger calls our attention to the 'self-collecting into the originary In-gathering [*das Sichsammeln auf die ursprüngliche Versammlung*], as which "the Logos" holds the essence of humanity gathered unto itself'.[111] The *homologein*, then, consists in a listening that recollects, that doubles, that echoes, that recalls the field of its activity, realizing its nature as dependent on the primordial laying-which-gathers and making the field audible in the world *as* that by grace of which our hearing, which is *itself* a laying-which-gathers, first becomes possible as such. Our listening *homologein* makes this primordial laying-which-gathers audible by letting it be heard *through* the laying-and-gathering character we ourselves have achieved. Thus, our listening becomes a *homo-*

logein when it achieves a character that *manifests as* the doubling, the mimesis, the echoing resonance, of the more originary laying-which-gathers.

The *homologein*, the 'homology' between mortal being and Being as such, takes place, then, when our hearing, having understood the gift initially given to it in its embodiment of a pre-ontological understanding, returns in recollection to gather up, to re-collect into itself, the pre-personal, pre-egological laying-which-gathers – the primordial In-gathering of Being, the *Logos* which, 'from the very beginning', and *as* that 'beginning', lays out an open field for our hearing. In the mimetic *homologein*, our hearing becomes genuinely hermeneutical, letting that primordial laying-which-gathers, the primordial opening-up of a field of sound, become audible, by virtue of its own laying-and-gathering character, *as* that by grace of which it is first made possible. The mimetic *homologein* thus makes audible an otherwise concealed *harmony* between our own hearing, the 'proper' hearing of mortals, and the gift (the *Es gibt*) of Being, the timely *Logos*, which is the opening-up and laying-out of a sonorous energy field, an elemental ground or atmosphere of sheer vibrancy, into the tonality of which our hearing is deeply gathered.

Let us read this interpretation in Heidegger. In 'Heraklits Lehre vom Logos', Heidegger states that hearkening establishes (lays out) 'a homologous connection [*Bezug*] between the human *logos* and the *one Logos*'.[112] And in his shorter 'Logos' study, he remarks that the gathering of the *homologein* involves 'letting whatever a letting-lie-before lays down before us lie gathered in its entirety [*in seinem Gesamt*]'.[113]

This last point is important, but obscure and confusing. How can we let the field of our hearing become audible in its entirety, its wholeness? The answer I suggest – an answer not to be found explicitly in Heidegger's works – is that we can accomplish this gathering of the field only by returning to retrieve our sense of *Zugehörigkeit*, the primordial gift of a preconceptually understood relationship to Being, a grace that consists in our inherence in, our belonging to, and our attunement by, the sonorous field as a whole: a primordial relationship into which we are initially cast, not as adults, but as infants. Thus, what we need to do is make contact with our presently felt sense of this *Zugehörigkeit*, because it is through such contact that we can retrieve a sense of the laying-which-gathers, as which, in an initially unconscious repetition, and echoing the primordial nature of the field itself, i.e. echoing its primordial opening up, laying out, and in-gathering of a field, our hearing always begins. (The passage from Merleau-Ponty's *Phenomenology of Perception*, quoted at the beginning of this section, was crucial for my thinking, here, because it helped me to realize that our perception is always involved – always and already involved, before any reflective self-awareness has been achieved – in a process of opening, laying-out, and gathering-in. Once I understood this, the mimetic, echoic task of the *homologein* suddenly became clear to me.)[114]

Since wholeness is an experience given first and foremost through our capacity for feeling, the retrieval of our sense, as auditory beings, of gathering and being-gathered is a process that requires the rooting of our hearing in feeling. Why? Because, as we grew out of infancy, we lost touch with the feeling dimension of our hearing; in short, our listening became increasingly dissociated from our 'mooded' being in the world. So our listening must first get in touch with the gathering of (in) feeling – *das Ge-müt*. (The *Ge-* in *Gemüt* reminds us, as Heidegger notes, that feeling is itself essentially a gathering.)[115]

In *Civilization and Its Discontents*, Freud is therefore compelled to concede that, in his words,

> The ego-feeling we are aware of now is thus only a shrunken vestige of a far more extensive feeling – a feeling which embraced the universe and expressed an inseparable connection of the ego with the external world.[116]

Through the rooting again of our hearing in the gatherings of feeling, we can begin to experience the *Logos*, Being itself, as a deeper gathering. We can begin to realize that our primordial relationship to Being is a relationship through which our hearing is *always* situated in a field of sonorous energies that have *already* been gathered for it in a 'layout' that sets the tone and gives it a 'proper' measure. But it is also through its rootedness in feeling that our hearing can learn how to become, itself, a corresponding gathering, a recollection of the silent reserve of Being, that echoes the primordial gathering within which we live, and makes its attunement, its environmental tonality, audible for our world.

'Mortals are skillful [*geschicklich*]', Heidegger says, 'when they measure the *Logos* as the *hen panta* and submit themselves to its measure.'[117] Elsewhere, but in the same text, he observes that 'Because it is appropriate [*Als ein schickliches*], such behaviour becomes skillful [*geschickt*]. This skillfulness, e.g., in hearing "properly", is "fateful" [*geschicklich*].'[118]

What makes our development of the *homologein* already inherent in our hearing so significant, what makes it, indeed, a 'fateful skill', is that it carries out a recollection of Being in the midst of a world being ravaged by nihilism. Perhaps we can now appreciate more fully a point I tried to emphasize in the Introduction to this study: the process of self-development and a response to the historical advent of nihilism are inseparable. Moreover, the cultivation of our capacity for listening turns out to be of singular importance for both: not only for our self-formation, but also for our attempt to overcome the closure to (the 'anarchy' of) Being that increasingly rules over our world.

Part VIII
The Fourfold: A Gathering of Sound

> When consciousness rules the ear, with the ear we can hear all sounds.
>
> *The Kaushitaki Upanishad*[119]

> The deep ear that discerns / At evening, things that attend it until it hears/ The supernatural prelude of its own.
>
> Stevens, 'The auroras of autumn'[120]

When I hear a flock of geese flying high over the lake, there is a sense in which I am there where they are, as well as here, in my house.[121] Perception spans the distance of space; it reaches out in all directions around me, forming a ring, a sphere, that extends as far as I can perceive. And I am everywhere within that sphere – to the extent that I am attentive, alert, caring. But in any case, our hearing is always a gathering.

Always – but also not yet. For, as I have argued, our hearing is a gift that we can cultivate and develop. Our hearing can always become more responsive, more caring, more compassionate. We can become more concerned about

– or take more of an interest in – a more extensive world, extending the reach and range of our listening, making this extension a practice.

Then we would hear things we had never heard before. And we would begin communicating with people we had never listened to before. We would find ourselves affected by these people, these strangers very near and very far, and our lives might be correspondingly changed. When we make our way through city streets, we would gather up into our ears all the sounds of city life: beautiful sounds, ugly sounds, painful sounds, joyful sounds, threatening sounds, peaceful sounds, sounds of human kindness, sounds of evil – people conversing, crying, shouting, fighting, greeting, and parting; the sounds of fire trucks and ambulances; the engines of cars, taxis, buses; trucks loading and unloading; doors opening and closing; the sounds of radios and television sets; the laughter and music of bars and restaurants; the sounds of an old building being torn down and of a new one being built; the sounds of a piano drifting through an open window; airplanes humming overhead, taking us with them to all parts of the world; the horn of a tugboat in the harbour. . . . The sounds of human life, a song of mortal existence, gathering all sounds, without exception, without passing judgment.

Leaving the city for a while, we would begin a kind of communion with the animals of nature. We would hear, as never before, the wild song of nature's world: the wind whispering through the pines, the creaking of an old oak, the waves breaking on the rocks, a muskrat jumping into the lake, a night heron about to take flight, the mating call of the tree frogs. We would hear all these sounds, all these soundful presences, gathered into the ring of a melodious song – a *mandala* of resonant beings, each one a centre of vibrant energy, each one, alive with its own song, contributing to the ring of a gathering.

The gatherings of sound I am trying to evoke here are gatherings that are possible only when our listening suspends its normal and habitual judgments – liking and disliking, approving and disapproving, accepting and rejecting. Since this gathering is *always* happening, whether or not we are present and aware, one may say that it is *already* taking place – that when we become aware of such a gathering, we realize that it has always and already been happening. Nevertheless, the 'already' must be followed by 'not yet', or 'not at this moment', because there is a world of difference between the gathering already taking place without our awareness and understanding, and the gathering that can take place only by virtue of a guardian awareness and an ontological understanding, relating the gathering to the song of Being as such. The gathering we are thinking through, here, is a gathering that comes as a gift to our ears when we have developed the art, the skill, of 'just listening'. It is a gathering that comes only when we let go and let be, letting whatever sounds forth have all the time-space, all the silence, all the openness and otherness of being it wants.

Only when we are able to give soundful beings this openness will they sound forth in a gathering of their songs. For it is the *embrace* of our openness, our silence, which gathers them into a great ring of sound, the melodious *Gestalt* that Heidegger called the *Geviert*, the Fourfold, a cosmological, cosmophonic *mandala* in which gods and mortals, earth and sky come together, echoing each other's songs. It is our *embrace* which gathers them; and it is our letting-go, our letting-be, which lets them *sing* with the resonance of the field as a whole, gathering into their ring the song of Being itself. There is, of course, a time and a place to be judgmental, accepting and rejecting. But there is also great value, a wisdom we can bring into daily life, in learning a *Gelassenheit* that embraces all sonorous beings and welcomes all sounds, regardless of their nature. If, even once, we have experienced this gathering of sound, all our listening encounters thereafter will benefit from the ontological spaciousness we would give to them.

In 'The principles of nature and grace, based on reason', Leibniz is perhaps attempting to convey a sense of this spaciousness when he writes that

> Each soul knows the infinite, knows all, but confusedly; as in walking on the seashore and hearing the great noise which it makes, I hear the particular sounds of each wave, of which the total sound is composed, but without distinguishing them.[122]

Part IX
Time and the Echo: A Gathering of Time

' . . . the ear, / The murmuring shell of time.
T. S. Eliot, *The Dry Salvages*[123]

For the heavenly ones are unable / To do everything, / Namely, the mortals / Reach the abyss. Thus the echo returns / With them. Long is / The time, but / What is true happens.
Friedrich Hölderlin, 'Mnemosyne'[124]

I am borne into personal existence by a time which I do not constitute.
Merleau-Ponty, *Phenomenology of Perception*[125]

For it is reflection which objectifies . . . whereas, when I perceive, I belong . . . to the world as a whole.
Merleau-Ponty, *Phenomenology of Perception*[126]

Time does not itself belong to motion but embraces it. The intratemporality of a being means its being embraced by time (now) as number (counted). The factor of the *periechesthai*, being embraced, stresses that time does not itself belong among the beings which are *in* time. So far as we measure a being, either in motion or at rest, by time, we come back from the time that embraces and measures the moving thing to that which is to be measured. If we remain with the image of the embrace, time is that which is farther outside, as compared with movements and with all beings that move or are at rest. It embraces or holds-around the moving and the resting things.
Heidegger, *The Basic Problems of Phenomenology*[127]

Into the awareness of the thunder itself the awareness of the previous silence creeps and continues; for what we hear when the thunder crashes is not thunder pure, but thunder-breaking-upon-the-silence-and-contrasting-with-it. . . . The feeling of the thunder is also a feeling of the silence just gone.
William James, *Principles of Psychology*[128]

> Each present reasserts the presence of the whole past, which it supplants, and anticipates that of all that is to come. . . . The present is not shut up within itself, but transcends itself toward a future and a past.
>
> Merleau-Ponty, *Phenomenology of Perception*[129]

> The past, therefore, is not past, nor the future future.
>
> ibid., 421

In his 'Theses on the philosophy of history', Walter Benjamin suggested a distinction between two orders or experiences of time.[130] The time we are accustomed to is homogeneous and empty. It is linear and irreversible, yet endlessly, reassuringly repetitive: always just more of the same. But there is also, he believed, a revolutionary time-order: a time of redemption, a time of decisive action, in which the redeeming potentials left behind in the past can be retrieved and fulfilled. For Benjamin, this other time-order allows for the possibility of what he termed a *Jetztzeit*: a present in which the utopian alternatives left unrealized in the past are brought, by virtue of our 'remembrance' (*Eingedenken*), into the living historical present, so that revolutionary praxis can pursue them.

Benjamin's thinking is provocative. For me, it generates a question that I want to take up in this part of the chapter: can we achieve a different experience of the order of time by developing our capacity to hear? In other words, does a different experience of time begin to form as we begin to learn *Gelassenheit* in listening? The burden of the present section is to argue an affirmative answer to these questions. As I will soon demonstrate, our experience in listening to echoes can contribute a crucial wisdom here, for the echo's position in our standard time-order – its relations to the past, the present, and the future – is irremediably problematic.

Adorno's work on music fills in a piece of the puzzle; but it also subverts the rest of our efforts. Characteristically, he gives support to our negative task – a critique of contemporary habits – but refuses to take part in any more 'constructive' efforts. Specifically, he argues that contemporary music betrays the fact that our listening has become fetishized and regressive – an 'atomized listening'.[131] And he touches on the thought that this degenerate listening is connected with our bondage to a repetitive, linear time-order. But his 'negative dialectics' encourages no consideration of a different way of listening and a different way of experiencing the temporal order. In a monograph on Wagner, Mahler, and Berg, for example, Adorno makes an emphatic assertion, no doubt fully conscious of the fact that he is repudiating the *Jetztzeit*, the redemptive present, of his friend: 'Only because it [recollection, remembrance] brings back the past as irretrievable does it grant it to the present.'[132] Adorno obviously wants to emphasize the 'irretrievable'. But Benjamin would want – with equal justification – to emphasize that the past *is* brought back and *is granted* to the living present.

Now, I certainly do not want to suppress our recognition of the sense in which the past is decisively irretrievable. In fact, I would continue the direction of thinking Adorno initiated when he said, in *Negative Dialectics*, 'that nothing is original except the goal, [and] that it is only from the goal that the origin will constitute itself'.[133] For I would add that there is a sense in which the present has never really been present – a conclusion on which, for different reasons, Benjamin and Derrida would converge. (For Benjamin, the now-present of the bourgeois time-order fails to fulfil its revolutionary – that is to say, emancipatory – potential. For Derrida, the now-present is always inscribed by absence.) However, in the phenomenological account to which we shall now turn, I would like to argue that the sense of 'irretrievability' that Adorno has in mind is conceptually bound up with the time-order he repudiates, and that, once we have rejected the hegemony of this 'degenerate' time-order, we can begin to think – and live – in terms of a time-order in which the 'bringing back' and the 'granting' give to the present a very significant and fulfilling present. It will turn out, though, that the possibility of this other time-order – and a radically different experience of the present – essentially depends on our capacity for exercising *Gelassenheit*. In making this argument, I will direct our attention, of course, to our experiences with listening.

We shall accordingly reflect on *listening-time* as an auditory in-gathering of Being as a whole; on *the recollection of Being* as a listening embrace of the In-gathering; and on the *echo* as a teacher of the wisdom, the *Gelassenheit*, we need for the ontological extension of this listening embrace.

For many years – at least since Freud – psychiatry has observed anxiety and rage in relation to change and impermanence; and it has treated the more extreme forms of this 'moodedness' (*Stimmung*) as symptoms of psychopathology.[134] But the aversion to change and the desire for permanence are pervasive determinants of our social and cultural life, not mere aberrations from the norm. Thus it is not really surprising that our metaphysics is committed to an ontology of constant and permanent presence, and that this commitment can be traced back to philosophers earlier than Plato. The 'eternity' of the philosophers is an antidote for lives sickened by their bondage to a time-order which ultimately *intensifies* the suffering, despite the fact that it constitutes an unconscious drive to impose on time the will of the ego.

The 'time' of our everydayness is not an absolute reality; it is an institutionalized projection of our self-limited condition. This condition is ruled by ego-logical attachments, and by the anxieties and defences these attachments bring out. We may, for example, become obsessively attached to the painfulness or the satisfaction that once filled our past, so that we are unable to let go, unable to forget, unable to let the past be past. Some people, people to whom Freud called our attention, are driven by what he called a 'repetition compulsion', endlessly repeating the pain of the past. Other people cannot let go of their past because they are fixated on its satisfactions. Such people cannot derive any pleasure from the present. But there are also people who suffer a paralysing anxiety in relation to the future, because they are absolutely certain that the future can only bring them more suffering. (They may be right.) And then there are people who are totally attached to the future – people who live *only* for the future, always disenchanted with the past and the present because they are caught up in their fantasies about the future. There are also people who withdraw into an empty present, cutting themselves off from their past and living without any hope, any openness to future possibilities.

These portraits of 'psychopathology' are easily recognizable; they are archetypes that mirror everyone. Most of the time, we are unable to accept the past and let it go; we cannot forget it, cannot forgo the getting of it. Most of the time, we are unable to greet the future with an open embrace, however it may come – and with whatever it may present. Most of the time, we are unable to be present in the present and take it just as it is. Most of the time, our being in time is therefore pathological, oppressive, because it is a way of patterning our experience that guarantees frustration, dissatisfaction, and suffering. The irony is that the time-order by which we live is itself entangled in this pathology: an effect that becomes, in turn, a cause.

The straight-arrow character of time, the irreversible linearity that times us, a series partitioned into pasts, now-presents, and futures, is a social manifestation of our egological condition and a source of unnecessary suffering, especially when we lose touch with, and forget, the body's felt experience of a temporality which embraced us at the beginning of our life and granted us a sense of its wholeness.

Once upon a time, it seems, we participated in the ecstatic gathering of temporality – a gathering that gathered us into its primordial openness. But, with the initiation of the ego into the pressures of worldly timing, this primordial temporality of Being, utterly open, was forgotten, and we were left to live out our lives in the irreversible order of worldly time – the linear, metaphysically structured time of *archē* and *telos*.

This time-order of our social life is, as such, a cause of suffering, because it installs us in a present, a 'now', that is essentially self-contained: isolated from 'its' past and discontinuous with 'its' future, this 'present' is supposed to be rich and full, since it is protected by segregation from loss, absence, dissemination. But in truth, this atomic now-point is thereby *emptied* of meaning – a present which somehow is never really present, never really lived.

We are not compelled, however, to subject ourselves to the rule of this painful time. Nothing compels us to restrict our being in time to the dimensions of this order. Here, then, I would like to go into the dimensions of the primordial temporality of Being: these are ecstatic dimensions that embrace our standard time-order, and to which we gain access through the wisdom of the body's capacity for feeling. We shall, of course, be working on our self-development as listening beings.

In *Living By Zen*, Suzuki Daisetz tells us that,

> When we hear a bell or see a bird flying . . .
> we hear the bell even prior to its ringing,
> and see the bird even prior to its flight.
> Once the bell rings and the bird flies, they
> are already in the [standardized everyday]
> world of the [commonly developed] senses,
> which means that they are differentiated,
> subject to intellectual analysis and synthesis.[135]

How is it possible, though, to hear a bell even prior to its ringing? How can it be that we see the bird's flight even before it has happened? The experiences about which Suzuki speaks require a radical change both in our perception and in our way of putting the essential temporality of our being *into* 'time'.

Something Heidegger wrote in his text on Nietzsche could perhaps be useful here. Drawing a distinction between 'scientific thinking' and 'a thinker's thinking', he suggested that 'whereas scientific thinking, figuratively speaking, always runs along a line and can continue from the place where it stopped earlier, a thinker's thinking must in advance make a leap into the whole for each step it takes and collect itself in the center of a circle'.[136] This distinction gives us an analogy, for 'scientific thinking' lives in the timing that rules over our world – a time-series that runs along a line; whereas the thinker's thinking leaps into the temporality of the whole, which correspondingly gives it, in return, the present of a hermeneutical timing.

The more I listen to the text from Suzuki, the more I begin to hear, thanks to its resonance, the unheard-of meaning given voice in Heidegger's assertion that mortals have 'always already heard', 'always already belonged'. Our work with listening earlier in this chapter should help us to clarify the Zen experience; but, conversely, we may be able to reachh a deeper understanding of the peculiar temporality of hearkening f we can work through, here, the paradox that Suzuki throws at us.

'To see', says Heidegger, referring, in 'The Anaximander fragment', to the sage, the holy seer, 'is to have seen.'[137] In the same way as the seer is one who has *always already* seen what is given to be seen, so the hearkening thinker is one who has always already *heard* whatever is given to be heard. By virtue of a more developed listening – that is to say, by virtue of a more developed ontological understanding – the thinker can hear the bell before it rings out. This is not at all, however, some occult power; on the contrary, it is simply a consequence of the thinker's commitment to 'take over' that being which he or she already is.[138]

At this point, I expect that some readers will protest that I am asking them to take leave of their senses. So I would like to quote again from Heidegger's *Nietzsche*, calling on a passage in which he is examining – that is to say, taking seriously – what Nietzsche has to say about truth: 'Strange logic! Certainly, but let us first try to comprehend before we hasten to elect as judge our all too straight and narrow understanding, condemning this doctrine of truth before it has reached our inner ear.'[139]

The fact of the matter is that the 'strange' hearing to which Heidegger and Suzuki are pointing is a universal potential, a gift we have all received, and one that Merleau-Ponty's phenomenology of time-consciousness makes explicit. In his *Phenomenology of Perception*, for example, he points out that

> The present still holds on to the immediate past without positing it as an object, and since the immediate past similarly holds its immediate predecessors, past time is wholly collected up and grasped in the present. The same is true of the imminent future, which will also have its horizons of imminence. But with my immediate past I have also the horizon of futurity which surrounded it, and thus I have my actual present seen as the future of that past. With the imminent future, I have the horizons of the past which will surround it, and therefore my actual present as the past of that future. Thus, through the double horizon of retention and protention, my present may cease to be a factual present quickly carried away and abolished by the flow of duration.[140]

Presumably, Merleau-Ponty is describing a universal structure of time-consciousness, so that what he is describing should be an experience of our temporality with which we would all be familiar. In fact, however, the experience he describes sounds rather more like the awareness we would attribute to a mystic. It is therefore necessary to conclude that, if the description formulates a universal truth about the nature of our experience, then it must be a hermeneutical truth, a truth in the making, a dialectical truth that convinces us only after it has changed our self-awareness, deepened our self-understanding, and enabled us to 'return' to ourselves, be *true* to ourselves. Once the description has altered our awareness, making the implicit explicit, we immediately realize that, though it *is* true *now*, it was, before our greater awareness, both true and not true -- both *always already* true and also *not yet* true. (The 'always already' depends on truth in the sense of *alētheia*, truth as unconcealment; the 'not yet' pertains to truth in the sense of 'correctness', an *adequatio* between the representation and the experience described.) This situation is not really a paradox; it is simply a consequence of the fact that phenomenological accounts are self-referential, self-reflective: phenomenological truth is unavoidably dialectical and hermeneutical; it cannot be interpreted in terms of the correspondence theory of truth.

But if Merleau-Ponty's description discloses the fact that there is a wonderful strangeness even in our most prosaic experiencing, it also shows that the Zen experience is not nearly so strange as at first it sounds. In fact, the Zen experience is really *everyday* experience, different only in being more conscious, more phenomenologically self-aware. As long as we remain fixated within the dimensions of everyday time-consciousness, the Zen experience will seem impossible. In order to realize its truth, it is necessary that we shift our attention. First of all, we must become aware of the protentional and retentional intertwinings, the interweaving of all temporal moments, the interplay of past, present and future, gathered together in the present. This, in turn, opens our awareness to the dimensionality of time as a whole: that openness, instanced in the present, within which our familiar time-series, a stretch of now-points, first receives its structural possibility.

At any moment, we are free in principle to make this dimensional shift from the time (*die Zeit*) in which we normally live to the temporality (*Temporalität*) by grace of which our being-in-time (*Zeitlichkeit*) first becomes possible. But our ability to accomplish the shift is conditioned by habits of timing that are not easily broken. Once the holistic feeling of our inherence in a primordial, ecstatic temporality has been partitioned and compressed; once we have lost touch with the protentional and retentional intertwinings, only the greatest exertion can recover it.

I take Merleau-Ponty's account to be describing, as he thinks, our pre-personal, pre-reflective, implicitly felt experience of temporality: that *sense* of time which underlies our familiar serial order, our self-limited way of timing ourselves. If we should go into that sense, we would accordingly find ourselves participating in the primordial In-gathering (*Versammlung*) of temporality (*Temporalität*), embraced by its measure. For it is first of all by way of our sense of being *gathered* by the protentional and retentional intertwinings that we are able, even without knowing it, and in fact long *before* knowing and understanding it, to experience the 'anteriority of the future to the present [and] of the whole to its parts'.[141] In fact, without such a bodily felt, 'inner' *sense* of our temporalization (*Zeitlichkeit*) in the intertwinings of a primordial field of temporality, we would not inhabit the serial order that we call 'time' at all. Consequently, when we get in touch with our underlying sense of being-in-time, an attunement by Being that is also our inherence in the ecstasy of a field of temporality, the whole of time – of serial time – can present itself, simultaneously *filling* the now-present and *opening it out* to absence. 'A past and a future spring forth', as Merleau-Ponty says, 'when I reach out to them.'[142] Of course, this 'reaching out' must be a gathering embrace, and not a gesture of grasping or fixating: an embrace reaching into the retentional and protentional intertwinings of past, present, and future, reaching these intertwinings through the body's felt sense of its inherent temporal wholeness.

Arguing against the psychology of associationism, Merleau-Ponty asserts that 'the unity of the thing in perception is not arrived at by association, but is a *condition* of association, and as such precedes the delimitations which establish and verify it, and indeed precedes itself'.[143] Similarly, he will argue that a sense of the whole of time – a sense, that is, of temporality as such – precedes our consciousness of times in the time-series and is in fact a condition of this series. The Zen experience is simply a deepening of this understanding, reaching into the abyss, the nothingness, of a temporality which 'precedes itself'.

In *Zugehörigkeit*, we correspond by natural attunement to the primordial In-gathering of temporality. In *Zugehörigkeit*, we belong, therefore, to the whole of time: we belong to, we inhere in, time in its unpartitioned, and consequently hermeneutical, wholeness. It is *in this sense* that we have always already heard that which is at any (given) time present to be heard – the ringing of a bell, for instance. However, since most people are split off from their experience of the temporal interplay and live entirely *inside* the ego's fixed partitions, the Zen experience can seem utterly fantastic, impossible. For these people, the 'always already' *is* true – but not yet.

If we are listening well, however, our recollection of the In-gathering temporality of Being may be assisted by the echo, which can carry us into the embrace of this primordial gathering, the deeper, more concealed temporality that determines the timing of all beings in relation to the openness of Being. The elusive echo, the returning of a sound, denies the exclusive reality of the ego's linear, monadically partitioned order of time and affirms the 'eternal return' of our earmarked times in the wholeness of the temporal field. The echo, eluding the ego's grasp of its hermeneutical timing, can always help us, if we are willing to submit and listen; it can help us to experience the In-gathering of temporality with an ontological understanding. For the echo's 'time' returns us to the differential interplay, there where the difference between the temporality of Being and the timing of beings takes place.

Most of us are not in touch with our inner, bodily felt sense of the in-gathering intertwinings that constitute our timing. (For more detail on contacting the body's felt sense, see Eugene Gendlin's contribution to *Phenomenology and the Social Sciences*: a paper entitled 'Experiential phenomenology'.) Unfortunately, 'conventional wisdom' tends to encourage our repression of the non-linear timing disclosed by the echo. Sooner or later, this fund of conventional wisdom, taken as our absolute point of reference, is always used to finance the 'truth' of our forgeries, our ontological concealments.

The Zen experience is a moment of 'vagabond' listening: a moment when we are radically open to whatever may sound forth – whatever the timing of temporality may give. It is a moment of 'just listening', akin to the practice of 'just sitting', i.e. *zazen*. It is possible if and only if we have broken the spell of everyday timing and reversed our inveterate tendency to press ourselves into the time of a specious present – a present made so full, so self-sufficient, so purely and totally present, that it is actually, in the final analysis, emptied of all meaning, isolated from its past and futures. Rather than persisting in this timing, however, we *can* move to break away from conventional wisdom, letting go of our habits and obsessions, anxieties and defences. Most of all, we must get beyond the 'metaphysical' need to fixate, our need for absolute constancy and permanence, our need for a present that is purely and totally present, cut loose from the differential intertwining of pasts, presents, and futures. The very same factors that block our experience of the echo's return to the abyss of Being also stand in the way of an experience of primordial temporality as a gathering embrace.

The temporality of Being can indeed, then, as Merleau-Ponty put it, be 'wholly collected up'. But only for a recollection that is willing to forget, to forgo the getting, to let go and let be.

The ego lives in a time-zone *between* the forgetting of Being and the beginning of an ontological recollection. This zone can become, therefore, a time of loss, of mourning and suffering. But there *is* a time of redemption echoing within the rhythms to which our ears are bound. Our listening must begin a recollection rooted in these rhythms, the song of these primordial intentionalities.

It is not memory but *non-memory* which gathers up the past.[144] The past *can* be 'wholly collected up', but only when we renounce our memory, our ego-logical habits of accumulative serial remembering. Recollection is a very different gathering – a gathering embrace that thinks, without grasping, holding, trying to possess, *into* the dimensionality of time as a whole. The Zen master's *Gelassenheit* in relation to the past manifests, therefore, in hearing as the ability to hear the echoing return of a bell's sound even *after* it has ceased to ring; for he follows the echo into the abyss, and does so precisely by letting it go. Likewise, the future can be 'wholly collected up', but only when we relinquish all expectations, all representations. The Zen master's *Gelassenheit* in relation to the future manifests, therefore, in hearing as the ability to hear the bell even *before* it has begun to ring. What is called for, here, is a *Gelassenheit* that makes a clearing, in the auditory field, for the embracing silence which precedes the ringing. We cannot have a present without a future that is future; so we must let the future *be* a future, be *absent* as future. But at the same time, we can, by virtue of our letting go, gather the whole of temporality into the present of recollection.

The metaphysics of presence, which I take to be, as Heidegger has argued, a metaphysical closure to the presencing, the *Es gibt*, of Being, depends on an essentially linear time that is stretched out between an *archē* and a *telos*. So if we are hoping to prepare ourselves for the possibility of an epochal break with metaphysics and its closure to Being, then we must work on breaking out of the understanding of time, and the experience of time, that have prevailed in our world. In other words, we must work on relinquishing our faith in the *archē* and *telos* of the linear time-order and attempt to develop our sense of the hermeneutical structure that is constitutive of an ecstatic temporality open to epochal disclosures, epochal discontinuities, epochal revolutions. Because of the role listening plays in the formation of the intersubjective Self, and because of the lessons on impermanence – the arising, persisting, and passing away of beings – that listening receives from timing, I am arguing that the development of our capacity for listening, and in particular, the working out of our experience with the echo, may hold us open to possibilities of the utmost importance, as we confront the historical challenge of overcoming the metaphysics of time, time as constant presence, within which our lives have been enframed.

Melodious, and like a song, is the gift of primordial temporality to the field of our hearing. Hearkening understands this. It listens for the return of the echo. It lets itself be gathered into the time of its celebration, into the soundings that take us into a dimension of temporality different from the timing of our worldly serial-time.

Hearkening has learned the wisdom of Periander of Corinth, one of the 'seven sages' of the West. It has learned *meleta to pan*: 'Take into care beings as a whole'.[145]

Part X
Belonging to Culture: A Gathering of History

> The constitution of others does not come after that of the body; others and my body are born together from an original ecstasy.
>
> Merleau-Ponty, 'The philosopher and his shadow'[146]

> In order to have some inkling of the nature of that amorphous [pre-personal] existence which preceded my own history, and which will bring it to a close, I have only to look within me at that time which pursues its own independent course, and which my personal life utilises, but does not entirely overlay.
>
> Merleau-Ponty, *Phenomenology of Perception*[147]

> Insofar as I have sensory functions, a visual,

> auditory and tactile field, I am already in communication with others.
>
> ibid., 353

> It is characteristic of cultural gestures to awaken in all others at least an echo if not a consonance.
>
> Merleau-Ponty, 'The indirect language'[148]

> The myths disclose . . . sacred and creative history. Moreover, through initiation, every young Aranda not only learns what happened in principle, but ultimately discovers that he was already there, that somehow he participated in these glorious events of the past. The initiation brings about an *anamnēsis*.
>
> Eliade, *The Quest: History and Meaning in Religion*[149]

In *The Claim of Reason*, Stanley Cavell points out that 'our access to belief [in contrast, for example, to our access to knowledge] is fundamentally through the ear, not the eye. The ear requires corroboration (and prompts rumour), the eye requires construction (and prompts theory).'[150] What he says is, for the most part, I suppose, correct. But I submit that he is unfair to the ear, hearing less in 'belief' and less in 'corroboration' than what, for example, Eliade and Merleau-Ponty have heard. For, what *they* can hear is the ear's contribution to the reproduction of social and cultural life: social cohesion, generational continuity, the preservation of cultural traditions, and the transmission of an accumulated wisdom, speaking in the voices of folklore, fairy tales, myths and legends, family history. Before they are old enough to read, children listen to stories and tales. Before the laws of ancient Greece were written down in the monotonous, univocal prose of jurisprudence, they were *nomoi*, melodious songs of praise for heroic deeds, the paradigms of virtue, honour, and noble intent. 'Corroboration' can mean renewal of spiritual connections, initiation into the religious life of a community, and communion with long-departed ancestors.

Here, at the conclusion of this chapter, this book, I would like to broach the question of our belonging to culture, interpreting it, in consonance with the topology that concerns us in this chapter, as our gathering into history. This interpretation will be the basis for the projection of what could, perhaps, be another historical 'beginning', a breach in the metaphysics of closure that has for so long ruled our civilization.

Before we leave our meditation on hearing, let us read – and together inwardly listen to – a story. This is the story of the echo and its gift to hearing: another episode. Returning from afar, a 'repetition', the echo brings with it our belonging to history. Because we do not understand the echo's gift; because we do not hear the *entrustment* of history to the guardian nature of our hearing, we are deprived of an historical belonging which we need and long for.

The song of this truth, the truth of our historical entrustment, has been sung many, many times, preserved in an echo of ancient, ancestral voices reverberating through time, binding generations to generations with a wisdom all its own. And yet, somehow, it has still not been heard; for in a sense we need to think, it can be heard only in a time which has awakened to its passing, the truth of its impermanence, its perishing, its irretrievable absence. Let us try, then, for a passing moment, to lend an ear to this song.

At the dawn of western civilization, history was entrusted to an oral/aural tradition of sages and poets, elders with voices pleasing to the ear. And the intimate bonds that brought mortals together to hear the stories of their history belonged to the under-standing of hearing. Once upon a time, hearing belonged to history; and history belonged to hearing. But now this kind of history, history in the keeping of our hearing, has virtually disappeared – except perhaps in some rural communities, isolated families, and urban ghettoes. Written history is not the same: it is bereft of the power in sound to touch, to penetrate, to move, to gather. When people ceased to tell one another their histories, myths, legends and tales, and ceased to listen, to take the time to listen, something of the element in which historical gathering lives passed away in silence. I think we really need to hear stories of this passage. But its song has not yet been sung.

'It is characteristic of cultural gestures to awaken in all others at least an echo if not a consonance.' In this sentence, Merleau-Ponty touches on the intercorporeality within which our cultural traditions are reproduced. These cultural gestures even echo from one generation to the next, passing on the life of a culture with the transpersonal constitution of an 'ancestral body', a living body of cultural tradition. We are not just individual bodies, private, personal bodies; and there have never been any monadic bodies. The human body belongs to history, to culture; and the body that is personal is therefore rooted in a body that is transpersonal: we are, from uterus on, rooted in a dimension of our auditory being that is constitutive of an 'ancestral body', a body belonging to its ancestors, as much as to its contemporaries.

When I listen to myself, to my words, to the sound of my voice, I can hear others: I hear others 'inside' myself. Living others, dead others; others near and others far. Conversely, when I listen to others, I can hear myself: I hear myself 'in', or 'through', the others of my world. We resonate and echo one another. I can hear my ancestors: their absence is present, their presence is the presence of an echo, an audible absence.

Deep within the living body of tradition, there echo the voices and gestures of history, gathering together the generations of mortals, those who are present and those who are absent – the living and the dead. In the echo of these voices, these gestures, we will hear repeated the story of our beginning, our initiatory belonging to an intercorporeal history, the intertwining of our historical lives. We can *develop* our sense of belonging to a transpersonal, transhistorical world by retrieving our auditory body's presently felt sense of its pre-personal coexistence with others. It is the listening body's pre-personal existence which makes a transpersonal development possible. This development is not the *extinction* of the individual person and its personality, but rather their *extension* into the communicative matrix of the flesh, where identities and destinies are inseparably intertwined.

Retrieving a sense of this intertwining, we assume responsibility for the intercorporeality that has always and already bound us together in a shared history and gathered and claimed us through its ontological attunement, and we open ourselves to the utopian dreams of the flesh – to the potential for their fulfilment in a different historical life. If we listen well to ourselves, we can hear within our embodiment resonances and echoes that confirm the *interconnectedness* of all beings and already bring us into communication with all other mortals, gathering us together for the making of a more thoughtful history. And if we listen well to the voices of history, we can hear within them a wisdom they pass on, even without any consciousness: a wisdom, namely, that speaks of our historical possibilities and present historical needs.[151]

Although the retrieval of the auditory gathering that takes

place in the pre-personal dimension of our embodied existence – and its transformation, of course, into a life consciously directed by the auditory capacity for a transpersonal gathering – will always mark an important, if seldom achieved, step in our self-development, it is *not yet* the historical life of which we are ultimately capable as listening beings. We need to commit, to bind, our capacity for listening to making the historical life into which we are cast an exemplary recollection of the resonance of Being in the midst of our daily lives.

In his *Nietzsche* book, Heidegger communicates his conviction that, 'because the relationship to beings as such and as a whole distinguishes man, he first attains his essence when he inheres in such a relationship and commits himself to history for that history's consummation'.[152] This conviction prompts him to write, because we need to hear it, to let it reverberate within us, that, 'for primordial questioning, the sole kind of thinking is one that attunes man to hear the voice of Being. It is a thinking that enables man to bend to the task of guardianship over the truth of Being.'[153]

Guardianship over the 'truth' of Being, over *alethēia*, the opening-up of beings to Being, means lending an ear to its soundings and serving as an organ for the dissemination of its audibility. But our guardianship requires an attunement that can take place only if we let ourselves be gathered into the history of its keeping and the keeping of its history. For this 'truth', as Heidegger says, 'always demands a humankind through which it is enjoined, grounded, communicated, and thus safeguarded'.[154] What does this imply? Since the 'truth' of Being is a 'voice' that can speak only through *human* voices, to be gathered into its history means that we participate in the ongoing cultural conversation, keeping it attuned to Being. It means speaking out, out of its resounding preserve, as fearlessly as we can; it means making a space of good listening for all the voices of history, all the *different* human voices, living and dead, through which the 'truth' of Being, polyphonic, melodious, full of harmonies and discords, speaks and has spoken; it means letting the *ground* of its different resonances, its different intonations, resound and reverberate – long enough, and loudly enough, to split wide open the world of our deaf indifference. It is only by virtue of our individual commitments to this collaborative task of listening that we will be gathered into a post-metaphysical history, gathered into the *making* of this history, gathered into the possibility of a new beginning.

Heidegger draws a distinction between 'origin' and 'beginning', arguing that the origin is always concealed by the unconcealment of (at) the beginning; that the beginning is always the withdrawal and concealment of the origin; and that, in and with the beginning, the origin is always already irrevocably forgotten. He also argues, correlatively, that we must draw a distinction between the 'ending' of metaphysics and the history of its 'closure'.[155] The forgetting of Being, the forgetting of the ontological difference, belongs to a history of closure; but this history is not at all the *ending* of metaphysics, which can continue – who knows how long? – in a condition of profound closure. *Seinsvergessenheit*, forgetfulness of Being, is, or has been, unavoidable: hence there is, or has been, an epoch of closure. But at least we bear some trace of sense, some nagging awareness, of the primordial self-concealment, and the beginning of our forgetfulness: hence there is no ending, and no persistence of closure as a pre-ordained fate.

Überwindung means 'ending'. In 'Overcoming metaphysics', Heidegger writes, instead, of *Verwindung*, that is to say: of closure. Joan Stambaugh translates this second term as 'incorporation', and she explains that 'when something is overcome in the sense of *verwunden*, it is, so to speak, incorporated. . . . Thus, to overcome metaphysics and, in particular, its closure would mean to incorporate metaphysics, perhaps with the hope, but not the certainty, of elevating it to a new reality.'[156] In the final chapter of this study, I have begun to explore what this 'incorporation' might signify, if it were to be understood as a process of recollection taking place in the body of the listening self.

To be sure, the recollection of Being is (to borrow some words from Merleau-Ponty that seem just right for the point) 'a movement toward what could not in any event be present to us in the original and whose irremediable absence would thus count among our originating experiences'.[157] Nevertheless, we must, to avoid total despair and nihilism, understand the fact that, with recollection, the difference between beings and Being does 'in a way' present itself, even though, of course, it also, as he says, 'keeps itself hidden in a strange incomprehensibility. Hence the difference remains veiled.'[158] Thus Heidegger denies us the fulfilment of perceptual presence, whilst naming a possible experience with hearing (namely, the 'resonance' of Being) and consequently calling attention to a claim on our capacity for listening: 'In this first appearance [of the ontological difference], the first resonance of the truth of Being still conceals itself, taking back into itself the precedence of Being with regard to its dominance.'[159] The resonance of the truth of Being – the resonance of the primordial *ecstasis* that opened up the auditory field – still conceals itself, still withdraws itself from audibility. Nevertheless, we can, we must, console ourselves with an essential experience of this ultimate inaudibility.

We need to listen well; we need to hear, as Ned Lukacher puts it, 'the space of the unheard rhythm, the space opened up by the withdrawal of the question of Being'.[160] This calls for a listening that comes from the body of pre-ontological understanding, a listening that draws its sense of time's gift of Being from the silent rhythms of this deeper body and incorporates within itself, without ever fully retrieving it, the originary *Legein* of the *Logos*, the originary laying-down and in-gathering of Being, an utterly open field of vibrant energies.

It is, I think, conceivable that, out of this listening, reversing the closure of metaphysics, we *could* make a new historical beginning, gathering into our recollection the concealment of, and at, the origin, that elusive, audibly inaudible, clearing silence by grace of which the history of mortal hearing first became a possibility – our gift, our task.

It is the ears, and not the eyes, rulers of the modern empire, which will reverse the history of closure. Metaphysics has been dominated by vision; our ontology is an optical projection. Listening, more sensitive to the passage of time, the great destroyer of this ontology, may alone provide the channels for a different historical life. Nietzsche perhaps intuited the historical significance of this difference, observing that 'the visual image orders our perception, while rhythm does the same for our hearing. From the eye we can never reach a representation of time, and from the ear we can never reach a representation of space.'[161] Listening belongs to time; and when it becomes recollection, it belongs to the *ecstasis* of a primordial temporality – belongs, in fact, to the *Es gibt*, the temporality that gives us Being.

Notes

Introduction The Gift and the Art

1 See Bernard Williams (1962) 'The idea of equality', in P. Laslett and W. C. Runciman (eds) *Philosophy, Politics and Society*, Oxford: Basil Blackwell, second series.
2 Seyla Benhabib (1986a) *Critique, Norm and Utopia: A Study of the Foundations of Critical Theory*, New York: Columbia University Press, 250.

Chapter One The Historical Call to Our Hearing

1 Terrence Des Pres (1976) *The Survivor: An Anatomy of Life in the Death Camps*, New York and London: Oxford University Press, 208.
2 Friedrich Nietzsche (1982) *Daybreak: Thoughts on the Prejudices of Morality*, Cambridge: Cambridge University Press, 73.
3 Concerning Nietzsche's interpretation of nihilism, see (1968) *The Will to Power*, New York: Random, 7–48.
4 See Max Horkheimer (1974b) *The Eclipse of Reason*, New York: Continuum-Seabury, 105–7. Also see Francis Barker (1984) *The Tremulous Private Body: Essays on Subjection*, London and New York: Methuen.
5 Horkheimer, *Eclipse of Reason*, 105–7. Also see ibid., 122, and Max Horkheimer and Theodor Adorno (1986) *The Dialectic of Enlightenment*, New York: Seabury.
6 See the interview with Jürgen Habermas in March 1969, reported in Martin Jay (1973) *The Dialectical Imagination: A History of the Frankfurt School and the Institute of Social Research, 1923–1950*, Boston, Mass.: Little, Brown, 271.
7 Ronald D. Laing (1968) *The Politics of Experience*, New York: Ballantine Books, 28.
8 Heidegger speaks of 'loss of Being' in (1977a) 'The age of the world picture', *The Question Concerning Technology and Other Essays*, New York: Harper & Row, 142. Also see my paper, 'Psychopathology in the epoch of nihilism', in David M. Levin (ed.) (1987) *Pathologies of the Modern Self*, New York and London: New York University Press.
9 Theodor Adorno (1970) *Über Walter Benjamin*, Frankfurt: Suhrkamp, 159.

10 ibid. Also see Adorno and Horkheimer, *The Dialectic of Enlightenment*, 230.
11 Martin Heidegger (1977b) 'The end of philosophy and the task of thinking', *The Basic Writings of Martin Heidegger*, New York: Harper & Row, 374. Also see Martin Heidegger (1973) 'Metaphysics as history of Being', 'Sketches for a history of being as metaphysics', and 'Overcoming metaphysics', *The End of Philosophy*, New York: Harper & Row, as well as Heidegger's (1961) *Introduction to Metaphysics*, New York: Doubleday, and his (1982) *Nietzsche*, vol. 4: *Nihilism*, New York: Harper & Row.
12 Heidegger, 'The end of philosophy and the task of thinking', 48.
13 Martin Heidegger (1977) 'The word of Nietzsche: "God is dead" ', *The Question Concerning Technology and Other Essays*, New York, Harper & Row, 112.
14 Martin Heidegger (1968) *What Is Called Thinking?*, New York: Harper & Row, 25. Also see ibid., 28, 36, 76.
15 Maurice Merleau-Ponty (1968) 'The intertwining – the chiasm', *The Visible and the Invisible*, Evanston, Ill.: Northwestern University Press, 155.
16 Heidegger, 'The word of Nietzsche: "God is dead" ', 111.
17 Horkheimer, *Eclipse of Reason*, 176.
18 Jürgen Habermas (Fall 1981) 'The dialectics of rationalization', *Telos* 49:7.
19 Arnold Mindell (1985) *Working with the Dreaming Body*, New York and London: Routledge & Kegan Paul, 74.
20 Richard Wolin (1982) *Walter Benjamin: An Aesthetic of Redemption*, New York; Columbia University Press, 93.
21 Martin Heidegger (1977b) 'The end of philosophy and the task of thinking', *The Basic Writings of Martin Heidegger*, New York: Harper and Row, 374.
22 Martin Heidegger (1971b) 'The thing', *Poetry, Language, Thought*, New York: Harper & Row, 181.
23 Heidegger, 'On the essence of truth', *Basic Writings*, 141.
24 Heidegger, 'The age of the world picture', 142.
25 Horkheimer and Adorno, *The Dialectic of Enlightenment*, 34–5.
26 Heidegger, 'The age of the world picture', op. cit., 154.
27 Heidegger, *What Is Called Thinking?*, 241–2.
28 Martin Heidegger (1975) 'The Anaximander fragment', *Early Greek Thinking*, New York: Harper & Row, 39.
29 ibid.
30 Heidegger, 'The age of the world picture', 150.
31 Heidegger, 'What are poets for?', *Poetry, Language, Thought*, 120. Also see 'The origin of the artwork', *Poetry, Language, Thought*, 25, wherein Heidegger thinks about a gaze giving to its object a 'free field'.
32 See Martin Heidegger (1966) *Discourse on Thinking*, New York: Harper & Row, 64–5.
33 John Sallis (October 1984) 'Heidegger/Derrida – presence', *Journal of Philosophy* 81 (10): 597.

34 See Erik Erikson (1965) 'Wholeness and totality: a psychiatric contribution', in Carl J. Friedrich (ed.) *Totalitarian Dictatorship and Autocracy*, New York: Praeger, 161, and Erik Erikson (1968) *Identity, Youth and Crisis*, New York: Norton, 80–1. Also see Martin Jay (1984) *Marxism and Totality*, Berkeley, Calif.: University of California Press, 22.
35 Erikson, *Identity, Youth and Crisis*, 81.
36 John Sallis (1986) *Delimitations: Phenomenology and the End of Metaphysics*, Bloomington, Ind.: Indiana University Press, 22.
37 ibid., 22–3.
38 Sallis, 'Heidegger/Derrida – presence', 597.
39 ibid., 598. Also see Derrida's own work, relating the hearing of the ears to his critique of metaphysics: Jacques Derrida (1982a) 'Tympanum', *Margins of Philosophy*, Chicago: University of Chicago Press, ix–xxix, and (1983) *D'un ton apocalyptique adopté naguère en philosophie*, Paris: Galilée, 60–1. Also see Ned Lukacher (1986) *Primal Scenes: Literature, Philosophy, Psychoanalysis*, Ithaca, NY and London: Cornell University Press, 74: 'What the philosopher listens to during the epoch of the beginning of the ending of metaphysics is the interminable "fading" of the voice, the death-in-life of memory and the logos.'
40 David Wood (1985) 'Difference and the problem of strategy', in David Wood and Robert Bernasconi (eds) *Derrida and Difference*, Coventry, Warks.: Parousia Press, University of Warwick, 102–3.
41 Aristotle (1946) *Metaphysics*, trans. John Warrington, London: Dent, 51.
42 Walter Benjamin (1986) 'One-way street', *Reflections: Essays, Aphorisms, Autobiographical Writings*, New York: Schocken, 92. On the question of western oculocentrism, also see Allan Megill (1985) *Prophets of Extremity: Nietzsche, Heidegger, Foucault, and Derrida*, Berkeley, Calif.: University of California Press; Evelyn Fox Keller and Christine Grontowski (1983) 'The mind's eye', in Sandra Harding and Merrill Hintikka (eds) *Discovering Reality: Feminist Perspectives on Epistemology, Metaphysics, Methodology and the Philosophy of Science*, Boston, Mass.: Reidel; Agnes Heller (Spring/Summer 1981) 'Enlightenment against fundamentalism: the example of Lessing', *New German Critique* 23: 13–26; Lucien Febvre (1982) *The Problem of Unbelief in the Sixteenth Century: The Religion of Rabelais*, Cambridge, Mass.: Harvard University Press; Robert Mandrou (1976) *Introduction to Modern France, 1500–1640: An Essay in Historical Psychology*, New York: Holmes & Meier; Marshall McLuhan and Quentin Fiore (1967) *The Medium is the Message*, New York: Bantam, 111; René Descartes (1965) *Discourse on Method, Optics, Geometry, and Meteorology*, Indianapolis, Ind.: Bobbs-Merrill; Richard Rorty (1979) *Philosophy and the Mirror of Nature*, Princeton, NJ; Princeton University Press; Rodolphe Gasché (1986) *The Tain of the Mirror: Derrida and the Philosophy of Reflection*, Cambridge, Mass.: Harvard University Press; Guy Débord (1970) *Society of the Spectacle*, Detroit, Mich.: Black and Red Publ.; Martin Jay (1986) 'In the empire of the gaze: Foucault and the denigration of vision in twentieth-

century French thought', in David Hoy (ed.) *Foucault: A Critical Reader*, New York and Oxford: Basil Blackwell, 175–204; Hans Jonas (1974) *Philosophical Essays: From Ancient Creed to Technological Man*, Chicago: University of Chicago Press, 224–36; Hans Jonas (1966) 'The nobility of sight: a study in the phenomenology of the senses', *The Phenomenon of Life: Towards a Philosophical Biology*, New York: Harper & Row, 135–56; Erwin Straus (1970) 'Born to see, bound to behold: reflections on the function of the upright posture in the aesthetic attitude', in Stuart Spicker (ed.) *The Philosophy of the Body: Reflections of Cartesian Dualism*, New York: Quadrangle, New York Times Book Co., 334–61; Rudolph Arnheim (1969) *Visual Thinking*, Berkeley, Calif: University of California Press; Donald M. Lowe (1982) *The History of Bourgeois Perception*, Chicago: University of Chicago Press; Michel Foucault (1980a) 'The eye of power', *Power-Knowledge: Selected Interviews and Other Writings, 1972–1977*, New York: Pantheon; Michel Foucault (1979) *Discipline and Punish: The Birth of the Prison*, New York: Vintage; and finally, David Michael Levin (1988) *The Opening of Vision*, New York and London: Routledge & Kegan Paul.

43 Horkheimer and Adorno, *The Dialectic of Enlightenment*, 6. Also see 24 and 42. The Enlightenment is characterized as 'patriarchal' on 17, 23, 33, 71–5, and as hostile to the pre-patriarchal culture on 31.

44 Hannah Arendt (1978a) *The Life of the Mind*, New York: Harcourt, Brace, Jovanovich, 122. Other pages to read are 19–53, 87, 104–12. Also see Arendt (1978b) 'Metaphor and the ineffable: illumination or the nobility of sight', in Stuart Spicker (ed.) *Organism: Medicine and Metaphysics*, Dordrecht: Reidel.

45 John Dewey (1927) *The Public and its Problems*, New York: Henry Holt, 218–19.

46 See Maurice Merleau-Ponty (1964a) 'The child's relations with others', *The Primacy of Perception*, Evanston, Ill.: Northwestern University Press, 138, and Julian Jaynes (1976) *The Origin of Consciousness in the Breakdown of the Bicameral Mind*, Boston, Mass.: Houghton Mifflin, 269.

47 See Heidegger, 'The Anaximander fragment', 33–6 and 'Moira', *Early Greek Thinking*, 97. Also see Heidegger, 'The question concerning technology', *The Question Concerning Technology*, 18.

48 Nietzsche, *The Will to Power*, 227.

49 See Martin Heidegger (1962) *Being and Time*, New York: Harper & Row, 88, 216, 237.

50 Stéphane Mallarmé (1945) 'Prose', *Oeuvres Complètes*, ed. Henri Mondor and G. Jean-Aubry, Paris: Editions Gallimard, 57.

51 Meister Eckhart (1969) 'Ubi est qui est Rex Judaeorum', in Raymond B. Blakney (ed.) *Meister Eckhart: A Modern Translation*, New York: Harper & Row, 108.

52 Erwin Straus (1966) 'The phenomenology of hallucinations', *Phenomenological Psychology*, New York: Basic Books, 285.

53 ibid., 286.

54 See Jürgen Habermas (1973a) *Theory and Practice*, Boston, Mass.: Beacon.
55 Horkheimer and Adorno, *The Dialectic of Enlightenment*, 37.
56 See Horkheimer, *The Eclipse of Reason*, 104, 174.
57 See Gerardo Reichel-Dolmatoff (1971) *Amazonian Cosmos: The Sexual and Religious Symbolism of the Tukano Indians*, Chicago: University of Chicago Press, 93. The Desana associate 'reason' and 'knowledge' with sight, and 'thinking' and 'understanding' with listening.
58 Straus, 'The phenomenology of hallucinations', 286.
59 Quoted in Fernand Pouillon (1985) *The Stones of the Abbey*, New York: Harcourt, Brace, Jovanovich, 110, and attributed to St Bernard of Clairvaux.
60 Thomas McCarthy (1978) *The Critical Theory of Jürgen Habermas*, Boston, Mass.: MIT Press, 208.
61 See Seyla Benhabib (1986a) *Critique, Norm and Utopia*, New York: Columbia University Press, 314–15.
62 Jürgen Habermas (1979a) *Communication and the Evolution of Society*, Boston, Mass.: Beacon, 97–8. On the structural homologies between individual development and social evolution, also see Jürgen Habermas (1974) 'On social identity', *Telos*, 19.
63 ibid. Also see McCarthy, *Critical Theory of Jürgen Habermas*, 233–71. Bracketed interpolations are my own.
64 Jürgen Habermas (1971) *Knowledge and Human Interests*, Boston, Mass.: Beacon.
65 Herbert Marcuse (1972) *Counter-Revolution and Revolt*, Boston, Mass.: Beacon, 71–2.
66 ibid., 64.
67 ibid., 71.
68 ibid.
69 ibid., 62.
70 ibid., 62–3.
71 John Rawls (1971) *A Theory of Justice*, Cambridge, Mass.: Harvard University Press, 415. Also see what Harry S. Sullivan says, in (1953) *The Interpersonal Theory of Psychiatry*, New York: Norton, 193, about 'the child's pleasure in manifesting any ability he has achieved'.
72 Karl Marx (1973) *Grundrisse*, Harmondsworth and Baltimore, Md: Penguin, 488.
73 Benhabib, *Critique, Norm and Utopia*, 112.
74 Herbert Marcuse (1969) *An Essay on Liberation*, Boston, Mass.: Beacon, 53.
75 Michel Foucault (1982) 'Why study power? The question of the subject', in Hubert Dreyfus and Paul Rabinow, *Michel Foucault: Beyond Structuralism and Hermeneutics*, Chicago: University of Chicago Press, 216.
76 Michel Foucault (1980) Howison Lecture on 'Truth and subjectivity', Berkeley, Calif., University of California Press, 20 October 1980, unpublished typescript.

77 Hubert Dreyfus and Paul Rabinow (1986) 'What is maturity?', in Hoy (ed.) *Foucault: A Critical Reader*, 111–12.
78 ibid.
79 The letter, written by Hubert Dreyfus, is dated 18 May 1981.
80 Heidegger, 'The turning', *The Question Concerning Technology and Other Essays*, 48.
81 Heidegger, *Being and Time*, 213. Bracketed interpolations are my own. I substituted the phrase 'experience itself' for the second use of 'find itself'.
82 ibid., 206. For the original German text, see Martin Heidegger (1963) *Sein und Zeit*, Tübingen: Max Niemeyer, 163.
83 Martin Heidegger (1968) *What Is Called Thinking?*, New York: Harper & Row, 25.
84 Martin Heidegger (Winter Semester Seminar, 1920–1921). 'Einleitung in die Phänomenologie der Religion'; bibliographical data missing.
85 Medard Boss (1979) *The Existential Foundations of Medicine and Psychiatry*, New York: Jason Aronson, 220.
86 ibid., 118.
87 ibid., 104.
88 Benhabib, *Critique, Norm and Utopia*, 314–15.
89 See Theodore F. Geraets (1971) *Vers une nouvelle philosophie transcendentale*, The Hague: Martinus Nijhoff, 193.
90 See Merleau-Ponty's work in *The Visible and the Invisible*.
91 Mary Daly (1978) *Gyn/Ecology: The Metaethics of Radical Feminism*, Boston, Mass.: Beacon, 2–3. Incidentally, 'uroboric' is a term which symbolizes the roundness and wholeness of the auditory experience of its field.
92 Søren Kierkegaard (1956) *Either/Or*, vol. 1, Princeton, NJ: Princeton University Press, 66.
93 See the two tables Erik Erikson offers in (1959) 'Identity and the life cycle', *Psychological Issues*, monograph 1, New York: International Universities Press, 120 and 166. Also see the table reproduced by Bruno Bettelheim in (1970) *The Children of the Dream: Communal Child-Rearing and American Education*, New York: Macmillan, 322.
94 See Lawrence Kohlberg (1987) *Essays on Moral Development*, vol. I: *The Philosophy of Moral Development*, New York: Harper & Row, esp. 296–305, 323–88. For serious and compelling criticisms of Kohlberg's model, see Carol Gilligan (1982) *In a Different Voice: Psychological Theory and Women's Development*, Cambridge, Mass.: Harvard University Press.
95 See Alfred Schmidt (1969) 'Adorno – ein Philosoph des realen Humanismus', *Neue Rundschau* 80 (4) and Martin Jay (Summer 1972) 'The Frankfurt School's critique of Marxist humanism', *Social Research* 39, (2).
96 Michel Foucault (1977) *Language, Counter-Memory and Practice: Selected Essays and Interviews*, Ithaca, NY: Cornell University Press, 228.
97 Heidegger, 'Letter on humanism', *Basic Writings*, 201.
98 ibid., 201–2. Italics added.

99 ibid., 202. Italics and bracketed interpolations are my own.
100 Søren Kierkegaard (1941) *Concluding Unscientific Postscript*, Princeton, NJ: Princeton University Press, 79.
101 See Nancy Fraser (Fall 1983) 'Foucault's body-language: a post-humanist political rhetoric?', *Salmagundi* 61: 58. Fraser finds, in humanism, its 'own immanent counter-discourse, its critical, self-reflective conscience'. Also see Hayden White (1987) 'Foucault's discourse: the historiography of anti-humanism'. *The Content of the Form: Narrative Discourse and Historical Representation*, Baltimore, Md: Johns Hopkins University Press, and (1986) 'Foucault decoded: notes from underground', *Tropics of Discourse: Essays in Cultural Criticism*, Baltimore, Md: Johns Hopkins University Press.
102 Jürgen Habermas (1984) *The Theory of Communicative Action*, vol. 1, Boston, Mass.: Beacon Press, 1.

Chapter Two Zugehörigkeit: Our Primordial Attunement

1 Martin Heidegger (1962) *Being and Time*, New York: Harper & Row, 44.
2 Maurice Merleau-Ponty (1962) *Phenomenology of Perception*, London: Routledge & Kegan Paul, 351.
3 Carl G. Jung (1968), 'The psychology of the child archetype', *The Collected Works of Carl G. Jung*, vol. 9: *The Archetypes and the Collective Unconscious*, Princeton, NJ: Princeton University Press, part 1, 52.
4 Merleau-Ponty, *Phenomenology of Perception*, 234.
5 ibid., 424.
6 David Bohm (1978) 'The enfolding-unfolding universe: a conversation', *Re-Vision* 1 (3–4) 25.
7 Merleau-Ponty, *Phenomenology of Perception*, 329.
8 The term 'implicate order' comes from David Bohm, a physicist who worked with Einstein during the master's early years at Princeton.
9 See Heidegger, *Being and Time*, 76, 173–6.
10 John Welwood (1977) 'Meditation and the unconscious: a new perspective', *Journal of Transpersonal Psychology* 9 (1): 4.
11 ibid, 9. On loss of 'psychic wholeness', see Erich Neumann (1976) *The Child: Structure and Dynamics of the Nascent Personality*, New York: Harper & Row, 33–4.
12 See Frederick Perls, Paul Goodman, and Ralph Hefferline (1951) *Gestalt Therapy: Excitement and Growth in the Human Personality*, New York: Delta, 51, 320–2.
13 See Erich Neumann (1972) *The Great Mother: An Analysis of the Archetype*, Princeton, NJ: Princeton University Press.
14 Aristotle (1953) *Nicomachean Ethics*, Harmondsworth: Penguin, book 1, ch. 13, 52. Also see his work (1942) *The Generation of Animals*, Cambridge, Mass.: Harvard University Press, 165–71. And see Isaiah Berlin (1980) *Personal Impressions*, New York: Viking, wherein he discusses Aldous Huxley's belief in a 'vegetative soul'.
15 Heidegger, *Being and Time*, 100.

16 Martin Heidegger (1982) *The Basic Problems of Phenomenology*, Bloomington, Ind.: Indiana University Press, 319.
17 Martin Heidegger (1975) 'The Anaximander fragment', *Early Greek Thinking*, New York: Harper & Row, 51.
18 Jacques Derrida (1982b) 'Sending: on representation', *Social Research*, 49: 312.
19 Merleau-Ponty, *Phenomenology of Perception*, 354.
20 ibid., 351.
21 See Martin Heidegger (1968) *What Is Called Thinking?*, New York: Harper & Row. 152.
22 Ned Lukacher (1986) *Primal Scenes: Literature, Philosophy, Psychoanalysis*, Ithaca, NY and London: Cornell University Press, 90.
23 Maurice Merleau-Ponty (1968) 'The intertwining – the chiasm', *The Visible and the Invisible*, Evanston, Ill.: Northwestern University Press, 159.
24 Martin Heidegger (1973) 'Overcoming metaphysics', *The End of Philosopy*, New York: Harper & Row, 91.

Chapter Three Everydayness: The Ego's World

1 William Blake (1978) *Milton*, Boulder, Colo.: Shambhala, 67.
2 Lame Deer, with Richard Erdoes (1972) *Lame Deer: Seeker of Visions*, New York: Simon & Schuster, 121.
3 C. G. Jung (1975a) 'Spirit and life', *The Collected Works of Carl G. Jung*, vol. 8: *The Structure and Dynamics of the Psyche*, Princeton, NJ: Princeton University Press, 324.
4 Martin Heidegger (1982) *The Basic Problems of Phenomenology*, Bloomington, Ind.: University of Indiana Press, 175.
5 Confucius (1979) *The Analects*, Harmondsworth and New York: Penguin, 63.
6 Martin Heidegger (1961) *An Introduction to Metaphysics*, New York: Doubleday, 109.
7 See Martin Heidegger (1968) *What Is Called Thinking?*, New York: Harper & Row. Also see his essay on the 'Logos' fragment attributed to Herakleitos, (1975) *Early Greek Thinking*, New York: Harper & Row, 65, and (1970) 'Logik: Heraklits Lehre vom Logos', *'Heraklit'*, *Gesamtausgabe*, vol. 55, Frankfurt am Main: Vittorio Klostermann, 246. Also see Don Ihde (1977) *Listening and Voice*, Athens, OH: Ohio University Press, 153.
8 Heidegger, *Introduction to Metaphysics*, 108.
9 Martin Heidegger (1962), *Being and Time*. New York: Harper & Row, 214.
10 ibid.
11 Heidegger, 'Logos', *Early Greek Thinking*, 67.
12 Martin Heidegger (1971) 'What are poets for?' *Poetry, Language, Thought*, New York: Harper & Row, 110.
13 John Welwood (1977) 'Meditation and the unconscious', *Journal of Transpersonal Psychology* 9(1): 22. Also Sigmund Freud (1962) *The Ego*

and the Id, New York: Norton, and (1975) *Three Essays on the Theory of Sexuality*, New York: Basic Books. Also see Geshey Ngarwang Dhargyey (1974) *The Tibetan Tradition of Mental Development*, Dharamsala: Library of Tibetan Works and Archives, 29–35, wherein the author analyses how the three *kléshas*, attraction, aversion, and ignorance-confusion, arise out of the primordial ground of awareness (the *alaya-vijnana, kun gzhi*).

14 Adrienne Rich (1976) *Of Woman Born*, New York: Norton, 267.

15 Carl Rogers (1969) *Freedom to Learn*, Columbus, OH: Charles E. Merrill, 227; also see 225.

16 Immanuel Kant (1960) *Religion within the Limits of Reason Alone*, New York: Harper & Row, book 2, 51.

17 Plato (1937) 'Laches', 188c–89a, *The Dialogues of Plato*, New York: Random.

Chapter Four Skilful Listening

1 Martin Heidegger (1962) *Being and Time*, New York: Harper & Row, 207; in the 1960 German edition (Tübingen: Max Niemeyer), see 164.

2 See Samuel J. Todes (1969) 'Sensuous abstraction and the abstract sense of reality', in James M. Edie (ed.) *New Essays in Phenomenology*, Chicago: Quadrangle, 15–23.

3 ibid., 23.

4 See Alphonso Lingis (1969) 'The elemental background', in Edie (ed.), *New Essays in Phenomenology*, 24–38.

5 See Rudolph Arnheim's discussion of the 'bodily resonance effect', in (1972) *Toward a Psychology of Art*, Berkeley, Calif.: University of California Press, 316–18. Also see Hans Heinz Drager (1958) 'The concept of "Tonal Body"', in Susanne Langer (ed.) *Reflections on Art*, Baltimore, Md: John Hopkins University Press, 174–85; Helmut Reinold (1958) 'On the problem of musical hearing', in Langer, *Reflections on Art*, 262–97; and Giséle Brelet (1958) 'Music and silence', in Langer, *Reflections on Art*, 103–21. Also see Theodor Adorno (1938) 'Über den Fetischcharakter in der Musik und die Regression des Hörens', *Zeitschrift für Sozialforschung*, 7 (3).

6 Maurice Merleau-Ponty, 'The intertwining–the chiasm', *The Visible and the Invisible*, Evanston, Ill., Northwestern University Press, 144.

7 Michael Taussig (1987) *Shamanism, Colonialism and the Wild Man: A Study in Terror and Healing*, Chicago: University of Chicago Press, 432.

8 Martin Heidegger (1971a) 'Andenken', *Erläuterungen zu Hölderlins Dichtung*, Frankfurt am Main: Vittorio Klostermann, 96.

9 ibid.

10 Johann Wolfgang von Goethe (1982) *Italian Journey, 1786–1788*, San Francisco: North Point Press, 78.

11 See Geshey Ngawang Dhargyey (1974) *The Tibetan Tradition of Mental Development*, Dharamsala: Library of Tibetan Works and Archives, 46, 127. Regarding hearing touched by the sufferings of other beings and even capable of taking over that suffering, see 117.

12 Gilles Deleuze, in a conversation with Foucault recorded 4 March 1972, published in *L'Arc* (no. 49, pp. 3–10) and reprinted in Michel Foucault (1977) *Lanaugage, Counter-Memory and Practice*, Ithaca, NY: Cornell University Press, 209.
13 Carl Rogers (1969) *Freedom to Learn*, Columbus, OH: Charles E. Merrill, 227.
14 ibid., 222–27.
15 See Eugene Gendlin (1981) *Focusing*, New York: Bantam.
16 See Jacques Lacan (1981) *The Four Fundamental Concepts of Psychoanalysis*, New York: Norton, 258: What we need, he says, is not a 'third ear', 'as if two were not enough to be deaf with', but rather a 'new way of listening'.
17 Martin Heidegger (1975) 'Logos', *Early Greek Thinking*, New York: Harper & Row, 67.
18 These words are attributed to Rilke by Maurice Blanchot, in (1982) *The Space of Literature*, Lincoln, Nebr.: University of Nebraska Press, 153, but so far I have not been able to locate them in my editions of Rilke's work.

Chapter Five Communicative Praxis

1 Jacques Derrida (1985) *The Ear of the Other*, (New York: Schocken, 35.
2 Herbert Marcuse (1962) *Eros and Civilization: A Philosophical Inquiry into Freud*, New York: Vintage Books, Random, 34.
3 Plato (1937) *Laws*, trans. Benjamin Jowett, in *The Dialogues of Plato*, New York: Random, book VII, 815, 569. Also see the chapters on 'Moral education' and 'The body politic' in my book (1985) *The Body's Recollection of Being*, London and Boston, Mass.: Routledge & Kegan Paul.
4 E. Adamson Hoebel (1964) *The Law of Primitive Man*, Cambridge, Mass.: Harvard University Press, 93.
5 Michel Foucault (1980a) 'Body/power', *Power/Knowledge: Selected Interviews and Other Writings, 1972–1977*, New York: Pantheon, 58–9. Foucault asks only what body our society needs. I ask: what society do our bodies need?
6 In *The Ear of the Other*, 28, Derrida attributes these words to Nietzsche's *Ecce Homo*.
7 Foucault, *Power/Knowledge*, 186.
8 Russell Jacoby (1975) *Social Amnesia: A Critique of Conformist Psychology from Adler to Laing*, Boston, Mass.: Beacon, 37.
9 Foucault, *Power/Knowledge*, 151–2.
10 Sigmund Freud (1962) *The Ego and the Id*, New York: Norton, 16.
11 Michel Foucault (1977) 'Nietzsche, genealogy, history', *Language, Counter-Memory and Practice*, Ithaca, NY: Cornell University Press, 148. Also see François Ewald (1975) 'Anatomie et corps politiques', *Critique* 343: 1229.
12 Joel Kovel (1982) *The Age of Desire: Reflections of a Radical Psycho-analyst*, New York: Pantheon, 258. Plato's *Republic* and *Laws* already articulate an amazing awareness of this understanding.

13 Nancy Fraser (Fall 1983) 'Foucault's body-language: a post-humanist political rhetoric?', *Salmagundi* 61: 63–4.
14 Charles Taylor (1986) 'Foucault on freedom and truth', in David Hoy (ed.) *Foucault: A Critical Reader*, London and New York: Basil Blackwell, 93. Also see Hubert Dreyfus (1984) 'Beyond hermeneutics: interpretation in late Heidegger and recent Foucault', in Gary Shapiro and Alan Sica (eds) *Hermeneutics: Questions and Prospects*, Amherst, Mass.: University of Massachusetts Press, 66–83.
15 See Sigmund Freud (1965) *New Introductory Lectures on Psycho-Analysis*, London: Hogarth, 98.
16 Karl Marx (1975) 'Manuscript of 1844', in Quinton Hoare (ed.) *The Early Writings of Karl Marx*, New York: Random, 335.
17 Theodor Adorno (1981) 'Notes on Kafka', *Prisms*, Boston, Mass.: MIT Press, 253.
18 Theodor Adorno (1974) *Minima Moralia*, London: New Left Books (Verso edition, 1978), 154.
19 Seyla Benhabib (1986a) *Critique, Norm and Utopia: A Study of the Foundations of Critical Theory*, New York: Columbia University Press, 175.
20 Kovel, *The Age of Desire*, 233.
21 ibid. But I cannot accept Kovel's identification of the 'transhistorical' with the body of instincts. This all-too-Freudian interpretation of the 'transhistorical' reinforces the conception of the body I am contesting: a conception, namely, that regards the body as a chaos of irrational Dionysiac drives, so extremely libidinal as to be totally anti-social.
22 ibid., 63.
23 ibid., 64.
24 See Nicos Poulantzas (1978) *L'État, le Pouvoir, le Socialisme*, Paris: Presses Universitaires de France.
25 Fraser, 'Foucault's body-language', 61.
26 Reiner Schürmann (December 1985) 'What can I do in an archaeological-genealogical history?' *Journal of Philosophy* 82: 542.
27 See, for example, Nancy Fraser (1987) 'Social movements versus disciplinary bureaucracies: the discourses of social needs', *CHS Occasional Papers*, no. 8, Minneapolis, Minn.: Center for Humanistic Studies, University of Minnesota. I agree entirely with the rest of the paper, which brilliantly integrates theoretical and practical levels of analysis.
28 Foucault, *Language, Counter-Memory, Practice*, 216.
29 Foucault, *Power/Knowledge*, 56, cited by Taylor in 'Foucault on freedom and truth', 86.
30 See Eugene Gendlin (1981) *Focusing*, New York: Bantam, and Eugene Gendlin (1987) 'A philosophical critique of the concept of narcissism: the significance of the Awareness Movement', in David M. Levin (ed.) *Pathologies of the Modern Self*, New York: New York University Press.
31 See Theodor Adorno (1979) 'Anmerkungen zum sozialen Konflikt heute', *Soziologische Schriften*, vol. 1, Frankfurt am Main: Suhrkamp, 93. Also see Theodor Adorno (1973) *Dissonanzen: Musik in der verwalteten*

Welt, Gesammelte Schriften, vol. 14, Frankfurt am Main: Suhrkamp, and *Hörmodelle, Gesammelte Schriften*, vol. 4, part 2, Frankfurt am Main: Suhrkamp.

32 John B. Thompson (1982) 'Universal pragmatics', in John Thompson and David Held (eds) *Habermas: Critical Debates*, Boston, Mass.: MIT Press, 116.

33 See Freidrich Beissner's commentary in the Stuttgart edition of Friedrich Hölderlin's (1946) *Sämtliche Werke*, Stuttgart: Kohlhammer, vol. 2, 495.

34 See Ralph Walso Emerson's letter to President Van Buren, written in 1838, reprinted (1956) *The Portable Emerson*, ed. Mark Van Doren, New York: Viking, 656.

35 Henry David Thoreau (1973) 'On the duty of civil disobedience' (1849), *Walden and Civil Disobedience*, New York: New American Library, 118–19.

36 Seyla Benhabib (1986a) 'The generalized and the concrete other: toward a feminist critique of substitutionality universalism', in E. Kittay and D. Meyers (eds) *Proceedings of the Women and Moral Theory Conference*, New Jersey: Rowman & Allenheld, 27.

37 Herbert Marcuse (1972) *Counter-Revolution and Revolt*, Boston, Mass.: Beacon, 79. Bracketed words are my own interpolation. See also Franco Basaglia (1987) *Psychiatry Inside Out: Selected Writings*, New York: Columbia University Press, esp. 231–63. Basaglia argues very eloquently that the suffering and misery of psychiatric patients can be directly related to the fact that, in the institutions of psychiatry, their voices cannot be heard, and they are not listened to.

38 Raymond Geuss (1981) *The Idea of a Critical Theory: Habermas and the Frankfurt School*, Cambridge: Cambridge University Press, 63. Also see an excellent study by Calvin O. Schrag (1986) *Communicative Praxis and the Space of Subjectivity*, Bloomington, Ind.: University of Indiana Press.

39 Jacoby, *Social Amnesia*, 100.

40 Jürgen Habermas (1971) *Knowledge and Human Interests*, Boston, Mass.: Beacon, 314–15.

41 Hannah Arendt (1963) *Eichmann in Jerusalem: A Report on the Banality of Evil*, New York: Viking, 23. Bracketed words are my own interpolation.

42 Tadeusz Borowski (1976) *This Way for the Gas, Ladies and Gentlemen*, New York and Harmondsworth: Penguin, 132.

43 Alasdair MacIntyre (1973) 'Ideology, social science, and revolution', *Comparative Politics* 5: 322.

44 See J. Habermas (1987) 'Marx and the thesis of internal colonisation', *The Theory of Communicative Action*, vol. 2, Boston, Mass.: Beacon.

45 ibid., 341–2.

46 ibid., 342.

47 ibid.

48 Max Horkheimer (1974a) *Critique of Instrumental Reason*, New York: Continuum-Seabury, 75.

49 Friedrich Nietzsche (1983) 'On the uses and disadvantages of history

for life', *Untimely Meditations*, Cambridge: Cambridge University Press, 119.

50 Friedrich Nietzsche (1982) *Daybreak: Thoughts on the Prejudices of Morality*, Cambridge: Cambridge University Press, 258.

51 Karl Marx, 'Economic and philosophical manuscripts of 1844', in Erich Fromm (1961) *Marx's Concept of Man*, New York: Frederick Ungar, 131.

52 Northrop Frye (1957) *The Anatomy of Criticism: Four Essays*, Princeton, NJ: Princeton University Press, 243.

53 Kovel, *The Age of Desire*, 249.

54 Michel Foucault, 'The subject and power', in H. Dreyfus and P. Rabinow, *Michel Foucault: Beyond Structuralism and Hermeneutics*, Chicago University of Chicago Press, 216.

55 Jürgen Habermas (1983) 'Walter Benjamin: consciousness-raising or rescuing critique?', *Philosophical-Political Profiles*, Boston, Mass. and London: MIT Press, 160. Note that he says 'transformed', not 'abandoned'. See Benhabib, *Critique, Norm and Utopia*, 329: 'The project of emancipation has increasingly been viewed not as the fulfillment, but as the transfiguration of the Enlightenment legacy.'

56 Max Horkheimer (1978) *Dawn and Decline: Notes 1916–1931 and 1950–1969*, New York: Continuum-Seabury, 162.

57 Michel Foucault (1984) 'What is enlightenment?', in Paul Rabinow (ed.) *The Foucault Reader*, New York: Pantheon, 48.

58 Jürgen Habermas (1979b) 'Moral development and ego identity', *Communication and the Evolution of Society*, Boston; Mass.: Beacon, 78.

59 Michel Foucault (1984b) 'On the genealogy of ethics: an overview of work in progress', in Rabinow (ed.), *The Foucault Reader*, 362.

60 Jacoby, *Social Amnesia*, 105.

61 ibid.

62 See Gendlin, 'A philosophical critique of the concept of narcissism'. Also see his paper (1986) 'Process ethics and the political question', in *The Focusing Folio*, Chicago: The Focusing Institute, vol. 5, no. 2, 69–87. And see my discussion of Gendlin in (1988) *The Opening of Vision*, London and New York: Routledge & Kegan Paul, 295–320.

63 Foucault, 'What is enlightenment?', 50.

64 ibid., 47.

65 See Freud, *The Ego and the Id*, 16.

66 Theodor Adorno (1973b) *Negative Dialectics*, New York: Continuum-Seabury, 297.

67 Anthony Giddens (1979) *Central Problems in Social Theory*, Berkeley, Calif.: University of California Press, 126.

68 Hugh C. Wilmott (March 1986) 'Unconscious sources of motivation in the theory of the subject: an exploration and critique of Giddens' dualistic models of action and personality', *Journal for the Theory of Social Behaviour* 16, 118.

69 ibid., 117.

70 See Jürgen Habermas (1987) 'Excursus on identity and individuation',

in *The Theory of Communicative Action*, vol. II, Boston, Mass.: Beacon Press, p. 106.

71 ibid. He makes a similar point in his 'Einführung' (10–11) to *Die Entwicklung des Ichs* (Koln, 1977), which he edited together with R. Döbert and C. Nunner-Winkler. The text is cited by Thomas McCarthy in (1978) *The Critical Theory of Jürgen Habermas*, Boston, Mass.: MIT Press, 342.

72 Benhabib, *Critique, Norm and Utopia*, 332. Also see 333.

73 See Lawrence Kohlberg (1981) *Essays on Moral Development*, vol. 1: *The Philosophy of Moral Development*, New York: Harper & Row. In some of his most recent work, work I have not yet had time to examine closely – especially (1983) *Moralbewusstsein und kommunikatives Handeln*, Frankfurt: Suhrkamp, and (1986) 'Gerechtigkeit und Solidarität: Eine Stellungnahme zur Diskussion über "Stufe 6"', in W. Edelstein and G. Nunner-Winkler (eds) *Zur Bestimmung der Moral: Philosophische und sozialwissenschaftliche Beiträge zur Moralforschung*, Frankfurt: Suhrkamp, 291–318 – Habermas moves away from the abstract universality of the Kantian and Rawlsian models, proposing a model based on interpersonal relationships between concrete individuals. In these two texts, Habermas takes issue with Gilligan; but he also contests very decisively the model advocated by Kohlberg.

74 See Carol Gilligan (1982) *In a Different Voice: Psychological Theory and Women's Development*, Cambridge & Mass.: Harvard University Press.

75 For criticisms of Habermas's attempt to patch up Kohlberg's theory, see Benhabib, *Critique, Norm and Utopia*, esp. 329–33. Also see Dieter Misgeld (Spring/Summer 1985) 'Critical hermeneutics versus neoparsonianism?', *New German Critique* 35: 55–82.

76 Habermas, 'Moral development and ego identity', 78. According to my way of understanding the 'ego', a way that distinguishes it from the 'self', Habermas should not be speaking of 'ego identity', but rather of the 'self'. What he has to say applies perfectly to the 'self', but not very well to the 'ego'. The interpolation of the phrase 'and the needs of others' is my own. The interpolation is necessary to avert a very egocentric interpretation here – to avert which is precisely the point of my ego/self distinction. For a critical discussion of the problems challenging the theory of moral development Habermas proposes in this text, see McCarthy, *The Critical Theory of Jürgen Habermas*, esp. the material on 'Psychoanalysis and social theory' (193–213) and 'Communication and socialization' (333–57).

77 Benhabib, *Critique, Norm and Utopia*, 336. Of particular significance, in this regard, is the recent work of my colleague at Northwestern, Nancy Fraser: (January 1986) 'Toward a discourse ethic of solidarity', *Praxis International* 5 (4): 425–9; (Winter 1987) 'Women, welfare, and the politics of need intepretation', *Hypatia: A Journal of Feminist Philosophy* 2, (1): 103–21, reprinted (1988) in Peter Lassman (ed.) *The Politics of Social Theory*, London: Tavistock, and (1987) 'Social movements versus disciplinary bureaucracies: the discourses of social

needs', *CHS Occasional Papers*, no. 8, Minneapolis, Minn.: Center for Humanistic Studies, University of Minnesota.

78 See Jürgen Habermas (1973) ' "Postscript" to *Knowledge and Human Interests*', *Philosophy of the Social Sciences* 5: 177.

79 Seyla Benhabib (Spring/Summer 1985) 'The utopian dimension in communicative ethics', *New German Critique* 35: 94.

80 ibid., 94–5. The words attributed to Habermas come from 'Moral development and ego identity', 93.

81 Benhabib, *Critique, Norm and Utopia*, 334.

82 ibid., 332–3.

83 See Fraser, 'Women, welfare, and the politics of need interpretation', in Lassman (ed.), *The Politics of Social Theory*.

84 Benhabib, *Critique Norm and Utopia*, 322.

85 Habermas, 'Moral development and ego identity', 93. The 'communicative fluidity' of needs, due to our ability to become articulate about them, is precisely what Foucault does not take into account. Nor, until recently, does Fraser.

86 Benhabib, *Critique, Norm and Utopia*, 333.

87 ibid., 314–15.

88 ibid., 314.

89 See Fraser, 'Women, welfare, and the politics of need interpretation'.

90 See Gendlin, 'Process ethics and the political question', a problematic also discussed in my book, *The Opening of Vision*, 295–320, and in Gendlin's paper, 'A philosophical critique of the concept of narcissism', in Levin (ed.), *Pathologies of the Modern Self*.

91 Harold Searles (1965) *Collected Papers on Schizophrenia and Related Subjects*, New York: International Universities Press, 340. Italics added.

92 ibid., 34. Also see 192–215, and see Shierry M. Weber (1970) 'Individuation as praxis', in Paul Breines (ed.) *Critical Interruptions: New Left Perspectives on Herbert Marcuse*, New York: Herder & Herder.

93 Maurice Merleau-Ponty (1968) *The Visible and the Invisible*, Evanston, Ill.: Northwestern Universities Press, 28.

94 Hugo Blanco (1972) *Land or Death: The Peasant Struggle in Peru*, New York: Pathfinder, 47.

95 Jürgen Habermas (1985) 'Questions and counterquestions', in Richard Bernstein (ed.) *Habermas and Modernity*, Cambridge, Mass. and London: MIT Press, 196–7. Italics added.

96 Christopher Lasch (1978) *The Culture of Narcissism: American Life in an Age of Diminishing Expectations*, New York: Norton, 74.

97 Friedrich Nietzsche (1968) *The Will to Power*, New York: Random, 358.

98 Maurice Merleau-Ponty (1963) *In Praise of Philosophy*, Evanston, Ill.: Northwestern University Press, 27.

99 Marx, letter to A. Ruge, September 1843. In Karl Marx (1975) *The Early Writings of Karl Marx*, New York: Vintage, 209.

100 Adrienne Rich (1976) *Of Woman Born: Motherhood as Experience and Institution*, New York: Norton, 21. Italics added.

101 Richard Wolin (1982) *Walter Benjamin: An Aesthetic of Redemption*, New York: Columbia University Press, 96. Also see 38.
102 Arnold Mindell (1985) *Working with the Dreaming Body*, New York and London: Routledge & Kegan Paul, 84.
103 Theodor Adorno (1971b) *Kritik*, Frankfurt am Main: Suhrkamp, 90–1.
104 Merleau-Ponty, 'Working notes', *The Visible and the Invisible*, 270.
105 ibid., 267.
106 ibid., 139.
107 ibid., 267.
108 *Diagnostic and Statistical Manual of Mental Disorders*, third edn, Washington, DC: American Psychiatric Association, 1980, 315. Also see Sigmund Freud (1957) 'On narcissism: an introduction', *Standard Edition of the Complete Works of Sigmund Freud*, vol. 14, London: Hogarth; Freud, *The Ego and the Id*; Sigmund Freud (1963) *Introductory Lectures on Psychoanalysis*, part III: 'General theory of the neuroses', vol. 16 of the *Standard Edition*, London: Hogarth; Sigmund Freud (1964) *New Introductory Lectures on Psycho-Analysis*, vol. 22 of the *Standard Edition*, London: Hogarth; Sigmund Freud (1964b) 'The splitting of the ego in the process of defence', *Standard Edition*, vol. 23, London: Hogarth. Also see Otto Kernberg (1975) *Borderline Conditions and Pathological Narcissism*, New York: Jason Aronson, and Richard Wollheim (1977) *Sigmund Freud*, New York: Viking.
109 See the *Diagnostic and Statistical Manual*, cited above.
110 ibid., 316.
111 See René Descartes (1955) 'Meditations on first philosophy', in E. Haldane and G. Ross (eds) *The Philosophical Works of Descartes*, vol. 1, New York: Dover. Also see Jacques Derrida (1978) 'Cogito and the history of madness', *Writing and Difference*, Chicago: University of Chicago Press; Bernard Flynn (1983) 'Descartes and the ontology of subjectivity', *Man and World* 16; Véronique Foti (June 1986) 'The Cartesian imagination', *Philosophy and Phenomenological Research* 46 (4); Michel Foucault (Autumn 1979) 'My body, this paper, this fire', *Oxford Literary Review* 4; English transl. by Geoff Bennington of an appendix to the second (1972) edn of *Histoire de la folie*, Paris: Plon (1961); and Harry Frankfurt (1979) *Demons, Dreamers, and Madmen*, Indianapolis, Ind.: Bobbs-Merrill.
112 See Lasch, *The Culture of Narcissism*; Nathan Schwartz-Salant (1982) *Narcissism and Character Transformation: The Psychology of Narcissistic Character Disorders*, Toronto: Inner City Books; and Herbert Marcuse (1955) *Eros and Civilization: A Philosophical Inquiry into Freud*, New York: Vintage, 1962; and 'On hedonism', in his (1968) *Negations: Essays in Critical Theory*, Boston, Mass.: Beacon.
113 On Lacan, see Jacques Lacan (1968) *The Language of the Self*, Baltimore, Md.: Johns Hopkins University Press, and (1977) *Écrits: A Selection*, ed. A. Sheridan, New York: Norton. Also see John P. Muller and William Richardson (1982) *Lacan and Language: A Reader's Guide to Écrits*, New York: International Universities Press. On Kohut, see

Heinz Kohut (1977) *The Restoration of the Self*, New York: International Universities Press.

114 Jacques Lacan (1977a) 'The mirror stage as formative of the function of the "I" as revealed in psychoanalytic experience', in Alan Sheridan (ed.) *Écrits: A Selection*, New York: Norton.

115 See Harry Stack Sullivan (1953) *The Interpersonal Theory of Psychiatry*, New York: Norton.

116 See Muller and Richardson, *Lacan and Language*.

117 ibid., 29. Also see John O'Neill (1982) 'The specular body: Merleau-Ponty and Lacan on self and other', paper read at the 1982 Merleau-Ponty Circle, published in *Proceedings of the Merleau-Ponty Conference*.

118 Muller and Richardson, *Lacan and Language*, 6.

119 ibid., 29.

120 ibid., 6.

121 ibid., 30.

122 ibid.

123 ibid., 28.

124 ibid., 31.

125 See Jacques Lacan (1977b) 'Aggressivity in psychoanalysis', in Sheridan (ed.) *Écrits*, discussed in Muller and Richardson, *Lacan and Language*.

126 See Maurice Merleau-Ponty (1964a) 'The child's relations with others', *The Primacy of Perception*, Evanston, Ill.: Northwestern University Press.

127 ibid., 114.

128 ibid., 146.

129 The 1977 study by Meltzoff and Moore, demonstrating the hitherto unrecognized existence of selective attention, perceptual discrimination, and interactive behaviours, even at the age of two weeks, is reported by Michael P. Coyle (1987) 'An experiential perspective on the mother-infant relationship', *Focusing Folio* 6 (1): 5–6. The *Folio* is published quarterly by the Focusing Institute of Chicago.

130 ibid., 14, 21, 22.

131 See Nancy Henley (1977) *Body Politics*, New Jersey: Prentice-Hall, 128.

132 Coyle, 'An experiential perspective', 22.

133 Merleau-Ponty, 'The child's relations with others', 119.

134 Coyle, 'An experiential perspective', 1. The empirical documentation of pro-social behaviour-patterns is now enormous. I catalogue only some of it here: Daniel Bar-Tal (1976) *Prosocial Behaviour: Theory and Research*, New York: Wiley; Z. F. Boukydis (1985) 'A theory of empathic relations between parents and infants: insights from a client-centred experiential perspective', *The Focusing Folio* 4 (1); T. B. Brazelton (1985) 'Early parent-infant reciprocity', *Progress in Reproductive Biology and Medicine*, vol. 2, 1–13; T. B. Brazelton, B. Klosowski, and M. Main (1974) 'The origins of reciprocity: the early mother-infant interaction', in M. Lewis and L. Rosenberg (eds) *The Effect of the Infant on its Caretaker*, New York: Wiley; G. Butterworth and M. Costello (1976) 'Coordination of auditory and visual space in

new-born human infants', *Perception* 5; J. Campos and C. Steinberg (1981) 'Perception, appraisals and emotion: the onset of social referencing', in M. E. Lamb and L. R. Sherwood (eds) *Infant Social Cognition: Empirical and Theoretical Considerations*, Hillsdale, NJ: Erlbaum; W. S. Condon and L. Sandler (1974) 'Synchrony demonstrated between movements of the neonate and adult speech', *Child Development* 45; W. Condon (1979) 'An analysis of behavioural organization', in S. Weitz (ed.) *Nonverbal Communication: Readings with Commentary*, New York: Oxford University Press; A. De Casper and W. Fifer (1980) 'Of human bonding: newborns prefer their mothers' voices', *Science* 208; Nancy Eisenberg (1982) *The Development of Prosocial Behaviour*, New York: Academic Press; R. Eisenberg (1964) 'Auditory behaviour in the human neonate: a preliminary report', *Journal of Speech and Hearing* 7; M. Haith (1980) *Rules That Babies Look By: The Organization of New-born Visual Activity*, Hillsdale, NJ: Erlbaum; J. M. Haviland, C. Maletesta, and M. L. Lelwien (1984) 'Emotional communication in early infancy', *Infant Mental Health Journal* 5 (3); M. L. Hoffman (1981) 'Is altruism part of human nature?', *Journal of Personality and Social Psychology* 3; J. Kagan, R. Kearsley, and P. Zelago (1978) *Infancy: Its Place in Human Development*, Cambridge, Mass.: Harvard University Press; Jerome Kagan (1984) *The Nature of the Child*, New York: Basic Books; Milton Klein (1981) 'On Mahler's autistic and symbiotic phases', *Psychoanalysis and Contemporary Thought* 4; L. Lipsitt (1982) 'Infancy and lifespan development', *Human Development* 25; A. N. Meltzoff and M. K. Moore (1977) 'Imitation of facial and manual gestures by human neonates', *Science* 198; A. N. Meltzoff and W. Barton (1979) 'Intermodal matching by human neonates', *Nature* 282; Paul Mussen and Nancy Eisenberg (1977) *The Roots of Caring, Sharing, and Helping*, New York: Freeman; J. D. Osofsky (ed.) (1979) *Handbook of Infant Development*, New York: Wiley; J. J. Parker (1984) 'Communication in early infancy: three common assumptions', *Human Development* 26; Jean Piaget (1964) *The Moral Judgement of the Child*, New York: Macmillan; H. Rosenfeld (1981) 'Whither conversational synchrony?', In K. Bloom (ed.) *Prospective Issues in Infancy Research*, Hillsdale, NJ: Erlbaum; E. Staub (1978) *Social Behaviour and Morality*, New York: Academic Press; D. Stern (1983) 'The early development of schemas of self, other, and self-with-other', in Samuel Kaplan and Joseph Lichtenberg (eds) *Reflections on Self Psychology*, Hillsdale, NJ: Analytic Press, Erlbaum; L. Stone, H. Smith, and L. Murphy (1973) *The Competent Infant*, New York: Basic Books; P. Stratton (ed.) (1982) *The Psychobiology of the Human Newborn*, New York: Wiley; E. Tronich and L. Adamson (1980) *Babies as People: New Findings on Our Social Beginnings*, New York: Collier-Macmillan; Marion Yarrow and C. Zahn-Wexler (1977) 'The emergence and founding of pro-social behaviours in young children', in R. Smart (ed.) *Readings in Child Development and Relationships*, New York: Macmillan. I should also mention, here, the work of George H. Mead (1962) *Mind, Self and Society*, Chicago: University of Chicago Press, and Max Scheler (1954)

The Nature of Sympathy, New Haven, Conn.: Yale University Press. I am grateful to Les Brunswick and Eugene Gendlin for steering me to the literature I have named in his catalogue.

135 Coyle, 'An experiential perspective', 2. Coyle refers to the work of D. Stern, cited in the preceding footnote.

136 Coyle, 'An experiential perspective', 6–8.

137 Merleau-Ponty, 'The child's relations with others', 148.

138 ibid., 150. Also see Elmar Holenstein (1985) *Menschliches Selbstverständnis: Ichbewusstsein, Intersubjektive Verantwortung, Interkulturelle Verständigung*, Frankfurt am Main: Suhrkamp.

139 Coyle, 14.

140 ibid., 15.

141 ibid., 16.

142 ibid.

143 Erik Erikson (1968) *Identity, Youth and Crisis*, New York: Norton, 113. Also see 98–118 on ego formation, mirroring, mother-child relations, and the 'associative transfer' of motor schemata by imitation.

144 Horkheimer, *Critique of Instrumental Reason*, 140–58.

145 Searles, *Collected Papers on Schizophrenia and Related Subjects*, 227–8. Also see Coyle, 'An experiential perspective', 13. Coyle points out that, even when there is consistent, reliable, and situationally appropriate *physical* care, in relation to the infant's basic *physiological* needs, the infant will show signs of developmental disturbance if there is inconsistent, inappropriate, excessive, or insufficient *empathic* responsiveness to the child's *emotional* nature – forms of responsiveness that do not allow the child periods of bodily felt sensing.

146 See Robert Romanyshyn (1987) 'Mirror as metaphor of psychological life', in K. Yardley and T. Honess (eds) *Self and Identity: Psychological Perspectives*, New York: Wiley, 297–305, and (1982) *Psychological Life: From Science to Metaphor*, Austin, Tex.: University of Texas Press.

147 Coyle, 'An experiential perspective', 11.

148 ibid., 20. Also see Sullivan's analysis of mother-child interaction processes, in *The Interpersonal Theory of Psychiatry*.

149 I am grateful to my colleague, Tom McCarthy, for his reminding me to say, here, that we form a sense of ourselves, not only in interactions with others, but also in interactions with the material world: thanks to negativities – perceptual surprises and disappointments, the frustration of egocentric expectations, and beliefs that turn out to be in error – we learn what is merely subjective.

150 McCarthy, *The Critical Theory of Jürgen Habermas*, 35.

151 Merleau-Ponty, 'The intertwining – the chiasm', *The Visible and the Invisible*, 136.

152 Merleau-Ponty, 'Working notes', *The Visible and the Invisible*, 210.

153 Merleau-Ponty, 'The intertwining – the chiasm', 139.

154 Merleau-Ponty, 'Interrogation and intuition', *The Visible and the Invisible*, 123.

155 Merleau-Ponty, 'Working notes', 259.

156 ibid., 255–6. Also see 'The intertwining – the chiasm', 139 for a definition of 'flesh'.
157 Merleau-Ponty, 'The intertwining – the chiasm', 147.
158 Merleau-Ponty, 'Interrogation and intuition', 123.
159 ibid., 122–3. Also see 'The intertwining – the chiasm', 147.
160 Merleau-Ponty, 'Interrogation and intuition', 123.
161 Merleau-Ponty, 'Working notes', 249.
162 ibid.
163 ibid., 250. See Michel de Montaigne (1965) *The Complete Essays*, Stanford, Calif.: Stanford University Press, book II, ch. 12: 'Even in my own writings, I do not always find again the sense of my first thought; I do not know what I meant to say.' He is perhaps the first one to deconstruct the 'metaphysics of presence'. And he does this using examples from writing. Derrida's work is not original.
164 Merleau-Ponty, 'Working notes', 254.
165 Merleau-Ponty, 'The intertwining – the chiasm', 134. Also see his 'Working notes', 266: For the *cogito* to be 'possessed' by the visible is, in effect, to be dispossessed by it.
166 Merleau-Ponty, 'Interrogation and intuition', 123.
167 Merleau-Ponty, 'The intertwining – the chiasm', 152.
168 Merleau-Ponty, 'Interrogation and intuition', 118.
169 See his 'Working notes', 249 and 256 for additional references to narcissism and the myth of Narcissus.
170 ibid., 245.
171 Merleau-Ponty, 'The intertwining – the chiasm', 139.
172 ibid. See Martin Dillon's interpretation, which argues persuasively against the symmetry of this reversibility, in (1983) 'Merleau-Ponty and the reversibility thesis', *Man and World* 16: 365–88.
173 See Dillon, 'Merleau-Ponty and the reversibility thesis', and Martin Dillon (Autumn 1978) 'Merleau-Ponty and the psychogenesis of the self', *Journal of Phenomenological Psychology* 9 (1–2).
174 Merleau-Ponty, 'The intertwining – the chiasm', 137.
175 ibid., 155. Also see 141–54.
176 Merleau-Ponty, 'Working notes', 264–5.
177 Merleau-Ponty, 'Interrogation and dialectic', *The Visible and the Invisible*, 49.
178 Merleau-Ponty, *Phenomenology of Perception*, 354.
179 Merleau-Ponty, 'The intertwining – the chiasm', 141.
180 ibid., 137.
181 ibid., 141.
182 Maurice Merleau-Ponty (1970) *Themes from the Lectures at the Collège de France. 1952–1960*, Evanston, Ill.: Northwestern University Press, 82.
183 Max Horkheimer (1974). *The Eclipse of Reason*, New York: Continuum-Seabury 179. Also see 115–16.
184 Mary Daly (1978) *Gyn/Ecology: The Metaethics of Radical Feminism*, Boston, Mass.: Beacon, 417.
185 Mindell, *Working with the Dreaming Body*, 80.
186 Adorno, *Negative Dialectics*, 221–2. I do not agree, however, that this

anamnēsis necessarily reinforces the ego. It *could*, instead, take us *beyond* the boundaries of the ego.

187 Benhabib, 'The utopian dimension in communicative ethics', 83. Italics added. Benhabib is commenting on Walter Benjamin and on Habermas's essay, 'Walter Benjamin: consciousness-raising or rescuing critique?'. I agree with what she says, but insist that such 'images and anticipations' are contained not only in the 'semantic heritage of a cultural tradition', i.e. in language, but *also* in the depths of the body – what Mindell is calling 'the dreambody'. In 'Body/power', *Power/Knowledge*, 55, Foucault rejects utopian images, whether or not embodied; but, in doing so, he throws 'the very bodies of individuals' to 'the materiality of power'. He is tragically in error.

188 Habermas, 'Moral development and ego identity', 78. Italics added; bracketed interpolations are mine. As I noted earlier, Habermas fails to distinguish ego and self. What he is really conceptualizing is not, despite his terminology, an ego-identity, but rather an identity, or character, *beyond* ego, namely, the identity, or character, of a Self. This explains my interpolation of 'self' inside the brackets.

189 Benhabib, *Critique, Norm and Utopia*, 336. Also see Harry C. Boyte (1984) *Community Is Possible: Repairing America's Roots*, New York: Harper & Row.

190 Foucault, *Power/Knowledge*, 190. Italics added. This assertion seems totally to contradict what he says in (1977) 'Revolutionary action: "until now" ', published in *Language, Counter-Memory, Practice*, Ithaca, NY: Cornell University Press: 'To imagine another system is to extend our participation in the present system' (230). Which of these views is strategically more progressive, more emancipatory? Perhaps there is a sense in which these views are complementary. Does it not depend on how we understand and practise the work of imagination? To 'dream' *can* be a way of escaping reality and avoiding the task of transforming society. But utopian 'dreaming' can also be a way of formulating our *sense* of what we want and need, clarifying what needs to change, and coherently organizing and directing our energies for the work of social change.

191 Coyle, 'An experiential perspective', 5. Italics added.

192 Merleau-Ponty, 'The child's relations with others', 118. Italics added. Also see Richard Cohen (Winter 1984), 'Merleau-Ponty, the flesh, and Foucault', *Philosophy Today*, 28.

193 Merleau-Ponty, *Phenomenology of Perception*, 354. Italics added.

194 ibid., 85. Italics added.

195 Merleau-Ponty, 'Reflection and interrogation', *The Visible and the Invisible*, 49. Italics and bracketed words added.

196 Merleau-Ponty, 'Working notes', 264. Italics added. On reversibility in relation to reciprocity and justice, see Kohlberg, 'Justice as reversibility: the claim to moral adequacy of a highest stage of moral judgement', *Essays on Moral Development*, vol. 1. 194.

197 Joel Whitebook (1985) 'Reason and happiness: some psychoanalytic

themes in critical theory', in Richard J. Bernstein (ed.) *Habermas and Modernity*, Cambridge, Mass.: MIT Press, 144.

198 Foucault, 'The subject and power', in Dreyfus and Rabinow, *Michel Foucault*, 216.

199 Merleau-Ponty, 'The intertwining – the chiasm', 144. Bracketed words added.

200 Merleau-Ponty, 'The child's relations with others', 119.

201 Merleau-Ponty, 'The concept of nature', *Themes from the Lectures at the Collège de France*, 82.

202 See Kohlberg, 'Justice as reversibility', *Essays on Moral Development*, vol. 1, 194.

203 See Benhabib, *Critique, Norm and Utopia*, 330–1.

204 ibid.

205 ibid.

206 Merleau-Ponty, 'The child's relations with others', 119.

207 See Merleau-Ponty, *Phenomenology of Perception*, 215, 216, 330, 352–4.

208 See an excellent study by Francis Barker (1984) *The Tremulous Private Body: Essays on Subjection*, London and New York: Methuen, 13.

209 Whitebook, 'Reason and happiness', 144. David Rappaport's text is (1967) 'A historical survey of psychoanalytic ego psychology', in Merton Gill (ed.) *The Collected Papers of David Rappaport*, New York: Basic Books, 753.

210 ibid.

211 Habermas, 'Moral development and ego identity', 90.

212 Searles, 'The effort to drive the other person crazy', *Collected Papers on Schizophrenia and Related Subjects*, 261.

213 See Michel Foucault (1977) *Discipline and Punish: The Birth of the Prison*, New York: Random House 228, 298–304.

214 See G. Snyders (1965) *La Pédagogie en France aux dix-septième et dix-huitième Siècles*, Paris: Plon. Also see the work of Lawrence Kohlberg, cited earlier.

215 Mindell, *Working with the Dreaming Body*, 81.

216 See Thomas McCarthy's 'Introduction' to Jürgen Habermas (1987) *The Philosophical Discourse of Modernity*, Boston, Mass.: MIT Press.

217 See Lasch, *The Culture of Narcissism*.

218 Maurice Merleau-Ponty (1964b) 'The philosopher and sociology', *Signs*, Evanston, Ill.: Northwestern University Press, 110.

219 Bernard Williams (1962) 'The idea of equality', in Peter Laslett and W. G. Runciman (eds) *Philosophy, Politics, and Society*, Oxford: Basil Blackwell, second series.

220 See John Rawls (September 1980) 'Kantian constructivism in moral theory', *Journal of Philosophy* 77, 525–7, and (1982) 'Social unity and primary goods', in Amartya Sen and Bernard Williams (eds) *Utilitarianism and Beyond*, Cambridge: Cambridge University Press, 165–6.

221 See Sullivan, *The Interpersonal Theory of Psychiatry*, 193, and John Rawls (1971) *A Theory of Justice*, Cambridge, Mass.: Harvard University Press, 415.

222 Alan Wolfe (1986) 'The return of values', *Tikkun* 1 (2): 63.
223 See Arendt, *The Life of the Mind*, note 86, 227.
224 Montaigne, *The Complete Essays*, book I, ch. 11.
225 Maurice Merleau-Ponty, 'The indirect language', *The Prose of the World*, Evanston, Ill.: Northwestern University Press, 94. Also see Henley, *Body Politics*, 128 for empirical confirmations.
226 Erikson, *Identity, Youth and Crisis*, 90. But I would add that it is not just a question of technology and scientific progress; it is also a question of social and poltical changes related to the Awareness Movement. Processes that promote and increase self-awareness also produce diversities and dissonances.
227 Heidegger, 'Poetically man dwells', *Poetry, Language, Thought*, 218–19.
228 Adorno, *Minima Moralia*, 103.
229 Benhabib, *Critique, Norm and Utopia*, 315.
230 ibid., 335.
231 ibid., 333.
232 ibid., 314.
233 Merleau-Ponty, *Phenomenology of Perception*, xx. Italics added.
234 Benhabib, *Critique, Norm and Utopia*, 329.
235 See Jürgen Habermas (1975) *Legitimation Crisis*, Boston, Mass.: Beacon.
236 Jürgen Habermas (Winter 1981) 'Modernity versus postmodernity', *New German Critique*, 22.
237 Merleau-Ponty, *Phenomenology of Perception*, xxi.
238 See Benhabib, *Critique, Norm and Utopia*, 286.
239 John Rawls (September 1980) 'Kantian constructivism in moral theory', *Journal of Philosophy* 77, 519.
240 Benhabib, 'The generalized and the concrete other', 8–9.
241 Benhabib, *Critique, Norm and Utopia*, 286.
242 ibid., 285.
243 Habermas, 'Moral development and ego identity', 88. Also see Don Johnson (1983) *Body*, Boston, Mass.: Beacon, 152–95, for a discussion of body-grounded consensus.
244 Merleau-Ponty, 'The child's relations with others', 109.
245 Merleau-Ponty, 'The intertwining – the chiasm', 144. Also see Hwa Yol Jung (Winter 1981), 'The Orphic voice and ecology', *Environmental Ethics*, 3:329–40, and (1979) *The Crisis of Political Understanding: A Phenomenological Perspective in the Conduct of Political Inquiry*, Pittsburgh, Penn.: Duquesne University Press, in which the author attempts to 'construct a theory of communication and social existence based on the metaphor of music'.
246 Foucault, 'Body/power', *Power/Knowledge*, 55.
247 See M. Foucault, *The Order of Things: An Archaeology of the Human Sciences*, xxii.
248 See J. G. Merquior, *Foucault*, 35–42.
249 See Arendt, *The Life of the Mind*, 104–12. I am grateful to Reiner Schürmann for calling my attention to these pages. Although my book was already finished, it was not too late for me to interpolate some references to her thoughts on vision and hearing.

250 See Reiner Schürmann (1987) *Heidegger on Being and Acting: From Principles to Anarchy*, Bloomington, Ind.: University of Indiana Press, 92. This is a superb book, which I regret getting to read only after I had already completed the final draft of my book. (The first draft of my book, finished in 1980, took shape around the hypothesis, inspired by my reading of Heidegger on the pre-Socratics, that we may be living now in a critical transition period between two epochal *epistemes*, two 'economies of presence': the modern, of course, visual; and the post-modern auditory.) Belatedly, I have been able to insert a very brief discussion of Schürmann's book at the very end of Chapter Five. But it is a book that merits and requires much more study and thought.

251 See Hans-Georg Gadamer (1975) *Truth and Method*, New York: Seabury Press, 420.

Chapter Six *Hearkening*: Hearing Moved by Ontological Understanding

1 William Carlos Williams (1963) *Paterson*, New York: New Directions, 201.

2 Maurice Merleau-Ponty (1968) 'Interrogation and intuition', *The Visible and the Invisible*, Evanston, Ill., Northwestern University Press, 121.

3 Martin Heidegger (1962) *Being and Time*, New York: Harper & Row, 207. In the German, see 163.

4 ibid., 188–9.

5 ibid. Also see 191. The bracketed interpolation is my own.

6 Martin Heidegger (1957) *Der Satz vom Grund*, Pfullingen: Günther Neske, 203.

7 Heidegger, *Being and Time*, 315.

8 Martin Heidegger (1975) 'Logos', *Early Greek Thinking*, New York: Harper & Row, 65.

9 See Heidegger's letter to Herr Büchner, published in his (1959) *Vorträge und Aufsätze*, Pfullingen: Günther Neske: an English translation has been published in Albert Hofstadter's edition of Heidegger's (1971) *Poetry, Language, Thought*, New York: Harper & Row, 183. Also see Martin Heidegger (1977) 'The question concerning technology', *The Question Concerning Technology and Other Essays*, New York: Harper & Row, 25. Bracketed interpolation is my own.

10 Heidegger, 'Logos', 65.

11 Friedrich Nietzsche (1983) 'On the uses and disadvantages of history for life', *Untimely Meditations*, Cambridge: Cambridge University Press, 83–4.

12 William Wordsworth (1972) *The Prelude*, New York and Harmondsworth: Penguin, book 2, 86.

13 Erich Neumann (1971) *Art and the Creative Unconscious*, Princeton, NJ: Princeton University Press, 172. Also see 169–72.

14 Maurice Merleau-Ponty (1964) *Themes from the Lectures at the Collège de France*, Evanston, Ill.: Northwestern University Press, 131.

15 Heidegger, *Being and Time*, 137. The bracketed words are mine.

16 Merleau-Ponty, 'Reflection and interrogation', *The Visible and the Invisible*, 32.
17 Maurice Merleau-Ponty (1962) *Phenomenology of Perception*, London: Routledge & Kegan Paul, 219. Also see 430.
18 Heidegger, 'Alētheia', *Early Greek Thinking*, 103. Also see Merleau-Ponty, *Phenomenology of Perception*, 320.
19 Heidegger, 'Logos', 66.
20 ibid., 65.
21 Wordsworth, *The Prelude*, book 2, 90. The chthonic, archetypally feminine symbolism comes to appearance in Geoffrey Hartman's reference to 'the ineluctable ear, its ghostly, cavernous, echoic depth'. See his (1981) *Saying the Text*, Baltimore, Md: Johns Hopkins University Press, 123. It is also evident in a work by Michel Leiris, *Biffures*, which evokes the 'deep country of hearing, described in terms of geology more than in those of any other natural science, not only by virtue of the cartilaginous cavern that constitutes its organ, but also by virtue of the relationship that unites it to grottoes, chasms, to all pockets hollowed out of the terrestrial crust whose emptiness makes them into resonating drums for the slightest of sounds'. Cited by Ned Lukacher in (1986) *Primal Scenes: Literature, Philosophy, Psychoanalysis*, Ithaca, NY: Cornell University Press, 194.
22 Martin Heidegger (1970) 'Logik: Heraklits Lehre vom Logos', 'Heraklit', *Gesamtausgabe*, vol. 55, Frankfurt am Main: Vittorio Klostermann, 247.
23 This text was quoted by Heidegger himself. See (1966) *Discourse on Thinking*, New York: Harper & Row, 57. What neither Heidegger nor Hebel make explicit, however, is that the naming of the realm of plants is also at the same time the acknowledging of the feminine archetypes and their traditional spirit.
24 Victor Perera and Robert Bruce (1982) *The Last Lords of Palenque: The Lacandon Mayas of the Mexican Rainforest*, Boston, Mass.: Little, Brown, 86. Silence is extremely significant in the lives of forest people, and their hearing tends to be very acute. See Colin Turnbull (1961) *The Forest People: A Study of the Pygmies of the Congo*, New York: Simon & Schuster.
25 Erich Neumann (1972) *The Great Mother*, Princeton, NJ: Princeton University Press, 248. 'Destiny' has often been symbolized, among the primal or pre-modern peoples, by weaving and unweaving – activities traditionally assigned to women. Thus, intimations of 'destiny' should be heard in Merleau-Ponty's concept of the intertwining – and also to be heard in this concept is the relevance of the traditional wisdoms borne by women.
26 Mary Daly (1978) *Gyn/Ecology*, Boston, Mass.: Beacon, 414.
27 Erich Neumann (1970) *The Origins and History of Consciousness*, Princeton, NJ: Princeton University Press, 324.
28 Carol Gilligan (1982) *In a Different Voice*, Cambridge, Mass.: Harvard University Press, 51.
29 Daly, *Gyn/Ecology*, 414.
30 Gilligan, *In a Different Voice*, 2.

31 Neumann, *The Great Mother*, Preface, xiii.
32 Gilligan, *In a Different Voice*, 4.
33 Neumann, *The Great Mother*, preface, xiii.
34 Heidegger, *Being and Time*, 275.
35 Gilligan, *In a Different Voice*, 12–13.
36 Neumann, *The Great Mother*, 331.
37 Daly. *Gyn/Ecology*, 412.
38 Neumann, *The Great Mother*, 226.
39 Nelle Morton, 'Beloved image', paper delivered at the National Conference of the American Academy of Religion, San Francisco, Calif., 28 December 1977. Reprinted in Daly, *Gyn/Ecology*, 412.
40 See Maria Sabina (1981) *Maria Sabina: Her Life and Her Chants*, transcribed by Alvaro Estrada and Henry Munn, Santa Barbara, Calif.: Ross-Erikson, 136, 180.
41 Daly, *Gyn/Ecology*, 424.
42 Helen Diner (1973) *Mothers and Amazons: The First Feminine Theory of Culture*, New York: Doubleday, 16.
43 Daly, *Gyn/Ecology*, 412.
44 Gilligan, *In a Different Voice*, 16.
45 George E. Marcus and Michael M. Fischer (1986) *Anthropology as Cultural Critique: An Experimental Movement in the Human Sciences*, Chicago: University of Chicago Press, 65.
46 Friedrich Nietzsche (1982) *Daybreak*, Cambridge: Cambridge University Press, 143.
47 Martin Heidegger (1979) *Nietzsche*, vol. 1: *The Will to Power as Art*, New York: Harper & Row, 51.
48 Heidegger, 'The origin of the artwork', *Poetry, Language, Thought*, 25.
49 See Eugene T. Gendlin (1973a) 'Experiential phenomenology', in Maurice Natanson (ed.) *Phenomenology and the Social Sciences*, Evanston, Ill.: Northwestern University Press; (1973b) 'Experiential psychotherapy', in Raymond Corsini (ed.) *Current Psychotherapies*, first edn only, Itasca, Ill.: Peacock; (1978–9) '*Befindlichkeit*: Heidegger and the philosophy of psychology', *Review of Existential Psychology and Psychiatry* 16, nos 1–3; and (1981) *Focusing*, New York: Bantam.
50 See Rodolphe Gasché (1986) *The Tain of the Mirror*, Cambridge, Mass.: Harvard University Press, 187–8.
51 See Gilligan, *In a Different Voice*, esp. 1–19, 29–30, 45, 62, 173.
52 See Eugene Gendlin, 'A philosophical critique of the concept of narcissism: the significance of the Awareness Movement', in David M. Levin (ed.) *Pathologies of the Modern Self*, New York: New York University Press.
53 Wordsworth, *The Prelude*, book 2, 95–6.
54 Katsuki Sekida (1977) *Two Zen Classics: The Mumonkan and Hekiganroku*, New York: John Weatherhill, 375.
55 Rainer Maria Rilke (1962) 'Gong', *Gesammelte Gedichte*, Frankfurt am Main: Insel.
56 See Phillip Wheelwright (1966) *The Presocratics*, New York: Odyssey 32.

57 Merleau-Ponty, *Phenomenology of Perception*, 234.
58 Wordsworth, *The Prelude*, book 3, 208.
59 See A. Kasamatsu and T. Hirai (1966) 'An electroencephalographic study of Zen meditation', *Folia of Psychiatric Neurology* 20. Cited by Roger Walsh, MD in (1979) 'Meditation research: an introduction and review', *Journal of Transpersonal Psychology* 11, 172.
60 David Shapiro (1965) *Neurotic Styles*, New York: Basic Books 87.
61 ibid.
62 Erik Erikson (1965) 'Wholeness and totality: a psychiatric contribution', in Carl Friedrich (ed.) *Totalitarian Dictatorship and Autocracy*, New York: Praeger.
63 See Maurice Merleau-Ponty (1964a) 'The child's relations with others', *The Primacy of Perception*, Evanston, Ill. Northwestern University Press.
64 Zenkei Shibayama (1974) *Zen Comments on the Mumonkan*, New York: New American Library, 223.
65 ibid., 257.
66 Hubert Benoit (1973) *Let Go*, New York: Samuel Weiser.
67 Martin Heidegger (1969) *Identity and Difference*, New York: Harper & Row, 64. Also see 'Science and reflection', in *The Question Concerning Technology and Other Essays*, 180.
68 Eugen Fink and Martin Heidegger (1979) *Heraclitus Seminar, 1966–1967*, University, Ala.: University of Alabama Press, 128.
69 ibid., 140.
70 See Lame Deer, with Richard Erdoes (1972) *Lame Deer: Seeker of Visions*, New York: Simon & Schuster, 155–6.
71 Perera and Bruce, *The Last Lords of Pelengue*, 214.
72 Martin Heidegger (1971a) 'Hölderlins Erde und Himmel', *Erläuterungen zu Hölderlins Dichtung*, Frankfurt am Main: Vittorio Klostermann, 178.
73 See Rilke's letter to his wife, Clara Rilke, in (1945) *Letters of Rainer Maria Rilke, 1892–1910*, New York: Norton 199.
74 Martin Heidegger (1972) 'The end of philosophy and the task of thinking', *On Time and Being*, New York: Harper & Row, 65.
75 Martin Heidegger (1949) 'What is metaphysics?', *Existence and Being*, ed. W. Brock, Chicago: Henry Regnery, 358. I have modified the translation, changing 'causes' to 'gives rise to'. Bracketed interpolations are my own.
76 See Katsuki Sekida's translation, with his own commentary, of the *Mumonkan*, 39.
77 G. Reichel-Dolmatoff (1971) *Amazonian Cosmos*, Chicago: University of Chicago Press, 94.
78 G. Reichel-Dolmatoff (1978) *Beyond the Milky Way: Hallucinatory Imagery of the Tukano Indians*, Los Angeles, Calif.: UCLA Latin American Center Publications. Latin America Series, vol. 42, 152.
79 ibid.
80 Reichel-Dolmatoff, *Amazonian Cosmos*, 94.

81 Reichel-Dolmatoff, *Beyond the Milky Way*, 152. Also see Lame Deer, *Lame Deer*, 134.
82 See Martin Heidegger (1971) 'The nature of language', *On the Nature of Language*, New York: Harper & Row, 108. In German, see (1959) *Unterwegs zur Sprache*, Pfullingen: Günther Neske, 29–30, 215.
83 Longchenpa (1976) *Kindly Bent to Ease Us*, vol. 3, Berkeley, Calif.: Dharma Publishing, 86–90. Interpolations are my own. I have taken the liberty of turning the author's verse into a continuous prose, in order to economize on space and facilitate reading.
84 Concerning *alētheia* and the correspondence theory of truth, see ch. 4 of my book, (1988) *The Opening of Vision*, New York and London: Routledge & Kegan Paul. Also see Roland Barthes (1974) *S/Z*, New York: Hill & Wang, 42.
85 See Heidegger, *Der Satz vom Grund*, 204–5. For the English translation of these lines, see Keith Hoeller's excellent translation in (August 1974) *Man and World* 7 (3): 217.
86 Gasché, *The Tain of the Mirror*, 118.
87 ibid., 120. My own interpolations.
88 Martin Heidegger (1987) *Nietzsche*, vol. 3: *The Will to Power as Epistemology and as Meraphysics*, New York: Harper & Row, 69. Italics added.
89 ibid., 238.
90 ibid., 180.
91 ibid. Also see Heidegger's discussion of language in ch. 1 of his (1968) *What Is Called Thinking?* New York: Harper & Row. He explicitly mentions 'univocity' there.
92 See ibid., 235. Also see my book, *The Opening of Vision*, ch. 4, where I characterize the difference between truth as correctness and truth as *alētheia* in terms of our experience with vision.
93 Heidegger, 'Logos', 66.
94 Martin Heidegger (1961) *An Introduction to Metaphysics*, New York: Doubleday, 123.
95 Merleau-Ponty, *Phenomenology of Perception*, 347. Italics added.
96 Carl Gustav Jung (1975a) 'Spirit and life', *The Collected Works of Carl G. Jung*, vol. 8: *The Structure and Dynamics of the Psyche*, Princeton, NJ; Princeton University Press, 325.
97 Fink and Heidegger, *Heraclitus Seminar*, 88. I have changed 'he' to 'we'.
98 Martin Heidegger (1973) 'Recollection in metaphysics', *The End of Philosophy*, New York: Harper & Row, 77.
99 Heidegger, 'Logos', 65.
100 ibid., 66.
101 ibid., 68.
102 ibid., 70.
103 Heidegger, *What Is Called Thinking?*, 62.
104 Lukacher, *Primal Scenes*, 46. Also see Heidegger, *Introduction to Metaphysics*, 109.
105 ibid., 146.

106 Heidegger, 'Logik: Heraklits Lehre vom Logos', 315.
107 Heidegger, 'Logos', 66.
108 Heidegger, 'Logik: Heraklits Lehre vom Logos', 315.
109 Heidegger, 'Logos', 66.
110 ibid.
111 Heidegger, 'Logik: Heraklits Lehre vom Logos', 275–6.
112 ibid., 296.
113 Heidegger, 'Logos', 66.
114 For more on the *homologein*, see my book (1985), *The Body's Recollection of Being*, London and Boston, Mass.: Routledge & Kegan Paul, ch. 1, and my paper (1984) 'Hermeneutics as gesture: a reflection on Heidegger's "Logos (Herakleitos B50)" study', in Michael Zimmerman (ed.) *Tulane Studies in Philosophy*, vol. 32, 69–77.
115 Heidegger, 'The question concerning technology', *The Question Concerning Technology*, 19: 'The original gathering from which unfold the ways in which we have feelings of one kind or another we name "Gemüt".'
116 Sigmund Freud (1961) *Civilization and Its Discontents*, New York: Norton, 15.
117 Heidegger, 'Logos', 75.
118 ibid., 68.
119 See *The Upanishads*, trans. and ed. Juan Mascaro (1965) New York and Harmondsworth: Penguin, 107. Also see Merleau-Ponty, 'Eye and mind', *The Primacy of Perception*, 170, on perception 'everywhere all at once'.
120 Wallace Stevens (1961) 'The auroras of autumn', *The Collected Poems of Wallace Stevens*, New York: Afred Knopf.
121 This is a point on which Heidegger, Merleau-Ponty, and Sartre all agree. All three explicitly say it. See Heidegger, 'Building dwelling thinking', *Poetry, Language, Thought*, 157; Jean-Paul Sartre (1956) *Being and Nothingness*, New York: Philosophical Library (Methuen edn, 1957), 325; Merleau-Ponty, *Phenomenology of Perception*, 140, 156, 288, 320, 353; Merleau-Ponty, 'Eye and mind', 170; and Merleau-Ponty, 'The intertwining – the chiasm', 133–4. Also see Medard Boss (1979) *The Existential Foundations of Medicine and Psychology*, New York: Jason Aronson, 42, 102–3.
122 Georg W. F. Leibniz (1951) 'The principles of nature and grace, based on reason', proposition 13, in Philip Wiener (ed.) *Leibniz Selections*, New York: Charles Scribner's Sons, 530.
123 T. S. Eliot (1963) 'The dry salvages', *Collected Poems, 1909–1962*, New York: Harcourt, Brace & World, 196.
124 Friedrich Hölderlin (1960) 'Mnemosyne', *Sämtliche Werke*, Berlin and Darmstadt: Tempel Verlag.
125 Merleau-Ponty, *Phenomenology of Perception*, 347.
126 ibid., 329.
127 Martin Heidegger (1986) *The Basic Problems of Phenomenology*, Bloomington, Ind.: University of Indiana Press, 252.

128 William James (1890) *Principles of Psychology*, New York: Henry Holt, 890.

129 Merleau-Ponty, *Phenomenology of Perception*, 420.

130 See Walter Benjamin (1969) 'Theses on the philosophy of history', *Illuminations*, New York: Schocken, 262–3.

131 See Theodor Adorno, 'Currents in music: elements of a radio theory', 26, cited in Martin Jay (1973) *The Dialectical Imagination*, Boston, Mass.: Little, Brown, 192 and 335. Also see (1938) 'Über den Fetischcharakter in der Musik und die Regression des Hörens', *Zeitschrift für Sozialforschung* 7 (3).

132 See Theodor Adorno (1971) 'Wagner, Mahler, Berg', *Gesammelte Schriften*, Frankfurt am Main: Suhrkamp, vol. 13, 350.

133 Theodor Adorno (1973b) *Negative Dialectics*, New York: Continuum Seabury, 155–6.

134 Sigmund Freud (1957) 'Thoughts for the times on war and death', *Standard Edition of the Complete Works*, vol. 14, London: Hogarth, 277. Also see Harold Searles (1965) 'Anxiety concerning change as seen in the psychotherapy of schizophrenic patients', *Collected Papers on Schizophrenia and Related Subjects*, New York: International Universities Press, 443–64. Also see my essay (October 1978) 'Painful time, ecstatic time', *The Eastern Buddhist* 11 (2): 74–112. But I especially recommend Tarthang Tulku (1978) *Time, Space and Knowledge*, Berkeley, Calif.: Dharma Publishing. This book contains a treasury of practical exercises, based on ancient Tibetan Buddhist wisdom, to facilitate the transformation of our habitual way of experiencing ourselves as living in time. I would add that, because of the connection between listening and time, and the way these two figure in the identity of the self, the development of our capacity for listening can change our experiencing of time – and, conversely, changes in the way we live time, changes in the way we experience ourselves as being-in-time, or being-timed, can affect the way we listen, e.g. increasing our listening patience and our tolerance of silence.

135 Suzuki Daisetz (1972) *Living By Zen*, New York: Samuel Weiser, 74.

136 Martin Heidegger (1987) 'The will to power as knowledge and as metaphysics', *Nietzsche*, vol. 3, New York: Harper & Row, 12.

137 Heidegger, 'The Anaximander fragment,' *Early Greek Thinking*, 34. On perception 'everywhere all at once', see Merleau-Ponty, 'Eye and Mind', *The Primacy of Perception*, 170.

138 Martin Heidegger (1927) *Sein und Zeit*, Tübingen: Max Niemeyer, 339.

139 Heidegger, *Nietzsche*, vol. 3, 32.

140 Merleau-Ponty, *Phenomenology of Perception*, 69.

141 ibid., 404.

142 ibid., 421.

143 ibid., 17.

144 See Herbert V. Guenther (1974) *The Royal Song of Saraha*, Boulder, Colo.: Shambhala, 48n, 119, 121.

145 Quoted by Heidegger in *Nietzsche*, vol. 3, 5. Also see Merleau-Ponty,

The Visible and the Invisible, 267, on an 'existential eternity' which is 'always the same'.

146 Maurice Merleau-Ponty (1964b) 'The philosopher and his shadow', *Signs*, Evanston, Ill.: Northwestern University Press, 174.
147 Merleau-Ponty, *Phenomenology of Perception*, 347. On the 'pre-personal', see 215, 216, 254, 347, 353. Also see *The Visible and the Invisible*, 187–8.
148 Maurice Merleau-Ponty (1973) 'The indirect language', *The Prose of the World*, Evanston, Ill.: Northwestern University Press, 94. Also see my book, *The Body's Recollection of Being*, chapters 1 and 2.
149 Mircea Eliade (1969) *The Quest: History and Meaning in Religion*, Chicago: University of Chicago Press, 85.
150 Stanley Cavell (1979) *The Claim of Reason*, New York and Oxford: Oxford University Press, 391.
151 See Heidegger, *Being and Time*, 424–55.
152 Heidegger, *Nietzsche*, vol. 3, 215.
153 ibid., 183.
154 ibid., 187.
155 See Heidegger, *What Is Called Thinking?*, 152.
156 See Joan Stambaugh's commentary on 'Overcoming metaphysics', 84, n. 1, in Martin Heidegger (1973) *The End of Philosophy*, New York: Harper & Row.
157 Merleau-Ponty, 'The intertwining – the chiasm', 159.
158 Heidegger, 'Overcoming metaphysics', 91.
159 ibid. Also see Lukacher, *Primal Scenes*, 68–93, wherein the processes of forgetting and remembering analysed in psychoanalytic discourse are connected to the forgetting and recollecting in Heidegger's discourse on metaphysics.
160 Lukacher, *Primal Scenes*, 177.
161 Friedrich Nietzsche (1969) *Le Livre du Philosophe*, Paris: Aubier-Flammarion, 135. I have not consulted the German original.

Bibliography

Adorno, T. (1938) 'Über den Fetischcharakter in der Musik und die Regression des Hörens', *Zeitschrift für Sozialforschung* 7.

Adorno, T. *et al.* (1950) *The Authoritarian Personality*, New York, Harper & Row.

Adorno, T. (1970) *Über Walter Benjamin*, Frankfurt am Main, Suhrkamp.

Adorno, T. (1971a) 'Wagner, Mahler, Berg', *Gesammelte Schriften*, vol. 13, Frankfurt am Main, Suhrkamp.

Adorno, T. (1971b) *Kritik*, Frankfurt am Main, Suhrkamp.

Adorno, T. (1973a) Hörmodelle', *Gesammelte Schriften*, vol. 14, part 2, Frankfurt am Main, Suhrkamp.

Adorno, T. (1973b) 'Dissonanzen: Musik in der verwalteten Welt', *Gesammelte Schriften*, vol. 14, Frankfurt am Main, Suhrkamp.

Adorno, T. (1973b) *Negative Dialectics*, New York, Continuum-Seabury.

Adorno, T. (1974) *Minima Moralia: Reflections from Damaged Life*, London, New Left Books.

Adorno, T. (1979) 'Anmerkungen zum sozialen Konflikt heute', *Soziologische Schriften*, vol. 1, Frankfurt am Main, Suhrkamp.

Adorno, T. (1981) *Prisms*, Boston, Mass., MIT Press.

Adorno, T. and Horkheimer, M. (1986) *The Dialectic of Englightenment*, New York, Continuum-Seabury.

Arendt, H. (1963) *Eichmann in Jerusalem: A Report on the Banality of Evil*, New York, Viking.

Arendt, H. (1978a) *The Life of the Mind*, New York, Harcourt, Brace, Jovanovich.

Arendt, H. (1978b) 'Metaphor and the ineffable: illumination or the nobility of sight', in S. Spicker (ed.) *Organism: Medicine and Metaphysics: Essays in Honour of Hans Jonas on his Seventy-Fifty Birthday*, Dordrecht, Reidel.

Aristotle (1942) *The Generation of Animals*, Cambridge, Mass., Harvard University Press, Loeb Classical Library.

Aristotle (1946) *Metaphysics*, trans. John Warrington, London, Dent.

Aristotle (1953) *Nicomachean Ethics*, Harmondsworth, Penguin.

Arnheim, R. (1969) *Visual Thinking*, Berkeley, Calif. University of California Press.

Arnheim, R. (1972) *Toward a Psychology of Art*, Berkeley, Calif., University of California Press.

BIBLIOGRAPHY

Barker, F. (1984) *The Tremulous Private Body: Essays on Subjection*, London and New York, Methuen.

Bar-Tal, D. (1976) *Prosocial Behaviour: Theory and Research*, New York, Wiley.

Barthes, R. (1974) *S/Z*, New York, Hill & Wang.

Basaglia, F. (1987) *Psychiatry Inside Out: Selected Writings*, New York, Columbia University Press.

Benhabib, S. Spring/Summer 1985 'The utopian dimension in communicative ethics', *New German Critique* 35.

Benhabib, S. (1986a) *Critique, Norm and Utopia: A Study of the Foundations of Critical Theory*, New York, Columbia University Press.

Benhabib, S. (1986b) 'The generalized and the concrete other: toward a feminist critique of substitutionality universalism', in E. Kittay and D. Meyers (eds) *Proceedings of the Women and Moral Theory Conference*, New Jersey, Rowman & Allenheld.

Benjamin, W. (1969) *Illuminations: Essays and Reflections*, New York, Schocken.

Benjamin, W. (1986) *Reflections: Essays, Aphorisms, Autobiographical Writings*, New York, Schocken.

Benoit, H. (1973) *Let Go*, New York, Samuel Weiser.

Berlin, I. (1980) *Personal Impressions*, New York, Viking.

Bettelheim, B. (1970) *The Children of the Dream: Communal Child-Rearing and American Education*, New York, Macmillan.

Blake, W. (1978) *Milton*, Boulder, Colo., Shambhala.

Blanchot, M. (1982) *The Space of Literature*, Lincoln, Nebr., University of Nebraska Press.

Blanco, H. (1972) *Land or Death: The Peasant Struggle in Peru*, New York, Pathfinder.

Bohm, D. (1978) 'The enfolding-unfolding universe', *Re-Vision* 1 (3–4).

Borowski, T. (1976) *This Way for the Gas, Ladies and Gentlemen*, New York and Harmondsworth, Penguin.

Boss, M. (1979) *The Existential Foundations of Medicine and Psychology*, New York, Jason Aronson.

Boyte, H. (1984) *Community Is Possible: Repairing America's Roots*, New York, Harper & Row.

Brelet, G. (1958) 'Music and Silence', in S. Langer (ed.) *Reflections on Art*, Baltimore, Md, Johns Hopkins University Press.

Bruce, R. and Perera, V. (1982) *The Last Lords of Palenque: The Lacandon Mayas of the Mexican Rainforest*, Boston, Mass., Little, Brown.

Cavell, S. (1979) *The Claim of Reason*, Oxford and New York, Oxford University Press.

Cohen, R. (Winter 1984) 'Merleau-Ponty, the flesh, and Foucault', *Philosophy Today* 28.

Confucius (1979) *The Analects*, Harmondsworth and New York, Penguin.

Coyle, M. (1987) 'An experiential perspective on the mother-infant relationship', *Focusing Folio*, 6, Chicago, The Focusing Institute.

Daly, M. (1978) *Gyn/Ecology: The Metaethics of Radical Feminism*, Boston, Mass., Beacon.

BIBLIOGRAPHY

Débord, G. (1970) *Society of the Spectacle*, Detroit, Mich., Black and Red Publ.

Derrida, J. (1978) 'Cogito and the history of madness', *Writing and Differance*, Chicago, University of Chicago Press.

Derrida, J. (1982a) *Margins of Philosophy*, Chicago, University of Chicago Press.

Derrida, J. (1982b) 'Sending: on representation', trans. Peter Caws, *Social Research*, 49.

Derrida, J. (1983) *D'un ton apocalyptique adopté naguère en philosophie*. Paris, Galilée.

Derrida, J. (1985) *The Ear of the Other*, New York, Schocken.

Descartes, R. (1955) 'Meditations on first philosophy', in E. Haldane and G. Ross (eds) *The Philosophical Works of Descartes*, vol. 1, New York, Dover.

Descartes, R. (1965) *Discourse on Method, Optics, Geometry, and Meteorology*, Indianapolis, Ind., Bobbs-Merrill.

Des Pres, T. (1976) *The Survivor: An Anatomy of Life in the Death Camps*, London and New York, Oxford University Press.

Dewey, J. (1927) *The Public and its Problems*, New York, Henry Holt.

Dewey, J. (1935) *Liberalism and Social Action*, New York, Putnam.

Dewey, J. (1944) *Democracy and Education*, New York, Macmillan.

Dewey, J. (1963) *Experience and Education*, New York, Collier-Macmillan.

Dhargyey, Geshey Ngarwang (1974) *The Tibetan Tradition of Mental Development*, Dharamsala, Library of Tibetan Works and Archives.

Diagnostic and Statistical Manual of Mental Disorders, third edn (1980), Washington, DC, American Psychiatric Association.

Dillon, M. (Autumn 1978) 'Merleau-Ponty and the psychogenesis of the self', *Journal of Phenomenological Psychology* 9 (1–2).

Dillon, M. (1983) 'Merleau-Ponty and the reversibility thesis', *Man and World* 16.

Diner, H. (1973) *Mothers and Amazons: The First Feminine Theory of Culture*, New York, Doubleday.

Drager, H. (1958) 'The concept of tonal body', in Susanne Langer (ed.) *Reflections on Art*, Baltimore, Md, Johns Hopkins University Press.

Dreyfus, H. (1984) 'Beyond hermeneutics: interpretation in late Heidegger and recent Foucault', in G. Shapiro and A. Sica (eds), *Hermeneutics: Questions and Prospects*, Amherst, Mass., University of Massachusetts Press.

Eckhart, Meister (1969) *Meister Eckhart: A Modern Translation*, ed. R. B. Blakney, New York, Harper & Row.

Eisenberg, N. (1982) *The Development of Prosocial Behaviour*, New York, Academic Press.

Eliade, M. (1969) *The Quest: History and Meaning in Religion*, Chicago, University of Chicago Press.

Eliot, T. S. (1963) *Collected Poems, 1909–1962*, New York, Harcourt, Brace & World.

Emerson, R. (1956) *The Portable Emerson*, ed. M. Van Doren, New York, Viking.

Erikson, E. (1950) *Childhood and Society*, New York, Norton.

Erikson, E. (1959) 'Identity and the life cycle', *Psychological Issues*, monograph 1, New York, International Universities Press.
Erikson, E. (1965) 'Wholeness and totality: a psychiatric contribution', in C. J. Friedrich (ed.) *Totalitarian Dictatorship and Autocracy*, New York, Praeger.
Erikson, E. (1968) *Identity, Youth and Crisis*, New York, Norton.
Erikson, E. (1980) *Identity and the Life Cycle*, New York, Norton.
Ewald, F. (1975) 'Anatomie et corps politiques', *Critique*, 343.
Febvre, L. (1982) *The Problem of Unbelief in the Sixteenth Century: The Religion of Rabelais*, Cambridge, Mass., Harvard University Press.
Fink, E. and Heidegger, M. (1979) *Heraclitus Seminar 1966–1967*, University, Ala., University of Alabama Press.
Fischer, M. and Marcus, G. (1986) *Anthropology as Cultural Critique: An Experimental Movement in the Human Sciences*, Chicago, University of Chicago Press.
Flynn, B. (1983) 'Descartes and the ontology of subjectivity', *Man and World* 16.
Foti, V. (June 1986) 'The Cartesian imagination', *Philosophy and Phenomenological Research*, 46 (4).
Foucault, M. (1970) The Order of Things: an Archaeology of the Human Sciences, New York, Random House.
Foucault, M. (1977) *Language, Counter-Memory, Practice: Selected Interviews and Essays*, Ithaca, NY, Cornell University Press.
Foucault, M. (1979) *Discipline and Punish: The Birth of the Prison*, New York, Random House.
Foucault, M. (Autumn 1979) 'My body, this paper, this fire', *Oxford Literary Review* 4.
Foucault, M. (1980a) *Power/Knowledge: Selected Interviews and Other Writings, 1972–1977*, New York, Pantheon.
Foucault, M. (1980b) 'Truth and subjectivity', Berkeley, Calif., University of California, Howison Lectures.
Foucault, M. (1982a) 'The subject and power', in H. Dreyfus and P. Rabinow, *Michel Foucault: Beyond Structuralism and Hermeneutics*, Chicago, University of Chicago Press.
Foucault, M. (1982b) 'Why study power? The question of the subject', in H. Dreyfus and P. Rabinow, *Michel Foucault: Beyond Structuralism and Hermeneutics*, Chicago, University of Chicago Press.
Foucault, M. (1984a) 'What is enlightenment?', in P. Rabinow (ed.) *The Foucault Reader*, New York, Pantheon.
Foucault, M. (1984b) 'On the genealogy of ethics: an overview of work in progress', in P. Rabinow (ed.), *The Foucault Reader*, New York, Pantheon.
Fox Keller, E. and Grontowski, C. (1983) 'The mind's eye', in S. Harding and M. Hintikka (eds.) *Discovery Reality: Feminist Perspectives on Epistemology, Metaphysics, Methodology and the Philosopy of Science*. Boston, Mass., Reidel.
Frankfurt, H. (1979) *Demons, Dreamers, and Madmen*, Indianapolis, Ind., Bobbs-Merrill.

Fraser, N. (Fall 1983) 'Foucault's body-language: a post-humanist political rhetoric?', *Salmagundi* 61.
Fraser, N. (January 1986) 'Toward a discourse ethic of solidarity', *Praxis International*, 5 (4).
Fraser, N. (1987) 'Social movements versus disciplinary bureaucracies: the discourses of social needs', *CHS Occasional Papers*, no. 8, Minneapolis, Minn., Center for Humanistic Studies, University of Minnesota.
Fraser, N. (1988) 'Women, welfare, and the politics of need interpretation', in P. Laslett (ed.) *The Politics of Social Theory*, London, Tavistock.
Freud, S. (1957) 'On narcissism', *Standard Edition of the Complete Works of Sigmund Freud*, vol. 14, London, Hogarth.
Freud, S. (1961) *Civilization and its Discontents*, New York, Norton.
Freud, S. (1962) *The Ego and the Id*, New York, Norton.
Freud, S. (1963) *Introductory Lectures on Psycho-analysis*, vol. 16 of the *Standard Edition of the Complete Works of Sigmund Freud*, London, Hogarth.
Freud, S. (1957) 'The splitting of the ego in the process of defence', *Standard Edition of the Complete Works of Sigmund Freud*, vol. 23, London, Hogarth.
Freud, S. (1965) *New Introductory Lectures on Psycho-analysis*, vol. 22 of the *Standard Edition of the Complete Works of Sigmund Freud*, London, Hogarth.
Freud, S. (1975) *Three Essays on the Theory of Sexuality*, New York, Basic Books.
Friedrich, C. (ed.) (1965) *Totalitarian Dictatorship and Autocracy*, New York, Praeger.
Fromm, E. (1961) *Marx's Concept of Man*, New York, Frederick Ungar.
Frye, N. (1957) *The Anatomy of Criticism: Four Essays*, Princeton, NJ, Princeton University Press.
Gasché, R. (1986) *The Tain of the Mirror: Derrida and the Philosophy of Reflection*, Cambridge, Mass., Harvard University Press.
Gendlin, E. (1962a) *Experiencing and the Creation of Meaning*, New York, Macmillan.
Gendlin, E. (1962b) 'A theory of personality change', in P. Worchel and D. Byrne (eds) *Personality Change*, New York, John Wiley.
Gendlin, E. (1973a) 'Experiential phenomenology', in M. Natanson (ed.) *Phenomenology and the Social Sciences*, Evanston, Ill., Northwestern University Press.
Gendlin, E. (1973b) 'Experiential psychotherapy', in R. Corsini (ed.) *Current Psychotherapies*, Itasca, Ill., Peacock, first edn only.
Gendlin, E. (1978–9) '*Befindlichkeit*: Heidegger and the philosophy of psychology', *Review of Existential Psychology and Psychiatry* 16 (1–3).
Gendlin, E. (1981) *Focusing*, New York, Bantam.
Gendlin, E. (1986) 'Process ethics and the political question', *The Focusing Folio*, vol. 5, no. 2, Chicago, The Focusing Institute.
Gendlin, E. (1987) 'A philosophical critique of the concept of narcissism: the significance of the Awareness Movement', in D. Levin (ed.) *Pathologies of the Modern Self: Postmodern Studies on Narcissism, Schizophrenia, and Depression*, New York, New York University Press.

Geraets, T. (1971) Vers une nouvelle philosophie transcendentale, The Hague, Martinus Nijhoff.

Geuss, R. (1981) *The Idea of a Critical Theory: Habermas and the Frankfurt School*, Cambridge, Cambridge University Press.

Giddens, A. (1979) *Central Problems in Social Theory*, Berkeley, Calif., University of California Press.

Gilligan, C. (1982) *In a Different Voice: Psychological Theory and Women's Development*, Cambridge, Mass., Harvard University Press.

Goethe, J. W. (1982) *Italian Journey, 1786–1788*, trans. W. H. Auden and Elizabeth Mayer, San Francisco, North Point Press.

Goodman, P. *et al.* (1951) *Gestalt Therapy: Excitement and Growth in the Human Personality*, New York, Delta.

Guenther, H. (1974) *The Royal Song of Saraha*, Boulder, Colo., Shambhala.

Habermas, J. (1971) *Knowledge and Human Interests*, Boston, Mass., Beacon.

Habermas, J. (1973a) *Theory and Practice*, Boston, Mass., Beacon.

Habermas, J. (1973b) ' "Postscript" to *Knowledge and Human Interests*', *Philosophy of the Social Sciences*, 5.

Habermas, J. (1974) 'On social identity', *Telos* 19.

Habermas, J. (1975) *Legitimation Crisis*, Boston, Mass., Beacon.

Habermas, J., (1979a) *Communication and the Evolution of Society*, Boston, Mass., Beacon.

Habermas, J. (1979b) 'Moral development and ego identity', *Communication and the Evolution of Society*, Boston, Mass., Beacon.

Habermas, J. (Fall 1981) 'The dialectics of rationalization', *Telos* 49.

Habermas J. (Winter 1981) 'Modernity versus postmodernity', *New German Critique* 22.

Habermas, J. (1983) *Philosophical-Political Profiles*, Boston, Mass. and London, MIT Press.

Habermas, J. (1984) *The Theory of Communicative Action*, vol. 1, Boston, Mass., Beacon.

Habermas, J. (1985) 'Questions and counterquestions', in R. Bernstein (ed.), *Habermas and Modernity*, Boston, MIT Press.

Habermas, J. (1987) *The Philosophical Discourse of Modernity*, Boston, Mass., MIT Press.

Hegel, G. (1984) *Letters*, Bloomington, Ind., University of Indiana Press.

Heidegger, M. (1963) *Sein und Zeit*, Tübingen, Max Niemeyer.

Heidegger, M. (1949) 'What is metaphysics?', in W. Brock (ed.) *Existence and Being*, Chicago, Henry Regnery.

Heidegger, M. (1959) *Vorträge und Aufsätze*, Pfullingen, Günther Neske.

Heidegger, M. (1957) *Der Satz von Grund*, Pfullingen, Günther Neske.

Heidegger, M. (1961) *An Introduction to Metaphysics*, New York, Doubleday.

Heidegger, M. (1962) *Being and Time*, New York, Harper & Row.

Heidegger, M. (1965) *Was ist Metaphysik?*, Frankfurt am Main, Vittorio Klostermann.

Heidegger, M. (1966) *Discourse on Thinking*, New York, Harper & Row.

Heidegger, M. (1968) *What Is Called Thinking?* New York, Harper & Row.

Heidegger, M. (1969) *Identity and Difference*, New York, Harper & Row.

Heidegger, M. (1970) 'Heraklit', *Gesamtausgabe*, vol. 55, Frankfurt am Main, Vittorio Klostermann.
Heidegger, M. (1971a) *Erläuterungen zu Hölderlins Dichtung*, Frankfurt am Main, Vittorio Klostermann.
Heidegger, M. (1971b) *Poetry, Language, Thought*, ed. A. Hofstadter, New York, Harper & Row.
Heidegger, M. (1971c) *On the Nature of Language*, New York, Harper & Row.
Heidegger, M. (1972) *On Time and Being*, New York, Harper & Row.
Heidegger, M. (1973) *The End of Philosophy*, New York, Harper & Row.
Heidegger, M. (1975) *Early Greek Thinking*, New York, Harper & Row.
Heidegger, M. (1977a) *The Question Concerning Technology and Other Essays*, New York, Harper & Row.
Heidegger, M. (1977b) *The Basic Writings of Martin Heidegger*, ed. D. Krell, New York, Harper & Row.
Heidegger, M. (1979) *Nietzsche*, vol. 1, *The Will to Power as Art*, New York, Harper & Row.
Heidegger, M. (1982) *Nietzsche*, vol. 4, *Nihilism*, New York, Harper & Row.
Heidegger, M. (1982) *The Basic Problems of Phenomenology*, Bloomington, Ind., University of Indiana Press.
Heidegger, M. (1987) *Nietzsche*, vol. 3: *The Will to Power as Epistemology and as Metaphysics*. New York, Harper & Row.
Held, D. and Thompson, J. (eds) (1982) *Habermas: Critical Debates*, Boston, Mass., MIT Press, 1982.
Heller, A. (Spring/Summer 1981) 'Enlightenment against fundamentalism: the example of Lessing', *New German Critique*, 23.
Henley, N. (1977) *Body Politics*, New Jersey, Prentice-Hall.
Hoebel, E. A. (1964) *The Law of Primitive Man*, Cambridge, Mass., Harvard University Press.
Hölderlin, F. (1960) *Sämtliche Werke*, Berlin and Darmstadt, Tempel Verlag.
Holenstein, E. (1985) *Menschliches Selbstverständnis: Ichbewusstsein, Intersubjektive Verantwortung, Interkulturelle Verständigung*, Frankfurt am Main, Suhrkamp.
Horkheimer, M., pseud. H. Regius (1934) *Dämmerung: Notizen in Deutschland*, Zürich, Oprecht & Helbling.
Horkheimer, M. (1936) 'Egoism and the movement for emancipation', *Zeitschrift für Sozialforschung*.
Horkheimer, M. (1974a) *Critique of Instrumental Reason*, New York, Continuum-Seabury.
Horkheimer, M. (1974b) *The Eclipse of Reason*, New York, Continuum-Seabury.
Horkheimer, M. (1978) *Dawn and Decline: Notes 1916–1931 and 1950–1969*, New York, Continuum-Seabury.
Horkheimer, M. and Adorno, T. (1986) *The Dialectic of Enlightenment*, New York, Continuum-Seabury.
Hoy, D. (ed.) (1986) *Foucault: A Critical Reader*, London and New York, Basil Blackwell.
Hwa Yol Jung (1979) *The Crisis of Political Understanding: A Phenomenological*

Perspective in the Conduct of Political Inquiry, Pittsburgh, Penn., Duquesne University Press.

Hwa Yol Jung (Winter 1981) 'The Orphic voice and ecology', *Environmental Ethics* 3.

Ihde, D. (1977) *Listening and Voice: The Phenomenology of Sound*, Athens, OH., Ohio University Press.

Jacoby, R. (1975) *Social Amnesia: A Critique of Conformist Psychology from Adler to Laing*, Boston, Mass., Beacon.

James, W. (1890) *Principles of Psychology*, New York, Henry Holt.

Jay, M. (Summer 1972) 'The Frankfurt School's critique of Marxist humanism', *Social Research*, 39 (2).

Jay, M. (1973) *The Dialectical Imagination: A History of the Frankfurt School and the Institute of Social Research, 1923–1950*, Boston, Mass., Little, Brown.

Jay, M. (1984) *Marxism and Totality*, Berkeley, Calif., University of California Press.

Jay, M. (1986) 'In the empire of the gaze: Foucault and the denigration of vision in twentieth-century French thought, in D. Hoy (ed.) *Foucault: A Critical Reader*, New York and Oxford, Basil Blackwell.

Jaynes, J. (1976) *The Origin of Consciousness in the Breakdown of the Bicameral Mind*, Boston, Mass., Houghton Mifflin.

Johnson, D. (1983) *Body*, Boston, Mass., Beacon.

Jonas, H. (1966) 'The nobility of sight: a study in the phenomenology of the senses', *The Phenomenon of Life: Toward a Philosophical Biology*, New York, Harper & Row.

Jonas, H. (1974) *Philosophical Essays: From Ancient Creed to Technological Man*, Chicago, University of Chicago Press.

Jung, C. (1968) *The Collected Works of Carl G. Jung*, vol. 9, *The Archetypes and the Collective Unconscious*, part 1, Princeton, NJ, Princeton University Press.

Jung, C. (1975) *The Collected Works of Carl G. Jung*, vol. 8, *The Structure and Dynamics of the Psyche*, Princeton, NJ, Princeton University Press.

Kant, I. (1960) *Religion within the Limits of Reason Alone*, New York, Harper & Row.

Kasamatsu, A. and Hirai, T. (1966) 'An electroencephalographic study of Zen meditation', *Folia of Psychiatric Neurology*, 20.

Kernberg, O. (1975) *Borderline Conditions and Pathological Narcissism*, New York, Jason Aronson.

Kierkegaard, S. (1941) *Concluding Unscientific Postscript*, Princeton, NJ, Princeton University Press.

Kierkegaard, S. (1956) *Either/Or*, Princeton, NJ, Princeton University Press.

Kohlberg, L. (1981) 'The philosophy of moral development', *Essays in Moral Development*, vol. 1, *The Philosophy of Moral Development: Moral Stages and the Idea of Justice*, New York, Harper & Row.

Kohlberg, L. (1984) 'The psychology of moral development', *Essays in Moral Development*, vol. 2, New York, Harper & Row.

Köhler, W. (1947) *Gestalt Psychology: An Introduction to New Concepts in Modern Psychology*, New York, New American Library.

Kohut, H. (1977) *The Restoration of the Self*, New York, International Universities Press.
Kovel, J. (1982) *The Age of Desire: Reflections of a Radical Psychoanalyst*, New York, Pantheon.
Lacan, J. (1968) *The Language of the Self*, Baltimore, Md, Johns Hopkins University Press.
Lacan, J. (1977a) 'The mirror stage as formative of the function of the "I" as revealed in psychoanalytic experience', in A. Sheridan (ed.) *Écrits: A Selection*, New York, Norton.
Lacan, J. (1977b) 'Aggressivity in psychoanalysis', in A. Sheridan (ed.) *Écrits: A Selection*, New York, Norton.
Lacan, J. (1981) *The Four Fundamental Concepts of Psychoanalysis*, New York, Norton.
Laing, R. (1968) *The Politics of Experience*, New York, Ballantine Books.
Lame Deer, with Erdoes, R. (1972) *Lame Deer: Seeker of Visions*, New York, Simon & Schuster.
Lasch, C. (1978) *The Culture of Narcissism: American Life in an Age of Diminishing Expectations*, New York, Norton.
Leibniz, G. (1951) 'The principles of nature and of grace, based on reason', in P. Wiener (ed.) *Leibniz Selections*, New York, Charles Scribner's Sons.
Leibniz, G. (1981) *New Essays on the Human Understanding*, Cambridge, Cambridge University Press.
Levin, D. (October 1978) 'Painful time, ecstatic time', *The Eastern Buddhist* 11 (2).
Levin, D. (1984) 'Hermeneutics as gesture: a reflection on Heidegger's "Logos (Herakleitos B50)" study', in M. Zimmerman (ed.) *Tulane Studies in Philosophy*, vol. 32.
Levin, D. (1985) *The Body's Recollection of Being; Phenomenological Psychology and the Deconstruction of Nihilism*, London and Boston, Mass., Routledge & Kegan Paul.
Levin, D. (1987a) 'Psychopathology in the epoch of nihilism', in D. Levin (ed.) *Pathologies of the Modern Self: Postmodern Studies on Narcissism, Schizophrenia, and Depression*, New York, New York University Press.
Levin, D. (1987b) 'Clinical stories: a modern self in the fury of being', in D. Levin (ed.) *Pathologies of the Modern Self*, New York, New York University Press.
Levin, D. (1988) *The Opening of Vision: Nihilism and the Postmodern Situation*, London and New York, Routledge & Kegan Paul.
Lingis, A. (1969) 'The elemental background', in J. Edie (ed.) *New Essays in Phenomenology*, Chicago, Quadrangle.
Longchenpa (1976) *Kindly Bent to Ease Us*, vol. 3, Berkeley, Calif., Dharma Publishing.
Lowe, D. (1982) *The History of Bourgeois Perception*, Chicago, University of Chicago Press.
Lukacher, N. (1986) *Primal Scenes: Literature, Philosophy, Psychoanalysis*, Ithaca NY and London, Cornell University Press.
McCarthy, T. (1978) *The Critical Theory of Jürgen Habermas*, Boston, Mass., MIT Press.

MacIntyre, A. (1973) 'Ideology, social science, and revolution', *Comparative Politics*, 5.

McLuhan, M. and Fiore, Q. (1967) *The Medium is the Message*, New York, Bantam.

Mallarmé, S. (1945) *Oeuvres Complètes*, ed. H. Mondor and G. Jean-Aubrey, Paris, Éditions Gallimard.

Mallin, S. (1979) *Merleau-Ponty's Philosophy*, New Haven, Conn., Yale University Press.

Mandrou, R. (1976) *Introduction to Modern France, 1500–1640: An Essay in Historical Psychology*, New York, Holmes & Meier.

Marcus, G. and Fischer, M. (1986) *Anthropology as Cultural Critique: An Experimental Movement in the Human Sciences*, Chicago, University of Chicago Press.

Marcuse, H. (1962) *Eros and Civilization: A Philosophical Inquiry into Freud*, New York, Vintage Books, Random.

Marcuse, H. (1968) *Negations: Essays in Critical Theory*, Boston, Mass., Beacon.

Marcuse, H. (1969) *An Essay on Liberation*, Boston, Mass., Beacon.

Marcuse, H. (1972) *Counter-Revolution and Revolt*, Boston, Mass., Beacon.

Marx, K. (1906) *Capital*, vol. 1, Chicago, Charles Kerr.

Marx, K. (1961) 'Economic and philosophical manuscripts of 1844', in E. Fromm, *Marx's Concept of Man*, New York, Frederick Ungar.

Marx, K. (1973) *Grundrisse: Outlines of a Critique of the Political Economy*, Harmondsworth and Baltimore, Md., Penguin.

Marx, K. (1975) *The Early Writings of Karl Marx*, ed. Quinton Hoare, New York, Random.

Megill, A. (1985) *Prophets of Extremity: Nietzsche, Heidegger, Foucault and Derrida*, Berkeley, Calif.: University of California Press.

Merleau-Ponty, M. (1962) *Phenomenology of Perception*, London, Routledge & Kegal Paul.

Merleau-Ponty, M. (1963) *In Praise of Philosophy*, Evanston, Ill., Northwestern University Press.

Merleau-Ponty, M. (1964a) 'The child's relations with others', *The Primacy of Perception*, Evanston, Ill., Northwestern University Press.

Merleau-Ponty, M. (1964b) *Signs*, Evanston, Ill., Northwestern University Press.

Merleau-Ponty, M. (1968) *The Visible and the Invisible*, Evanston, Ill., Northwestern University Press.

Merleau-Ponty, M. (1970) *Themes from the Lectures at the Collège de France*, Evanston, Ill., Northwestern University Press.

Merleau-Ponty, M. (1973) *The Prose of the World*, Evanston, Ill., Northwestern University Press.

Merquior, J. G. (1985) *Foucault*, London, Fontana Paperbacks, and Berkeley, University of California Press.

Mindell, A. (1985) *Working with the Dreaming Body*, London and New York, Routledge & Kegan Paul.

Misgeld, Dieter (Spring/Summer 1985) 'Critical hermeneutics versus neoparsonianism?', *New German Critique*, 35.

Montaigne, M. de (1965) *The Complete Essays*, ed. D. Frame, Stanford, NJ, Stanford University Press.
Muller, J. and Richardson, W. (1982) *Lacan and Language: A Reader's Guide to Écrits*, New York, International Universities Press.
Mussen, P. and Eisenberg, N. (1977) *The Roots of Caring, Sharing and Helping*, New York, Freeman.
Neumann, E. (1970) *The Origins and History of Consciousness*, Princeton, NJ, Princeton University Press.
Neumann, E. (1971) *Art and the Creative Unconscious*, Princeton, NJ, Princeton University Press.
Neumann, E. (1972) *The Great Mother: An Analysis of the Archetype*, Princeton, NJ, Princeton University Press.
Neumann, E. (1976) *The Child: Structure and Dynamics of the Nascent Personality*, New York, Harper & Row.
Nietzsche, F. (1960) *Joyful Wisdom*, New York, Frederick Ungar.
Nietzsche, F. (1968) *The Will to Power*, New York, Random.
Nietzsche, F. (1969) *Le Livre du Philosophe*, Paris, Aubier-Flammarion.
Nietzsche, F. (1982) *Daybreak: Thoughts on the Prejudices of Morality*, Cambridge, Cambridge University Press.
Nietzsche, F. (1983) *Untimely Meditations*, Cambridge, Cambridge University Press.
O'Neill, J. (1982) 'The specular body: Merleau-Ponty and Lacan on self and other', *Proceedings of the Merleau-Ponty Conference*.
Perera, V. and Bruce, R. (1982) *The Last Lords of Palenque: The Lacandon Mayas of the Mexican Rainforest*, Boston, Mass., Little, Brown.
Perls, F., Goodman, P., and Hefferline, R. (1951) *Gestalt Therapy: Excitement and Growth in the Human Personality*, New York, Delta.
Piaget, J. (1965) *The Moral Judgement of the Child*, New York, Macmillan.
Plato (1937) *The Dialogues of Plato*, trans. Benjamin Jowett, New York, Random.
Pouillon, F. (1985) *The Stones of the Abbey*, New York, Harcourt, Brace, Jovanovich.
Poùlantzas, N. (1978) *L'État, le Pouvoir, le Socialisme*, Paris, Presses Universitaires de France.
Rabinow, P. (ed.) (1984) *The Foucault Reader*, New York, Pantheon.
Rawls, J. (1971) *A Theory of Justice*, Cambridge, Mass., Harvard University Press.
Rawls, J. (September 1980) 'Kantian constructivism in moral theory', *Journal of Philosophy*, 77(9).
Rawls, J. (1982) 'Social unity and primary goods', in A. Sen and B. Williams (eds) *Utilitarianism and Beyond*, Cambridge, Cambridge University Press.
Reichel-Dolmatoff, G. (1971) *Amazonian Cosmos: The Sexual and Religious Symbolism of the Tukano Indians*, Chicago, University of Chicago Press.
Reichel-Dolmatoff, G. (1978) *Beyond the Milky Way: Hallucinatory Imagery of the Tukano Indians*, Los Angeles, Calif., UCLA Latin American Center Publications, Latin America Series, vol. 42.

Reinold, H. (1958) 'On the problem of musical hearing', in S. Langer (ed.) *Reflections on Art*, Baltimore, Md, Johns Hopkins University Press.
Rich, A. (1976) *Of Woman Born: Motherhood as Experience and Institution*, New York, Norton.
Richardson, W. and Muller, J. (1982) *Lacan and Language: A Reader's Guide to Écrits*, New York, International Universities Press.
Ricoeur, P. (1970) *Freud and Philosophy: An Essay on Interpretation*, New Haven, Yale University Press.
Rilke, R. (1945) *Letters of Rainer Maria Rilke, 1892–1910*, New York, Norton.
Rilke, R. (1962a) *Gesammelte Gedichte*, Frankfurt am Main, Insel.
Rilke, R. (1962b) *Sonnets to Orpheus*, New York, Norton.
Rogers, C. (1969) *Freedom to Learn*, Columbus, OH, Charles E. Merrill.
Romanyshyn, R. (1982) *Psychological Life: From Science to Metaphor*, Austin, Tex., University of Texas Press.
Romanyshyn, R. (1987) 'Mirror as metaphor of psychological life', in K. Yardley and T. Honess (eds) *Self and Identity: Psychological Perspectives*, New York, Wiley.
Rorty, R. (1979) *Philosophy and the Mirror of Nature*, Princeton, NJ, Princeton University Press.
Sabina, M. (1981) *Maria Sabina: Her Life and Her Chants*, transcribed and ed. by A. Estrada and H. Munn, Santa Barbara, Calif., Ross-Erikson.
Sallis, J. (October 1984) 'Heidegger/Derrida – presence', *Journal of Philosophy*, 81(10).
Sallis, J. (1986) *Delimitations: Phenomenology and the End of Metaphysics*, Bloomington, Ind., Indiana University Press.
Sartre, J. (1956) *Being and Nothingness*, New York, Philosophical Library.
Schmidt, A. (1969) 'Adorno – ein Philosoph des realen Humanismus', *Neue Rundschau* 80 (4).
Schrag, C. (1986) *Communicative Praxis and the Space of Subjectivity*, Bloomington, Ind., University of Indiana Press.
Schürmann, R. (December 1985) 'What can I do in an archaeological-genealogical history?'. *Journal of Philosophy*, 82.
Schürmann, R. (1987) *Heidegger on Being and Acting: From Principles to Anarchy*, Bloomington, Ind., University of Indiana Press.
Schwartz-Salant, N. (1982) *Narcissism and Character Transformation: The Psychology of Narcissistic Character Disorders*, Toronto, Inner City Books.
Searles, H. (1965) *Collected Papers on Schizophrenia and Related Subjects*, New York, International Universities Press.
Sekida, K. (1977) *Two Zen Classics: The Mumonkan and Hekiganroku*, New York, John Weatherhill.
Shapiro, D. (1965) *Neurotic Styles*, New York, Basic Books.
Shapiro, G. and Sica, A. (eds) (1984) *Hermeneutics: Questions and Prospects*, Amherst, Mass., University of Massachusetts Press.
Shibayama, Z. (1974) *Zen Comments on the Mumonkan*, New York, New American Library.
Snyders, G. (1965) *La Pédagogie en France aux dix-septième et dix-huitième Siècles*, Paris, Plon.

Stevens, W. (1954) *The Collected Poems of Wallace Stevens*, New York, Alfred Knopf.
Straus, E. (1966) *Phenomenological Psychology*, New York, Basic Books.
Straus, E. (1970) 'Born to see, bound to behold', in S. Spicker (ed.) *The Philosophy of the Body: Reflections of Cartesian Dualism*, New York, Quadrangle.
Sullivan, H. (1953) *The Interpersonal Theory of Psychiatry*, New York, Norton.
Suzuki, D. (1972) *Living By Zen*, New York, Samuel Weiser.
Tarthang Tulku (1978) *Time, Space and Knowledge*, Berkeley, Calif., Dharma Publishing.
Taussig, M. (1987) *Shamanism, Colonialism and the Wild Man: A Study in Terror and Healing*, Chicago, University of Chicago Press.
Taylor, C. (1986) 'Foucault on freedom and truth', in D. Hoy (ed.) *Foucault: A Critical Reader*, London and New York, Basil Blackwell.
Thompson, J. and Held, D. (eds) (1982) *Habermas: Critical Debates*, Boston, Mass., MIT Press.
Thompson, J. (1981) *Critical Hermeneutics: A Study in the Thought of Paul Ricoeur and Jürgen Habermas*, Cambridge, Cambridge University Press.
Thoreau, H. (1947) *The Portable Thoreau*, ed. C. Bode, New York, Viking.
Thoreau, H. (1973) *Walden and Civil Disobedience*, New York, New American Library.
Thoreau, H. (1981) *Walden*, New York, Bantam.
Todes, S. (1969) 'Sensuous abstraction and the abstract sense of reality', in J. Edie (ed.) *New Essays in Phenomenology*, Chicago, Quadrangle.
Turnbull, C. (1961) *The Forest People: A Study of the Pygmies of the Congo*, New York, Simon & Schuster.
The Upanishads, trans. and ed. J. Mascaro (1965), New York and Harmondsworth, Penguin.
Walsh, R. (1979) 'Meditation research; an introduction and review', *Journal of Transpersonal Psychology*, 11 (2).
Weber, S. (1970) 'Individuation as praxis', in P. Breines (ed.) *Critical Interruptions: New Left Perspectives on Herbert Marcuse*. New York, Herder & Herder.
Welwood, J. (1977) 'Meditation and the unconscious: a new perspective', *Journal of Transpersonal Psychology*, 9 (1).
Wheelwright, P. (1966) *The Presocratics*, New York, Odyssey.
White, H. (1986) 'Foucault decoded: notes from underground', *Tropics of Discourse: Essays in Cultural Criticism*, Baltimore, Md, Johns Hopkins Universty Press.
White, H. (1987) 'Foucault's discourse: the historiography of anti-humanism', *The Context of the Form: Narrative Discourse and Historical Representation*, Baltimore, Md, Johns Hopkins University Press.
Whitebook, J. (1985) 'Reason and happiness: some psychoanalytic themes in critical theory', in R. Bernstein (ed.) *Habermas and Modernity*, Boston, Mass., MIT Press.
Williams, B. (1962) 'The idea of equality', in P. Laslett and W. Runciman (eds) *Philosophy, Politics and Society*, Oxford, Basil Blackwell.
Williams, W. C. (1963) *Paterson*, New York, New Directions.

Wilmott, H. (March 1986) 'Unconscious sources of motivation in the theory of the subject: an exploration and critique of Giddens' dualistic models of action and personality', *Journal for the Theory of Social Behaviour*, 16 (1).
Wolfe, A. (1986) 'The return of values', *Tikkun*, 1 (2).
Wolin, R. (1982) *Walter Benjamin: An Aesthetic of Redemption*, New York, Columbia University Press.
Wollheim, R. (1977) *Sigmund Freud*, New York, Viking.
Wood, D. (1985) 'Difference and the problem of strategy', in D. Wood and R. Bernasconi (eds) *Derrida and Differance*, Coventry, Warks., Parousia Press, University of Warwick.
Wordsworth, W. (1972) *The Prelude*, Harmondsworth and New York, Penguin.
Yarrow, M. and Zahn-Wexler, C. (1977) 'The emergence and founding of pro-social behaviours in young children', in R. Smart (ed.) *Readings in Child Development and Relationships*, New York, Macmillan.

Index

Abhidharma 226–7
abstraction: sensuous 82–4
abyss 214, 238, 251, 258, 266–8
Adorno, Theodor xvi-xvii, 4, 8, 15, 29, 35, 62–4, 94–5, 101, 104, 106–7, 120, 141–2, 167, 172, 174–5, 188, 259–60
aesthetic attitude 81–4
alētheia 199, 202, 238, 244–6, 264, 273–5; *see also* truth
alienation 108, 208; in mirroring 148–64; of meaning 8
always already 25, 46, 67, 70–5, 172, 177, 194, 207, 211, 219, 222, 247–50, 254–7, 270, 274
anagnōrisis 164
anamnēsis 167, 174–5, 270
ancestral body 271
ancestral voices 271–2
Anaximander 21
Anwesen(heit) 24–8, 198
anxiety 78–9, 83, 260–1, 267
appropriation: *see* ontological
archē 15, 262, 268
archetrace 220
Arendt, Hannah xiv, 29, 105, 187, 201–3
Aristotle 28–9, 39, 60–1, 69, 123, 184, 186–7
art of hearing 111
attention: *see* channeling; intentionality
auditory distortion 111
authenticity: and truth 138; in listening 207–8, 230, 249–51; in practices of self-development 115–23
authoritarian personality type 26, 226
autonomy 61, 108, 122, 124–6, 130, 132, 154, 167–8, 186, 189, 194, 221
awareness movement 116–19, 222

background 68–9, 83; *see also* ground
Bendaña, Alejandro 110
Benhabib, Seyla 2, 40, 43, 95, 104, 122, 127–31, 167–8, 173–5, 188–92
Befindlichkeit 68, 209, 219
beginning: as different from origin 54, 274
Being 5–6; claim of 7, 114–15,

207–8, 249–52; in closure 6, 15–18, 45–7, 199–200, 210, 249–52, 255, 268, 270–1, 274–5; loss of 20, 55; organ of 16, 206–8, 219, 224, 251, 273; question of 5–7, 15–16, 22, 44, 48–9, 64, 233; song of 206, 256–7
belief: in contrast to knowledge 270
Benjamin, Walter xxv, 8, 15, 20, 29, 141, 201, 259–60
Bergson, Henri 29
Bernard of Clairvaux 34
Bildungsprozesse 37, 91, 121–2, 126, 177–9, 185–6, 207; *see also* education; self; self-development
binding 209, 211–12, 273
biologism 180
Blake, William 76
Blanco, Hugo 136–7
body 91–2, 212, 219, 222; and capitalism 127–8, 204; and education 178–9; and history 92–103; and knowledge 245; and listening 4, 16–17, 21–2, 71–5; and power 97, 178–9, 197; as anti-social 176; as organized by and for meaning 98–100; as self 32; as surface 92, 99–100; as totally imprinted by history 92–103; capacities of the 103; Foucault's two concepts of 92–103, 163–4, 180; idealities of the 98–9, 103, 161, 177–80; in culture 271–2; in synchronization with others 151; libidinal 39; normativity of 98–9, 103, 127, 161, 177–80; of auditory experience 4, 14, 16, 17, 21–2, 25, 38, 46, 65, 71–3, 75, 88, 97–8, 100–3, 109, 121, 166, 174, 222; of depths 91, 97, 99–100; 179; of dreaming 167, 174, 177, 181, 183, 272; of needs 38, 132, 172; of ontological understanding 46; of pre-ontological understanding 251, 275; of tradition 271–2; original ecstasy of 269; politic 90–103, 138, 140–204; *see also* felt sense
Bohm, David 67, 138
bonding: natal 209–12
Book of Psalms 1
Borowski, Tadeusz 90, 105
Boss, Medard 43
Buddha's hearing 227

capacities 1–8, 17, 38–65, 67, 102, 109, 113–14, 127–31, 135–6, 154–5, 183–4, 222, 249–54; fulfilled in the *homologein* 252; moral claims of 67, 79, 108, 110, 114–15, 136–7, 139–40, 183–4, 207–8;
capitalism 38–40, 91, 100–1, 180; and the body 127–8; and the ego 180, 204; and social justice 204
care: in relationships 218; *see also* ethics
Cartesian metaphysics 11–12; *see also* metaphysics
Cavell, Stanley, 270
centres of experiencing 57–8
channeling: and power 111; of perception 18–19, 31, 44–5, 48, 54, 56–7, 67–71, 77–8, 83, 176, 195, 203, 225–7; *see also* intentionality
character 1, 3, 52–3, 69–70, 78, 115, 126, 137, 139–140, 186, 218, 221–50; and the *homologein* 253; modelled by intercorporeal mimesis 154–5
chiasm 121, 164–5, 169; *see also* double-crossing: reversibility
child 209–11; body of the 178; of joy 211; *see also* education
claim: of Being 7, 17, 67, 208, 249–52; on our perceptual

capacities 67, 114–15, 183–4, 207–8, 249–52
closure: as challenged by the echo 237; of metaphysics 6, 15–18, 45–7, 199–200, 210, 249, 255, 268, 271, 274–5
cogito 158, 162, 164, 222, 237, 240; *see also* ego
cognitive dissonance 197
cognitivism 106, 125, 184
collectivity: anonymous 152; *see also* subjectivity, universalism
colonialism 12
communication 102–10, 116, 121; and listening 29–37
communicative ethics 35–7, 124–32, 188–91, 203; *see also* communicative rationality; ethics
communicative rationality 33, 35–7, 39, 53, 124–8, 130–2, 138, 188–90; *see also* reason
community: ideal 172; initial, 152, 172
compassion 89, 255
competitive model 221
conformity 53, 77, 91, 120, 185, 202, 208; in truth, 244–5
Confucius 77
conscience 105, 111–13
consciousness: philosophy of 124, 203
consensus 3, 5, 80, 133, 135, 171, 176–7, 181, 186–98; *see also* reason
contemplation 20
cooperative model 221
corporeal images 148–50, 167, 173–4, 178–9, 197, 221, 272; *see also* corporeal schematism
corporeal schematism 97, 100, 126–8, 138, 140–98; *see also* body
correspondence 245–6
Coyle, Michael 152, 155, 168
critical ontology 41, 119
culture 91, 187, 269–75; as intercorporeal, 271
curiosity 30–1, 77–8; *see also* channeling; desire; intentionality

Daly, Mary 44, 166, 213–15, 217
deafness 56, 79, 85–6, 103–11, 140, 273
death: fear of 78; of God 13–18; sounds of 79
deep self 99–100
defensiveness: of the ego-logical structure 78–83, 233, 267
delegitimation 190
Deleuze, Gilles 86
democratic procedures 37
depressions 14; *see also* nihilism; psychopathology
Derrida, Jacques xv, 25, 27–8, 73, 90, 159, 220, 244, 260
Descartes, René, 35, 72, 119, 123, 142–3, 146, 150–1, 156–64, 186
desire: to hear 77–9, 233
Des Pres, Terrence 9
destiny: symbol of 213, 216, 272
Dewey, John xviii, 29, 178
Diagnostic and Statistical Manual of Mental Disorders 145–6
Différance 160
difference 6, 186–98, 234; *see also* figure/ground difference; interplay; ontological difference
Dillon, Martin 163
Diner, Helen 217
dispensations of Being 5–6
dissonance 101–2, 114, 136, 183, 187, 195–6; cognitive 197
domination 40, 98–9, 109, 220; and education 178–9; and ego 120; and hearing 140; and mimesis 166
double-crossing 158, 162, 165; and the feminine

intertwining 217; *see also* chiasm; intertwining
dreambody 167, 174, 177, 181, 183, 197, 272; *see also* body; corporeal schematism; needs
Dreyfus, Hubert 41, 117
drives: psychology of 170–6, 186
dualisms: of modernity 12, 120
Durkheim, Emile 122

ears: as portals 90; as a shell 78, 258; lust of 111; passion of 78; of our thinking xxiv; of the earth 67; of the State 104; of the world 104
earth: Great Mother of the 69, 212–23; Song of the 212; symbol of the 69, 212–14, 218–19, 223
Écarts 159; *see also* difference; ecstasis; ontological difference
echo 74, 251–4; and the ego 235–40, 266–7; and history 270–2; and metaphysics 237–8; and the play of differences 234; and presence 237–8; and time 258–69; and truth 237–8, 244–5; as measure 236–8; in the formation of culture 187; in self-forming relations with others 61–2, 66, 87, 134–5, 142, 153–60, 165, 170–1, 182, 187, 195, 224, 257–8, 272; motor 150, 170–1
Eckhart, Meister 31–2
ecstasis 7, 45–6, 50–1, 54–5, 68, 70–1, 238–44, 246, 262, 266, 269, 275; of infancy 30, 71, 269; see also infancy; *Zugehörigkeit*
ecstasy: see *ecstasis*
education 177–9, 185–6
EEG responsiveness: and *Gelassenheit* 225
ego 14, 20, 32, 47, 50–2, 54, 56, 76, 78, 132, 167, 234; and echo 235–40, 266–7; and needs 127; and primordial openness 266–7, 231–2; and object of representation 20, 234; and other 12, 175; and patriarchy 3, 12, 220; and security 78, 120; and social domination 120, 175; and sounds 34, 234; and time 261; and the will to power 9–29; as bourgeois 12, 180, 204; as different from the self 8, 11–12, 47, 49, 56, 64, 117–25, 145, 160, 170, 202, 221–2; as embodied 92; as masculine 11–12; as surface 92, 99–100, 120; *cogito* 158, 162, 164, 222; deconstruction of 175, 179–80, 182–3, 204; development of 47–54, 143–5, 148–9, 156, 160–1, 177; disappearance of 57; identity of 194; in capitalism 127–8, 180, 204; psychology 170, 172, 174, 176, 220
Eichmann, Adolph 105
Eliade, Mircea 270
Eliot, T. S. 258
emancipation 4–5, 11, 13, 20, 33, 37–9, 97, 115–18, 124, 127, 130, 172, 260; of the senses xxv-xxvii, 37–8, 41, 43
embrace: temporal 257–67; *see also* gathering; time
Emerson, Ralph W. 104
Enlightenment 5, 11, 13, 29–35, 59, 61, 184, 190–1
epistēmē: as different from *sophia* 31
epistemes 199–202
epistemological narcissism 157–9
equality 187
Ereignis 72, 243
Erikson, Erik 26, 50–3, 60, 154–5, 178, 187, 194, 200, 221, 226

Erinnerung 73, 75; *see also* recollection
Es gibt 5, 7, 70–1, 207, 235, 241, 247, 250, 253, 268, 275
eternity 261
ethics 35–7, 124–32, 188–91, 203; of care and responsibility 123, 171–2, 194, 221–2; of rights and duties 123, 221
evil 105
experience: importance of 14; inner 115, 155: politics of 98–9; *see* also body

face: the human 99–100, 120; in the face-to-face relationship 128; *see also* deep self
feeling: capacity for 21–2, 83, 209, 212, 218–19, 254
felt sense: as a bodily process 17, 21–2, 51, 55, 67, 73–4, 179, 195, 211, 219, 231, 245, 267; in identity formation 151–5; *see also* body; focusing
feminine archetypes 49, 212–23; wisdom of the 32, 44
figure/ground difference 4, 6, 31, 44–5, 48, 56–7, 68–9, 227, 235, 240–7; reversal 206; *see also* difference; ground; interplay; ontological difference
Fink, Eugen 229–32, 248
Fischer, Michael 218
flesh 96–7, 100, 103, 121, 126, 140–86, 206, 247; and the deconstruction of the ego 150, 158; communicativeness of the 150, 162, 272; dreams of the 272; idealities in the 99–103, 127, 161, 177–80; *logos* in the 180, 203; non-egological 204; universal 164–5, 169
focal attention 68–9; *see also* channeling; intentionality
focusing 101; *see also* body; felt sense
forgetfulness of Being 5, 6, 49, 55, 72, 75, 210, 246, 274; *see also* recollection
Fourfold 75, 198, 203, 255–7
Foucault, Michel 2, 8, 40–1, 62–4, 91–2, 96–8, 100–1, 107–8, 110, 112–13, 116–19, 127, 130–1, 133, 139, 163, 168–9, 175, 179, 185–6, 197, 199, 203; and two conceptions of the body 92–3, 103, 180
Fraser, Nancy 97, 133
freedom 38–9
Freud, Sigmund 7, 30, 55, 69, 92, 94, 99, 120, 152, 156, 161–2, 185–6, 254, 260–1; on narcissism 142–7
friendship 123, 129
frontal ontology 31
Frye, Northrop 112
future time 259–69

Gadamer, Hans-Georg 204
Gasché, Rodolphe 220, 243–4
gathering 49, 52, 75, 203, 227, 246–75; as feeling 254; of time 258–69
Gelassenheit 21, 28, 48–9, 52, 126, 199, 202, 223–35, 238, 241, 243, 246, 257–60, 268
Gemüt 254
Gendlin, Eugene 101, 119, 134, 178, 219, 222, 267
Geschick 233
Gestalt formation 3, 20–2, 26–8, 31, 43–4, 47–9, 53, 57, 126, 148, 199–200, 226–7, 231–2, 234
Gestell 21, 26, 31, 47–9, 199–200, 220, 242
Geuss, Raymond 104–7
Geviert 26, 49, 52, 199–200; *see also* gathering
Gilligan, Carol 50, 52, 120, 122, 125, 130, 214–21

God: death of 13–18
gods: as embodied normative ideals 52, 203
Goethe, Wolfgang 85
Greek culture: as different from Jewish 201
greeting the sound 17–18, 85, 225, 234, 257
ground 6, 35, 44, 56, 67, 71, 78, 210, 214, 216, 227, 240–7, 250; and metaphysics 235; of silence 75; principle of the 35, 235, 240–7; *see also* difference; figure/ground difference; metaphysics
Guardian awareness 227, 233, 257
Guenther, Herbert 305

Habermas, Jürgen 2, 8, 18, 30, 33, 35–6, 41, 53, 65, 102, 105–8, 112–13, 121, 124–38, 155, 167, 170, 172–7, 182–3, 190, 193–4, 196
happiness 39, 60, 79, 89, 130, 167, 169, 184
harmony 61–2, 76, 79–80, 136, 140, 180, 195–6, 240–2, 246, 253
hearing: and technology 113; as different from vision (sight) xiv, 29–35, 200–3, 218–19, 246, 249, 270, 275; Buddha's 227; scientific account of 77–8; *see also* listening
hearkening 48–9, 56, 205–75
Hebel, Johann 212
Hebrew tradition 35, 199, 201
Hegel, Georg xxiii, 33–4, 122
Heidegger, Martin xix, xxii, xxiv, 8, 14–18, 20–8, 41–2, 45–8, 62–4, 200
Hekigan-roku 223
Henley, Nancy 151
Herakleitos 136, 208, 211, 246–9, 252
Hermeneutics 54–5, 58, 199–201, 204
historical determinism 133–4, 197
historicism 131, 180
history: gathering of 269–75
Hobbes, Thomas 176–7
Hoebel, Adamson 91
Hölderlin, Friedrich 237, 258
holism 83; *see also* wholes; wholeness
holistic experience 45, 68, 70, 265
homelessness 13
homologein 251–5
Horkheimer, Max xvi-xvii, xx, 5, 8, 12, 18, 29, 35, 62–3, 109–10, 113, 154–5, 165–6, 172, 174–5
humanism xvii-xix, 12, 35, 58, 62–5, 184
human nature 54, 58–64, 94–6, 117–18, 120, 133–4
Husserl, Edmund 82, 97, 119, 183

idealities: of the flesh 98–103, 127, 161, 177–80
ideal listening situation 194–5
ideal speech situation 183, 192–5
identity: social imposition of 161; *see also* ego; self
ideology 88, 104, 106, 109, 111, 118, 134, 135–6, 138–40, 195–6, 203; as different from truth 138; as dissonance 101–2
implicate order 67, 138, 165, 185, 222
incorporation 166, 274
indifference 56, 273
individuation 114–16, 145, 152, 167, 170, 176–7, 181, 221; non-egological 161, 180, 204
infancy 49, 54–5, 60–1, 67, 70–2, 75, 147–52, 209, 231, 253; and narcissism 144; ecstasy of 30, 71, 269; inter-

corporeality in 151–2; perception in 30, 45–51
inner experience 14, 98–9, 115
inner nature 127–36, 167, 172, 174
inner self 95, 98; *see also* self
instrumental attitude 22–3, 52, 56
intentionality 18–19, 22, 31, 33, 59, 68–71, 78, 82–4, 206, 225–35, 268; *see also* channeling
interconnectedness 213, 221, 272; *see also* intertwining
intercorporeality 135, 151–2, 155, 164–6, 171, 173, 175–7, 179, 183, 195, 271–2
interests 133
interplay: differential 83, 220, 234–5, 246, 267
interrelatedness 47, 51; *see also* interconnectedness; intertwining
intersubjectivity 37, 109–27, 124, 126, 130, 132, 143, 171, 173, 204
intertwining 50–1, 117, 142, 150–82, 194, 212–23, 228, 234, 272; as feminine 217

Jacoby, Russell 91, 105, 118
James, William 258
Jay, Martin 278–9, 281
Jetztzeit 259
Jewish culture 35, 199, 201
Jonas, Hans 201, 203
joy 210, 234; child of, 211
Jung, Carl 8, 66, 76, 220–1, 248
juridification 107
justice 3–5, 56, 105, 130–1, 167, 172, 191–2, 203; sense of 48, 182–98
just listening 223, 233–5, 244, 257, 267

Kant, Immanuel 10, 33–5, 53, 106, 119, 123–4, 128–9, 188, 190, 195–6, 240
Kaushitaki Upanishad 255
Kehre 68, 203, 249
Kierkegaard, Søren, 45, 50–1, 64
knowledge: in contrast to belief 270
Kohlberg, Lawrence 50, 52–3, 109, 122–6, 130–1, 177, 194, 202, 221
Köhler, Wolfgang 147
Kohut, Heinz 145–6
Kovel, Joel 92, 95–6, 112
Kyōgen 236

labyrinth 205, 214, 216–17, 247; *see also* abyss; chiasm; intertwining
Lacan, Jacques 142–50, 156–7, 160–2, 164, 185
Laing, R. D. 14
Lame Deer 76, 232
language: acquisition of 193–4; capacity for 195; new processes in 174; Samoan 218
Lasch, Christopher 138, 182
laying-down 203, 207, 246, 250–3; *see also legein*; *Logos*
Layout 207, 254; *see also legein*; *Logos*
legein 67, 74, 203, 207–8, 246–55, 275; *see also Logos*
legitimation: political 189–90, 199, 202
Leibniz, Gottfried xxi, 257
letting be: *see Gelassenheit*
letting go: *see Gelassenheit*
Lévinas, Emmanuel 64
listening: and community 29–37; as different from vision 200–1, 218–19; as therapeutic 79, 86–8, 134–5; ideal situation for 194–5
logic 214, 216, 240
logocentrism 125, 237, 247
Logos 67, 74, 180, 203, 207–8, 246–55, 275; *see also legein*
Long-chen rab 'byams-pa 238–40

loss: of Being 20, 55; of joy, 210; of meaning, 2–13
Lukacher, Ned 74, 251, 275
lust: of the ears 111

MacIntyre, Alasdair 106
male consciousness 215, 218; *see also* masculine archetypes
Mallarmé, Stéphane 30, 71
Mandala: of sounds 256–7
Marcus, George 218
Marcuse, Herbert xxvii 8, 37–40, 90, 92, 104, 172, 174, 185
Marx, Karl xxvi, 8, 33, 36–8, 40, 91, 94–5, 108, 112, 122, 141, 175, 179
masculine archetypes 12, 30, 44, 218–20
maturation 135; *see also* self-development
Mayan Indians 212–13, 232
McCarthy, Thomas 35, 155, 182
Mead, George 122
meaning: alienation from 8; body's immanent organization of 98–100, 132–6; need for 251; *see also* nihilism
measure 9–11, 33, 40, 254–5, 258; and the echo 236–8
memory 268
Merleau-Ponty, Maurice 7, 16–17, 43, 51
Mersenne, Père 72
metaphysics 7–8, 15–29, 186; and the echo 237–8; and the ground 235, 240–7; and vision 29–35; the closure of 7; the end of 7, 274; the history of 7–8; Cartesian 11–12; of presence 31, 159–60, 201, 204, 268; the overcoming of 44, 74–5, 204; the transgression of 28–9
mimesis 75, 153–54, 165–6, 251–4; see also *homologein*
Mindell, Arnold 141, 167, 181
mirroring 145–60, 165, 170, 182; alienation in 148–50, 156, 160–4
modernity: dualisms of 12, 120; and narcissism 146; rationality dominant in 188–9
monotones: and laws 270; and truth 245, 247
Montaigne, Michel de 160, 187
moral character 1, 3, 52–3, 69–70, 78, 115, 126, 139–40, 218, 221
moral claims: on our capacities 79, 108, 114–15, 136–7, 139–40, 183–4, 194
moral self-development 36, 124–32, 152, 178, 194
Morton, Nelle 216
Mother: Great Earth 69, 213–17; as related to the flesh 141
Mumonkan 227
music 80, 84, 206–7, 210–11, 217, 223, 227, 233–4, 243–5, 256, 259–60; of the spheres 87
mutual recognition: *see* recognition

narcissism 9–15, 141–86; epistemological 157–9; *see also* psychopathology; will to power
natal bonding 141, 209–12; *see also Zugehörigkeit*
natural attitude 82
nature: as inner 129, 132, 134, 167, 172, 174
needs 3, 38, 40, 86, 88, 91, 98–103, 114–18, 127–36, 172, 174, 188; and meaning 251; and ego 127; body of 132, 172, 174; formation of new 132–5, 181, 188; informing rationality 138
Neumann, Erich 209, 213–16
neurotic perception 225–6
neutralization 233; *see also* channeling; *Gelassenheit*; intentionality

new critical paradigm 122–7
Nietzsche, Friedrich 8, 10–13, 30, 78, 91, 94, 111, 137, 140, 163, 185, 209, 218, 245, 263, 275
nihilism 3–29, 41, 58, 166, 200–1, 208, 233, 255
non-memory 268
not yet 67–8, 70–5, 211, 222, 249–50, 254–60, 263–6, 273

obaudire 32, 34, 52, 224
obedience 42, 52, 91, 126, 185, 189, 194, 196, 202, 224, 235
objectification 78, 258
objectivity 13–14
objects 13–22, 46–50, 71, 120–3, 158, 173, 175, 209–11, 220, 228, 233–4, 243, 250
oculocentrism 30, 35, 188, 200, 202, 204
ontological appropriation 48, 206–8, 240, 249
ontological difference 6, 35, 48, 56, 72–5, 207, 234, 240–7, 274; indifference 56; interpretation 215; understanding 46, 67, 205–75; *see also* difference; *écarts*; interplay
ontology: is fiction 240; of objects and persons 202
openness: primordial 67–75, 226–7, 231–4, 242–7, 249–54, 257, 275; *see also ecstasis*
organ of Being: *see* Being
organismic a priori 16, 67, 178
organismic order: and need fulfillment 93, 100–3, 132, 177, 183–5
origin: as different from beginning 274; as irretrievable 260
others 104, 122–31, 163, 169, 191, 195–6, 202, 204, 272

pain 86, 89, 115–16, 181, 184, 261–2; ideological distortion of 106–8
parrhēsia 119, 139; *see also* truth
Pascal, Blaise 10
passion, of the ears 78
past time 259–69
patriarchy 3, 12, 30, 44, 79, 218, 220, 222–3
perception: and social change xxv-xxvii, 37–43; and technology 41, 70, 113; as a gathering 255; fulfilled in the *homologein* 252; in a patriarchal hierarchy of powers 218; neurotic 225–6
Periander of Corinth 269
periechesthai 258
Perls, Frederick 200
persons: ontology of, as not reducible to objects 202
Pestalozzi, Johann 178
phrōnēsis 2
Piaget, Jean 122, 178, 221
plants: symbolism of 69, 212–13, 219, 223
Plato 80–2, 90–1, 113, 136, 140, 153, 178, 240, 246, 261
play: in listening 233–5
pluralism: democratic 190
power 9–29, 178, 197; and self-development 107–14; *see also* will to power
practices of the self 2, 17, 23, 25, 35, 38–62, 68, 117–20, 126, 138–9, 212, 256; *see also* self; self-development
preconceptual understanding 21, 231, 250–3
pre-egological experience 46, 49–51, 69, 73, 253
pre-ontological understanding 16–17, 25, 45–6, 49–50, 55, 67, 72–5, 172, 206, 219, 229–30, 253, 275
prepersonal experience 46, 50–1, 69, 176, 250, 253, 265, 272–3
presence 15, 18–29, 31, 54,

159–60, 198, 201, 204, 241–4, 268; and the echo 237–8
present that never is (was) 54–5, 74–5, 244, 259–60, 262, 274
present time 259–69
primary process 69
primordial attunement; *see* *Zugehörigkeit*; experience 72
principle of the ground 35, 235, 240–7; *see also* figure/ground difference; ground
procedural justice 123
progress 187, 189–90
progression: in developmental process 54, 57–8
pro-social behaviour 185–6; *see also* corporeal schematism; socialization
proto-social embodiment 152, 178; *see also* corporeal schematism; socialization
Protagoras 9–10
psychoanalysis 99, 141, 160, 170, 186
psychopathology 2–5, 14–15, 26–7, 57–8, 68, 143, 182, 220, 226; in the experiencing of time 261–2
psychosis 86

question of Being 5–7, 15–16, 22, 44, 48–9, 64, 233

Rabinow, Paul 41, 117
radio 41, 113
rationality: *see* reason
Rawls, John 39, 60, 106, 122, 184, 190–1
reality principle 90
reason 29–39, 53, 124–32, 138, 188–90; and consensus 196; and feeling 219; and power 11–12; as different from thinking xxiv, 17; as disembodied 130; as embodied 34, 65, 97, 138, 191; as monological 35–7, 188–9, 196; as speculative 17, 20, 188–9; as instrumental 12–15, 33, 166, 190, 195; listening to 240, 246–7; loss of faith in 13; subject-centred 143, 203, 206; traditional conception of 247; universal 11, 13, 33, 35; voice of 65; *see also* communicative rationality
reciprocity 3, 37, 48, 53, 135–6, 143, 145, 150, 152, 157, 163–4, 166, 169, 171–2, 177, 183–94
recognition: mutual 156, 163, 181
recollection of Being 5–8, 16, 32, 48–56, 203–8, 219–22, 244–74; as embodied process 72–5
reflection: as objectifying 258
reflexivity 171
regression xvi 55–8, 143
Reichel-Dolmatoff, Gerardo 236–7
Renaissance 11
repetition compulsion 261
representation 17–29, 234, 242–6; as deferment, 19
repression 78, 95
resistance 97–116
response-ability 2, 8, 43, 47, 67, 117–18, 165, 194, 203, 252
retrieval: of experience of Being 55, 231, 250, 253, 272; *see also* recollection
reversibility 37, 48, 53, 124–8, 131, 142–97
revolution 112–13
Rich, Adrienne 79, 141
Richardson, William 147–9
rigidity: in personality and perception 226
Rilke, Rainer 67, 78, 89, 206, 223, 235
Rogers, Carl 79, 86–8, 178
rootlessness 13
Rousseau, Jean-Jacques 178

Sabina, Maria 216–17
Sallis, John 27
Sartre, Jean-Paul 97
schematization: *see* corporeal schematism
schizophrenia 14, 54, 134, 155
Schrag, Calvin 287
Schürmann, Reiner, 99, 203
Searles, Harold 134, 155, 177, 181
seer 263
Seinsgeschick 67
self: and other 130; and society 95, 115–18; as different from ego 8, 11–12, 47–57, 64, 117–25, 145, 160, 170, 202, 221–2; as self-made man 12; deep 99–100, 120; developmental stages of 2–8, 37, 39–62, 68, 89, 110, 167, 171, 194, 222, 273; California cult of the 117–19; fulfillment of the 56, 58, 59, 100–3, 123; inner 95, 98; moral 122–8; sense of 155; traditional 122–5; *see also* practices of the self
self-development: and social evolution 36–7
sensation: pure 81
sense: a bodily felt 17, 21–2, 55, 67, 73–4, 179, 195, 211, 219, 231, 245, 267; of justice 48, 182–98
sensibility 140, 220, 227; and social change xxv-xxvii, 37–43
sensuous abstraction 82–4
sensus communis 135
setting the tone 230, 240, 246–50, 253–4; *see also* tonality
Shapiro, David 225
slight: *see* vision
silence 74, 79, 232–3, 238, 241, 247, 251, 254, 258, 268; ground of 75
skilfulness 233, 254–5
sociability: syncretic 152
social change xxv–xxvii, 37–9, 41, 43, 115–17; and individual development 36–7
socialization 46–9, 54, 70, 77, 94, 98–100, 116, 130, 134, 156, 166, 177–80, 183, 185, 211; biological roots of 169–76
Socrates 80, 136, 139–40, 218
solidarity 123, 129, 221
solipsism 158, 160
Song: of the Earth 212
sophia 31–2, 216
speculation 24; *see also* reason
speech: ideal situation for 183, 193–4
Stambaugh, Joan 74, 274
Stevens, Wallace 255
Stimmung 68, 222, 261
Straus, Erwin 34
subject-object structure 20–2, 46–50, 71, 78, 120–3, 158, 173, 175, 209–11, 220, 228, 233–34, 243, 250
subjectivity: and objectivity 13–14; and resistance 116; as anonymous 175–6, 179; as intersubjectivity 124; as monadic 206; as self-grounding 34, 206; authentic 116–23; is not subjugation 116; metaphysics of 143, 150, 158, 206; new forms of 21, 40–4, 112–18, 156, 169–72, 182–6, 202, 222; true and false 118
Sullivan, Harry 145, 147, 149, 184
Suzuki, Daisetz 262–8

Tarthang Tulku 305
Taussig, Michael 84–5
Taylor, Charles 93
technology 41, 70, 113
telos 262, 268
Temporalität 265–6
temporality: and echoes 258–69; and sounds 34; as different

from timing of time 265–6; as embrace 258, 260; primordial 247, 262–9, 275; protentional structure of 265–6; retentional structure of 265–66; subordination to spatial totalization 201
theoretical attitude 23, 30
therapeutic listening 79, 86–8, 134–5
Thompson, John 102
Thoreau, Henry 104, 106–7
time: and the echo 258–69; and the ego 261–9; and suffering 261–9; as bourgeois 260; as different from temporality 265–6; as a gathering 258–69; as linear 259–69; metaphysics of 269; of loss 268; of mourning 268; psychopathology of 260–9
Todes, Samuel 81–4
tonality 5, 17–18, 67, 74, 226–7, 230, 237, 251; double 48, 234, 240, 242–3, 246–7, 250–3; setting of 240, 246–50, 253–4
totalism 107
totalitarianism 26, 29–30, 198
totalities: as different from wholes 26–8, 34, 44, 49, 226
traces 54, 66, 73–5, 105, 169, 251–2, 274
tradition: living body of 271–2
transhistorical nature 95–6, 179–80, 185
transpersonal experience 50–1, 272
truth 136–40, 192–3, 201–3, 244–6; and authenticity 138; and conformity 244–5; and echoes 237–8, 244–5; and univocity 245, 247, and will to power 246; as *alētheia* 199, 202, 238, 244–6, 273–5; as correctness of representation 201–2; as different from ideology 138; as monotone 245, 247; consensus theory of 190–2; control of 246–7; correspondence theory of 244–5; of Being 21, 273, 275; representational 199, 201–3; resonance of 245–7; telling the 139
Tukano Indians 236–7
typification 22

universal flesh 87, 164–5, 169; *see also* flesh
universalism 87, 104–6, 123–5, 128–32, 175–6, 187–92, 195–7
univocity 105; and truth 245, 247; in laws 270
Upanishad: Kaushitaki 255
utopian images and dreams 124, 136, 166–8, 173–4, 197, 200, 272; *see also* body; flesh; corporeal schematism
utopian-emancipatory potential 88, 176, 190, 201–2

values 178; and the body 185
vegetative soul 69–70
Vernunft: as different from *Verstand* 33–4
vision: and metaphysics 29–35; as different from hearing xiv, 27, 29–35, 200–3, 218–19, 246, 249, 270, 275; paradigm dominance of 183, 199–201
Vorhandensein 22–6, 30, 70

Wallon, Henri 147
weaving: symbolism of 216–17, 221; see also destiny: feminine archetypes; intertwining; plants
Weber, Max 33
Welwood, John 68, 78
Whitebook, Joel 169–70, 172–3, 176
wholeness 187, 215, 220, 223–4, 248, 269
wholes: as different from totalities 26, 28, 34, 43–4, 49, 226; *see also* totalities

Wiederholung 73–5, 231
Williams, Bernard 1, 184
Williams, William 203
Wilmott, Hugh 120
will to power, 3, 9–35, 78; and truth as correctness 246; *see also* ego; narcissism; nihilism
Wolfe, Alan 185
Wolin, Richard 20, 141
women's movement 122–6, 130
Wood, David 28
Wordsworth, William 205, 209, 212, 223–4

Xenophanes 224

Zeit 265
Zeitlichkeit 265–6
Zen 225, 236, 262–8
Zugehörigkeit 25, 45–6, 54–8, 66–75, 121, 172–7, 203, 209, 229–31, 253, 266; *see also ecstasis*; infancy
Zuhandensein 22–6, 64, 70